WEIRD, SCARY & UNUSUAL

Stories & Facts

WEST SIDE PUBLISHING

Contributing Writers: Jeff Bahr, Fiona Broome, Eric Paul Erickson, Mary Fons, Linda Godfrey, J. K. Kelley, Susan McGowan, Jason Rip, Cheri Sicard, Troy Taylor, Wesley Treat, James Willis, Anna Zaigraeva

Special thanks to James Willis for additional consulting and for lending his expertise on many things weird, scary, and unusual.

Cover Illustrator: Adrian Chesterman

Interior Illustrator: Dan Grant

Factual Verification by: Darcy Chadwick, Diane Dannenfeldt, Anne Geiberger, Lawrence Greenberg, Mindy Hicks, Maureen McGerty, Carl Miller, and Katrina O'Brien

Contents

A Confession from the Publisher

I must confess one of my personal guilty pleasures. I've always been just a little bit fascinated by evidence of the weird in real life—the unknown, the things that give you goose bumps or evoke a sense of disbelief, the things that make you ask, "How did *that* happen?" or "What the *heck*?" In short, those events or circumstances that bring out the curiosity seeker in all of us.

Here at the Armchair Reader™, we've collected bizarre tidbits from newspapers and magazines, peculiar snippets from the Internet, and other quirky stories, and put them together for your enjoyment in *Armchair Reader™: Weird, Scary & Unusual*. Some stories are a bit creepy, some will cause you to scratch your head in disbelief, and some may trigger your "Wow!" button. Any way, they'll grab your attention—and some might not let it go, instead leaving a lasting impression of how twisted human nature can be. Prepare yourself for such mind-boggling delights as:

- The Watseka Wonder—one of the most authentic cases of spirit possession in history

- Eyewitness accounts of UFOs, USOs (unidentified submerged objects), and other unexplained phenomena, such as crying statues and disappearing ships

- The White House Ghosts—find out which former president paid a visit to Winston Churchill from "the other side"

- The mysterious handprint that reappears in an old jail in Pennsylvania despite extensive efforts to remove it

Feel free to kick back, recline, and get ready for the twists and turns found on this ride into the outer limits of the natural, the unnatural, and even the supernatural.

Allen Orso
Publisher

Animal Crime and Punishment

Rats declared public enemies, pigs hung in the town square, wolves tried and executed…it's hard to imagine animals held criminally responsible for their actions, but it has happened!

Ox Murderers
Perhaps the earliest recorded mention of legal prosecution of an animal is an Old Testament verse in Exodus chapter 21, verse 28: "When an ox gores a man or a woman to death, the ox shall be stoned, and its flesh shall not be eaten; but the owner of the ox shall not be liable."

It's unknown how many Israelite oxen were actually stoned and left uneaten after jabbing unwary citizens, but it's clear that such events were backed by ancient Biblical edict.

The Case of the Reticent Rats
In medieval France, rats were legally charged with the crime of eating barley. But it was extremely difficult to get the rats to appear in court, as villagers of Autun discovered in 1522. The village judge appointed a defense lawyer for the rats and waited for them to show up. The lawyer argued that his clients inhabited many towns so one summons was insufficient to reach them all. The rats were given more time, and villagers were advised to keep their cats from eating any court-bound rats. Eventually, the case was dismissed.

Marauding Mice
Perhaps the people of Autun had heard about a similar action taken in 1519 in Glurns, Switzerland. A farmer asked the court to charge area field mice with damage to his hay. But he was careful to request counsel for the mice so they would receive

a fair trial. The farmer claimed he had observed mice eating area hay fields for at least 18 years and found corroborating testimony from a field worker and another farmer.

The defense counsel asserted that the mice were also helpful, assisting in insect control in the fields. He asked for a safe field for the mice to live in and for relocation assistance for any pregnant mice. The sentence allowed the mice two weeks to move out of the damaged fields and banned them for eternity. In a show of leniency, pregnant mice and infants were allowed an extra 14 days to relocate.

Insect Indictments

Rats were not the only creatures to prey upon barley and other staple crops. Weevils, locusts, and worms were regularly charged by formal courts during the Middle Ages. Because most courts were administered by the church, insect pests could even be excommunicated or formally barred from services and the Lord's Supper.

One famous case again occurred in France. In 1546, a massive population of weevils that threatened the barley crop was miraculously decimated when the villagers practiced some extreme religion and performed many penitent acts. The weevils stayed away for four decades but returned with a vengeance in 1586. This time a full trial was held, defense counsel was hired for the weevils, and a settlement was attempted. The peasants offered the weevils their own tract of land if they would just stay there, but the defense persuaded the court that the land in question was not fertile enough to support his clients. Ironically, insects ate the final record of judgments in the case, leaving the fate of the barley weevils unknown.

Prosecuting Porky

In ancient times, livestock were often left to roam village streets and squares, foraging for garbage and other "found" food. Accidents were bound to happen, and pigs attacked children and other vulnerable humans from time to time. Records of pig prosecution exist in a number of European countries and show that they were by far the most common species brought to trial for murder of humans. Suspected pigs were usually kept in the same jail as human criminals and were sometimes tortured for "evidence," their frantic grunts and screams accepted as confessions. Execution methods included hanging or live burial. In 1457, a sow and her six piglets were accused of killing a five-year-old boy and were sentenced to death. The sow was hung by her hind legs on a gallows, but the piglets were forgiven due to their youth and the fact that they were corrupted by their mother.

Kitty Kriminals

The old wives' tale that cats smother infants dates back at least to 1462 when a cat was tried for just such a crime. It was found guilty and hanged. During the great witch trials of the Middle Ages, cats were often thought to be spirit companions of accused witches and were often killed with their owners.

Beasts of the Burden of Proof

Bulls, horses, oxen, and goats were often tried as humans, especially in cases of bestiality. However, in 1750, a female donkey was found not guilty in a case in France because a group of respectable citizens all signed a document testifying that they had been acquainted with the animal for her entire life and she had never acted scandalously. The creature's human assaulter, however, was sentenced to death.

Beavers in Contempt

A resident of Pierson, Michigan, received a letter from the state government in December 1997, threatening to charge the "unauthorized" contractors building two wood dams in nearby Spring Pond $10,000 a day if they did not stop. The government was informed by the resident's landlord that the illegal builders were a couple of beavers and that if these two animals were forced to pay fines, beavers all over the state would have to be treated similarly. The state dropped its case.

A Favorite Celebrity Haunt

💀 💀 💀 💀 💀

*San Diego's grand Hotel del Coronado sparkles in the Cali-
fornia sun. It's a popular seaside resort, a National Historic
Landmark, and a very haunted hotel. Affectionately called "the
Del," the hotel is proud of Kate Morgan, its resident ghost. Her
story is just one of the hotel's many spine-tingling tales.*

The Mysterious Mrs. Morgan

On November 24, 1892, Kate Morgan checked into the Hotel
del Coronado under the name Lottie A. Bernard from Detroit.
She looked pale and said she wasn't feeling well. She mentioned that she was planning to meet her brother, a doctor.

After a few days, the staff began to worry. The mysterious
woman had checked in with no luggage. Her brother hadn't
arrived, and she had barely left her room.

On Monday, November 28, the woman went into town and
purchased a gun. Her body was found early the next morning on stairs that led from the hotel to the beach. From the
gunshot wound to her head, it appeared she had committed
suicide. When police investigated, they found few personal
belongings in her hotel room.

Murder or Suicide?

After Kate's death, police determined that "Lottie A. Bernard"
was an alias. They sent a sketch of her to newspapers, which
described her as "the beautiful stranger." Further investigation
uncovered that "Lottie" had been born Kate Farmer in Iowa,
and married Tom Morgan in 1885.

Morgan was reputed to be a conman and a gambler. He
allegedly worked the rails and enlisted Kate's help in stealing
money from train passengers. According to a witness, somewhere between Los Angeles and San Diego, Kate and Morgan
had an intense argument on a train. Morgan departed before
reaching San Diego; Kate continued on the train and then
checked into the Del.

Some people claim that the clues at the scene add up to murder rather than suicide. Attorney Alan May's 1990 book, *The Legend of Kate Morgan,* claims the bullet that killed Kate was a different caliber than the gun she'd purchased.

Haunting in Room 302

Whatever happened, Kate's ghost has lingered at the Del. She often manifests as eerie eyes and lips appearing in the mirror or reflected in the window of her room. Kate's spirit may be responsible for strange noises and unexplained breezes around her room as well. The curtains on closed windows billow for no reason, and lights and televisions turn themselves on and off. Kate also appears as a pale young woman in a black lace dress. A sweet fragrance lingers after her apparition disappears.

Kate stayed in Room 302. Later, during remodeling the hotel changed the room number to 3327. The haunted room is so popular that people ask for it as "the Kate Morgan room." The hotel welcomes questions about the ghost, and everyone treats Kate as an honored guest.

The Mysterious Maid

Room 3519 at the Del is also haunted, perhaps even more intensely than Kate's room.

In 1983, a Secret Service agent stayed in Room 3519 while guarding then-Vice President George H.W. Bush. The special agent bolted from the room in the middle of the night claiming that he'd heard unearthly gurgling noises and that the entire room seemed to glow.

The Secret Service agent may have encountered a ghost related to the Kate Morgan mystery. According to one legend, while Kate was at the hotel, a maid stayed in what would later be Room 3519. In some versions of the story, the maid was traveling with Kate; in others, the maid had simply befriended her. Whatever the connection between the two, the maid allegedly vanished the same morning Kate was found dead.

That's not the only ghost story connected with Room 3519. Another story goes that in 1888, the year the hotel was built, a wealthy man kept his mistress in that room. When the woman found out she was pregnant, she killed herself. Her body was removed from the Del, and nothing else is known about her, not even her name. Ghost hunters believe she is the one who causes the lights in the room to flicker and is responsible for the unexplained cold spot in front of the room's door.

The Blonde on the Beach

In recent years, some hotel guests have reported sightings of the ghost of Marilyn Monroe. She loved the Hotel del Coronado when she stayed there to film the movie *Some Like it Hot*. Monroe's ghost has appeared at several of her favorite places, including Hollywood's Roosevelt Hotel, where people see her in the lobby's mirror.

At the Del, Monroe is supposedly seen outdoors as a fleeting, translucent apparition near the door to the hotel or on the beach nearby. Those who see Monroe's ghost comment on her windswept blonde hair and her fringed shawl that flutters in the breeze. Others have allegedly heard her light giggle in the second and third floor hallways.

Whether they're from a rural farm or the silver screen, guests and ghosts love the Hotel del Coronado. If you choose to stay in one of its most haunted rooms, just remember that you're never alone.

Tree House Dream House

An 83-year-old man in eastern India has been living in a tree for more than 50 years after an argument with his wife. For years Gayadhar Parida has turned down pleas from his wife and children to return home. "We quarreled over a tiny issue," his wife explained. Parida claims that his tree home has helped him grow spiritually and overcome tension. He spends days at a time in the tree, often going without food, and only coming down to get water from a nearby pond.

Joseph Pujol, King of Farts

Most musical performers produce sound by vibrating the upper part of the digestive tract, but French entertainer Joseph Pujol gained great notoriety in the early 20th century for "singing" from his system's lower end.

Going by the stage name of *Le Petomane,* or "The Farting Maniac," Pujol wowed audiences with the sheer scope and variety of sounds he was able to create on command. He could mimic everything from earthquakes to cannons.

The Start of the Fart

Pujol attributed his bizarre ability to an incident in his early teens. Born in 1857 in Marseille, France, at the prophetic address of 13 Rue des Incurables, Pujol's life was unremarkable until he took a dip in the ocean one day. While holding his breath underwater, he experienced a strange, freezing sensation in his colon. He swam gasping to the shore, where he discovered water inexplicably gushing from his rear. He consulted a doctor who told him if he wished to avoid repeating the strange phenomenon, he should simply stay out of the ocean.

The experience taught Pujol that he possessed the ability to suck water into his anus and then forcefully expel it as far as ten feet away! With practice, he soon progressed from taking in water to "inhaling" air, which could be ejected in different amounts and pressures by controlling his sphincter muscles.

Pujol first showed off his talent to fellow soldiers in the French Army. When he became a civilian again, he apparently provided customers in his bakery with a performance that involved the imitation of various musical instruments. The act was such a hit that he began performing on stage, first in Marseille and then Paris in 1892. Even the king of Belgium covertly attended his show.

Floating Fluffies for Fun and Profit

The first thing Pujol did on stage was assure his audience
that gas masks would not be necessary because his toots were
odorless. He even joked that his parents had gone broke paying for perfume for his intestines. Impeccably dressed in a red
coat and black breeches, he broke wind in the classic position:
leaning forward, knees slightly bent, rear turned to the audience for maximum effect. His repertoire was varied—he could
mimic the lengthy rip of a merchant tearing a bolt of fabric
or sound off the grunts, barks, and moos of a menagerie of
farm animals.

Although gentlemanly in public, Pujol was not too prudish
to exhibit more of himself for private gatherings. Instead of his
elegant satin breeches, he would perform wearing pants with a
wide opening in the back seam so that the truly curious could
observe the "art of *petomanie*" as well as hear it.

Extreme Emissions

Not content with his own nonamplified equipment, the enterprising Pujol strategically inserted a three-foot-long rubber
tube for the second part of his act. With the aid of the tube,
he could anally smoke a cigarette, play a flute, and blow out
candles. Soon he was collecting almost three times the daily
pay of famed actress Sarah Bernhardt.

But with success came imitation. After Pujol's gig at the
Moulin Rouge ended over a minor legal flap, the theater
began advertising a female "flatulist." But she was no match
for *Le Petomane* as she was soon found cheating with a bel-
lows placed under her wide skirt. A Paris newspaper criticized
her act, and a flurry of lawsuits followed. The lady's career was
blown.

How It All Came Out

Pujol started his own traveling show and, until World War I,
farted his way from Algeria to Belgium. When his tour ended,
Pujol became a baker in Marseille once more. And until his
death in 1945 at age 88, the only cheese he cut in public was as
a side dish for his pastries.

Red Eyes Over Point Pleasant: The Mysterious Mothman

In 1942, the U.S. government took control of several thousand acres of land just north of Point Pleasant, West Virginia. The purpose was to build a secret facility capable of creating and storing TNT that could be used during World War II. For the next three years, the facility cranked out massive amounts of TNT, shipping it out or storing it in one of the numerous concrete "igloo" structures that dotted the area. In 1945, the facility was shut down and eventually abandoned, but it was here that an enigmatic flying creature with glowing red eyes made its home years later.

"Red Eyes on the Right"

On the evening of November 15, 1966, Linda and Roger Scarberry were out driving with another couple, Mary and Steve Mallette. As they drove, they decided to take a detour that took them past the abandoned TNT factory.

As they neared the gate of the old factory, they noticed two red lights up ahead. When Roger stopped the car, the couples were horrified to find that the red lights appeared to be two glowing red eyes. What's more, those eyes belonged to a creature standing more than seven feet tall with giant wings folded behind it. That was all Roger needed to see before he hit the gas pedal and sped off. In response, the creature calmly unfolded its wings and flew toward the car. Incredibly, even though Roger raced along at speeds close to 100 miles per hour, the red-eyed creature was able to keep up with them without much effort.

Upon reaching Point Pleasant, the two couples ran from their car to the Mason County Courthouse and alerted Deputy Millard Halstead of their terrifying encounter. Halstead couldn't be sure exactly what the two couples had seen, but whatever it was, it had clearly frightened them. In an attempt to calm them down, Halstead agreed to accompany them to the TNT factory. As his patrol car neared the entrance, the police radio suddenly emitted a strange, whining noise. Other than that, despite a thorough search of the area, nothing out of the ordinary was found.

More Encounters

Needless to say, once word got around Point Pleasant that a giant winged creature with glowing red eyes was roaming around the area, everyone had to see it for themselves. The creature didn't disappoint. Dubbed Mothman by the local press, the creature was spotted flying overhead, hiding, and even lurking on front porches. In fact, in the

last few weeks of November, dozens of witnesses encountered the winged beast. But Mothman wasn't the only game in town. It seems that around the same time that he showed up, local residents started noticing strange lights in the evening sky, some of which hovered silently over the abandoned TNT factory. Of course, this led some to believe that Mothman and the UFOs were somehow connected. One such person was Mary Hyre of *The Athens Messenger*, who had been reporting on the strange activities in Point Pleasant since they started. Perhaps that's why she became the first target.

Beware the Men in Black

One day, while Mary Hyre was at work, several strange men visited her office and began asking questions about the lights in the sky. Normally, she didn't mind talking to people about the UFO sightings and Mothman. But there was something peculiar about these guys. For instance, they all dressed exactly the same: black suits, black ties, black hats, and dark sunglasses. They also spoke in a strange monotone and seemed confused by ordinary objects such as ballpoint pens. As the men left, Hyre wondered whether they had been from another planet. Either way, she had an up-close-and-personal encounter with the legendary Men in Black.

Mary Hyre was not the only person to have a run-in with the Men in Black. As the summer of 1967 rolled around, dozens of people were interrogated by them. In most cases, the men showed up unannounced at the homes of people who had recently witnessed a Mothman or UFO sighting. For the most part, the men simply wanted to know what the witnesses had seen. But sometimes, the men went to great lengths to convince the witnesses that they were mistaken and had not seen anything out of the ordinary. Other times, the men threatened witnesses. Each time the Men in Black left a witness's house, they drove away in a black, unmarked sedan. Despite numerous attempts to determine who these men were and where they came from, their identity remained a secret. And all the while, the Mothman sightings continued throughout Point Pleasant and the surrounding area.

The Silver Bridge Tragedy

Erected in 1928, the Silver Bridge was a gorgeous chain suspension bridge that spanned the Ohio River, connecting Point Pleasant with Ohio. On December 15, 1967, the bridge was busy with holiday shoppers bustling back and forth between West Virginia and Ohio. As the day wore on, more and more cars started filling the bridge until shortly before 5:00 P.M., when traffic on the bridge came to a standstill. For several minutes, none of the cars budged. Suddenly, there was a loud popping noise and then the unthinkable happened: The Silver Bridge collapsed, sending dozens of cars and their passengers into the freezing water below.

Over the next few days, local authorities and residents searched the river hoping to find survivors, but in the end, 46 people lost their lives in the bridge collapse. A thorough investigation determined that a manufacturing flaw in one of the bridge's supporting bars caused the collapse. But there are others who claim that in the days and weeks leading up to the collapse, they saw Mothman and even the Men in Black around, on, and even under the bridge. Further witnesses state that while most of Point Pleasant was watching the Silver Bridge collapse, bright lights and strange objects were flying out of the area and disappearing into the winter sky. Perhaps that had nothing to do with the collapse of the Silver Bridge, but the Mothman has not been seen since…or has he?

Mothman Lives!

There are reports that the Mothman is still alive and well and has moved on to other areas of the United States. There are even those who claim that he was spotted flying near the Twin Towers on September 11, 2001, leading to speculation that Mothman is a portent of doom and only appears when disasters are imminent. Some believe Mothman was a visitor from another planet who returned home shortly after the Silver Bridge fell. Still others think the creature was the result of the toxic chemicals eventually discovered in the area near the TNT factory. And then there are skeptics who say that the initial sighting was nothing more than a giant sand crane and that mass hysteria took care of the rest. Whichever theory you choose to believe, the Mothman Lives Web site compiles all sightings of the creature from the 1960s to the present.

Just Mail Him His Sentence, Already

In late 2007, convicted armed robber Walter Barrett, 37, was determined not to attend his sentencing before a county judge in Florida. After he was awakened for his court appearance, Barrett refused to dress. Then he coated himself with his own excrement and pelted corrections officers with the excess. It took a dozen deputies to prepare Barrett for court, but appear he did.

He had previously lost two public defenders by spitting on them, and his third attorney argued that he was incompetent to stand trial.

Extreme Sports:
Playing on the Edge

*The following activities exist well off sport's mainstream path.
From 1,000 feet below ground to at least that high overhead,
endorphin-hounds risk it all in pursuit of "epic" moments.*

"Swabbing" the Swabbie

Water (or sea) jousting captures all the action of medieval
jousting without that sport's messy mauling and death. Nevertheless, it features fearsome competitors such as the "Unroot-
able" Casimir Castaldo and Vincent Cianni, "the man of
100 victories."

The drill is simple: Two boats are rowed toward each other.
When helm nears helm, competitors perched on protruding
platforms draw their lances and get busy. Last one standing gets the girl, or at least a moment of glory. And the vanquished? That wet critter gets to joust another day.

The sport dates back to 2780 B.C., when Egyptian bas-reliefs
depicted nautical jousts that were possibly a genuine form of
warfare. The most prestigious event is the Tournament de la
Saint-Louis held in Sète, France, every August. Since 1743 it
has attracted hordes of enthusiastic followers who come to see
their least favorite competitors get "bumped off."

I Can't Believe I Ate the Whole Thing

Nathan's Famous is the name most associated with eating con-
tests, but there are many more out there. At the 2007 Coney
Island event, 230-pound Californian Joey "Jaws" Chestnut
rammed 66 hot dogs and buns down his gullet in 12 minutes
to set a new world record.

Consider these impossible-sounding world marks: 22 slices of 16-inch-diameter pizza downed in ten minutes by 190-pound Chicagoan Patrick Bertoletti in August 2007. Or how about 8.31 pounds of Armour Vienna sausage wolfed down in ten minutes? This eat feat was accomplished by petite Sonya Thomas in May 2005. At 105 pounds, Thomas proves far and away that physical size is not necessary to produce records.

Underwater Pursuits

Scuba diving is risky business, but cave diving ups the ante even more. Here practitioners do underwater what spelunkers do underground. The difference? If a spelunker gets lost, it's usually an inconvenience. To a cave diver equipped with limited oxygen, it can mean death.

Experts explore ever deeper and more distant passages, but even the greatest can have an off day. Sheck Exley of Jacksonville, Florida, was a pioneer in cave diving. The 45-year-old had captured numerous world records in the sport before he met with tragedy in 1994 at Zacatón, a forbiddingly deep sinkhole in Mexico. When his body was recovered a few days later, his depth gauge showed a maximum depth of 879 feet. To many, he was the absolute best; unfortunately, statistics show he probably won't be the last.

Peak Performance

Ordinary skiing features lifts that take people to the top of groomed trails, but heliskiing uses helicopters to deliver skiers to wild, often untouched terrain. Reaching a mountain's absolute peak opens up a brave new world of virgin powder and incomparable alpine views, as well as extreme avalanches and bone breaks. The latter two occur often enough that outfitters generally provide clients with GPS transponders to help locate them in the event of an accident or avalanche.

Heliskiing isn't cheap. On average, heliskiers can expect to pay between $500 and $1,000 for three to four full runs. But it's worth it, according to aficionados who are willing to pay the price and risk their lives for solitude on the slopes and the chance to ski thousands more feet per run.

The Ultimate (Ground) Rush

B.A.S.E. jumping—an acronym for Building, Antenna, Span, Earth—is the practice of skydiving from these four different, ground-anchored points. Popularized by endorphin-junkies in the 1970s, the sport continues to grow despite inherent risks.

Though no single venue is typical, West Virginia's famed New River Gorge Bridge is revered as a glorious step-off spot. Once there, jumpers toss themselves into the 876-foot high abyss. Freefall time before chutes open? About four seconds. Time from takeoff to "splat!" if they don't? Approximately eight seconds. Since 1981, more than 116 unlucky B.A.S.E. jumpers have been killed pursuing the sport.

Shredding the Tarmac

Street luge (aka butt-boarding) is where speed freaks go when the melt is on. As with winter luge, the first to reach the bottom wins. Unlike the snowy version, steep paved roadways of varying lengths are used for propulsion.

Street lugers lay flat on their backs, but because there is no ice, they ride an elongated version of a skateboard. Steering is accomplished with leg pressure and by shifting body weight.

Born in the 1970s by skateboarders searching for greater speed, a modern "boarder" can hit speeds in excess of 70 miles per hour, with handling that boggles the mind. Even so, accidents happen, and when they do, they're generally spectacular.

Freestyle Walking

Despite its unimposing name, freestyle walking represents an all-new level of extreme sport. Using an urban landscape as their playground, practitioners outfitted with nothing more than their bodies fluidly jump from building to building, swing from fences, dive over benches and walls, and hop, skip, and jump over just about everything else. Unaware observers might think they're watching the filming of an action flick.

The extreme part of this sport kicks in when grip is lost, distances are misjudged, or Murphy's Law comes into play. Since the early 1990s, the sport has attracted a youth culture that constantly raises the bar by attempting ever-more dicey moves.

Wakeboarding Gets Gnarly

Occasionally, an expert in a given sport asks, "How can I make this *less* safe?" This seems to be the case with rail-sliding, a relatively new addition to the wakeboardist's bag of tricks.

Here's how it works: A wakeboarder is towed by a boat, as if waterskiing, toward a stationary rail in the water. The widths of these beams vary from a few inches to more than a foot, and some reach 90 feet in length. At the last second, the boarder bunny hops on top of this slicker-than-glass surface, landing his board in a standing position with feet straddling the rail.

If all goes well, he slides along to glory. If not, a host of really bad things can happen, including back-crushing "kick-outs" (backward falls onto the rail), agonizing face plants (a kickout performed in reverse), and worse.

A Pick and a Prayer

Leave it to rock climbers to devise ever-more dangerous pastimes. Ice climbing raises the bar and offers a way to climb in the dreaded winter off-season.

With pickax in hand and crampons (metal spikes that attach to boots) strapped to feet, the climber advances…until he or she hears an ominous cracking sound. Though this scenario is infrequent, it does happen. When it doesn't, ice climbers enjoy the same rush as rock climbers.

With soft ice, falling ice, and avalanches posing additional risks, ice climbing is thought to be even more perilous than rock climbing. But that doesn't stop the adventurous from taking a swing at it—the swing of an ax, that is.

Down the Chute

Imagine whooshing down an icy luge track at breakneck speed, the course moving by in a blur. Now imagine lying *headfirst* on a sled and doing the same. Welcome to skeleton luge, where one false move produces one serious headache.

Competitors, or "sliders," must first run 100 feet while pushing their sleds. Then they jump aboard, navigate the course with their body movements, and hope all goes according to plan. The sled follows a steeply banked track, and there are no brakes. Fastest time wins the day. After hitting speeds of 80 miles per hour and pulling up to four Gs on a skeleton luge, the neighborhood toboggan hill will never look the same.

Getting into It

Straight from New Zealand comes zorbing, an offbeat ball sport invented in the 1990s that's practiced inside a giant ball. Here's the drill: The zorbian (zorbing enthusiast) straps himself inside a fully inflated plastic ball. Then, with common sense jettisoned in favor of high adventure, an assistant sets the ball rolling down a steep hill. Happy shrieks can be heard as the zorbian attains speeds up to 25 miles per hour. If the ball veers off course or takes a bad bounce, shrieks of a far different sort can be heard.

Clearly on a roll, this sport has spread into Norway, Sweden, Switzerland, China, Japan, England, and the United States, among other countries.

Behind the Mouse Ears

- *Since 1967, there's been a private club in Disneyland's New Orleans Square called Club 33. It's the only place in the park where alcohol is sold. Despite a $7,500 initiation fee and $2,250 annual dues, the club has about 400 members and a three-year waiting list to join.*

- *Until the late 1960s, men with long hair were denied admission to the park. Disneyland had an unwritten dress code and guests were admitted based upon the impression they made on the ticket takers at the front gate.*

- *When Soviet premier Nikita Khrushchev visited the United States in 1959, he wanted to visit Disneyland, but authorities said they could not ensure his security and denied his request. Instead he was given a tour of Los Angeles public housing.*

- *Science-fiction author Harlan Ellison was hired as a writer for Disney, but his tenure only lasted a half-day. In the commissary, he joked about making a pornographic Disney film, a comment that was overheard by studio boss Roy O. Disney, Walt's brother, who promptly fired Ellison.*

- *During World War II, Disney released a series of instructional cartoons for the troops. They also developed an animated film in 1946 called* The Story of Menstruation, *which was used in girl's health classes for several decades.*

- *Although his fortune was built on the back of Mickey Mouse, Walt Disney was allegedly afraid of mice.*

- *Until 2000, Disney park employees were not allowed to have facial hair. Now male employees are allowed to sport well-groomed mustaches.*

The Body Farm

When will an employee not be reprimanded for laying down on the job? When that worker is a Body Farm recruit. Hundreds of rotting corpses get away with such shenanigans every day at the University of Tennessee's "Body Farm," and they have yet to be written up for it. In fact, they are praised for their profound contributions to science.

A Eureka Moment

Forensic anthropologist William M. Bass had a dream. As an expert in the field of human decomposition, he couldn't fathom why a facility devoted to this under-studied process didn't exist. So, in 1972, working in conjunction with the University of Tennessee, he founded the Body Farm or, more specifically, the University of Tennessee Forensic Anthropology Facility.

Body Snatchers

If you're going to start a body farm, it doesn't take a forensic anthropologist to realize that there might be a problem in obtaining bodies. One way is to use bodies that have been donated for medical studies. Another focuses on cadavers that rot away each year at medical examiners offices, with nary a soul to claim them. Enter Bass and his associates. Like "pods" from *Invasion of the Body Snatchers,* these scientists grab every body they can lay their hands on.

A Creepy Joint

Just outside of Knoxville, the eerie three-acre wooded plot that Bass claimed for his scientific studies—which is surrounded by a razor wire fence (lest the dead bodies try to escape)—is where an unspecified number of cadavers in various states of decomposition are kept. While some hang out completely in the open, others spend their time in shallow graves or entombed in vaults. Others dip their toes and other body parts in ponds. And a few spend eternity inside sealed car trunks.

Dying for the Cause

So why is this done? What can be learned from observing human flesh and bone decay in the hot Tennessee sun? Plenty, according to scientists and members of the media who have studied the Body Farm. "Nearly everything known about the science of human decomposition comes from one place—forensic anthropologist William Bass' Body Farm," declared CNN in high praise of the facility. The bodies are strewn in different positions and under varying circumstances for reasons far from happenstance. Each cadaver will display differing reactions to decomposition, insect and wildlife interference, and the elements. These invaluable indicators can help investigators zero-in on the cause and time of death in current and future criminal cases.

Stiff Legacy

Bass himself claims that knowledge gleaned from Body Farm studies has proven especially helpful to murder investigations. "People will have alibis for certain time periods, and if you can determine death happened at another time, it makes a difference in the court case," said Bass. Even the prestigious FBI uses the Body Farm as a real-world simulator to help train its agents. Every February, representatives visit the site to dig for bodies that farm hands have prepared as simulated crime scenes. "We have five of them down there for them," explains Bass. "They excavate the burials and look for evidence that we put there."

Such is life down on the Body Farm.

As Seen on TV

Keen on disproving a key point made in an episode of *CSI*, a 55-year-old South Dakota man was killed in 2007 after shooting himself in the stomach. The man was trying to prove that a woman featured in the episode could indeed shoot herself in the stomach, despite a script that showed otherwise. Sadly, he was absolutely correct.

Nessie: Shock in the Loch

The legend of Nessie, the purported inhabitant of Scotland's Loch Ness, dates back to the year 565 when a roving Christian missionary named St. Columba is said to have rebuked a huge water monster to save the life of a swimmer. Rumors persisted from that time on, but it wasn't until the 20th century that the creature became internationally famous.

Monster Ahoy

In 1933, one witness said he saw the creature three times; that same year, a vacationing couple claimed they saw a large creature with flippers and a long neck slither across the road and then heard it splash into the lake. These incidents made news around the world, and the hunt for Nessie was on.

Sightings multiplied and became more and more difficult to explain away. In 1971, a priest named Father Gregory Brusey saw a speedy long-necked creature cruising through the loch. One investigator estimates that more than 3,000 people have seen Nessie. The witnesses come from every walk of life, including teachers, doctors, police officers, and scientists.

Monster Media Madness

As technology has advanced, Nessie has been hunted with more sophisticated equipment, often with disappointing results. In 1934, a doctor snapped the famous "Surgeon's Photo," which showed a dinosaurlike head atop a long neck sticking out of the water. It has since been proven a hoax and what was thought to be Nessie was actually a picture of a toy submarine. Many other photos have been taken, but all are inconclusive.

Since 1934, numerous expeditions have been mounted in search of Nessie. Scuba divers and even submarines have scoured the lake to no avail because the amount of peat in the water makes visibility extremely poor.

In 2003, the British Broadcasting Corporation undertook a massive satellite-assisted sonar sweep of the entire lake, but again with no results. And in 2007, cameras were given to 50,000 people attending a concert on the lake's shore in hopes that someone might get lucky and snap a shot of Nessie. But apparently she doesn't like rock music—Nessie was a no-show.

The Ness-essary Debate

Theories about Nessie's true nature abound. One of the most popular ideas, thanks to the oft-reported long neck, flippers, and bulbous body, is that Nessie is a surviving plesiosaur—a marine reptile thought to have gone extinct 65 million years ago. Critics insist that even if a cold-blooded reptile could exist in the lake's frigid waters, Loch Ness is not large enough to support a breeding population of them. Other theories suggest that Nessie is a giant eel, a string of seals or otters swimming

in formation, floating logs, a porpoise, or a huge sturgeon.

Locals have hinted that the creature is actually a demon. Stories of devil worship and mysterious rituals in the area have gone hand in hand with rumors of bodies found floating in the loch. In the early 1900s, famed occultist Aleister Crowley owned a home on the lake's southern shore where he held "black masses" and conducted other ceremonies that may have aimed to "raise" monsters. And for centuries, Scots have repeated folktales of the kelpie, or water horse, a creature that can shape-shift in order to lure the unwary into the water.

Whatever the truth about Nessie, she has made quite a splash as a tourist attraction. Every year thousands of people try their luck at spotting and recording the world's most famous monster.

The Restless Spirits
of the LaLaurie Mansion

There is no city in the American South as haunted as New Orleans, which is not surprising given its dark history of death, murder, war, slavery, and on occasion, downright depravity. New Orleans is a city that stands as a prime example of the deeds of the past creating the hauntings of today.

There are scores of ghost stories in the city, but there is no story as famous as that of the LaLaurie Mansion. It has long been considered the French Quarter's most haunted house, and in many early writings of the city, its infamy was so great that it was simply referred to as "the haunted house."

The origins of the ghostly tales centering on 1140 Royal Street began around 1832, when Dr. Louis LaLaurie and his wife, Delphine, moved into the mansion. It was regarded as one of the finest houses in the city and one that befit their social status—the family was noted for its grand affairs and respected for its wealth and prominence.

Madame LaLaurie was considered one of the most intelligent, beautiful, and influential women in the city. She was known for her grand dinner parties that showed off her fine china and imported rugs and fabrics. One of the things that nearly all of her guests recalled about her was her extraordinary kindness.

A Darker Side

This was the side of Madame LaLaurie that her friends and admirers saw. But beneath the delicate and refined exterior was a cruel, cold-blooded, and possibly insane woman—a side that some were forced to see on a regular basis.

The finery of the LaLaurie house was attended to by dozens of slaves. Many guests to the mansion remembered the finely dressed servants, who made sure that guests wanted for nothing. Other slaves, sometimes glimpsed in passing, were not so elegant. In fact, they were surprisingly thin and hollow-chested. Rumors began to swirl that Madame LaLaurie abused these slaves. It was said that she kept her cook chained to the kitchen's fireplace and that many other slaves were subjected to treatment that went far beyond mere cruelty.

Mr. Montreuil, a neighbor on Royal Street, was one of the first to become suspicious that something was not quite right with the slaves in the LaLaurie house. Parlor maids were replaced with no explanation, and stable hands suddenly disappeared, never to be seen again. Montreuil made a report to the authorities, but little, if anything, was done.

One day, another neighbor heard a scream and saw Madame LaLaurie chasing a young servant girl across the courtyard with a whip. The neighbor watched as the girl was pursued from floor to floor until she and Madame LaLaurie at last appeared on the rooftop. The child ran down the steeply pitched roof and vanished. Moments later, the neighbor heard a horrible thud as the child's small body struck the flagstones below. Stunned, the neighbor watched the house that night and told authorities that she witnessed the girl being buried in a shallow grave.

When the authorities investigated the neighbor's claims, the LaLaurie slaves were impounded and sold at auction. Unfortunately, Madame LaLaurie coaxed some relatives into secretly buying them back for her. The entire incident had been a terrible accident, she said. Some believed her, but many others didn't, and the LaLaurie social standing began to slowly decline. Soon, everyone would know the truth.

Unspeakable Horrors

In April 1834, a huge fire broke out in the kitchen of the LaLaurie Mansion. The story goes that the fire was set by the cook, who couldn't handle any more torture at the hands of Madame LaLaurie. As the fire swept through the house and smoke filled the rooms, the streets outside began filling with people. Soon the volunteer fire department was on hand carrying buckets of water, and bystanders began crowding into the house, trying to offer assistance.

Throughout the chaos, Madame LaLaurie remained calm. She directed the volunteers to carry out expensive paintings and smaller pieces of furniture. She was intent on saving the house but would not allow panic to overcome her.

Montreuil, the neighbor who had been suspicious of Madame LaLaurie, came to assist during the fire. He asked if the slaves were in danger from the blaze and was told by Madame LaLaurie not to interfere in her family business. Montreuil appealed to a local official who was also present. They began searching for the rest of the servants and were joined by several firefighters. They tried to enter the attic but the door was locked, so firefighters broke it down.

What they saw in the attic was unlike anything they could have imagined. They found slaves chained to the walls. Cruel experiments had been carried out with mouths sewn shut, eyes poked out, limbs removed, and skulls opened while the slaves were still alive. The men were overwhelmed by the terrifying sight, as well as the stench of death and decaying flesh permeating the confined chamber.

Although the chamber contained a number of dead bodies, many of the slaves were still alive. Some were unconscious and some cried in pain, begging to be killed and put out of their misery. The men fled the scene in disgust, and once the fire was extinguished, bystanders helped the surviving slaves out of the attic and provided them with food and water.

It is uncertain just how many slaves were found in Madame LaLaurie's torture chamber. Only a few were strong enough to leave the chamber of horrors under their own power.

As the mutilated slaves were carried out of the house, a crowd gathered outside. Nothing happened for hours, but word of the atrocities began to spread. Madame LaLaurie alone, it was said, was responsible for the atrocities in the house, and the people wanted vengeance. Threats were shouted as the crowd grew restless.

Suddenly, the gates to the mansion opened and a carriage clattered onto the street. The coach sped past, carrying its passengers out of sight. Madame LaLaurie had escaped, fleeing to a ship that took her far away from New Orleans.

The seething mob on Royal Street was enraged. They decided to take their anger out on the mansion the LaLauries had left behind. They broke furniture, shattered windows, and looted the fine china, expensive glassware, and imported foods before the authorities arrived and restored order. The house was eventually closed and sealed, and it sat on Royal Street, completely empty for years. Or so it seemed at the time.

The Haunted House on Royal Street

Recently discovered letters signed by Madame LaLaurie show that she escaped to France where her dark past was unknown. No legal action was ever taken against her, and she was never seen in New Orleans, or her mansion, again. The same cannot be said for her victims....

Tales of ghosts at 1140 Royal Street began soon after the LaLauries fled. As the mansion began to fall into disrepair, neighbors and passersby claimed to hear cries of terror from the deserted property. They saw apparitions of slaves peering out from the windows and walking in the overgrown gardens.

The house was eventually sold, but the first owner kept it for only three months. He heard groaning sounds and cries in the darkness and soon abandoned the place. He attempted to operate it as a boarding house, but renters usually only stayed for a few days and then moved out. Finally, he gave up, and the house was abandoned again.

The LaLaurie house switched owners several times until the late 1890s, when it was converted into a boarding house for recent immigrants.

A number of strange events occurred during that time. One story told of a tenant being attacked by a naked man in chains, who quickly vanished. There were stories of children being chased by a spectral woman with a whip; screams and weeping sounds from the attic; and on one occasion, a mother was frightened to see a woman in a formal gown gazing into the crib where her infant slept. Even cheap rent was not enough to convince tenants to stay for longer than a week or two, and soon the house was empty once again.

The Haunted Saloon

Over the years, the house served as a saloon, a furniture store, and a refuge for poor and homeless men. In 1969, the mansion was converted into 20 apartments before a new owner, a retired New Orleans doctor, purchased it. The house was restored to its original condition and turned into condominiums. Apparently, tenants are a little easier to keep today than they were a century ago.

That owner did not observe any supernatural occurrences in the house, but past tenants have told of doors that opened and closed by themselves, water faucets that inexplicably turned on, toilets that flushed under their own power, and other small irritations. Others told of a lingering scream that was sometimes heard in the courtyard at night.

The LaLaurie Mansion was recently purchased by actor Nicholas Cage, who previously bought another property in the Garden District from famous horror writer Anne Rice. The house has been quiet as of late, but perhaps Cage will draw out the spirits of this terrible tragedy.

Madame LaLaurie's Secret Graveyard

During a remodeling of the house that took place some years ago, workers discovered an unmarked graveyard under the floorboards of the house. The skeletal remains had been placed there haphazardly and with no sense of organization or ceremony. When officials investigated, they found the remains to be from the early to mid-1800s. Some believe that Madame LaLaurie may have buried these bodies in secret, solving the mystery of why some of the slaves simply disappeared.

But how many of her slaves did she kill? And how many of them have never found peace?

Scarab beetles, also known as dung beetles, roll fresh manure into balls several inches in diameter before pushing them to a safe place to eat.

Dinner with a Ghost

Next time you enjoy a meal at your favorite restaurant, know that you may be dining with some unseen guests. Here are a few eateries where a ghostly good time is always on the menu.

Stone's Public House, Ashland, Massachusetts

Since 1834, Stone's Public House has been serving up food and drink to area residents and visitors alike. Should you choose to stop in for a bite, first take a good look at the photo of John Stone hanging over the bar's fireplace, so you'll be sure to recognize his ghost when it appears. Stone's spirit is said to be one of a handful that haunt the inn. Other spirits include a man that Stone accidentally murdered in an argument during a card game. According to the legend, Stone and several friends buried the man in the basement. The spirits make their presence known by breaking glasses, causing cold breezes, and appearing as shadowy figures.

Arnaud's, New Orleans, Louisiana

The ghost of a man dressed in an old-fashioned tuxedo is often spotted near the windows of the main dining room. But this ghost, believed to be that of Arnaud Cazenave, the first owner of the establishment, is not alone. A ghostly woman has been seen walking out of the restroom and moving silently across the restaurant before disappearing into a wall.

Country House Restaurant, Clarendon Hills, Illinois

As the story goes, many years ago, a woman who was dating one of the restaurant's bartenders stopped in and asked him to watch her baby for a while. When he refused, the woman put the baby back in her car, sped off down the road, and promptly crashed into a tree, killing herself and her child. That should have been the end to this sad tale, but apparently the ghost of both the young woman and her baby found their way back to the restaurant. The young woman's ghost has been blamed for banging on walls and doors and the jukebox playing on its own. She has also been seen walking through the restaurant and sometimes people outside see the ghostly woman in an upstairs window. Patrons and employees have also reported hearing a baby cry, even when there were no babies present.

Poogan's Porch, Charleston, South Carolina

Originally built as a house in 1888, the building underwent major renovations and reopened as a restaurant in 1976. Perhaps it was those renovations that brought the ghost of Zoe St. Amand, former owner of the house, back to see what all the fuss was about. Zoe's ghost is described as an older woman in a long black dress who silently wanders through the establishment at all hours of the day and night.

Big Nose Kate's Saloon, Tombstone, Arizona

Named after Mary Katherine Haroney, thought to be the first prostitute in Tombstone, the building was originally known as the Grand Hotel. At this establishment, there are several ghosts who seem to enjoy passing the time touching patrons and employees, moving objects, and appearing in the occasional photograph. The most famous ghost, however, is that of a man known as the Swamper. Legend has it that the man lived in the basement of the saloon and had dug a secret tunnel under the street and into a nearby silver mine. He would sneak into the mines late at night and make off with untold amounts of silver. The strange sounds and muffled voices still coming from this long-abandoned tunnel seem to prove that even in death, the Swamper continues his underhanded and illegal mining practices.

More than 1,400 people studied at the Ringling Brothers and Barnum & Bailey Clown College before it closed in 1997.

Nostradamus: Seer of Visions

Nostradamus was born in December 1503 in Saint-Rémy-de-Provence, a small town in southern France. Little is known about his childhood except that he came from a very large family and that he may have been educated by his maternal great-grandfather. In his teens, Nostradamus entered the University of Avignon but was only there for about a year before the school was forced to close its doors due to an outbreak of the plague. He later became a successful apothecary and even created a pill that could supposedly protect against the plague.

Looking to the Future

It is believed that some time in the 1540s, Nostradamus began taking an interest in the occult, particularly in ways to predict the future. His preferred method was scrying: gazing into a bowl of water or a mirror and waiting for visions to appear.

Nostradamus published a highly successful almanac for the year 1550, which included some of his prophecies and predictions. This almanac was so successful that Nostradamus wrote more, perhaps even several a year, until his death in 1566. Even so, it was a single book that caused the most controversy, both when it was released and even today.

Les Prophéties

In addition to creating his almanacs, Nostradamus also began compiling his previously unpublished prophecies into one massive volume. Released in 1555, *Les Prophéties* (*The Prophecies*) would become one of the most controversial and perplexing books ever written. The book contained hundreds of quatrains (four-line stanzas or poems), but Nostradamus worried that some might see his prophecies as demonic, so he encoded them to obscure their true meanings. To do this, Nostradamus did everything from playing with the syntax of the quatrains to switching between French, Greek, Latin, and other languages.

When first released, some people did think that Nostradamus was in league with the devil. Others simply thought he was insane and that his quatrains were nothing more than the ramblings of a delusional man. As time went on, though, people started looking to Nostradamus's prophecies to see if they were coming true. It became a common practice that after a major event in history, people would pull out a copy of *Les Prophéties* to see if they could find a hidden reference to it buried in one of Nostradamus's quatrains. It is a practice that has continued to this day and only gets more and more common as the years go by.

Lost in Translation

One of the interesting and frustrating things about Nostradamus's *Les Prophéties* is that due to the printing procedures in his time, no two editions of his book were ever alike. Not only were there differences in spelling or punctuation, but entire words and phrases were often changed, especially when translated from French to English. Presently, there are more than 200 editions of *Les Prophéties* in print, all of which have subtle differences in the text. So it's not surprising that people from all over the world have looked into their version and found references to the French Revolution, Napoleon, the rise of Hitler, the JFK assassination, even the *Apollo* moon landing. But of all the messages reportedly hidden in Nostradamus's quatrains, the most talked about recently are those relating to the terrorist attacks on September 11, 2001.

Soon after the Twin Towers fell, an e-mail started making the rounds, which claimed that Nostradamus had predicted the events and quoted the following quatrain as proof:

In the City of God there will be a great thunder,
Two Brothers torn apart by Chaos,
While the fortress endures,
The great leader will succumb,
The third big war will begin when the big city is burning

—Nostradamus, 1654

Anyone reading the above can clearly see that Nostradamus is describing September 11, the Twin Towers ("Two Brothers") falling, and the start of World War III. Pretty chilling, except Nostradamus never wrote it. It's nothing more than an Internet hoax that spread like wildfire. It's a pretty bad hoax, too. First, Nostradamus wrote quatrains, which have four lines. This one has five. Also, consider that the date Nostradamus supposedly penned this—1654—was almost 90 years after he died. Nostradamus might have been able to see the future, but there's no mention of him being able to write from beyond the grave.

However, others believe Nostradamus did indeed pen a quatrain that predicted September 11. It is quatrain I.87, which when translated reads:

> *Volcanic fire from the center of the earth*
> *Will cause tremors around the new city;*
> *Two great rocks will make war for a long time*
> *Then Arethusa will redden a new river.*

Those who believe this quatrain predicted September 11 believe that the "new city" is a thinly-veiled reference to New York City. They further state that Nostradamus would often use *rocks* to refer to religious beliefs and that the third stanza refers to the religious differences between the United States and the terrorists. Skeptic James Randi, however, believes that the "new city" referred to is Naples, not New York. So who's right? No one is really sure, so for now, the debate continues…at least until the next major catastrophe hits and people go scrambling to the bookshelves to see what Nostradamus had to say about it.

When glass breaks, the cracks move faster than 3,000 miles per hour. To photograph the event, a camera must shoot at a millionth of a second!

Spotting Sasquatch

💀　💀　💀　💀　💀

Throughout the world, it's called Alma, Yeti, Sasquatch, the Abominable Snowman, Wildman, and Bigfoot. Whatever the name, people agree that it's tall, hairy, doesn't smell good, and has a habit of showing up in locations around the globe— especially in North America.

Jasper, Alberta, Canada (1811)

This was the first known Bigfoot evidence found in North America. An explorer named David Thompson found 14-inch footprints in the snow, each toe topped by a short claw. He and his party didn't follow the tracks, fearing their guns would be useless against such a large animal. In his journal he wrote that he couldn't bring himself to believe such a creature existed.

British Columbia, Canada (1924)

In 1957, prospector Albert Ostman was finally able to come forward about a chilling event that happened to him more than 30 years prior. While camping at the head of Toba Inlet near Vancouver Island, Ostman was snatched up, still in his sleeping bag, and taken to a small valley where several Bigfoot

were living. Held captive for several days, Ostman was only able to escape when one of the larger creatures tried to eat his snuff and chaos ensued.

Wanoga Butte, Oregon (1957)

After a long, uneventful morning hunting, Gary Joanis and Jim Newall were ecstatic when Joanis felled a deer with a single shot. But when a hairy creature "not less than nine feet tall" emerged from the woods, threw the deer over its shoulder, and lumbered off, the two men were left speechless.

Monroe, Michigan (1965)
On August 13, Christine Van Acker and her mother were driving when a large, hairy creature came out of the nearby woods. Frightened by the creature, the mother lost control of the car and grazed the beast. The car stalled and while the mother struggled to start it, the creature put its arm through the window, struck Christine in the face and slammed her mother's head against the car door, leaving both women with black eyes, photos of which were widely circulated in the press.

Bluff Creek, California (1967)
The famous sighting by Roger Patterson and Bob Gimlin yielded the first home-movie footage of Bigfoot. Although critics said it was obviously a man in a gorilla suit, Patterson denied the hoax allegations until his death in 1972. As of 2008, Gimlin still contends that the footage wasn't faked.

Spearfish, South Dakota (1977)
Betty Johnson and her three daughters saw two Bigfoot in a cornfield. The larger of the two was eight-feet tall; the other, slightly smaller. They both appeared to be eating corn and making a whistling sound.

Paris Township, Ohio (1978)
Herbert and Evelyn Cayton reported that a seven-foot-tall, 300-pound, fur-covered creature appeared at their house so frequently that their daughter thought it was a pet.

Jackson, Wyoming (1980)
On June 17, Glenn Towner and Robert Goodrich went into the woods on Snow King Mountain to check out a lean-to built by a friend of theirs. After hearing moaning and growling, the pair was chased out of the woods by a 12-foot-tall creature covered in hair. The creature followed them back to civilization,

where it was last spotted standing briefly beneath a streetlight before vanishing back into the woods.

Crescent City, California (1995)
A TV crew was driving in their RV, filming the scenery in Jedediah Smith Redwoods State Park, when an eight-foot-tall hairy giant crossed their path and was caught on tape.

Cotton Island, Louisiana (2000)
Bigfoot surprised lumberjacks Earl Whitstine and Carl Dubois while they were clearing timber. The hairy figure returned a few days later, leaving behind footprints and hair samples.

Selma, Oregon (2000)
While hiking with his family near the Oregon Caves National Monument on July 1, psychologist Matthew Johnson smelled a strange musky odor. Hearing odd grunting noises coming from behind some trees, Johnson went to investigate and saw something very tall and hairy walking away. When asked to describe it, Johnson said that it could be "nothing else but a Sasquatch."

Granton, Wisconsin (2000)
As James Hughes was delivering newspapers early one morning, he saw a shaggy figure, about eight feet tall, carrying a goat. However, sheriffs called to the scene couldn't find any footprints or missing goats.

Mt. St. Helens, Washington (2002)
Jerry Kelso made his wife and two-year-old child wait in the car, while he chased what he thought was a man in a gorilla suit. When he was about 100 feet away, he realized that it wasn't a gorilla suit and that the seven-foot-tall creature was carrying a club.

Cranbrook, British Columbia, Canada (2007)
Snowplow driver Gord Johnson drove by a large, hairy figure with a "conical head" walking along a snowy road.

Back from the Dead

Nothing is certain but death and taxes...yet sometimes that's not so true. History is riddled with strange tales of people who just weren't content staying dead.

- After a major automobile accident in 2007, Venezuelan Carlos Camejo was declared dead. The coroner had just begun the autopsy by cutting into Camejo's face when the man began to bleed. Immediately realizing that the crash victim was still alive, the doctor became even more stunned when Camejo regained consciousness as he was stitching up the incision. "I woke up because the pain was unbearable," Camejo told reporters after his ordeal.

- Ann Greene, a young servant in Oxford, England, was convicted of killing her illegitimate newborn child after the baby was stillborn in 1650. After she was hanged, Greene's body was cut down and transported to Oxford University where it was to be used for anatomy classes. As the lesson progressed, Greene began to moan and regained consciousness. The students helped revive her and treated her injuries. Eventually she was given a pardon, gained a level of celebrity, married, and had several children.

- In 1674, Marjorie Erskine died in Chirnside, Scotland, and was buried in a shallow grave by a sexton with less than honorable intentions. Erskine was sent to her eternal rest with some valuable jewelry the sexton was intent on adding to his own collection. After digging up her body, the sexton was trying to cut off her finger to steal her ring when, much to his surprise, she awoke.

- After being found unconscious and sprawled on the floor of her Albany, New York, apartment by paramedics in 1996, Mildred Clarke, 86, was pronounced dead by a coroner. About 90 minutes later an attendant noticed that the body bag containing Clarke was, in fact, moving. Clarke recovered but unfortunately only lived for another week, giving into the stress of age and heart failure.

- When 19th-century Cardinal Somaglia took ill and passed out, he was thought to be dead. Being a high-ranking church official, embalming was begun immediately so he could lie in state, as was customary. As a surgeon began the process by cutting into the cardinal's chest, he noticed that the man's heart was still beating. Somaglia awoke and pushed the knife away. However, the damage was done, and he died from the embalming process.

- Oran was a devout sixth-century monk on Iona, a small island off the coast of Scotland. According to legend, he was buried alive by his own urging to sanctify the island but was dug up three days later and found alive. He told his fellow monks that he had seen heaven and hell and a host of other sights. "There is no such great wonder in death, nor is hell what it has been described," he claimed as he was pulled from the ground. The head monk, Columba, ordered that he be reburied immediately as a heretic. To this day, when someone in the region broaches an uncomfortable subject, people will tell the person to "throw mud in the mouth of St. Oran."

- In 1740, 16-year-old William Duell was convicted of rape and murder and sentenced to death by hanging. After his lifeless body was removed from the gallows it was taken to the local college for dissection. His body was stripped and laid out in preparation for the process when a servant who was washing the corpse noticed it was still breathing. After a full recovery, he was returned to prison, but it was decided that instead of being hanged again he would be exiled to the then-prison state of Australia.

- A victim of the horrors of war, three-year-old Lebanese Hussein Belhas had his leg blown off in an Israeli attack in 1996. Declared dead, the boy's body was placed in a morgue freezer, but when attendants returned he was found alive. After he recovered from his injuries, Belhas took a stoic stance on his fate. "I am the boy who died, and then came back to life. This was my destiny," he said.

- In late 1995, Daphne Banks of Cambridgeshire, England, was declared dead. On New Year's Day, 1996, as she lay in the mortuary, an undertaker noticed a vein twitching in her leg. Examining closer, the attendant could hear snoring coming from the body. The 61-year-old Banks was quickly transferred to a local hospital where she made a full recovery.

- As mourners sadly paid their last respects to the Greek Orthodox bishop Nicephorus Glycas on the island of Lesbos in 1896, they were met with quite a shock. Glycas had been lying in state for two days as preparations for his burial were being made. Suddenly, he sat up and looked around at the stunned congregation. "What are you staring at?" he reportedly asked.

- During the 16th century, a young man named Matthew Wall died in the village of Braughing, England. As pallbearers were carrying him to his final resting place, they dropped his coffin after one of them stumbled on a stone. When the coffin crashed to the ground, Wall was revived and went on to live a full life. When he actually did pass away years later, the terms of his will stipulated that Old Man's Day be celebrated in the village every October 2, the anniversary of his return from the dead.

Ernest Vincent Wright wrote a novel that contains more than 50,000 words—none of them with the letter E.

Strange Theme Restaurants

Eating at a restaurant is so boring. You sit down, you order, you eat, blah, blah, blah. Why not eat from a toilet-shape bowl or watch medieval knights joust each other while you dine?

Banana Restaurant, Taiwan

Oh, if only it was actually a banana-themed restaurant. Nope, this Taiwanese restaurant has a *condom* theme that just cloaks the concept with a euphemism. Condom-inspired art decorates the place, the dishes are visually suggestive and named with sexual innuendos, and every guest receives a free condom with their meal. The proprietors say the restaurant is condom-themed to promote safe sex and AIDS awareness.

Medieval Times, Numerous Locations

One of the most famous theme restaurants is also one of the strangest. Started in Spain in 1973, the Medieval Times Dinner & Tournament is now a nationwide chain in the United States. Diners enter a huge arena, receive paper crowns, and eat stew and bread with their bare hands while armored knights joust each other on horseback. Fair maidens are saved and villains are vanquished—all in a suburb near you!

The Toilet Bowl Restaurant, Taiwan

Matong means "toilet" in Chinese, and toilets are what you get at this restaurant, which opened in 2004. Patrons sit on converted toilet seats and dine from toilet-shaped bowls. Neon-lit faucets and urinals line the walls, and favorite dishes include chunky soups and soft-serve chocolate ice cream. We don't need to point out why those items are on the menu, do we?

O. Noir, Montreal, Quebec, Canada

Don't bother getting dressed up for dinner at O. Noir—no one will be able to see your outfit. Everything happens in the dark at this restaurant. Customers eat, converse, and order in pitch darkness. We're not sure how it all works in the kitchen, but the owners say that diners have a heightened sense of the food's flavors because one of their five senses is taken away. Five percent of the restaurant's profits are donated to local organizations that serve the blind and visually impaired.

Fortezza Medicea, Italy

For some, getting into this restaurant is easier than getting out. Located inside a maximum-security prison outside of Pisa, Fortezza Medicea is a restaurant staffed by criminals. Murderers, thieves, and various other convicts pour wine and serve tasty Italian dishes to diners who line up for a seat at the simple wooden tables. But be prepared to eat with plastic forks and knives—the real stuff is contraband.

X-Rated Sushi

It's nothing new in Japan, but in the past few years, the time-honored tradition of eating sushi off a naked woman is gaining ground in the United States. Known as *nyotaimori* or "body sushi," restaurants that offer this dining experience are usually just regular sushi joints hoping to bring in new customers for a meal and an eyeful. The women who participate aren't totally naked: they commonly wear plastic wrap and enough lingerie to cover their private parts. Sushi is placed on their abdomens only and patrons use chopsticks to select their food. It comes as no surprise that a lot of women's rights groups are enraged by the idea, but eating raw fish off a warm body doesn't disgust enough people to keep them from doing it.

The average adult's skin weighs approximately 9 pounds, measures 21 square feet, and houses more than 11 miles of blood vessels.

FREAKY FACTS: DEER

- In Blacksburg, Virginia, in 2003, a six-point buck ran into a supermarket. The deer leapt over soup cans and knocked over displays before escaping out a back door, where he was hit, but not killed, by a passing vehicle.

- The legend of a ghost deer echoes through the canyons of Mt. Eddy in northern California. Hunters describe a giant buck with 12 points on one antler and 10 on the other. Those who have shot at it say bullets pass right through, and its tracks are said to disappear at natural barriers such as great ridges or bodies of water.

- On August 1, 2003, Joshua Laprise spotted a pure white albino deer eating in a field in Rhode Island. The chances of seeing an adult albino white-tailed deer in the wild are about one in a million. Most albinos do not live more than a few years due to lack of protective coloration but are protected by law in Illinois, Iowa, Tennessee, and Wisconsin.

- In the late 1940s, white-colored deer began populating what is now known as the Conservation Area (CA) in Seneca, New York. It seems that some of the white-tailed deer in the CA carried a gene for white coloration. Today, there are more than 200 white deer living in the CA, making it the only place in the world with such a large population of white deer.

- The antlers of white-tailed deer can become self-defeating traps—if two battling males lock horns, they may be unable to separate and consequently starve to death or be killed by a predator.

The Devil Is Alive and Well...
And Living in New Jersey

💀　　💀　　💀　　💀　　💀

The Pine Barrens consist of more than a million acres of forested land in central and southern New Jersey. So named because the area's sandy, acidic soil is bad for growing crops, it has proven a fertile home for an amazing collection of trees and plants. Of course, if the stories are true, the area is also home to a bizarre winged creature known as the Jersey Devil.

Birth of the Devil

There are many legends concerning the origin of the Jersey Devil. The most popular involves the Leeds family, who came to America from Europe in the 1730s and settled in the southern area of the Pine Barrens. The Leeds family quickly grew by leaps and bounds, and before long, their house was filled with a dozen children. Needless to say, when Mother Leeds found out she was pregnant with child number 13, she was less than enthusiastic. In fact, she supposedly yelled out that she was done having children and that this child "could be the devil" for all she cared. Apparently someone was listening, for when the 13th child was born, it allegedly resembled a devil, complete with wings, a tail, and cloven hooves. Once born, the child devoured its 12 siblings and its parents, then promptly disappeared into the Pine Barrens, where it still lives to this day.

The First Sightings

One of the first, and most intriguing, sightings of the Jersey Devil took place in the early 1800s when Commodore Stephen Decatur saw a bizarre creature flying overhead as he was test-firing cannons at the Hanover Iron Works. Perhaps wishing to test the accuracy of the cannons, Decatur took aim and fired upon the creature overhead, striking one of its wings. To the amazement of Decatur and the other onlookers, the creature didn't seem to care that it had just been shot by a cannonball and casually flew away.

From the mid-1800s until the early 1900s, there were numerous sightings of the Jersey Devil throughout the Pine Barrens and beyond. Those who actually witnessed it described it as being everything from short and hairy to tall and cranelike. But there was one thing everyone agreed upon—whatever the creature was, it was not of this earth.

1909: The Year of the Devil

At the beginning of 1909, thousands of people encountered the beast in the span of a week. On Saturday, January 16, a winged creature believed to be the Jersey Devil was spotted flying over the town of Woodbury, New Jersey. The following day, residents of Bristol, Pennsylvania, also reported seeing something strange flying in the sky. Later the same day, bizarre tracks were discovered in the snow. Then on Monday, January 18, residents of Burlington, New Jersey, and neighboring

towns were perplexed by the strange tracks in the snow on their rooftops. They had no clue as to who or what left them. All the while, reports kept coming in of something strange flying overhead with a head resembling a horse and hooves for feet.

In the early morning hours of January 19, Nelson Evans and his wife got up close and personal with the Jersey Devil outside their Gloucester, New Jersey, home. At approximately 2:30 A.M., a creature standing more than eight feet tall with a "head like a collie dog and a face like a horse" peered into the Evanses' window. Although they were petrified, Nelson mustered up the courage to open the window and yell at the creature. Startled, the creature turned, made a barking sound, and then flew off. Later that day, two Gloucester hunters claimed they had tracked strange footprints in the snow for nearly 20 miles. As they followed the tracks, they noticed that whatever this creature was, it not only had the ability to fly or leap over large areas, but it could also squeeze underneath fences and through small spaces.

By Wednesday, January 20, local towns were forming posses intent on tracking down the Jersey Devil. They were all unsuccessful, although they did have several sightings of the winged creature flying toward neighboring towns. Then on Thursday, things really got out of hand. The day began with the Devil reportedly attacking a trolley car in Haddon Heights. It was also during this time that local farmers reported finding some of their livestock missing or dead. And in Camden, New Jersey, a dog was attacked by the Jersey Devil and only managed to survive when its owner chased the beast away.

By Friday, the Devil had been spotted all over New Jersey and in parts of Pennsylvania. During that time, the creature had been shot at (and was supposedly struck by several bullets) and was even hosed down by a local fire department, but this didn't seem to phase the beast at all.

Sightings Continue

As news of the Jersey Devil spread, it seemed that the entire nation descended upon New Jersey in an attempt to catch a glimpse of or, better yet, capture, the creature. But despite all the searching and even a $10,000 reward for the beast's capture, it was never caught.

It appears that after its very busy week in 1909, the Jersey Devil decided to lay low. In fact, though sightings did continue through the years, they were few and far between. Because of this, people started to believe that the Jersey Devil was a harbinger of doom and would only be sighted when something bad was going to happen. Of course, this did not stop hundreds of people from wandering through the Pine Barrens in search of the beast. But no matter how hard people looked, not a single photograph or piece of video exists of the creature. Part of the reason certainly has to be that the Pine Barrens has remained virtually the same vast and undeveloped area, making it the perfect place for a devil to hide. So for now, the Pine Barrens is keeping its secret.

Outrageous Media Hoaxes

Fair and balanced hasn't always been the mantra of the media.
In fact, some newspapers used to pride themselves on the out-
landish stories they could come up with. Here are a few of the
most outrageous hoaxes in journalism.

Man on the Moon

In 1835, in one of America's earliest media hoaxes, *The New York Sun* reported that a scientist had seen strange creatures on the moon through a telescope. The story described bat-like people who inhabited Earth's neighbor. Readers couldn't get enough of the story, so other publishers scrambled to create their own version. When faced with criticism, *The Sun* defended itself, stating that the story couldn't be proven untrue, but eventually the stories were revealed as hoaxes.

Hoaxer Ben Franklin

For nearly a decade, Ben Franklin perpetrated a hoax continually claiming that Titan Leeds, the publisher of the main competitor to Franklin's *Poor Richard's Almanac,* was dead. This greatly decreased Leeds's circulation, since no one wanted to read the ramblings of a dead man. Leeds protested, but year after year, Franklin published annual memorials to his "deceased" competitor. When Leeds really did pass away, Franklin praised the man's associates for finally admitting he was dead.

Anarchy in London

In 1926, a dozen years before *The War of the Worlds,* the BBC staged a radio play about an anarchic uprising. The "news-cast" told of riots in the streets that led to the destruction of

Big Ben and government buildings. The population took the play so seriously that the military was ready to put down the imaginary rioters. The following day the network apologized and the government assured the public that the BBC would not be allowed such free range in the future. The British were ridiculed worldwide, especially in the United States, where the public had not yet been introduced to a young actor named Orson Welles.

Wild Animals on the Loose in New York City

In 1874, the *New York Herald* published stories detailing how animals at the city zoo had escaped and were rampaging through the streets. The mayor ordered all citizens to remain in their homes while the National Guard grappled with the situation. The problem was that the stories weren't true. In fact, the final line of the article read, "Of course, the entire story given above is pure fabrication." Apparently, no one read that far as the city was thrown into a panic. When the smoke cleared, the editor wasn't fired…he was given a bonus for raising the newspaper's circulation.

Mr. Hearst's War

Media mogul William Randolph Hearst had no problem with manipulating the truth to sell newspapers. One of his most famous hoaxes was a series of misrepresentations of what was really occurring in Cuba during the lead-up to the Spanish–American War. He sent artist Frederic Remington to the island to capture the atrocities, but the artist found none. "You furnish the pictures, I'll furnish the war," Hearst replied. But Hearst's misuse of pictures was not limited to that event. Consumed with a passion to defeat the communists, he once ordered his editors to run pictures showing an imaginary Russian famine. However, on the same day, they unwittingly published truthful stories about the rich harvest Russia was enjoying.

Poe's Prank

Though Edgar Allan Poe is best known for his macabre works of fiction, he had his hand in a few works of journalistic fiction as well. One of his best known was a piece that ran in *The New York Sun* in 1844, the same year he wrote his classic poem "The Raven." The article claimed that daring adventurer Monck Mason had crossed the Atlantic Ocean in a hot air balloon. Mason had only intended to cross the English Channel but had been blown off course and arrived 75 hours later in South Carolina. When readers investigated the claim, Poe and *The Sun* conveniently admitted they had not received confirmation of the story.

Millard Fillmore's Bathtub Bunk

Everyone seems to know that Millard Fillmore was the first president to have a bathtub installed in the White House. The only problem is, it isn't true. The story, along with a detailed history of the bathtub, was all a hoax perpetrated by writer H. L. Mencken when he worked for *The New York Evening Mail*. "The success of this idle hoax, done in time of war, when more serious writing was impossible, vastly astonished me," Mencken later wrote. The excitement around his piece and the public's inability to accept the truth affected Mencken, and he began to wonder how much of the rest of history was indeed, in his words, "bunk."

Keystone Cops

Cunning 19-year-old Timothy Rouse came up with a foolproof way to get sprung from the Kentucky Correctional and Psychiatric Center in LaGrange. In April 2007, he simply offered jailors a crudely written, grammatically incorrect fax that ordered him freed by order of the state supreme court, even though the fax's originating line showed it came from a local grocery store. Nevertheless, authorities released Rouse. Two weeks later, when they realized that they had been conned, they rearrested Rouse at his mother's house without further drama.

A Haunting on Chicago's Magnificent Mile

💀 💀 💀 💀 💀

Chicago's Water Tower stands more than 150 feet tall along the world-famous Magnificent Mile—one of the city's most popular tourist attractions. However, many visitors don't realize that the site is haunted by a hero who died during the Great Chicago Fire of 1871.

Mrs. O'Leary Lit a Lantern in the Shed

On the evening of October 8, 1871, the Great Chicago Fire began behind the home of Patrick O'Leary. Contrary to popular belief, the fire was not started by a cow kicking over a lantern. Nevertheless, the flames spread quickly from the O'Leary's barn.

When the smoke cleared a couple of days later, charred buildings and ashes littered the city. The fire had cut a path nearly a mile wide and four miles long, leaving more than 100,000 people homeless. Approximately 300 people died in the fire, but the heat was so intense that only 125 bodies were recovered. One of those bodies was a suicide victim found inside the Chicago Water Tower.

A Hero's Last Resort?

According to legend, a lone fireman remained steadfast at the water-pumping station in Chicago's Streeter-ville neighborhood trying to save as many nomes as possible. But as the flames closed in around him, he realized it was a losing battle. With his back to the Chicago Water Tower, there was no place to run.

As the fire edged closer, the brave fireman considered his options. Apparently, a slow death by fire seemed more frightening than a quicker end by his own hand. So the story goes that the fireman climbed the stairs inside the water tower, strung a rope from a beam near the top of the structure, and, in a moment of desperation, looped the rope around his neck and jumped to his death.

The Solitary Ghost
The heat of the fire did not destroy the Chicago Water Tower, but it scorched everything inside. The heroic fireman's identity was never known, but his spirit lingers. Hundreds of people have seen the sad figure of the hanging man and smelled a suggestion of smoke inside the tower, especially on October nights around the anniversary of the tragedy.

From outside the historic structure, some people see a pale man staring down at them from a window near the top of the tower. His expression is sad and resigned, and he seems to look right through those on the ground.

Other visitors have reported an eerie, sorrowful whistling that seems to come from inside the structure. It echoes through the tower, and then it stops abruptly.

However, most people who've seen the Water Tower ghost describe him with a rope around his neck, swinging and turning slowly. His face is twisted, grotesque, and highlighted as if flames are just beneath him. The ghost appears so real that many witnesses have called police to report a suicide. But responding officers, who have often seen the apparition themselves, know that he's a ghost…and a reminder of valor during a tragic fire more than a century ago.

Ten percent of the weight of a six-year-old pillow is from the waste and dead remains of the common bed mite.

Mythical Creatures

From the time man first began telling tales around the camp-
fire, every human culture has described creatures with characteristics quite different from run-of-the-mill animals. The
legends of horses and snakes with wings, behemoths with
horns in odd places, or other conglomerations live on to tease
us with questions of their existence.

Dragons: Real Scorchers

One of the oldest and most universal mythical creatures is the
dragon. Huge, winged lizards or serpents with greenish scales
and flaming breath are found in tales from ancient China to
medieval Europe.

In China, the dragon originally represented the rising sun,
happiness, and fertility. Sumerians included dragons in their
religious art as early as 4000 B.C. The ancient Greeks called
their dragon *Draco* and pictured it as a massive, winged snake
emitting light and squeezing victims to death in its coils.

In the British Isles, dragons were associated with the legendary King Arthur and St. George, and though it is generally
accepted that dragons do not exist, some think ancient man's
glimpses of giant sea snakes may have inspired dragon myths.

People Acting Fishy: Mermaids and Mermen

The ancient Babylonians worshipped a half-human/half-fish
creature named Oannes who gave them the gift of civilization.
The contemporary mermaid, a beautiful woman with the lower
body of a fish, may have been popularized by Danish writer
Hans Christian Andersen's tale *The Little Mermaid.* Some
think that mermaids spotted at sea by lonesome sailors are
nothing more than manatees—large flat-tailed mammals.

Unicorns: Creatures that Make a Point

Variations of the unicorn, a horse with a single, long horn growing out of its forehead, appear in myths worldwide. It is possible that a similar, actual creature may have appeared at one time to inspire these myths. In the 1800s, a French woman grew a single, ten-inch horn from her forehead. A wax casting of the horn is preserved in Philadelphia's Mütter Museum. More recently, in 2003, a 95-year-old Chinese woman began growing a similar horn. By May 2007, it was five inches long. These are called cutaneous (skin-related) horns and, if possible in humans, could also logically occur in other large mammals. Unicorns are usually portrayed as snow white, gentle, noble creatures—each with a very long, twisted horn that comes to a sharp point.

Pegasus: Cloud Galloper

Greek legend has it that when Poseidon, god of the sea, got together with Medusa, the gorgon with the snake-infested hair, their offspring was Pegasus, a great white horse with wings. Pegasus became the mount of the hero Bellerophon, and together they slew the bizarre Chimera (a fire-breathing monster with the head of a lion, body of a goat, and tail of a snake). Pride in the great deed made Bellerophon think he could ride Pegasus to Mt. Olympus, home of the gods, so he sprang away for the heavens. But the mortal Bellerophon was thrown back to Earth by Zeus, who kept the winged horse for himself. There is a constellation named for Pegasus.

Cyclops: Keeping an Eye Out

They were not pretty, according to Greek legend. The small group of grotesque, one-eyed giants called Cyclopes (in the plural) was warlike and given to eating human flesh. Their one skill was an astonishing talent for creating weapons for the gods, such as swords and arrows. Could such people ever have existed? Humans inflicted with an endocrine disorder known as gigantism have been known to reach a height of eight feet, and very rarely humans may also be born with a birth defect that gives them a single eye, so perhaps this monster has roots in a long-forgotten, actual human being.

Having a Lot of Faun
Very similar to goat-man creatures called satyrs but not at all related to baby deer (fawns), fauns looked like men from the navel up, except for the goat horns sprouting from their temples. They also bounded about on goat legs and hooves. Fathered by the Greek god Faunus, fauns protected the natural world, especially fields and woods. They were also similar in appearance to Pan, Greek god of nature, who gave us the word *panic* for the fright he could inspire by blowing on his magical conch shell. Mr. Tumnus from C. S. Lewis's *The Lion, the Witch, and the Wardrobe* was a faun.

Centaurs: When Horse and Rider are Truly One
A skilled rider will often appear as one with his or her galloping steed, so it isn't hard to see how ancient Greeks may have envisioned a creature that was humanlike from the trunk up but with the legs and body of a stallion—it makes for truly seamless horsemanship. Centaurs were meat-eating revelers who loved to drink, according to Greek legend, except for one gentle man-horse named Chiron known for his wisdom and teaching abilities. Chiron lives on as the centaur constellation Sagittarius, and centaurs are still seen on the coats of arms of many old European families.

Trolls: Mammoth Mountain Men
Although the descriptions of these ugly, manlike beings vary from country to country, trolls originated in Scandinavian lands, where they were said to be gigantic, grotesque humanoids who lived in the hills or mountains, mined ore, and became wondrous metalsmiths. Trolls could turn to stone if caught in the sun, and Norway's ancient rock pillars are said to be evidence of this belief. But perhaps legends of trolls are

based on a few individuals with a disorder that would not have been understood in ancient times. A rare hormonal disorder called gigantism causes excessive growth of the long bones, and, thus, greatly increased height.

Griffins: In the Cat-Bird Seat?

Depictions of these folk monsters can be found in artwork from ancient Egypt and other cradles of civilization as early as 3300 B.C. Mainly a lion-eagle combo, griffins featured a lion's body and an eagle's wings, head, and legs. But they also sported big ears and fierce, ruby-colored eyes. Griffins often guarded rich treasure troves and viciously defended their turf with their sharp beaks and talons. They have survived in modern fantasy fiction, including Lewis Carroll's *Alice's Adventures in Wonderland*.

Fairies: Not Always Tinkerbell

Fairies, also known as wood nymphs, sprites, pixies, and many other names in cultures around the world, are usually thought of as attractive little spirit beings, proportioned like humans and charmingly dressed in wildflowers and acorns. In modern times, they are often depicted as sweet little beings with translucent wings. But in medieval times, the *fée* or *fay,* as they were called in Old French or English, could be naughty or nice.

One Irish tradition maintains that fairies often stole babies, substituting an old, wrinkled fairy or even a bundled log in place of the infant. Some European folk traditions believed fairies were descended from an old, superior race of humanoid creatures, and others thought they were fallen angels that had landed in woods or meadows. Shakespeare's play, *A Midsummer Night's Dream*, with its royal fairies Oberon and Titania, helped popularize the notion of fairies as small, magical people living in their own kingdom among humans. And folk belief worldwide still insists that these little people must be treated respectfully and given offerings and gifts to keep them from pulling nasty tricks on their human neighbors.

Frightening Flicks

There are many freaky films out there to cause you to spill your popcorn or cower beneath the covers. But this "Devilish Dozen" are a slash above—true masters of the skill to chill.

Alien (1979)

This movie is able to get more jumps out of a cat named Jones than most movies are able to fit into an entire picture. It's also famous for showing a baby alien popping out of John Hurt's stomach. On a socio-political note, Sigourney Weaver's Ripley provided the world with one of the first action heroines.

The Amityville Horror (1979)

This bone-chilling tale, supposedly based on actual events, tells the story of George and Kathy Lutz, who purchase a house knowing that a previous tenant had murdered his entire family there just a year before. From the start, strange things happen, such as a bloodlike substance oozing down the walls, nightmares about the house's murderous past, and an evil, disembodied voice commanding a priest to "Get out!" when he tries to bless the house. Eventually, the family flees in the middle of the night, leaving their possessions—and their possessed house—behind.

The Blair Witch Project (1999)

Sure, this phenomenally successful indie film became famous largely because of a marketing campaign that tried to persuade viewers that the events depicted in the film had actually happened, but still, the slow stalking of Heather, Mike, and Josh by a never-seen presence offers bonafide chills, to say nothing of the nausea inspired by the jittery camera work.

Carrie (1976)

Lots of people got picked on in school but not like poor Carrie White, who was bogusly elected Prom Queen and then doused with pig's blood. Can you blame her for enacting brutal telekinetic revenge on John Travolta and the rest of her classmates? This was the first movie based on a Stephen King novel.

The Exorcist (1973)
Lame sequels aside, this movie tops more "Scariest Movie Ever" lists than any other. The idea of demonic possession (especially of an innocent child) still holds immense power, and scenes involving pea-soup vomit and a 360-degree head swivel are considered classic moments in the horror genre.

Halloween (1978)
John Carpenter's pioneering horror film single-handedly established the slasher genre. Michael Myers (wearing an inside-out William Shatner mask) kills his sister, gets sent to an asylum, gets out, kills a lot more people, gets shot by Donald Pleasance, and then stumbles off to wait for the sequel. Jamie Lee Curtis was cast not only for her screaming abilities but also because she was the daughter of Janet Leigh of *Psycho* fame.

A Nightmare on Elm Street (1984)
Sure, once you get a good look at him, Freddy Krueger's deep-fried face loses a lot of its shock value, but the first movie in a long sequence of *Nightmare* films knew enough to keep its dream-invading boogeyman in the shadows. With a young Johnny Depp getting devoured by his own bed, this film makes you pity real estate brokers selling property on any Elm Street.

Pet Sematary (1989)
This movie, which makes extensive use of zombielike cats and children, scares the dickens out of its viewers as it explores the consequences of bringing loved ones back from the dead by planting them in the supernatural soil of the old pet cemetery. Poor Fred Gwynne (aka Herman Munster) gets his Achilles tendon cut by a toddler!

Poltergeist (1982)
One of the scariest movies that's actually about ghosts—as opposed to demons or demented humans—this Steven Spiel-

berg film is famous for its extra-nimble clown doll and its truly interactive TV set ("They're heeeere!"). Two cast members from the original film (including Heather O'Rourke, who played Carol Anne) died tragically at a young age, leading to talk of a *Poltergeist* curse.

The Shining (1980)
Jack Nicholson's performance as Jack Torrance, a slowly degenerating novelist and hotel caretaker, anchors this film, which made cinematic currency out of the phrases "red rum" and "Heeeere's Johnny!" Based on a novel by Stephen King (who apparently hates the film), Stanley Kubrick's only horror movie really packs a punch. Everyone's been afraid of their dad at some point, but has he ever chased you with an ax?

The Texas Chain Saw Massacre (1974)
Surprisingly understated for having such a shocking title, this movie, about the exploits of Leatherface and the rest of his homicidal kinfolk, quickly became a cult classic. Who can forget Leatherface's manic dance-steps when his prey eludes him at the end of the film? Believe it or not, *The Texas Chain Saw Massacre* and *Psycho* were both inspired by the real-life crimes of cannibalistic killer Ed Gein.

The Thing (1982)
Widely acclaimed as one of John Carpenter's most frightening films, *The Thing* delves into the depths of fear and paranoia as a band of Antarctic research scientists is set upon by a hostile alien that takes over the bodies of those it kills. Team members fight each other to survive as they race to uncover who is real and who has already been taken. One famous scene features a severed head sprouting legs and walking away like a spider.

In 2005, there were more than 1.2 billion land-based telephone lines in use worldwide but approximately 2.1 billion cellular phones.

Strange Eating Habits
of the Rich and Famous

💀 💀 💀 💀 💀

*Ah, to be a celebrity. Massive paychecks, VIP treatment,
magazine covers, and the right to demand a truly weird meal.
Some of the people on this list, however, were weird eaters long
before anyone paid attention.*

H. P. Lovecraft

The influential "cosmic-horror" writer reportedly grew up on
candy and other sweets given to him by doting aunts in the late
1890s. Lovecraft might be a cult figure now, but he was relatively unknown while he lived and spent most of his life in poverty, eating whatever was most economical. His usual dinner
consisted of baked beans and ice cream. In the end, his poor
diet may have contributed to his death from intestinal cancer.

Beyoncé Knowles

To whittle her bootyliscious figure down to a more slender
silhouette for the movie *Dreamgirls,* singer-actress Beyoncé
drank a mixture of lemon juice, honey, and cayenne pepper
for weeks at a time and watched the pounds melt away. But
she made it clear in interviews that such a diet was strictly for
movie actresses who need to drop weight fast for a role—not
for the general public. Of course, that certainly didn't stop the
Master Cleanse from becoming the diet du jour.

Marcel Proust

French author, critic, and hero to highbrow conversationalists
everywhere, Marcel Proust lived off barbiturates and café au
lait during the last years of his life. In 1922, he apparently

suffered a negative reaction to the drug Adrenalin, which caused internal burns to his throat and stomach. He survived on ice cream and cold beer for the next month.

Mariah Carey
If it's purple, this pop diva will eat it. If it isn't, take it away. Eating foods purple in color is just one of the ways Carey has approached her diet in recent years. Apparently, Carey believes that mauveish-colored foods (i.e., eggplant, radishes, blueberries, plums) help reduce inflammation and wrinkles, things that a public personality like Carey just can't have.

Victoria Beckham
Spice Girl, wife to soccer legend David Beckham, and media darling Victoria Beckham is seriously skinny. Rumors abound when famous women's collarbones jut out—could it be an eating disorder? Drug use? One report claims that Vicks eats three things and three things only: lettuce, edamame (steamed soy beans), and strawberries.

Howard Hughes
This super-wealthy producer could have afforded anything he wanted to eat, but as Hughes aged and became more and more eccentric, he limited his diet to medium-rare steak, salad, peas, vanilla ice cream, and cookies. Not a bad meal, unless you eat it every day to the exclusion of everything else. And Hughes did just that—he wouldn't even venture outside the box for a different flavor of ice cream.

Give Me a Cheeseburger or I'll Shank You
A 13-year-old Tampa girl acted oddly upon her release from juvenile detention in early 2008. Within 90 minutes of gaining her freedom, the teen was at the rear entrance of a Burger King wearing pajamas and socks while confronting an employee with a knife and demanding a cheeseburger. The employee fled, but the teen pursued, whereupon other employees tackled and subdued her until police returned her to juvie.

Crazy Entertainment Acts

☠ ☠ ☠ ☠ ☠

From Vaudeville of old to today's Cirque du Soleil, wacky enter-
tainers have always tried to rule the showman's roost. Here are
a few acts that fall outside the traditional entertainment genre,
but astound, confound, and mesmerize just the same.

David Blaine

Audience members will grow old and gray before they see
magician David Blaine pull a rabbit from a hat or saw an assistant in half. What they will see, however, perplexes as much
as it entertains, and it often flirts with danger. One illusion
called "Frozen in Time" saw Blaine encased between transparent blocks of ice. He remained a human ice cube for nearly
62 hours before being freed by chain saws. How he beat hypothermia is anyone's guess, but he was hospitalized for a week
after the ordeal.

   Not every stunt in Blaine's act is death defying. During
street performances, Blaine sometimes levitates and hovers
a foot or more above the ground for several seconds. Upon
seeing this, amazed witnesses often believe they've seen something ethereal. And with David Blaine, they just might have.

Beautiful Jim Key

Starting in the late 1800s, Doc Key and his horse "Beautiful
Jim Key" made a mighty strong case for the infinite power
of kindness. From 1897 to 1906, the pair thrilled audiences
with Jim's uncanny humanlike abilities. Billed as the "Marvel
of the Twentieth Century" and "The Greatest Crowd Drawer
in America," Jim could read, write, sort mail, tell time, use
a cash register and a telephone, and perform a host of other
humanlike tasks. But it wasn't always so. In 1889, Jim Key was

a sickly, near-lame colt that owner Doc Key half-expected to die. Nurtured by medicines of Doc Key's own concoction, as well as an abundance of love, the misfit colt was eventually transformed into a gorgeous mahogany bay. People were so taken by Jim Key's abilities that they joined the Jim Key Band of Mercy to the tune of two million members. Their peaceful pledge? "I promise always to be kind to animals."

Growing Man

Billed as "the man who grows before your eyes," Clarence E. Willard could control his muscular and skeletal systems with such astounding ease that he could voluntarily lengthen and shorten his frame by some six inches. From the 1930s through the 1950s, Willard's ability confounded the scientific community as well as his audiences as he stretched from 5'10" to 6'4."

Signora Jo Girardelli

Known as the "incombustible lady," Signora Girardelli had a way with fire. Born in Italy around 1780, the fire-eater distinguished herself by performing daring feats above and beyond those of more pedestrian acts. She went to great lengths to prove that she was actually *eating* or defying fire. Her mediums consisted of nitric acid, molten metal, boiling oil, melted wax, and lit candles. In a performance designed to prove her mettle, Girardelli would fill a pan with boiling oil, drop the white of an egg into it so all could see it cook, fill her mouth with the burning liquid, swish it about for a few seconds for added effect, then spit it out into a brazier where it would instantly blaze up, proving that it was indeed hot oil.

Another favorite found Girardelli flaunting her prowess with hot metal. This feat involved heating a shovel until red hot then setting wood ablaze with it. With this accomplished, the performer would stroke her arms, feet, and hair with the burning-hot shovel. No smoke or scorching of any kind was detectable by the audience. At this point, Girardelli was just getting warmed up. The real showstopper arrived seconds later when she *licked* the shovel and an audible hiss was heard from her tongue.

White House Ghosts

The colonial-style mansion at 1600 Pennsylvania Avenue may be America's most famous address, as well as one of the most haunted. Day and night, visitors have seen spirits that include presidents William Henry Harrison, Andrew Jackson, and Abraham Lincoln. The spirits of these men are almost as powerful today as when they ruled America.

William Henry Harrison Feels a Little Blue

William Henry Harrison was the first American president to die in office. While giving his inauguration speech on an icy, windy March 4, 1841, Harrison caught a cold that quickly turned to pneumonia.

There are stories about Harrison, half-conscious with fever, wandering the corridors of the White House, looking for a quiet room in which to rest. Unfortunately, there was no escape from the demands of his office…nor from the doctors whose treatments likely killed him. While Harrison's lungs filled with fluid and fever wracked his body, his doctors bled him, then treated him with mustard, laxatives, ipecac, rhubarb, and mercury. It is speculated that the president died not from the "ordinary winter cold" that he'd contracted, but from the care of his doctors. William Henry Harrison died April 4, 1841, just one month after taking office.

Harrison's translucent ghost is seen throughout the White House, but especially in the residential areas. His skin is pale blue, and his breathing makes an ominous rattling noise. He appears to be looking for something and walks through closed doors. Some believe that he's looking for rest or a cure for his illness. Others say he's searching for his office, so he can complete his term as president.

Andrew Jackson Likes the Ladies

If you'd prefer to see a happier ghost, look for Andrew Jackson. He's probably in the Queen's Bedroom where his bed is displayed. But Jackson may not necessarily be looking for his old bed—in life he was quite the ladies' man and, today, the Queen's Bedroom is reserved for female guests of honor.

Mary Todd Lincoln frequently complained about the ghost of Andrew Jackson cursing and stomping in the corridors of the White House. When she left the presidential estate, Jackson stopped complaining.

Visitors may simply sense Jackson's presence in the Queen's Bedroom or feel a bone-chilling breeze when they're around his bed. Others have reported that Jackson's ghost climbs under the covers, sending guests shrieking out of the room. But Jackson isn't the only president who haunts this room.

Two Wartime Leaders Meet

During World War II, the Queen's Bedroom was called the Rose Room, and it wasn't reserved for women. While visiting the White House during the war, Winston Churchill strolled into the Rose Room completely naked and smoking a cigar after taking a bath. It was then that he encountered the ghost of Abraham Lincoln standing in front of the fireplace with one hand on the mantle, staring down at the hearth. Always a quick wit, Churchill said, "Good evening, Mr. President. You seem to have me at a disadvantage."

According to Churchill, Lincoln smiled at him then vanished. Churchill refused to stay in that room again, but Lincoln wasn't finished surprising guests.

Lincoln Wakes Up the Queen

When Queen Wilhelmina of The Netherlands stayed in the Queen's Bedroom in 1945, she was hoping to get a good night's sleep. Instead, she was awakened by noisy footsteps in the corridor outside her room. Annoyed, she waited for the person to return to his room, but he stopped at her door and knocked loudly, several times. When the queen finally opened her door, she was face to face with the specter of Abraham Lincoln. She said that he looked a bit pale but very much alive and was dressed in travel clothes, including a top hat and coat. The queen gasped, and Lincoln vanished.

Lincoln's ghost may be the most solid-looking and "real" spirit at the White House, and hundreds of people have encountered it. Strangely enough, Lincoln, who seemed to be in touch with "the other side" even before he died, claimed he once saw his own apparition and talked about it often.

Abraham Lincoln Sees His Own Ghost

The morning after Abraham Lincoln was first elected president, he had a premonition about his death. He saw two reflections of himself in a mirror. One image was how he usually appeared, fit and healthy. In the other reflection, his face was pale and ghostly. Lincoln and his wife believed it predicted that he wouldn't complete his second term in office.

Later, Lincoln saw his own funeral in a dream. He said that he was in the White House, but it was strangely quiet and filled with mourners. Walking through the halls, he entered the East Room, where, to his horror, he saw a body wrapped in funeral vestments and surrounded by soldiers.

He said he approached one of the soldiers to find out what had happened. "Who is dead in the White House?" Lincoln demanded in his dream. "The president," the soldier replied. "He was killed by an assassin!"

A few days later, that fateful day when he attended Ford Theatre for the last time, President Lincoln called a meeting of his cabinet members. He told them that they would have important news the following morning. He also explained that he'd had a strange dream…one that he'd had twice before. He saw himself alone and adrift in a boat without oars. That was all he said, and the cabinet members left the president's office with a very uneasy feeling.

The following morning, they received news that the president had been assassinated.

Lincoln Never Leaves

Lincoln's apparition has been seen clearly by hundreds of people, including Eleanor Roosevelt's maid, who saw Abe sitting on a bed, removing his boots. Franklin Roosevelt's valet ran out of the White House after encountering Lincoln's spirit.

Calvin Coolidge's wife saw Lincoln's face reflected in a window in the Yellow Oval Room.

President Lincoln has been seen in many places in the White House but most frequently in the Lincoln Bedroom. Although the late president's bed is now in this room, during his lifetime, it was the cabinet room in which he signed the Emancipation Proclamation.

Ghosts of Presidents' Families and Foes

Abigail Adams used to hang laundry on clotheslines in the White House's East Room. Her ghost appears there regularly in a cap and wrapped in a shawl. She's usually carrying laundry or checking to see if her laundry is dry.

Dorothea "Dolley" Madison defends the Rose Garden that she designed and planted. When Woodrow Wilson's second wife, Edith, ordered gardeners to dig up the garden for new plants, Dolley's apparition appeared and allegedly insisted that no one was going to touch her garden. The landscaping ceased, and Dolley's roses remain exactly as they were when the Madisons lived in the White House in the early 1800s.

Abraham Lincoln's son Willie died in February 1862 after a brief illness. Soon after, the First Lady began holding séances in the White House to communicate with him. The president was equally obsessed with his son's death and had his coffin reopened at least twice, just to look at him. Willie's apparition has been seen at the White House regularly since then, most often appearing in the second-floor bedrooms where his presence was witnessed by Lyndon Johnson's daughter Lynda.

However, Lynda's bedroom may have been haunted by other spirits as well. Harry Truman's mother died in that room, and Lynda used to report unexplained footsteps in the bedroom. Sometimes, her phone would ring in the middle of the night and, when she answered, no one was on the line.

Also on the second floor, people have heard the ghost of Frances Cleveland crying, perhaps reliving a time when her husband, Grover, was diagnosed with cancer.

One very out-of-place spirit appears to be a British soldier from around 1814 when the White House was sieged and burned. The uniformed soldier looks lost and is holding a torch. When he realizes that he's been spotted, he looks alarmed and vanishes.

The White House's Oldest Ghost

David Burns may be the oldest ghost at the White House. He donated the land on which the house was built. One day, Franklin Roosevelt heard his name being called, and when he replied, the voice said that he was Mr. Burns.

FDR's valet, Cesar Carrera, told a similar story. Carrera was in the Yellow Oval Room when he heard a soft, distant voice say, "I'm Mr. Burns." When Carrera looked, no one was there.

Later, during the Truman years, a guard at the White House also heard a soft voice announce himself as Mr. Burns. The guard expected to see Truman's Secretary of State, James Byrnes, but no one appeared. What's more, the guard checked the roster and learned that Byrnes hadn't been in the building at all that day.

The White House may be America's most haunted public building. Ghosts are seen there, day and night. On the White House's Web site, staff members talk about their regular ghostly encounters. In the words of Harry Truman, the White House is haunted, "sure as shooting."

Until Lincoln Cries

In 2007, Paul Brant walked into a Frankfort, Indiana, auto dealership and plunked down enough cash to purchase a new Dodge Ram truck—more than $25,000—all in rolled coins! The 70-year-old claims to have amassed his metallic fortune by dropping loose change into coffee cans, water jugs, and piggy banks over the years. The dealership summoned an armored car to count and redeem the mountain of coins. But this wasn't the first time Brant had made a large purchase with coins. In 1994, he dropped $36,000 in coinage on a Dodge Neon and a Dodge Pickup.

The Clairvoyant Crime-Buster

Before there were TV shows like Ghost Whisperer *and* Medium, *which make the idea of solving crimes through ESP seem almost commonplace, there was psychic detective Arthur Price Roberts. And his work was accomplished in the early 1900s, when high-tech aids like electronic surveillance and DNA identification were still only far-fetched dreams. Police in those times* needed *psychics to break many cases.*

He Saw Dead People

A modest man born in Wales in 1866, Roberts deliberately avoided a formal education because he believed too much learning could stifle his unusual abilities. He moved to Milwaukee as a young man where, ironically, the man who never learned to read was nicknamed "Doc."

One of his earliest well-known cases involved a baffling missing person incident in Peshtigo, Wisconsin, a small town northwest of Milwaukee. A man named Duncan McGregor had suddenly gone missing in July 1905, leaving no clue as to his whereabouts. Police searched for him for months, and finally his desperate wife decided to go to the psychic detective who had already made a name for himself in Milwaukee. She didn't even have to explain the situation to Roberts; he knew immediately upon meeting her who she was.

Roberts meditated on the vanished husband, then sadly had to tell Mrs. McGregor that he'd been murdered and that his body was in the Peshtigo River, caught near the bottom in a pile of timber. Roberts proved correct in every detail.

Mystery of the Mad Bombers

Roberts solved numerous documented cases. He helped a Chicago man find his brother who had traveled to Albuquerque and had not been heard from for months; Roberts predicted that the brother's body would be found in a certain spot in Devil's Canyon, and it was.

After coming up with new evidence for an 11th hour pardon, Roberts saved a Chicago man named Ignatz Potz, who had been condemned to die for a murder he didn't commit. But his biggest and most famous coup came in 1935 when he correctly predicted that the city of Milwaukee would be hit by six large dynamite explosions, losing a town hall, banks, and police stations. People snickered; such destruction was unheard of in Milwaukee. Roberts made his prediction on October 18 of that year. In little more than a week, the Milwaukee area entered a time of terror.

First, a town hall in the outlying community of Shorewood was blasted, killing two children and wounding many other people. A few weeks later, the mad bombers hit two banks and two police stations. Federal agents descended upon the city, and several local officers were assigned to work solely on solving the bombings. Finally, the police went to Roberts to learn what was coming next. Roberts told them one more blast was in the works, that it would be south of the Menomonee River, and that it would be the final bomb. Police took him at his word and blanketed the area with officers and sharpshooters.

And sure enough, on November 4, a garage in the predicted area blew to smithereens in an explosion that could be heard as far as eight miles away. The two terrorists, young men 18 and 21 years old, had been hard at work in the shed assembling 50 pounds of dynamite when their plan literally backfired. Few people argued with Roberts's abilities after that.

His Final Fortune

Roberts's eeriest prediction, however, may have been that of his own death. In November 1939, he told a group of assembled friends that he would be leaving this world on January 2, 1940. And he did, passing quietly in his own home on that exact date. Many of his most amazing accomplishments will probably never be known because a lot of his work was done secretly for various law enforcement agencies. But "Doc" Roberts had an undeniable gift, and he died secure in the knowledge that he had used it to help others as best he could.

Odd and Unusual Structures

Whether they're made out of bones or toilet paper tubes, the
following structures rank among some of the most creative and
outlandish in the world.

Sedlec Ossuary: The Skeleton Sanctuary

A chandelier made of every bone in the human skeleton, a
heap of 14th century skulls with arrow wounds, and a skull and
crossbones atop a tower all make the little chapel known as the
Sedlec Ossuary a most unusual church.

Located just outside the medieval silver-mining center of
Kutna Hora, Czech Republic, in a suburb now called Sedlec,
the chapel was predated by a cemetery made famous in 1278
after a church official sprinkled it with soil from the Holy
Land. The chapel was built in 1400, but by 1511, the cemetery
was so overcrowded that bones were dug up and stored inside.
In 1870, a woodcarver named Frantisek Rindt was hired to
organize the bones of the 40,000 people stashed in the ossuary,
so he decided to assemble them into a fantastic assortment of
altars, sculptures, and other furnishings and decorations.

Dancing House of Prague: A Building that Boogies

Originally named the "Astaire and Rogers" building after the
famous dance duo, the modern building's swaying towers
suggest a dancing couple. The building, which houses a popular restaurant, was designed by architects Vlado Milunic and
Frank Gehry and built in the mid-1990s. Set in a traditional
neighborhood of Baroque, Gothic, and Art Nouveau buildings,
the crunched appearance of the Dancing House inspired great
local controversy when first proposed.

Bangkok Robot Building: Banking on Robots

The world's first robot-shape building houses the United Overseas Bank headquarters in Bangkok, Thailand, and was designed to reflect the hope that robots will someday release humanity from the burden of drudgework. Designed by Dr. Sumet Jumsai and built mostly of native materials, the energy-efficient, 20-story "robot" includes a day-care center and an 18th floor dining room with a sweeping view of the city. The building, finished in 1986, is complete with reflective glass eyes, lightning rod "antennae," and bright blue walls.

Topsy-Turvy in Tennessee

Imagine that a colonnaded building from some genteel laboratory was transported in a windstorm to land upside down, where it remained…chock-full of strange anomalies for visitors to explore. That's the scenario operators of Wonder Works in Pigeon Forge, Tennessee, and Orlando, Florida, hope paying guests will believe. Both places appear to be upside down on the inside, too, and patrons can experience a re-creation of the 1989 San Francisco earthquake among other interactive displays. The Orlando attraction was built in 1998, and its sister structure plopped in Pigeon Forge in 2006.

Poland's Crooked House: Wavy-Walled Wonder

Tipsy bar patrons who wander outside the Crooked House in Sopot, Poland, may rightly wonder if their eyes deceive them. But whether viewed with or without an alcoholic haze, the curving facade is purposely out-of-kilter, and its green shingles are intended to look like the scales of a dragon. The building is home to several pubs, coffee shops, and other businesses and has become a favorite attraction since it opened in 2004.

Shigeru Ban's Houses of Cardboard

In the 1980s, Japanese architect Shigeru Ban began making buildings from cardboard tubes because he felt good structure should be affordable to anyone and that a new kind of architecture could arise from so-called "weak materials." Ban has used his idea to develop inexpensive yet durable shelters for refugees from natural disasters. But he has also designed spectacular buildings from what he calls "improved wood." One of the most famous is his Nomadic Museum, made out of approximately 150 shipping containers that can be sent and reassembled anywhere from Manhattan to Tokyo. Inside, it features giant curtains made from thousands of recycled tea bags.

Futuro Flying Saucer Homes

In the 1960s, people were looking forward to a futuristic tomorrow, while at the same time waves of UFO sightings swept the world. Finnish architect Matti Suuronen combined the two social phenomena to create houses that resembled flying saucers. Suuronen's Futuro units were made from fiberglass and measured 26 feet in diameter and 11 feet high. Like any good spaceship, the Futuro homes had windows that

looked like portholes and visitors entered units through a lower hatch. The inside featured a set of built-in plastic chairs, a kitchenette, and a tiny bedroom and bathroom arranged around a fireplace. Suuronen envisioned the Futuro units as the ultimate mobile home, designed to be moved easily. Although the oil embargo of the early 1970s drove up petroleum prices so high that plastic houses were no longer affordable, about 100 models were produced and several still exist.

Houston Beer Can House: The Six-Pack Shack

The ultimate in recycling projects, John Milkovisch's Houston home, which is covered with siding made from smashed beer cans, has proven that even a six-pack-a-day habit can be eco-friendly. That's about what it took to provide materials over the course of 20 years. After his retirement from the railroad in 1968, Milkovisch started the project just to have something to do and drank some 40,000 cans of Coors, Bud Light, and Texas Pride to create his unique habitat. For a bit of flair, he added wind chime curtains made from pulltabs and arranged horizontal rows of cans to provide decorative fences. Both Milkovisch and his wife, Mary, are now deceased, so an arts preservation foundation now owns the property.

South Korea Toilet House: The Potty House

South Korean lawmaker Sim Jae-Duck is flushed with pride over the house he built in Suwon in 2007—the home is shaped like a giant toilet. Sim Jae-Duck, who built the home for a meeting of the World Toilet Association, said he hoped to persuade people to think of toilets not just as a "place of defecation" but also a "place of culture." The two-story home is outfitted with four actual toilets, including one encased in motion-sensitive glass that fogs up for privacy. The house's staircase spirals where the drain would be if the structure were actually a toilet. The 4,520-square foot house sits on the site of Sim Jae-Duck's former home, which was tanked for the new project.

The Haines Shoe House: A Boot-iful Home

Anyone wanting a place to just kick back should focus solely on a boot-shape home near Hellam, Pennsylvania. The 25-foot tall building was created in 1948 by shoe magnate Mahlon Haines to help publicize his wares. The house was designed to function as an actual house with a kitchen, two baths, three bedrooms, and a living room. It's currently an ice cream shop but has also served as an inn.

A Tisket, a Tasket, That Building's a Basket!

One of the most creative corporate headquarters anywhere is the Longaberger building in Newark, Ohio. Built to mimic the company's product—woven baskets—the structure includes a giant version of the gold-plated Longaberger brand tag and trademark "bent wood" handles balancing over the top. The building stands seven stories high with windows set in indentations of the synthetic basket-weave exterior.

Grave Curiosities

Gravesites offer us a chance to make one final statement, one that will hopefully last for all eternity. Here are a few that certainly make walking through a cemetery a unique experience!

Davis Memorial

John Davis was a successful farmer in Hiawatha, Kansas. When his wife, Sarah, passed away in 1930, Davis spent the next seven years, and nearly all his money, building a memorial to honor his wife and their life together.

Created in stages, the memorial uses life-size granite and Italian marble statues to depict John and Sarah's life together. Beginning with statues of John and Sarah as a young couple, visitors follow the couple literally to their graves. The final "scene" involves miniature versions of John and an angellike Sarah kneeling over their own graves. The most touching, however, is the previous carving, which portrays John, sitting in an oversize chair and looking quite sad, shortly after Sarah's death. Next to him, where Sarah should be, is an empty chair marked "The Vacant Chair."

Yield to Oncoming Grave

When Nancy Barnett passed away on December 1, 1831, her family was determined to make sure her final resting place stayed just that—final. So, in the early 1900s, when it was announced that the proposed route for a new highway near Franklin, Indiana, was going to cut through the small cemetery where Nancy was buried, the family knew they had to act fast. When local workers showed up to exhume the bodies and relocate them to another cemetery, they found Barnett's grandson sitting on her grave, holding a shotgun. He made it clear that under no circumstances was he going to allow Nancy's body to be moved. The workers figured if they ignored him, he would eventually go away. But each day they returned, Nancy's grandson was there with his shotgun. Eventually, the authorities decided to leave Nancy where she was and build the road around her grave. Today, motorists traveling down County Road 400 just south of Franklin notice signs alerting them that there's a divided highway up ahead—divided because cars have to go around the grave in the middle of the road.

Victim of the Beast

With just four words and three numbers, a gravesite in Salt Lake City Cemetery creeps people out. Lying quietly amongst the other tombstones is one belonging to Lilly E. Gray. Her stone is simple, containing only her name, birth and death dates, and the following statement: "Victim of the Beast 666." The first time people see the stone, they naturally assume that it's a hoax. It's not, but the meaning behind the cryptic statement is unclear. Theories range from "the Beast" being Lilly's husband, Elmer, to one that claims "666" is actually a reference to the local road, Route 666, and that Lilly might have had a bad accident there. If so, she survived the crash because her death certificate lists no clues other than that she died at a local hospital from "natural causes."

Ray's Mercedes

Friends say that Raymond Tse, Jr., always wanted to own a Mercedes Benz. Sadly, those dreams all but died in 1981 when Ray passed away at just 15 years of age…or did they? In an effort to fulfill his brother's dream, David Tse had a life-size replica of a 1982 Mercedes Benz 2400D limousine carved from a single block of granite. It took nearly two years and $250,000 to create, and when finished, it was "parked" behind the Tse mausoleum, complete with "RAY TSE" vanity plates.

Bill's Not Here

El Campo Santo is one of the oldest cemeteries in San Diego. When Bill Marshall met his untimely death in December

1851, he was buried in the far corner of the cemetery. However, as time went by, people stopped looking after El Campo Santo so much that when a new streetcar line was going in, the town took over much of the cemetery's property. When a new cemetery wall was erected in the 1930s, it was discovered that Bill Marshall's body, along with many others, was now outside the cemetery grounds. Today, visitors to El Campo Santo Cemetery will find a marker that reads "Bill Marshall is not here but on the other side of the wall" with a carved hand pointing toward the wall.

Midnight Mary's Grave

Just inside the entrance to Evergreen Cemetery in New Haven, Connecticut, is the gravestone of Mary Hart, aka Midnight Mary. At first glance, there seems to be nothing special about the stone until you read the words carved on it:

> *At high noon,*
> *Just from, and about to renew*
> *Her daily work, in her full strength of*
> *Body and mind,*
> *Mary E. Hart*
> *Having fallen prostrate,*
> *Remained unconscious until she died at midnight,*
> *October 15, 1872*
> *Born December 16, 1824*

Sure, the words are strange enough, but they don't hold a candle to the frightening words emblazoned in raised, black letters in an arch over the stone:

> *The people shall be troubled at midnight and pass away*

No one knows for sure who Mary Hart was, but legend has it that she was a witch who used her tombstone to curse all those who persecuted her while she was alive. Another popular story claims that Mary was accidentally buried alive, and by the time the mistake was realized, she was already dead from suffocating in her coffin.

Ghastly Medieval Torture Devices

💀   💀   💀   💀   💀

The following devices, designed to maim, torture, and kill, prove that mankind has far to go in its quest for civility.

The Rack

During medieval times, being interrogated meant experiencing excruciating pain as one's body was stretched on the infamous Rack. The operating premise was diabolically simple. Victims laid on their backs with arms extended while straps anchored the hands and feet to opposite ends of the table. The torture began when the operator rotated rollers at each end in opposing directions. At the very least, severe joint dislocations occurred. At worst, limbs were ripped clean off and death would result. Even when the tortured victim was subsequently released, they'd often be incapable of standing erect since muscle fibers stretched beyond a certain point lose their ability to contract.

The Iron Maiden

The Iron Maiden torture device differs wildly from the popular heavy metal band of the same name, even if both could ultimately make one's ears bleed. Insidious in its intent, the sarcophagus-shape instrument opened to allow the victim to step inside. Once there, protruding spikes on the front and back halves would spear the occupant as the door was closed. Agonies were prolonged because spikes were strategically positioned to find the eyes, chest, and back but not vital organs. As a result, death occurred only after the victim had bled out, an agonizing process that could sometimes last for days.

The Pear

Despite sharing its name with a sweet fruit, there was nothing at all sweet about the Pear. Designed to be inserted in the most sensitive of the body's orifices (i.e., mouth, rectum, vagina), the pear-shape torture tool was used as a punishment for those who had committed sexual sins or blasphemy. Once put in place, a screw mechanism caused pointed outer leaves to expand ever wider, resulting in severe internal mutilation.

The Tongue Tearer

Self-explanatory in name, the Tongue Tearer worked precisely as advertised. Resembling a wire cutter with an eye bolt passing through its end grips, a victim's mouth was forced open as the Tongue Tearer was employed. After finding purchase on its slippery quarry, the eye bolt at the opposite end of the device was tightened, ever so slowly, until the tongue became completely detached from the horrified victim's mouth.

The Lead Sprinkler

With its innocuous sounding name, one might expect to find this item gracing a formal garden, not doing the devil's handiwork in a dank dungeon. Shaped like a maraca, the Lead Sprinkler held molten lead inside a perforated spherical head. The torturer would simply hold the device over the victim and give it a shake. The ensuing screams were the only music to come from this instrument.

Next Time, Just Withhold His Allowance

Angela Cancio, 38, of Tampa, was arrested and charged with child abuse in 2007 after stabbing her teenage son in the arm with scissors.

The trouble evidently began when Cancio offended her son's girlfriend. The son stuck up for his belle, and another boy stuck up for Mom. While the boys fought, Mom stabbed her son. Just to make sure that the girlfriend didn't feel neglected, a fourth youth slapped her.

The Windy City's Famous Phantom: Resurrection Mary

Most big cities have their share of ghost stories, and Chicago is no different. But beyond the tales of haunted houses, spirit-infested graveyards, and spooky theaters, there is one Chicago legend that stands out among the rest. It's the story of a beautiful female phantom, a hitchhiking ghost that nearly everyone in the Windy City has heard of. Her name is "Resurrection Mary" and she is Chicago's most famous ghost.

The Girl by the Side of the Road

The story of Resurrection Mary begins in the mid-1930s, when drivers began reporting a ghostly young woman on the road near the gates of Resurrection Cemetery, located on Archer Avenue in Chicago's southwestern suburbs. Some drivers claimed that she was looking for a ride, but others reported that she actually attempted to jump onto the running boards of their automobiles as they drove past.

A short time later, the reports took another, more mysterious turn. The unusual incidents moved away from the cemetery and began to center around the Oh Henry Ballroom (known today as Willowbrook Ballroom), located a few miles south of the graveyard on Archer Avenue. Many claimed to see the young woman on the road near the ballroom and sometimes inside the dancehall itself. Young men claimed that they met the girl at a dance, spent the evening with her, then offered her a ride home at closing time. Her vague directions always led them north along Archer Avenue until they reached the gates of Resurrection Cemetery—where the girl would inexplicably vanish from the car!

Some drivers even claimed to accidentally run over the girl outside the cemetery. When they went to her aid, her body was always gone. Others said that their automobiles actually passed through the young woman before she disappeared through the cemetery gates.

Police and local newspapers began hearing similar stories from frightened and frazzled drivers who had encountered the mysterious young woman. These first-hand accounts created the legend of "Resurrection Mary," as she came to be known.

Will the Real Resurrection Mary Please Stand Up?

One version of the story says that Resurrection Mary was a young woman who died on Archer Avenue in the early 1930s. On a cold winter's night, Mary spent the evening dancing at the Oh Henry Ballroom, but after an argument with her boyfriend, she decided to walk home. She was killed when a passing car slid on the ice and struck her.

According to the story, Mary was buried in Resurrection Cemetery, and since that time, she has been spotted along Archer Avenue. Many believe that she may be returning to her eternal resting place after one last dance.

This legend has been told countless times over the years and there may actually be some elements of the truth to it—although, there may be more than one "Resurrection Mary" haunting Archer Avenue.

One of the prime candidates for Mary's real-life identity was a young Polish girl named Mary Bregovy. Mary loved to dance, especially at the Oh Henry Ballroom, and was killed one night in March 1934 after spending the evening at the ballroom and then downtown at some of the late-night clubs. She was killed along Wacker Drive in Chicago when the car that she was riding in collided with an elevated train support. Her parents buried her in Resurrection Cemetery, and then, a short time later, a cemetery caretaker spotted her ghost walking through the graveyard. Stranger still, passing motorists on Archer Avenue soon began telling stories of her apparition trying to hitch rides as they passed by the cemetery's front gates. For this reason, many believe that the ghost stories of Mary Bregovy may have given birth to the legend of Resurrection Mary.

However, she may not be the only one. As encounters with Mary have been passed along over the years, many descriptions of the phantom have varied. Mary Bregovy had bobbed, light-brown hair, but some reports describe Resurrection Mary as having long blonde hair. Who could this ghost be?

It's possible that this may be a young woman named Mary Miskowski, who was killed along Archer Avenue in October 1930. According to sources, she also loved to dance at the Oh Henry Ballroom and at some of the local nightspots. Many people who knew her in life believed that she might be the ghostly hitchhiker reported in the southwestern suburbs.

In the end, we may never know Resurrection Mary's true identity. But there's no denying that sightings of her have been backed up with credible eyewitness accounts. In these real, first-person reports, witnesses give specific places, dates, and times for their encounters with Mary—encounters that remain unexplained to this day. Besides that, Mary is one of the few ghosts to ever leave physical evidence behind!

The Gates of Resurrection Cemetery

On August 10, 1976, around 10:30 P.M., a man driving past Resurrection Cemetery noticed a young girl wearing a white dress standing inside the cemetery gates. She was holding on to the bars of the gate, looking out toward the road. Thinking that she was locked in the cemetery, the man stopped at a nearby police station and alerted an officer to the young

woman's predicament. An officer responded to the call, but when he arrived at the cemetery, the girl was gone. He called out with his loudspeaker and looked for her with his spotlight, but nobody was there. However, when he walked up to the gates for a closer inspection, he saw something very unusual. It looked as though someone had pulled two of the green-colored bronze bars with such intensity that handprints were seared into the metal. The bars were blackened and burned at precisely the spot where a small woman's hands would have been.

When word got out about the handprints, people from all over the area came to see them. Cemetery officials denied that anything supernatural had occurred, and they later claimed that the marks were created when a truck accidentally backed into the gates and a workman had tried to heat them up and bend them back. It was a convenient explanation but one that failed to explain the indentions that appeared to be left by small fingers and were plainly visible in the metal.

Cemetery officials were disturbed by this new publicity, so, in an attempt to dispel the crowds of curiosity-seekers, they tried to remove the marks with a blowtorch. However, this made them even more noticeable, so they cut out the bars with plans to straighten or replace them.

But removing the bars only made things worse as people wondered what the cemetery had to hide. Local officials were so embarrassed that the bars were put back into place, straightened, and then left alone so that the burned areas would oxidize and eventually match the other bars. However, the blackened areas of the bars did not oxidize, and the twisted handprints remained obvious until the late 1990s when the bars were finally removed. At great expense, Resurrection Cemetery replaced the entire front gates and the notorious bars were gone for good.

A Broken Spirit Lingers On

Sightings of Resurrection Mary aren't as frequent as in years past, but they do still continue. Even though a good portion of the encounters can be explained by the fact that Mary has become such a part of Chicago lore that nearly everyone has heard of her, some of the sightings seem to be authentic. So whether you believe in her or not, Mary is still seen walking along Archer Avenue, people still claim to pick her up during the cold winter months, and she continues to be the Windy City's most famous ghost.

Share a Toast with a Ghost

Visitors to the Golden Fleece, a 16th-century pub and inn in York, England, can spend a few minutes or a full night with numerous ghosts at the city's most haunted site. Located at the end of one of Europe's best-preserved medieval streets known as "the Shambles," the Golden Fleece is a well kept but ancient building surrounded by a mysterious atmosphere.

Enjoy Some Spirits with Some Spirits

Upon entering the Golden Fleece, visitors sense spirits from the pub's past. Even when the front room is nearly empty, many visitors glance around nervously, expecting to see other guests standing in a dark corner. Unexplained shadows move and then vanish, and the sound of phantom glasses clinking can be heard. It's truly an eerie place.

Many guests will witness the Golden Fleece's ghosts if they go looking for them. For the best ghostly encounters, explore the pub's quirky corridors and cozy public rooms. Ghosts have been reported in every part of the pub and also in the haunted yard immediately behind it. Most people see the spirits as flickering figures, off to one side. Others see full apparitions, such as the colorful ghost of Lady Alice Peckett.

Lady Peckett Kept Her Head, But Thomas Percy Didn't

Lady Alice Peckett haunts both the Golden Fleece and Lady Peckett's Yard directly behind it. Her husband, John, who owned the building, was the Lord Mayor of the city of York in 1701. He left the pub when he died, but his wife decided to stay. No one is certain why she lingers, but some claim that she was too spirited and fun-loving for her more serious politician husband. Perhaps she doesn't want to miss out on anything at the Golden Fleece.

Lady Alice generally manifests as an older woman wearing sweet perfume, but don't let her serene demeanor fool you.

She's a mischievous ghost who likes to surprise people by walking through solid walls around the Function Room.

Another ghost to keep an eye out for is Thomas Percy, the Seventh Earl of Northumberland. Also know as the Headless Earl, Percy, a relatively harmless ghost, floats around the Shambles, near the entrance to the Golden Fleece, in search of his missing head.

During the reign of Queen Elizabeth I, when Catholics were burned at the stake, Percy held steadfast in his Catholic beliefs. Despite this, Percy was a favorite of the queen for many years. Unfortunately, Thomas didn't realize his vulnerability. In 1569, he led a rebellion against Elizabeth and planned to replace her with her Catholic cousin, Mary, Queen of Scots. When the rebellion failed, Percy was beheaded in a public execution not far from the Golden Fleece. Though his body was buried, his head was left on public display as a warning to others. After some time, the head was simply thrown away.

A Fine "Cold Spot" in the Pub

If the weather is sultry or the pub is crowded, find a seat at the booth in the back corner of the pub. The spirits will oblige by keeping that corner cool and breezy. During a June 2007 visit, a group of American tourists complimented the staff on how well the booth was cooled. They were startled to learn that there is no air conditioning in the pub.

The chilling effect may be thanks to "One Eyed Jack," a 17th-century ghost dressed in a red coat, wig, and crisply pressed breeches. He's sometimes seen carrying a flintlock pistol and creates a refreshing breeze as he paces up and down the room, waiting to be served.

A Full Night of Good Spirits

Above the pub is an inn, and guests can spend the night encountering various spirits. Look for the gruesome, blue-tinted face of an inebriated World War II airman who fell to his death from a window.

Or listen for the confused whimpering of a little boy who appears in Victorian clothing. In the late 1800s, he was crushed to death as a cart backed up to the pub door to deliver ale. He's often seen around the front room of the pub and has even been known to pick pockets.

If you encounter a ghost wearing a noose, that spirit has escaped from the pub's basement. After being executed, corpses were sometimes stored in the cellar of the Golden Fleece, but in many cases, the bodies were never claimed, and they may be buried in the basement. Perhaps they're wandering the Golden Fleece hoping that someone will recognize them and give them a proper burial.

Most often, overnight guests at the Golden Fleece hear music and loud laughter from downstairs. When they investigate the noise, they discover that the pub is closed, the lights are off, and the downstairs rooms are empty…unless you count the ghosts, of course.

Just remember that if you see a Roman soldier who seems to be walking on his knees, nothing terrible happened to his legs. He's haunting from a time when the streets of York were several feet lower than they are now. That's the level where his ghostly feet are.

The Mysterious Coral Castle

💀 💀 💀 💀 💀

It's a typical boy-meets-girl, boy-proposes-to-girl, boy-gets-jilted-at-the-altar-builds-cryptic-modern-day-castle-in-Florida-to-win-her-back story. Nothing too out of the ordinary.

It's Not You, It's Me

Born in Latvia in 1887, Ed Leedskalnin was a skinny kid who never grew much more than five feet tall. But his diminutive stature didn't keep him from falling in love in a big way: When he was 26, he fell hard for 16-year-old Agnes Scuffs. The two were engaged and Leedskalnin was overjoyed. But the night before the wedding, Agnes had an abrupt change of heart and left Ed, claiming he was "too old and too poor."

Leedskalnin never recovered from the jilting. He left Latvia heartbroken, ending up in American lumberyards, working to support himself while nursing his broken heart. After a nasty bout with tuberculosis, he made his way to Florida, where he purchased a small plot of land in Florida City.

That'll Show Her!

Somewhere along the way, Leedskalnin decided to do a little construction project. Specifically, he wanted to build an impressive stone castle. Not only could he experiment with magnetic field engineering (he had been fascinated with magnets since being sick and claimed magnets had cured his TB), but perhaps he could even win back Agnes.

Leedskalnin harvested more than 1,000 tons of coral rock from his property in Florida City. From this he created movable walls, enormous pieces of furniture, towers, and massive fountains on the grounds of what he called Rock Gate Park. And Leedskalnin (who, remember, was about 5′0″, 100 pounds, and left school after the fourth grade) did so without the use of electricity, hydraulics, or high-tech machinery. It's hard to know exactly how he *did* construct Rock Gate Park because the eccentric man reportedly worked in total seclusion at night using only the light of a lantern. And although each three-foot-thick wall in the park weighs approximately 58 tons, no cranes were ever seen on Ed's property and there are no reports of him hiring a crew.

Magnet-o-rama?

It took Leedskalnin 28 years to build his coral universe, including a three-year stretch when he moved the whole operation ten miles up the road to the town of Homestead.

So, you must be wondering, how did he do all this?

Leedskalnin self-published a variety of pamphlets detailing his beliefs and research about magnetic fields. Some believe that he was able to move such enormously heavy rocks by harnessing the power of magnets with a "perpetual motion holder." Those same people tend to think this is what helped build the Great Pyramids and Stonehenge and that Leedskalnin was a misunderstood genius born to bring the power of the ancients to modern times.

In order to bring in an income, Ed gave tours of Rock Gate Park. For 25 cents, he would lead visitors through the bizarre grounds. When asked why he spent so many years building a castle out of raw stone, he always replied, "It's for my Sweet Sixteen" and claimed he was still "waiting for Agnes."

Ed died in 1951 from a combination of malnutrition, kidney failure, and stomach cancer. Three days before he passed away, he stuck a sign on the entrance to the park with the words, "Going to the hospital." His property was given to a nephew after his death and was eventually sold to a corporation that now manages the tourist traffic at the renamed "Coral Castle." The company markets the grounds as a kind of grand, romantic gesture by a heartsick man. Though that may be true, the more compelling story is in the mysterious methods used by an eccentric man to move tons of rock without the help of modern machines.

Epilogue: Agnes Scuffs died having never seen the fruits of her ex-fiancé's labor.

Strange Collections

Judging from the number of online museums and collectors' guides, it seems that many people are trying to make a name for themselves with one-of-a-kind collections. American Idol contestant Brandon Green even proudly displayed his toenail and fingernail collection for a national television audience.

Navel Fluff

In 1984, Graham Barker of Perth, Australia, started collecting his navel lint. Since then, he has seldom missed a day's "harvest" and collects an average of 3.03 milligrams each day; he currently has about 2½ jars of lint. He was rewarded for his efforts in 2000 when *Guinness World Records* declared his navel lint collection the world's largest. Barker also collects his own beard clippings, bakery bags, fast-food tray inserts, and ski-lift tickets.

Adhesive Bandages

Marz Waggener of Long Beach, California, has been collecting (unused) adhesive bandages since February 1994, after convincing her mother that she needed a box of Incredible Crash Dummies bandages for a Girl Scout badge. Fourteen years later, her collection had reached 3,300 different bandages, including a 1979 Superman bandage and some rare samples from the 1950s.

Traffic Signs and Signals

Stephen Salcedo asks visitors to his Web site to refrain from calling the cops on him—all 500-plus traffic signs and signals in his collection were obtained legally. Salcedo started his collection in 1986 at age five. The Fort Wayne, Indiana, collector has always been attracted to the graphic design aspect of road signs and has a special fondness for older ones (pre-1960). The "treasure" of his collection is the street sign that stood on the corner near his childhood home in Merrillville, Indiana.

Police and Prison Restraints

If the handcuff-collecting world has a celebrity, it is Stan Willis of Cincinnati. Since 1969, Willis has been collecting police and prison restraints and has built his reputation selling rare cuffs to other collectors. In 2003, *Guinness World Records* recognized his collection as the largest—it now contains nearly 1,400 items. He also collects police and fire department-related items, such as badges, lanterns, and helmets.

Mustard

Barry Levenson began his mustard collection in October 1986, with 12 jars he bought to soothe his grief when the Boston Red Sox lost to the New York Mets in the World Series. He vowed to assemble the largest collection of prepared mustard in the world. In April 1992, he opened the Mount Horeb Mustard Museum in Mount Horeb, Wisconsin. He now displays nearly 5,000 mustards from all 50 states and more than 60 countries, as well as historic mustard memorabilia. He is currently working on getting widespread recognition of the first Saturday in August as World Mustard Day, which is already celebrated at the museum.

Toothpaste

Dentist Val Kolpakov began collecting toothpaste and dental artifacts in March 2002 as a way to advertise his new dental practice. His hobby became a mission, however, and he now displays more than 1,400 tubes in his Saginaw, Michigan, office. Although the star of his collection is a rare silver Georgian tooth powder box from 1801, he is especially interested in vintage toothpastes, tubes from around the world, toothpastes from TV and movie sets, and flavors other than the traditional mint. Dr. Kolpakov boasts a variety of liquor-flavored pastes (including bourbon, Scotch, wine varietals, and champagne) as well as curry, lavender, and pumpkin pudding. Kolpakov believes his to be the largest collection in the world and is in the process of applying for a Guinness Record Certificate.

Barf Bags

Although Steve Silberberg of Massachusetts has never been out of the United States, his 2,000-plus barf bags come from around the world. Silberberg began collecting "happy sacks"—as they're known in piloting circles—in 1981 and now has a wide range of bus, car, train, and helicopter bags as well. Although not the largest collection in the world (he guesses it might be the tenth largest), he does have the largest collection of non-transportation bags, including novelty bags not intended for use, as well as political and movie sickness bags. The treasures of his collection include those given away on the Disneyland Star Tours ride and one from the Space Shuttle.

Mechanical Memorabilia

Marvin Yagoda has been a pharmacist for 50 years, but he is best known for his hobby of collecting mechanical novelties, vintage oddities, strange curiosities, and wonders, as he calls them. He started his collection of vintage coin-operated games and toys in the early 1960s and displayed some pieces in a local food court. After the food court closed in 1988, he opened Marvin's Marvelous Mechanical Museum in 1990—a 5,500-square-foot building in a strip mall in Farmington Hills, Michigan. Yagoda has packed the 40-foot ceilings with such things as fortune-tellers-in-a-box, nickelodeons, a carousel, more than 50 model airplanes, antique electric fans, animatronic dummies, vintage arcade games (from the early 1900s through present day), prize machines, one of the infamous P. T. Barnum Cardiff Giant statues, the electric chair from Sing Sing Prison, and much, much more. More than a thousand electrical outlets power the machines, which are all in working condition. Even the walls are not overlooked, sporting his collection of magic posters and 20-foot-long carnival canvases. Admission to his museum is free, but be sure to come with a few rolls of quarters.

H. H. Holmes:
Serial Killer at the World's Fair

H. H. Holmes has secured a place in history as one of the cruelest, most horrifyingly prolific killers the world has ever seen. From his headquarters at a Chicago hotel, Holmes slaughtered at least 27 people starting in the early 1890s.

Many filmmakers, scholars, and authors have tried to understand the mind of the madman Holmes. Here is an overview of the twisted, convoluted details of the real-life "Doctor Death."

Troubled Child

Born in May 1860, Herman Webster Mudgett was a highly intelligent child and did well in school, but he was constantly in trouble. As a teen, he became abusive to animals and small children—a classic characteristic of serial killers.

Fascinated with bones, skeletons, and the human body, Mudgett decided to pursue a degree in medicine. He changed his name to H. H. Holmes, married Clara Lovering, and with her inheritance, enrolled in medical school in Burlington, Vermont.

Swindler, Liar, Cheat

In medical school, Holmes was able to be around skeletons, cadavers, and fresh corpses all the time, which suited him just fine. Very soon, however, it was obvious that Holmes wasn't in the medical field for humanitarian reasons. Ever the swindler, Holmes came up with a scheme whereby he'd take insurance policies out on family members he didn't actually have. He would steal cadavers from the school, make them look as if they'd had an accident, then identify the bodies as those of his family members to collect the insurance money. Some of these frauds brought in $10,000 or more per body.

When authorities became suspicious of all these dead "family members," Holmes abandoned Clara and their newborn baby. Where he went after that is a little murky, as the next six or so years of Holmes's life are not well documented. But by the mid-1880s, Holmes was back on the radar as a charming, intelligent, bold-faced liar and thief with murderous intentions. This time, his mark was Chicago. The city would become the site of Holmes's biggest, deadliest swindle of all.

The Roots of a Murderous Plan

If you lived in Chicago in the late 1800s, you were likely consumed with thoughts of the World's Fair. Officially known as the World's Columbian Exposition of 1893, the colossal event had most of the Midwest working for its success. It was to be the event that would make America a superstar country and make Chicago one of the country's A-list cities. The Great Fire of 1871 had demolished the town; the World's Fair vowed to bring it back in a big way.

It was during the years of preparation for the big fair that Holmes began his path of murder. With so many people flooding the city every day looking to nab one of the thousands of new jobs in the area, Chicago was experiencing a population boom that made it very easy to lose track of people. Holmes recognized this as an opportunity to lure women into his clutches while most people had their focus elsewhere.

He married his second wife, Myrtle, in 1885, even though he had never actually divorced Clara. While Myrtle lived in suburban Wilmette, Holmes took a place in Chicago, and the couple lived apart for most of their marriage. Holmes needed to be in the city because he was working at a drugstore in Chicago's Englewood neighborhood. He worked for the elderly Mrs. Holdens, a kind woman who was happy to have such an attractive young doctor help out at her busy store. When Mrs. Holden disappeared without a trace in 1887 and Holmes purchased the store, no one suspected a thing.

Holmes (who now had full access to a well-stocked drugstore with countless medical tools, chemicals, and medicines) purchased a vacant lot across the street from the drugstore and began construction on a house with a strange floor plan he'd designed himself. The three-story house would have 60 rooms, more than 50 doors placed in an odd fashion throughout the structure, trap doors, secret passageways, windowless rooms, and chutes that led down to a deep basement. Holmes hired and fired construction crews on a regular basis, and it was said that his swindler's streak got him out of paying for most (or perhaps all) of the materials and labor used to create what would later be known as the "Murder Castle."

Death: Up & Running

As construction of the "castle" wrapped up, Holmes made plans for several of his employees. The bookkeeper Holmes had at the store around 1890 was Ned Connor, a man who had come to Chicago with his lovely wife, Julia, and their baby daughter, Pearl. Holmes found Julia irresistible and quickly put the make on her, firing Ned so his wife could take his place. It is believed that as his new bookkeeper, Julia was possibly an accomplice in the fraudulent actions at the drugstore, which eased Holmes's mind and allowed him to concentrate on his new building.

Advertised as a lodging for World's Fair tourists, the building opened in 1892. Holmes placed ads in the newspaper to rent rooms, but also listed fake classifieds, calling for females interested in working for a start-up company. He also placed ads for marriage, posing as a successful businessman in need of a wife. Any woman who answered these fake ads was interviewed by Holmes, was told to keep everything a secret, and was instructed to withdraw all funds from her bank account in order to start a new life with him as his worker, wife, or whatever role he had offered. Holmes was a brilliant liar and quite the charmer, and naive 19th-century women fell for it. Once they passed Holmes's tests, these women became his prisoners, doomed to meet their grisly ends.

Gas pipes were secretly installed throughout the house with nozzles that piped noxious fumes into the rooms. Holmes would turn on the gas so that the victim du jour would drop to the floor unconscious. While she was out cold, Holmes would usually rape her, then send the girl down to the basement via the chute. Once there, he would perform experiments on her at his dissection table or torture her with various equipment. He reportedly listened to the screams of the victims from an adjacent room.

Once he had brutalized the unfortunate soul, he would dump her body into a vat of lime acid to completely destroy the evidence. Other times, he sold bones and organs to contacts in the medical field. Holmes murdered at least 22 people in his home, mostly women, though every once in awhile a worried male neighbor or a concerned relative looking for a missing young woman would get too suspicious for Holmes's liking and go missing themselves.

While the "Murder Castle" was in operation, Holmes continued to marry various women and carry out insurance fraud and other deviant acts. After the World's Fair ended, creditors put pressure on him again, and Holmes knew it was time to flee. He traveled across the United States and Canada, scamming and murdering along the way. Strange as it seems, when Holmes was finally caught and brought to justice, it wasn't initially for homicide; a horse-swindling scheme he attempted to pull off with longtime partner in fraud Ben Pietzel was what gave authorities enough evidence to arrest Holmes. When they searched Holmes's Chicago dwelling, their investigation turned up a lot more than they anticipated.

The End of "Doctor Death"
Over the years, one detective had been hot on Holmes's trail. Detective Frank Geyer, a veteran Pinkerton detective, had done his best to follow this creepy man whose identity changed with the weather. Geyer had traced many of the missing World's Fair women back to Holmes's lodging house and had discovered trails that pointed to his fraudulent activities. In 1895, Holmes entered a guilty plea for the horse-fraud case, and Geyer took that opportunity to expand the investigation. He was particularly interested in the whereabouts of three children—Howard, Nellie, and Alice Pietzel, children of Holmes's now murdered accomplice, Ben Pietzel.

Geyer traced the children—and then Holmes—by following his mail. When his search took him to Canada, Geyer knocked on doors all over Toronto to track down Holmes. Finally, he found a house where Holmes had allegedly stayed with several children in tow. Buried in a shallow grave in the backyard were the bodies of the two Pietzel girls. The boy was found several months later in an oven in an Indianapolis home.

When the evidence was brought back to court, Geyer got full clearance to investigate every dark nook and cranny of Holmes's house and business, and one of America's most chilling stories of murder and crime officially broke. As detectives and police officers uncovered layer after layer of hideous evidence, the public became more and more frightened—and fascinated. The *Chicago Tribune* published the floor plan of the "Murder Castle," tourists flocked to ogle the building, and tabloids ran horrifying descriptions of what had happened to the victims inside, events both real and embellished. Then, in August 1895, Holmes's house of horrors burnt to the ground.

While all that took place, inside his heavily guarded cell, Herman Webster Mudgett confessed to his crimes. He officially confessed to 27 murders, six attempted murders, and a whole lot of fraud. What he didn't confess to, however, were any feelings of remorse. Holmes claimed at times to be possessed by the devil, though depending on the day, he'd also claim to be innocent of any wrongdoing whatsoever. All told, estimates of his victims may have hit the 200 mark. Just because he confessed to 27 murders doesn't mean that's what his final tally was—indeed, with the kind of liar Holmes was, it's pretty certain that the number isn't accurate at all.

Holmes was executed by hanging in 1896. He was buried in a coffin lined with cement, topped with more cement, and buried in a double grave—instructions he gave in his last will and testament so that "no one could dig him back up." Was he ready to rest eternally after a life of such monstrosity? Or was he afraid that someone would conduct experiments on him as he had done to so many hapless victims?

In 2003, Mexico reported three deaths from acne.

FREAKY FACTS:
WORLD'S WEIRDEST ANIMALS

- The female boomslang, a type of African tree snake, looks so much like a tree branch that birds—its main prey—will land right on it.

- Tiny shrews, sometimes only a few inches long, may be the fiercest of all mammals because they eat their own weight in food over the course of the day and can kill prey twice their size—everything from insects and snakes to mice and rats. They are able to do this partly because their saliva contains a paralyzing substance similar to cobra venom.

- The koala, which is not actually a bear but a primitive marsupial that has existed in its present form for more than a million years, gets almost all the liquid it needs from licking dew off tree leaves.

- When the male snowy owl wishes to arouse a female, he dances while swinging a dead lemming from his beak.

- The emperor penguin of the Antarctic has equality of the sexes down pat—the female lays the egg, but the male has the "brood pouch," a roll of skin and feathers between his legs that drops over the egg. He then must protect the egg and keep it still for two months until it hatches and the female returns to feed the chick.

- In a Mediterranean species of the cardinal fish, the male takes part in mouthbrooding—holding the fertilized eggs in his mouth until they are ready to hatch.

- The roadrunner takes a no-holds-barred approach to killing a rattlesnake. It jabs the snake with its sharp bill, shakes it, body-slams it, then administers a final peck in the head before devouring its prey headfirst.

Fireball in the Sky

While playing football on the afternoon of September 12, 1952, a group of boys in Flatwoods, West Virginia, saw a large fireball fly over their heads. The object seemed to stop near the hillside property of Bailey Fisher. Some thought the object was a UFO, but others said it was just a meteor. They decided to investigate.

Darkness was falling as the boys made their way toward the hill, so they stopped at the home of Kathleen May to borrow a flashlight. Seeing how excited the boys were, May, her two sons, and their friend, Eugene Lemon, decided to join them. The group set off to find out exactly what had landed on the hill.

Walking Through the Darkness

As they neared the top of the hill, the group smelled a strange odor that reminded them of burning metal. Continuing on, some members of the group thought they saw an object that resembled a spaceship. Shining their flashlights in front of them, the group was startled when something not of this world moved out from behind a nearby tree.

The Encounter

The description of what is now known as the Flatwoods Monster is almost beyond belief. It stood around 12 feet tall and had a round, reddish face from which two large holes were visible. Looming up from behind the creature's head was a large pointed hood. The creature, which appeared to be made of a dark metal, had no arms or legs and seemed to float through the air. Looking back, the witnesses believe what they saw was a protective suit or perhaps a robot rather than a monster.

When a flashlight beam hit the creature, its "eyes" lit up and it began floating toward the group while making a strange hissing noise. The horrible stench was now overpowering and some in the group immediately felt nauseous. Because she was at the head of the group, Kathleen May had the best view of the monster. She later stated that as the creature was moving toward her, it squirted or dripped a strange fluid on her that resembled oil but had an unusual odor to it.

Terrified beyond belief, the group fled down the hillside and back to the May house, where they telephoned Sheriff Robert Carr, who responded with his deputy, Burnell Long. After talking with the group, they gathered some men and went to the Fisher property to investigate. But they only found a gummy residue and what appeared to be skid marks on the ground. There was no monster and no spaceship. However, the group did report that the heavy stench of what smelled like burning metal was still in the air.

The Aftermath

A. Lee Stewart, a member of the of the search party and copublisher of the *Braxton Democrat,* knew a good story when he saw one, so he sent the tale over the news wire, and almost immediately, people were asking Kathleen May for interviews. On September 19, 1952, May and Stewart discussed the Flatwoods Monster on the TV show *We the People.* For the show, an artist sketched the creature based on May's description, but he took some liberties, and the resulting sketch was so outrageous that people started saying the whole thing was a hoax.

Slowly, though, others came forward to admit that they too had seen a strange craft flying through the sky near Flatwoods on September 12. One witness described it as roughly the size of a single-car garage. He said that he lost sight of the craft when it appeared to land on a nearby hill.

Since that night in 1952, the Flatwoods Monster has never been seen again, leaving many people to wonder what exactly those people encountered. A monster? An alien from another world? Or perhaps nothing more than a giant owl? One thing is for sure: There were far too many witnesses to deny that they stumbled upon something strange that night.

Psychic Detectives

When the corpse just can't be found, the murderer remains unknown, and the weapon has been stashed in some secret corner, criminal investigations hit a stalemate and law enforcement agencies may tap their secret weapons—individuals who find things through some unconventional methods.

"Reading" the Ripper: Robert James Lees

When the psychotic murderer known as Jack the Ripper terrorized London in the 1880s, the detectives of Scotland Yard consulted a psychic named Robert James Lees who said he had glimpsed the killer's face in several visions. Lees also claimed he had correctly forecasted at least three of the well-publicized murders of women. The Ripper wrote a sarcastic note to detectives stating that they would still never catch him. Indeed, the killer proved right in this prediction.

Feeling Their Vibes: Florence Sternfels

As a psychometrist—a psychic who gathers impressions by handling material objects—Florence Sternfels was successful enough to charge a dollar for readings in Edgewater, New Jersey, in the early 20th century. Born in 1891, Sternfels believed that her gift was a natural ability rather than a supernatural one, so she never billed police for her help in solving crimes. Some of her best "hits" included preventing a man from blowing up an army base with dynamite, finding two missing boys alive in Philadelphia, and leading police to the body of a murdered young woman. She worked with police as far away as Europe to solve tough cases but lived quietly in New Jersey until her death in 1965.

The Dutch Grocer's Gift: Gerard Croiset

Born in the Netherlands in 1909, Gerard Croiset nurtured a growing psychic ability from age six. In 1935, he joined a Spiritualist group, began to hone his talents, and within two years had set up shop as a psychic and healer. After a touring lecturer discovered his abilities in 1945, Croiset began assisting law enforcement agencies around the world, traveling as far as Japan and Australia. He specialized in finding missing children but also helped authorities locate lost papers and artifacts. At the same time, Croiset ran a popular clinic for psychic healing that treated both humans and animals. His son, Gerard Croiset, Jr., was also a professional psychic and parapsychologist.

Accidental Psychic: Peter Hurkos

As one of the most famous psychic detectives of the 20th century, Peter Hurkos did his best work by picking up vibes from victims' clothing. Born in the Netherlands in 1911, Hurkos lived an ordinary life as a house painter until a fall required him to undergo brain surgery at age 30. The operation seemed to trigger his latent psychic powers, and he was almost immediately able to mentally retrieve information about people and "read" the history of objects by handling them.

Hurkos assisted in the Boston Strangler investigation in the early 1960s, and in 1969, he was brought in to help solve the grisly murders executed by Charles Manson. He gave police many accurate details including the name Charlie, a description of Manson, and that the murders were ritual slayings.

The TV Screen Mind of Dorothy Allison

New Jersey housewife Dorothy Allison broke into the world of clairvoyant crime solving when she dreamed about a missing local boy as if seeing it on television. In her dream, the five-year-old boy was stuck in some kind of pipe. When she called police, she also described the child's clothing, including the odd fact that he was wearing his shoes on the opposite feet. When Allison underwent hypnosis to learn more details, she added that the boy's surroundings involved a fenced school and a factory. She was proven correct on all accounts when the boy's body was found about two months after he went missing, floating close to a pipe in a pond near a school and a factory with his little shoes still tied onto the wrong feet.

Allison, who began having psychic experiences as a child, considered her gift a blessing and never asked for pay. One of her more famous cases was that of missing heiress Patty Hearst in 1974. Although Allison was unable to find her, every prediction she made about the young woman came true, including the fact that she had dyed her hair red.

Like a Bolt Out of the Blue: John Catchings

While at a Texas barbeque on an overcast July 4, 1969, a bolt of lightning hit 22-year-old John Catchings. He survived but said the electric blast opened him to his life's calling as a psychic. He then followed in the footsteps of his mother, Bertie, who earned her living giving "readings."

Catchings often helped police solve puzzling cases but became famous after helping police find a missing, 32-year-old Houston nurse named Gail Lorke. She vanished in late October 1982, after her husband, Steven, claimed she had stayed home from work because she was sick. Because Catchings worked by holding objects that belonged to victims, Lorke's sister, who was suspicious of Steven, went to Catchings with a photo of Gail and her belt. Allegedly, Catchings saw that Lorke had indeed been murdered by her husband and left under a heap of refuse that included parts of an old, wooden fence. He also gave police several other key details. Detectives were able to use the information to get Steven Lorke to confess his crime.

Among many other successes, Catchings also helped police find the body of Mike Dickens in 1980 after telling them the young man would be found buried in a creek bed near a shoe and other rubbish, including old tires and boards. Police discovered the body there just as Catchings had described it.

Fame from Fortunes: Irene Hughes

In 2008, famed investigative psychic Irene Hughes claimed a career tally of more than 2,000 police cases on her Web site.

Born around 1920 (sources vary) in rural Tennessee, Hughes shocked her church congregation at age four when she shouted out that the minister would soon leave them. She was right and kept on making predictions, advised by a Japanese "spirit guide" named Kaygee. After World War II, Hughes moved to Chicago to take a job as a newspaper reporter. She financed her trip by betting on a few horse races using her psychic abilities! She gained fame in 1967 when she correctly prophesied Chicago's terrible blizzard and that the Cardinals would win the World Series. By 1968, she was advising Howard Hughes and correctly predicted his death in 1976.

Hughes's more famous predictions included the death of North Vietnamese premiere Ho Chi Minh in 1969 (although she was off by a week), the circumstances of Ted Kennedy's Chappaquiddick fiasco, and that Jacqueline Kennedy would marry someone with the characteristics of her eventual second husband, Aristotle Onassis. Hughes operated out of a luxurious office on Chicago's Michigan Avenue and commanded as much as $500 an hour from her many eager clients. She hosted radio and TV shows, wrote three books, and in the 1980s and '90s, wrote a much-read column of New Year's predictions for the *National Enquirer*. Now in her eighties, she still works out of her home and writes a regular astrology column.

Massive Movement

Following a horrific car crash in July 2007, fire engulfed a vehicle near Augusta, Georgia. It had already claimed one life and was about claim another. Luckily, a quick-thinking driver from a local plumbing firm saw the incident unfold and took action. He released 1,500 wet gallons onto the vehicle—a heroic move that extinguished the deadly flames and saved the passenger's life. It had been a stroke of luck that the plumber had just pumped a payload from a nearby client. But then, sucking *raw sewage* from septic tanks did comprise the bulk of his work.

Medical Atrocities on Display at Philadelphia's Mütter Museum

Located at the College of Physicians of Philadelphia, the Mütter Museum is perhaps the most grotesque, or at least one of the most shockingly fascinating museums in the United States. Its collection of human skulls, preserved brains (eyes included), and freaks of nature will entertain those with even the most morbid curiosities.

It's also one of the most elegant museums open to the public, with red carpet, brass railings, and redwood-lined display cases. It might even appear a bit high-brow if the curators themselves didn't acknowledge what a uniquely abnormal exhibit they were pushing—a refreshing attitude evident in their motto "Disturbingly Informative."

The museum originated in 1859, when Dr. Thomas Mütter donated several thousand dollars and his personal collection of 1,700 medical specimens to the College of Physicians. Merging it with their own meager collection, the institution used Mütter's money to build new quarters to house it all and opened it to both students and the public.

Further acquisitions expanded the museum's collection tremendously, as doctors contributed specimens they acquired through their own private practices and studies. A large number of them have been skeletal, such as a woman's rib cage that became cartoonishly compressed by years of wearing tight corsets and the 19th-century Peruvian skulls showing primitive trephinations (holes cut or drilled in the head). There are also the combined skeletons of infants born with a shared skull and the bones of a man suffering a condition in which superfluous bone grows in patches, eventually fusing the skeleton together and immobilizing it and its owner. Most popular, though, is the skeleton of a man measuring 7'6", the tallest of its kind on display in North America, which stands next to that of a 3'6" female dwarf.

Other items include heads sliced like loaves of bread, both front to back and side to side, and outdated medical instruments, many of which look torturous. Curators also have in their possession more than 2,000 objects removed from people's throats and airways, a vintage iron lung, and photographs of some of medicine's most bizarre human deformities.

The museum even has its own celebrities of sorts. For example, there's Madame Dimanche, an 82-year-old Parisian whose face and the drooping, ten-inch horn growing from her forehead have been preserved in lifelike wax. There's also the unidentified corpse of a woman known simply as the Soap Lady, whose body was unearthed in 1874. The particular composition of the soil in which she was buried transformed the fatty tissues in her body, essentially preserving her as a human-shape bar of soap. And who can forget Eng and Chang, the conjoined brothers who toured the world with P. T. Barnum and inspired the term "Siamese twins"? The Mütter Museum not only has a plaster cast of their torsos, but also their actual connected livers.

STRANGE STATS

- *The basenji is an African hunting dog that washes itself like a cat and yodels and chortles, although it does not naturally know how to bark (but can mimic other dogs barking).*

- *Seven percent of Americans say they have been abducted by aliens or know someone who has.*

- *Some frogs eat so many fireflies that they glow themselves.*

- *Mistletoe was originally used to ward off witches and evil spirits.*

- *One person in two billion will live to age 116 or older.*

- *Buzz Aldrin's mother's maiden name was Moon.*

The Bell Witch of Tennessee

There is perhaps no haunting in America that resonates quite like the event that occurred on the farm of John Bell in rural Tennessee. The story stands unique in the annals of folklore as one of the rare cases in which a spirit not only injured the residents of a haunted house but also caused the death of one of them! For this reason, even though the haunting occurred in the early 1800s, it has not yet been forgotten.

The story of the Bell Witch will be forever linked to the small town of Adams in northwestern Tennessee. In 1804, John Bell, his wife, Lucy, and their six children came to the region from North Carolina. He purchased 1,000 acres of land on the Red River, and the Bell family settled quite comfortably into the community. John Bell was well liked and kind words were always expressed about Lucy, who often opened her home to travelers and hosted social gatherings.

Bumps in the Night

The Bell haunting began in 1817 after John Bell and his son Drew spotted odd creatures in the woods near their farm. When they shot at the strange beasts, they vanished.

Soon after, a series of weird knocking, scraping, and scratching sounds began on the exterior of the house and then at the front door. Shortly thereafter, the sounds moved inside and seemed to emanate from the bedroom belonging to the Bell sons. This continued for weeks, and before long, the irritating sounds were heard all over the house. They continued from room to room, stopping when everyone was awake and starting again when they all went back to bed.

The Bells also heard what sounded like a dog pawing at the wooden floor or chains being dragged through the house. They even heard thumps and thuds, as though furniture was being overturned. These sounds were frightening, but not as terrifying as the noises that followed—the smacking of lips, gurgling, gulping, and choking—sounds seemingly made by a human.

The nerves of the Bell family were starting to unravel as the sounds became a nightly occurrence.

The Coming of the Witch

The disembodied sounds were followed by unseen hands. Items in the house were broken and blankets were yanked from the beds. Hair was pulled and the children were slapped and poked, causing them to cry in pain. The Bells' daughter Betsy was once slapped so hard that her cheeks stayed bright red for hours.

Whatever the cause of this unseen force, most of its violent outbursts were directed at Betsy. She would often run screaming from her room in terror as the unseen hands prodded, pinched, and poked her. Strangely, the force became even crueler to her whenever she entertained her young suitor, Joshua Gardner, at the house. Desperately seeking answers, John Bell enlisted the help of some of his neighbors to investigate.

Even in the presence of these witnesses, the strange sounds continued, chairs overturned, and objects flew about the room. The neighbors formed an investigative committee, determined to find a cause for the terrifying events.

Regardless, the household was in chaos. Word began to spread of the strange happenings, and friends and strangers came to the farm to witness it for themselves. Dozens of people heard the banging and rapping sounds and chunks of rock and wood were thrown at curious guests by unseen hands.

As the investigative committee searched for answers, they set up experiments, tried to communicate with the force, and kept a close eye on the events that took place. They set up overnight vigils, but the attacks only increased in intensity. Betsy was treated brutally and began to have sensations that the breath was being sucked out of her body. She was scratched and her flesh bled as though she was being pierced with invisible pins and needles. She also suffered fainting spells and often blacked out for 30 to 40 minutes at a time.

Soon, a raspy whistling sound was audible, as if someone was trying to speak. It progressed until the force began to talk in a weak whisper. The voice of the force told them that it was a spirit whose rest had been disturbed, and it made many claims as to its origins, from being an ancient spirit to the ghost of a murdered peddler.

The excitement in the community grew as word spread that the spirit was communicating. People came from far and wide to hear the unexplained voice. Hundreds of people witnessed the activity caused by the witch. There were those who came to the Bell farm intent on either driving out the witch or proving that the entire affair was a hoax. But without fail, each of them left the farm confessing that the unusual events were beyond their understanding.

A Strange Affliction

John Bell began to complain of a curious numbness in his mouth that caused his tongue to swell so greatly that he was unable to eat or drink for days at a time. As the haunting progressed, he began to suffer other inexplicable symptoms, most notably bizarre facial tics that rendered him unable to talk or eat and often made him lose consciousness. These odd seizures lasted from a few hours to a week, and they increased in severity as time wore on.

No one knows why John Bell was targeted by the spirit, but from the beginning, the witch made it clear that it would torment him for the rest of his life. Bell was also physically abused by the witch and many witnesses recalled him being slapped by unseen hands or crying out in pain as he was stabbed with invisible pins. Bell's doctor was helpless when it came to finding a cure for his ailments. The witch laughed at his efforts and declared that no medicine could cure him.

Some believe the reason for Bell's suffering was revealed one night when the spirit claimed to belong to Kate Batts, an eccentric neighbor who had disliked Bell because of some bad business dealings in the past. Whether the spirit was Batts is unknown, but people began calling the witch Kate.

The Death of John Bell

By 1820, John Bell's physical condition had worsened. His facial jerks and twitches continued, as did the swelling of his tongue and the seizures that left him nearly paralyzed for hours or days at a time. In late October, he suffered another fit and took to his bed. He would never leave the house again. As Bell writhed in pain, Kate remained nearby, laughing and cursing at the dying man.

On the morning of December 19, 1820, Lucy checked on her husband who appeared to be sleeping soundly. An hour later, she returned to the bedroom and realized that he was in a stupor. When John, Jr., went to get his father's medicine, he discovered that all of his father's prescriptions had vanished. In place of them was a small vial that contained a dark-colored liquid. No one knew what had happened to the medicines or what was in the vial.

Suddenly, Kate's voice took over the room. She claimed that she had poisoned Bell with the contents of the dark vial and that he would never rise from his bed again. The mysterious liquid was tested on a family cat, and the animal was dead in seconds.

John Bell never did recover. On December 20, he took one last shuddering breath and died. Laughter filled the house as the witch stated that she hoped John Bell would burn in hell.

Bell was laid to rest in a small cemetery, a short distance from the family home. As mourners left the cemetery, the voice of Kate returned, echoing loudly in the cold morning air. She cheered the death of the man she hated so much.

This ended the most terrifying chapter of a haunting that left an indelible mark in the annals of supernatural history. But the Bell Witch was not finished—at least not quite yet.

The Broken Engagement

After the funeral, the activities of the witch seemed to subside, but she was not totally gone. Kate remained with the family throughout the winter and spring of 1821, but she was not quite as vicious as she had been, not even to Betsy, around whom her activities continued to be centered.

During the haunting, it was clear that Betsy would be punished as long as she allowed herself to be courted by Joshua Gardner. But Betsy and Joshua refused to give in to Kate's wishes. In fact, on Easter Sunday 1821, the couple became engaged, much to the delight of their family and friends.

But their joy would not last long as the antics of the witch returned with horrific force. Realizing that the witch would never leave her alone as long as she stayed with Joshua, Betsy broke off the engagement and never saw him again.

The Return of the Witch

In the summer of 1821, the witch left the Bell family, promising to return in seven years. In 1828, she came back and announced her return in the same manner as when the original haunting first began—scratching and other eerie sounds inside and outside the house, objects moving, and blankets pulled from the beds.

The Bells decided to ignore the activity, and, if spoken to by the spirit, they ignored it as well. In this way, they hoped the visitation might end quickly. And so it did—the witch left the house after a few weeks.

However, much of the activity during the witch's 1828 visit took place at the home of John Bell, Jr., who had built a house on land that he had inherited from his father. The witch allegedly made several accurate predictions about the future, including the Civil War, the end of slavery, the rise of the United States as a world power, and the coming of World Wars I and II. She even predicted the end of the world, stating that the world would end with the temperature of the planet rising so high that it would become uninhabitable.

Kate stayed with John Bell, Jr., for several months. Before she left, she promised to return again in 107 years (1935), and though there is no record that she ever did so, there are some that maintain that the Bell Witch has never left Adams, Tennessee. Strange events still occur where the old Bell farm stood. Old Kate is still talked about today and you'd have to travel far to find someone who does not believe that something very strange occurred there in the early 1800s. What was it exactly? No one knows for sure, but there's no question that it made an indelible mark on American history.

FREAKY FACTS: TASTE BUDS

- *Babies are born with taste buds on the insides of their cheeks and overall have more taste buds than adults, but they lose them as they grow older.*

- *Adults have, on average, around 10,000 taste buds, although an elderly person might have only 5,000.*

- *One in four people is a "supertaster" and has more taste buds than the average person—more than 1,000 per square centimeter.*

- *Twenty-five percent of humans are "nontasters" and have fewer taste buds than other people their age—only about 40 per square centimeter.*

- *A taste bud is 30 to 60 microns (slightly more than $\frac{1}{1000}$ inch) in diameter.*

- *Taste buds are not just for tongues—they also cover the back of the throat and the roof of the mouth.*

- *Cats' taste buds cannot detect sweetness.*

- *The "suction cups" on an octopus' tentacles are covered in taste buds.*

- *A butterfly's taste buds are on its feet and tongue.*

- *Attached to each taste bud are microscopic hairs called microvilli.*

- *Taste buds are regrown every two weeks.*

- *About 75 percent of what we think we taste is actually coming from our sense of smell.*

- *Along with sweet, salty, sour, and bitter, there is a fifth taste, called umami, which describes the savory taste of foods such as meat, cheese, and soy sauce.*

Odd Scientific Experiments

Popular culture often credits scientists with a sort of noble eccentricity. Sometimes, though, even a genuine experiment can seem less off the bell curve and more off the bell tower.

Will Eat Vomit to Graduate

In 1804, Stubbins H. Ffirth, a medical student at the University of Pennsylvania, set out to prove that yellow fever could not be transmitted from person to person. He smeared himself with blood, urine, sweat, saliva, and fresh black vomit from yellow fever patients. When this failed to make him ill, Ffirth heated more vomit in a sand bath and inhaled the fumes. Then he made the residue into pills, swallowed them, and chased them with more vomit. Having emerged from this crucible in glowing health, Ffirth wrote up the results of his work for his graduation thesis. (For the record: Yellow fever is highly contagious, but it is most effectively transmitted by mosquitoes directly into the bloodstream. Ffirth was incredibly lucky.)

Gua, the "Human" Ape

If a human child raised by wolves starts acting like a wolf, would a baby chimp adopted by humans begin to act human? This was the question Winthrop Kellogg sought to answer in 1931 when he adopted a 7½-month-old female chimp named Gua. For the next nine months, Kellogg's baby son, Donald, had a "sister." The two were treated exactly the same by adults, and soon Gua was playing with her "brother," kissing her "parents," opening and closing doors, wearing clothes and shoes, eating with a spoon, and even walking upright—all the same tasks that Donald learned. The only thing she could not master was speech. One can only imagine what she might have said.

Which Is Worse: Nail Biting or Sleep Deprivation?

In the summer of 1942, Lawrence LeShan of the College of William and Mary in Williamsburg, Virginia, tried to get a group of boys to stop biting their nails through subliminal messages. While the boys slept, LeShan played a record in their dormitory with one single phrase recorded on it: "My fingernails taste terribly bitter." When the record player broke down, LeShan took up the slack by repeating the phrase himself all night. By the end of the summer, 40 percent of the boys had kicked the habit, but LeShan was presumably ready for a long nap.

Bow-Wow Holy Cow

In 1954, Soviet surgeon Vladimir Demikhov presented a bizarre creature to the world: an adult German shepherd with the head, neck, and front legs of a puppy grafted onto its neck. The heads snarled at each other, nibbled each other's ears, and lapped milk in tandem. Demikhov created 20 such Franken-pups, but none lived for more than a month before tissue rejection set in. Demikhov's main research focus was cardiology and the development of surgical techniques for heart transplants. He even performed the first canine heart transplant in 1946, followed by a lung transplant on a dog the following year.

Remote-Control Bull

In 1965, Jose Delgado, a professor at the Yale School of Medicine, stepped into a bull-fighting ring in Spain. A bull was released and charged the matador's red cape, but moments before the beast's horns made contact, the professor pressed a button on a radio transmitter, and the bull braked to a halt. The professor then pressed another button, and the animal trotted away. The day before, Delgado had implanted several wires into the bull's brain, and he was now effectively remote-controlling—or at least remotely influencing—the bull's movements. He performed similar experiments on other animals and undoubtedly influenced countless science-fiction writers through his work.

Impending Doom

In the early 1960s, the U.S. Army loaded ten soldiers into a plane for what was supposed to be a routine training mission. Mid-flight, one of the propellers failed, and the pilot announced over the intercom that the plane was about to crash into the ocean. A steward then began distributing insurance forms for the soldiers to fill out. After the last one was finished, the pilot suddenly revved the propeller back up and made a second announcement: The emergency had been a joke. The Army was simply conducting an experiment on whether people made more mistakes under the stress of imminent death. The soldiers must have gotten a kick out of that one.

Tripping Elephant

On August 3, 1962, psychiatrists from the University of Oklahoma injected 297 milligrams of LSD into the rump of a 14-year-old elephant named Tusko. They wanted to determine whether the acid—3,000 times the typical human dose—would plunge the animal into musth, a state of temporary madness and sexual aggression in bull elephants. Things didn't go quite as planned: After stumbling and lurching around his pen, poor Tusko keeled over dead. Defending themselves later to the public, the researchers claimed that they hadn't expected such a severe reaction to the drug, since some of them used LSD themselves.

Brains vs. Body

What does it take to excite a turkey? This important question was investigated by Penn State University researchers Martin Schein and Edgar Hale in the 1960s. It turns out that a female turkey really doesn't need much to arouse a male's interest—not even a body. When researchers constructed a lifelike model of a female turkey and then dismantled it piece by piece, they observed that the males retained interest in the "female" even when nothing remained of the model except a head on a stick. Oddly enough, the same males showed little interest in courting a headless body.

Death...Isn't It Ironic?

💀   💀   💀   💀   💀

No matter who you are, it's inevitable your time on this earth will end. But some people have a way of shuffling off this mortal coil with a bit more ironic poignancy.

- In 1936, a picture of baby George Story was featured in the first issue of *Life* magazine. Story died in 2000 at age 63, just after the magazine announced it would be shutting down. *Life* carried an article about his death from heart failure in its final issue.

- In the early 1960s, Ken Hubbs was a Gold Glove second baseman for the Chicago Cubs. The young standout had a lifelong fear of flying, so to overcome it, he decided to take flying lessons. In 1964, shortly after earning his pilot's license, Hubbs was killed when his plane went down during a snowstorm.

- While defending an accused murderer in 1871, attorney Clement Vallandigham argued that the victim accidentally killed himself as he tried to draw his pistol. Demonstrating his theory for the court, the lawyer fatally shot himself in the process. The jury acquitted his client and Vallandigham won the case posthumously.

- Private detective Allan Pinkerton built his career on secrecy and his ability to keep his mouth shut. However, biting his tongue literally killed him when he tripped while out for a walk, severely cutting his tongue. It became infected and led to his death in 1884.

- When he appeared on *The Dick Cavett Show* in 1971, writer and healthy living advocate Jerome I. Rodale claimed, "I've decided to live to be a hundred," and "I never felt better in my life!" Moments later, still in his seat on stage, the 72-year-old Rodale was dead of a heart attack. The episode never aired.

- South Korean Lee Seung Seop loved playing video games more than anything. His obsession caused him to lose his job and his girlfriend and eventually took his life as well. In August 2005, after playing a video game at an Internet café for 50 consecutive hours, he died at age 28 from dehydration, exhaustion, and heart failure.

- Jim Fixx advocated running as a cure-all, helping develop the fitness craze of the late 20th century. However, in 1984, he died from a heart attack while jogging. Autopsy results showed he suffered from severely clogged and hardened arteries.

- Thomas Midgley, Jr., was a brilliant engineer and inventor who held 170 patents. After contracting polio at age 51, he turned his attention to inventing a system of pulleys to help him move around in bed. In 1944, he was found dead, strangled by the pulley system that he had invented.

- At least two of the Marlboro Men—the chiseled icons of the cigarette culture—have died from lung cancer. David McLean developed emphysema in 1985 and died from lung cancer a decade later. Wayne McLaren portrayed the character in the 1970s, and, although he was an anti-smoking advocate later in life, he still contracted cancer. Despite having a lung removed, the cancer spread to his brain, and he died in 1992.

- Author Olivia Goldsmith wrote *The First Wives Club,* a book that became an icon for older women whose husbands had tossed them aside for younger trophy wives. A generation of women embraced their wrinkles and weren't afraid to let the world know. Ironically, Goldsmith died while undergoing cosmetic surgery.

- Shortly before he died in a high-speed car crash, James Dean filmed a television spot promoting his new film *Giant.* The interviewer asked Dean if he had any advice for young people. "Take it easy driving," he replied. "The life you save might be mine."

Monsters Across America

💀　💀　💀　💀　💀

*Dracula, Frankenstein, the Wolf Man—these are the monsters
who strike fear into the hearts of children—the same ones
that parents chase away and tell their kids there's no such
thing as monsters. But are they wrong?*

Dover Demon

For two days in 1977, the town of Dover, Massachusetts, was
under attack from a bizarre creature that seemed to be from
another world. The first encounter with the beast—nicknamed
the Dover Demon—occurred on the evening of April 21. Bill
Bartlett was out for a drive with some friends when they saw
something strange climbing on a stone wall. The creature
appeared to be only about three feet tall but had a giant, oversize head with large, orange eyes. The rest of the body was tan
and hairless with long, thin arms and legs.

Several hours later, the same creature was spotted by
15-year-old John Baxter, who watched it scurry up a hillside.
The following day, a couple reported seeing the Demon, too.
When authorities asked for a description, the couple's matched
the ones given by the other witnesses except for one difference:
The creature the couple encountered appeared to have glowing
green eyes. Despite repeated attempts to locate it, the creature
was never seen again.

Momo

In the early 1970s, reports came flooding in of a strange creature roaming the woods near the small town of Louisiana, Missouri. Standing nearly seven feet tall, Momo (short for Missouri Monster) was completely covered in black fur with glowing orange eyes. The first major report came in July 1971 when
Joan Mills and Mary Ryan claimed to have been harassed by a
"half ape, half man" creature that made bizarre noises at them
as they passed it on Highway 79. Even though the creature
didn't make physical contact with them, both women believed

it would have harmed them had it been given the chance. That seemed to be confirmed the following year when, on July 11, 1972, brothers Terry and Wally Harrison spotted a giant, hairy beast carrying a dead dog. The boys screamed, alerting family members, who caught a glimpse of the creature before it disappeared into the woods. Sightings continued for a couple of weeks, but Momo hasn't been seen since.

Lawndale Thunderbird

If you're ever in Lawndale, Illinois, keep an eye out for giant birds lest they sneak up on you and whisk you away. That's what almost happened in 1977 when Lawndale residents noticed two large black birds with white-banded necks and 10- to 12-foot wingspans flying overhead. The birds, though enormous, seemed harmless enough. That is, until they swooped down and one of them reportedly tried to take off with ten-year-old Marlon Lowe while he played in his yard. The boy was not seriously injured, but the thunderbird did manage to lift the terrified boy several feet off the ground and carry him for nearly 40 feet before dropping him. Over the next few weeks, the birds were seen flying over various houses and fields in nearby towns, but, thankfully, they did not attack anyone else. And though they appear to have left Lawndale for good, reports of thunderbird sightings continue across the United States. The most recent one was on September 25, 2001, in South Greensburg, Pennsylvania.

Ohio Bridge Trolls

In May 1955, a man driving along the Miami River near Loveland, Ohio, came across a frightening sight. Huddled under a darkened bridge were several bald-headed creatures, each three to four feet tall. Spellbound, the man pulled over and watched the creatures, which he said had webbed hands and feet. Though they made no sound, the man said the creatures appeared to be communicating with each other and did not notice him watching them. However, when one of the creatures held up a wand or rod that began emitting showers of sparks, the man quickly left. He drove straight to the local police station, which dispatched a car to the bridge. A search of the area turned up nothing, and, to this day, there have been no more reported sightings of these strange creatures.

Maryland's Goatman

Think goats are cute and fuzzy little creatures? If so, a trip through Prince George's County in Maryland just might change your mind. Since the 1950s, people have reported horrifying encounters with a creature known only as the Goatman. From afar, many claim to have mistaken the Goatman for a human being. But as he draws nearer, his cloven feet become visible, as do the horns growing out of his head. If that's not enough to make you turn and run, reports as recent as 2006 state that the Goatman now carries an ax with him.

Gatormen

The swamplands of Florida are filled with alligators, but most of them don't have human faces. Since the 1700s, tales of strange half-man, half-alligator creatures have circulated throughout the area. Gatormen are described as having the face, neck, chest, and arms of a man and the midsection, back legs, and tail of an alligator. Unlike most other monsters and strange beasts, Gatormen reportedly prefer to travel and hunt in packs and even appear to have their own verbal language. What's more, recent sightings have them traveling outside the state of Florida and taking up residence in the swamplands of Louisiana and swimming around a remote Texas swamp in 2001.

Skunk Ape

Since the 1960s, a creature has been spotted in the Florida Everglades that many call Bigfoot's stinky cousin: the skunk ape. The beast is said to closely resemble Bigfoot with one minor difference—it smells like rotten eggs. In late 2000, Sarasota police received an anonymous letter from a woman who complained that an escaped animal was roaming near her home at night. Included with the letter were two close-up photographs of the creature—a large beast that resembled an orangutan standing behind some palmetto leaves, baring its teeth.

Lizard Man

At around 2:00 A.M. on June 29, 1988, Christopher Davis got a flat tire on a back road near the Scape Ore Swamp in South Carolina. Just as the teen finished changing the tire, he was suddenly attacked by a seven-foot-tall creature with scaly green skin and glowing red eyes. Davis was able to get back into his car and drive away but not before the Lizard Man managed to climb onto the roof and claw at it, trying to get inside. As he drove, Davis could see the creature had three claws on each of its "hands." Eventually, the creature fell from the car and Davis was able to escape. A search of the scene later that day turned up nothing. Despite numerous subsequent sightings, the creature has yet to be apprehended.

Devil Monkeys

Far and away, some of the strangest creatures said to be roaming the countryside are the Devil Monkeys. Take an adult kangaroo, stick a monkey or baboon head on top, and you've got yourself a Devil Monkey. By most accounts, these creatures can cover hundreds of feet in just a few quick hops. They're nothing to tangle with, either. Although Devil Monkeys have traditionally stuck to attacking livestock and the occasional family pet, some reports have them attempting to claw their way into people's homes. Originally spotted in Virginia in the 1950s, Devil Monkeys have now been spotted all across the United States. On a related note, in May 2001, residents of New Delhi, India, were sent into a panic when a four-foot-tall half-monkey, half-human creature began attacking them as they slept.

A Condemned Man Leaves His Mark

In 1877, Carbon County Prison inmate Alexander Campbell spent long, agonizing days awaiting sentencing. Campbell, a coal miner from northeastern Pennsylvania, had been charged with the murder of mine superintendent John P. Jones. Authorities believed that Campbell was part of the Molly Maguires labor group, a secret organization looking to even the score with mine owners. Although evidence shows that he was indeed part of the Mollies, and he admitted that he'd been present at the murder scene, Campbell professed his innocence and swore repeatedly that he was *not* the shooter.

The Sentence

Convicted largely on evidence collected by James McParlan, a Pinkerton detective hired by mine owners to infiltrate the underground labor union, Campbell was sentenced to hang. The decree would be carried out at specially prepared gallows at the Carbon County Prison. When the prisoner's day of reckoning arrived, he rubbed his hand on his sooty cell floor then slapped it on the wall proclaiming, "I am innocent, and let this be my testimony!" With that, Alexander Campbell was unceremoniously dragged from cell number 17 and committed, whether rightly or wrongly, to eternity.

The Hand of Fate

The Carbon County Prison of present-day is not too different from the torture chamber that it was back in Campbell's day. Although it is now a museum, the jail still imparts the horrors of man's inhumanity to man. Visitors move through its claustrophobically small cells and dank dungeon rooms with mouths agape. When they reach cell number 17, many visitors feel a cold chill rise up their spine, as they notice that Alexander Campbell's handprint is still there!

"There's no logical explanation for it," says James Starrs, a forensic scientist from George Washington University who investigated the mark. Starrs is not the first to scratch his head in disbelief. In 1930, a local sheriff aimed to rid the jail of its ominous mark. He had the wall torn down and replaced with a new one. But when he awoke the following morning and stepped into the cell, the handprint had reappeared on the newly constructed wall! Many years later Sheriff Charles Neast took his best shot at the wall, this time with green latex paint. The mark inexplicably returned. Was Campbell truly innocent as his ghostly handprint seems to suggest? No one can say with certainty. Is the handprint inside cell number 17 the sort of thing that legends are made of? You can bet your life on it.

STRANGE STATS

- *Thirty-seven percent of Americans believe the U.S. government is in contact with aliens.*

- *There are places in Panama where the sun rises over the Pacific and sets in the Atlantic.*

- *If left unchecked, 100 fleas can produce 500,000 offspring.*

- *Vampire bats can—and do—drink their sleeping victims' blood for 30 minutes without waking them.*

- *Since 1884, there have been 23 documented cases of humans born with true vestigial tails.*

- *The U.S. Mint has made enough pennies to circle Earth more than 137 times.*

- *The United States ranks seventh in the world in deaths by power lawn mower.*

- *Seven percent of American workers admit to wasting more than three hours each workday.*

Who Wants to Be a Troglodyte?

Lots of creatures sleep in cozy caves or burrows—rabbits, bats, and moles, for example. Here are a few cave-based hotels and inns that are sure to make the animals green with envy.

Beckham Creek Cave Haven, Parthenon, Arkansas

This combination cave and cabin was built on a 530-acre estate in the Ozark Mountains. It makes the most of its gorgeous surroundings with big windows on its outside-facing wall, a rock waterfall, and a stalactite-studded ceiling. Below ground, guests have plenty of elbow room, and can divide their time between the 2,000-square-foot great room, spacious kitchen, game room, and five bedrooms tucked into rocky crevices.

Les Hautes Roches, Rochecorbon, France

This hotel is comprised of an 18th-century castle and the caves that were created when stone was quarried for the Loire Valley château. Over the years, the cave was used as a refuge from war, to house monks from a nearby abbey, to grow mushrooms, and to store wine before becoming the first cave hotel in France. It now offers guests 15 rooms (12 of which are underground). A cave bar still contains the original fireplace and bread oven. Many guests use the hotel as a home base for exploring nearby mushroom caves.

Yunak Evleri, Urgup (Cappadocia), Turkey

The "fairy towers" and underground spaces carved out of Cappadocia's tuff (soft volcanic rock) were once used as hiding places from armies. Today, tourists use them to find seclusion. One of the many hotels built into the area's caves, the Yunak

Evleri contains 30 rooms. The hotel actually consists of six fifth- and sixth-century cave houses and a 19th-century Greek mansion. Each room features whitewashed rock walls, hardwood floors, and antique Turkish rugs.

Kokopelli's Cave Bed & Breakfast, Farmington, New Mexico

This 1,650-square-foot, one-bedroom "luxury cliff dwelling" was not built in a natural cave. In 1980, geologist Bruce Black excavated the cave out of 40-million-year-old sandstone and turned it into an office 70 feet below the earth. During the next 15 years, Black worked to make the cave habitable. Bruce and his wife live in the cave, and since 1997, they've been welcoming paid guests. The cave entrance is located in the cliff face and is accessible via a steep path, 150 hand-hewn sandstone steps, and a short ladder. Guests are encouraged to pack light.

PJ's Underground B&B, White Cliffs, Australia

White Cliffs was home to the first commercial opal mine in Australia. Because it is self-supporting and easy to carve, the local sandstone made it easy for miners to create dugouts. In fact, most residents of White Cliffs dug their own dwellings with only a jackhammer and a wheelbarrow. Low humidity and constantly cool temperatures (70°F year-round) make the dugouts comfortable living spaces. PJ's offers guests six underground rooms, an underground cottage, homegrown vegetables, homemade bread, and help arranging visits to the opal mines.

Las Casas–Cueva, Galera, Spain

In ancient times, when a woman from the Andalusia region of Spain discovered she was pregnant, her first chore was to dig the baby's bedroom out of the limestone walls of her cave. Today, a tourist complex known as Las Casas–Cueva de Galera, sits at the top of the hilly, prehistoric village of Galera. It is the biggest cave hotel in the region. Each cave includes a fireplace, kitchen, and Jacuzzi.

Fooled Ya!: Famous Hoaxes

Whether for fun, notoriety, or profit, hoaxers have moved amongst us since the beginning of humankind. Here are some of the boldest hoaxes of recent times.

Milli Vanilli

Milli Vanilli, Germany's pop singing duo, who won a coveted Grammy Award for the Best New Artist of 1989, ultimately proved too good to be true. The handsome, dreadlocked duo of "Fab" Morvan and Rob Pilatus sold more than 30 million singles and 14 million albums before their secret came out.

In July 1990, while performing their hit song "Girl You Know It's True," at a theme park in Connecticut, an obvious problem erupted when the first four words of the song repeated over and over again. Their obvious lip-syncing wasn't a deal-breaker in itself, but it did cause critics to take notice.

By November, under intense scrutiny, it was learned that Morvan and Pilatus hadn't sung *any* of the tracks for which they'd become famous. In reality, the songs were recorded by session musicians, and Morvan and Pilatus were simply chosen for their looks. To fans, it was an unforgivable transgression.

As a result, the artists were stripped of their Grammy and were treated as pariahs by their once adoring fans. In a sad footnote, Pilatus died in April 1998 at age 32 when he overdosed on prescription drugs.

Sibuxiang Hoax

In an unintentional hoax that mimicked America's famed "War of the Worlds" radio broadcast, an entire city in northern China was emotionally traumatized on September 19, 1994, when television warnings were repeatedly broadcast to viewers in Taiyuan. In a scrolled message, viewers were warned about the gruesome Sibuxiang Beast, a creature with a deadly bite. "It is said that the Sibuxiang is penetrating our area from Yanmenguan Pass and within days will enter thousands of homes," read the ominous type. "Everyone close your windows and doors and be on alert!"

With this "official" announcement acting as impetus, the good people of Taiyuan launched into a panic as some barricaded themselves inside their homes. Local officials were soon swamped with telephone calls.

It seems it had all been one giant misunderstanding. The Sibuxiang Beast was real enough, but it wasn't an animal. In fact, it was nothing more than a new brand of liquor. The townspeople had, in fact, been watching a commercial.

The ad's creator was fined $600 for causing a public panic, but the incident had turned Sibuxiang liquor into a household name virtually overnight. Three months after the incident, the owner reported that his client base had quadrupled.

Cardiff Giant

On October 16, 1869, a ten-foot-tall "petrified" man was discovered by workers digging a well in Cardiff, New York. Shortly thereafter, property owner William C. Newell began charging 50 cents to see the amazing man up close, and thousands anteed-up for the privilege. Speculation ran wild. Who could the giant be? How old was he? Was he even human?

The "Cardiff Giant" was purchased by businessmen for $37,500 (a vast sum at the time) and shipped to Syracuse for display. There, the petrified man was more closely examined and the truth emerged. It had all been a divine hoax that Newell and his friend George Hull had concocted. For an investment of $2,600, the devilish pair had created the statue out of gypsum and buried it on Newell's farm.

Oddly, the giant proved even more popular after the truth came out, and people came from far and wide to see it. P. T. Barnum offered the new owners $60,000 for the giant. They declined, so Barnum constructed an exact plaster replica of the Cardiff Giant and placed it on display in his New York City museum. It drew even bigger crowds than the original, which is now on display at the Farmer's Museum in Cooperstown, New York. Barnum's replica can be seen at Marvin's Marvelous Mechanical Museum in Farmington Hills, Michigan.

Hitler's Diaries

In 1983, when German magazine *Stern* claimed to have discovered Adolf Hitler's diaries, more than a few took notice.

They shouldn't have. After paying nine million German marks (at the time about $5 million U.S.) to Gerd Heidemann, a German journalist who claimed to have discovered the diaries in an East German barn, the magazine realized that they'd been conned. But they were not alone.

Before the scam came to light, noted World War II historians Eberhard Jäckel, Gerhard Weinberg, and Hugh Trevor-Roper deemed the diaries authentic. Two weeks later, the diaries were revealed as fakes that had been produced on modern paper using modern ink. Notorious forger Konrad Kujau was found to be the grand architect of the scheme, and both he and Heidemann were sentenced to 42 months in prison.

I Buried Paul

In 1969, news broke that Beatles member Paul McCartney had died in a car crash three years before. The fantastic story claimed that McCartney's bandmates, stricken with fear that their popularity might wane, had installed a body double named William Campbell in Paul's place.

To stir up interest, the mop-tops allegedly left clues, such as a line at the end of "Strawberry Fields Forever," which uttered the words, "I buried Paul."

The story had publicity stunt written all over it, but many still believed Paul was dead. A report by NBC anchorman John Chancellor summed things up: "All we can report with certainty is that Paul McCartney is either dead or alive."

Then, *Life* magazine discovered a very much alive Paul McCartney and snapped some photos. Confronted with the damning evidence, the clearly annoyed Beatle grudgingly granted *Life* an interview and the hoax was laid to rest.

The origin of the hoax remains unknown. Many believe the Beatles were directly involved since the boys had a penchant for mischief and a good joke. And to this day, there are some who *still* believe that William Campbell is standing in for Paul.

The Kuano River Boy

Around the world, feral (or wild) children have reportedly been raised by wolves, monkeys, and even ostriches, but a boy seen splashing about the banks of a river in northern India in the 1970s was rumored to have been raised by fish or lizards.

From the Black Lagoon

The boy, about 15 years old when first discovered in 1973 by residents of the small town of Baragdava, had blackish-green skin and no hair. His head appeared malformed in a strange bullet shape, and he was entirely naked. "Lizard people" complete with green scales have been reported from time to time around the world, but this boy lacked scales, gills, or even webbed toes.

He lived amid the crocodiles in the Kuano River without fear of attack and was able to hold his breath and stay underwater longer than thought humanly possible. But strangest of all, hundreds of people, including police and reporters, saw him run across the surface of the water. This may have been explained by the slightly submerged dam surface. A person dashing across it might have appeared to be running on water to observers at a distance. Either way, there was no question that the boy was strangely at home in the river habitat.

Son of a Water Spirit

Although his initial appearance was a shock, a village woman named Somni, who found the boy lying in a field one day, noticed a birthmark on his back that was identical to that of the infant son she had lost in the swirling river several years earlier. Somni even had an explanation for why her son, whom she'd named Ramchandra, ended up as a "merman." Somni claimed that she had been raped and impregnated by a giant water spirit during a rainstorm. Villagers accepted Somni's story; however, her husband displayed the same bullet-shape skull as the River Boy.

The Amphibious Life

Although Ramchandra, if that was indeed his true identity, preferred to remain in the river most of the time, he did seem curious about the human villagers living nearby and would sometimes approach them. Several times he was captured and brought to the village by force. He enjoyed eating vegetables left for him along the riverbank, although his main sustenance came from raw fish and frogs that he gulped from the river without using his hands.

Not Easy Being Green

For nine years, the River Boy interacted with the villagers of Baragdava, but eventually he came to a terrible end. In 1982, after two policemen tried to catch him, he made an escape from what had been his home village and swam to another river town about 12 miles away. There he approached a woman tending a small tea shop. The woman was so frightened by his naked, greenish appearance that she doused him with a pan of boiling water. Ramchandra ran back to the river where he died from severe burns. His body was eventually retrieved floating on the water. The Kuano River Boy's age at the time of his tragic death was estimated at 24.

The River Boy's green-tinted skin was never definitively explained, although it was presumed to have been from long-time contact with the river water and perhaps algae. But strangely, there are records of other green children of unknown origin. In 1887, some field workers observed a boy and a girl as they timidly emerged from a cave in Banjos, Spain. The skin of both children was bright green, and they wore clothing made from an unrecognizable fabric. They spoke a language no one understood, but when the girl learned some Spanish, she told the villagers that a whirlwind had brought them to the cave from another land where the sun was never seen. Both children perished young—the boy after some days and the girl after about five years—but their skin turned a paler and paler green the longer they were out of the cave.

Scream Machines and Vomit Comets

💀   💀   💀   💀   💀

Today's crop of thrill rides stagger the imagination. From a heart-stopper that shoots riders higher than the Eiffel Tower, to a mind-boggler that reaches 100 miles per hour faster than any production car, the following scream machines electrify the senses as they agitate the innards.

Big Shot

Ranked as the highest thrill ride in the world, Big Shot, located at the Stratosphere Hotel and Casino in Las Vegas, has been scaring the tar out of adrenaline junkies since its debut in 1996. This compressed-air vertical "blast" ride launches riders 160 feet into the air. Seems rather tame until you consider that Big Shot's launch pad is 921 feet off the ground on the side of the Stratosphere Tower. Less than three seconds after blast-off, newly acrophobic riders find themselves an astounding 1,081 feet from terra firma.

Timber Tower

As its name suggests, Timber Tower, located at Dollywood in Pigeon Forge, Tennessee, gives riders the sensation that the 65-foot-tall cylindrical tower they are sitting atop has broken free from its base and tumbled over like a freshly chopped tree falling toward the ground. Add to the mix the fact that riders are spinning horizontally around that tower as it falls and then rights itself only to fall in the opposite direction over and over again, and what you get is a circumstance where riders see death rushing toward them and then they don't; then they do; then they don't, as if trapped in a continuous loop.

Kingda Ka

Officially the tallest and fastest roller coaster in the world, Kingda Ka, located at Six Flags Great Adventure in Jackson, New Jersey, has effectively thrown down the gauntlet to its challengers. With an overall height of 456 feet and an actual drop of 418 feet, this monster is only beginning to puff its chest. But Kingda Ka's greatest strength lies in its blistering speed. Shot from ground-level into a 90-degree vertical spiral, riders accelerate from 0 to 128 miles per hour in just 3.5 seconds! In comparison, an aircraft carrier catapult launch excels planes from 0 to 150 miles per hour in roughly 2 seconds.

Mega Drop

Found at amusement parks and traveling carnivals, the Mega Drop's 115-foot-tall objective is simple: Twelve passengers sit around a ring that's slowly raised to the top of the tower. Then, without warning the vehicle is released and free-falls downward at 69 feet per second (approximately 47 miles per hour). A magnetic braking system decelerates the plummeting cab until it is stopped by four beefy shock absorbers.

Superman Ultimate Flight

If you've ever wanted to fly like a superhero, then head over to a Six Flags theme park in Georgia, Illinois, or New Jersey, where this ride's specially designed cars tilt passengers facedown into a flying position, so that they're suspended horizontally from the track above. Riders get a bird's-eye view at the top of a 109-foot hill before sailing through the air at 60 miles per hour in a series of loops, spirals, turns, and rolls. This truly is a unique thrill ride.

Son of Beast

As wooden roller coasters go, this monster at Kings Island in Cincinnati, Ohio, is without peer. Built in 2000, it is currently the world's fastest wooden roller coaster at 78 miles per hour, the world's tallest at 218 feet, and features not only the world's loftiest first drop for a "woody" at 214 feet but the world's greatest second drop (164 feet) as well. Beyond these records there is one honor that no longer applies. When Son of Beast opened, it was the only "looping" wooden roller coaster in the world, but the loop was removed before the 2007 season. These days, the mighty "Son" carries on the grand tradition set forth by the original Beast, also at Kings Island.

The Screamer

The Screamer, a 168-foot-tall, 3.5 g-force-inducing swinging pendulum ride at Sacramento's Scandia Family Fun Center, lives up to its name with startling regularity, as do most thrill rides that rocket their riders toward the ground at 65 miles per hour. But the ride's name has proven prophetic in more ways than one. Fed up with listening to the banshee shrieks, area residents complained shortly after the ride opened in 2007. Since then, a rigidly enforced "no scream" policy has been in effect. If anyone is caught screaming on the ride, it is stopped and the offending party is sent to the back of the line. Ironically, the park's motto is, "It's a Scream!"

Man Assaults Police, Steals Squad Car

For Walter J. Brois, it all went downhill in a hurry. In January 2008, two sheriff's deputies in Florida stopped Brois for doing wheelies on his motorcycle. He fled, crashed his bike, then pepper-sprayed the officers. Once apprehended and subdued in the police car, Brois complained of chest pains. The officers let him out, whereupon he stole the squad car, dragged the two officers for approximately 75 feet, then drove the car through three fences before fleeing on foot. Soon after, a local resident reported his truck stolen, and Brois was apprehended three days later.

The Bloodthirsty Countess

Born to George and Anna Bathory in August 1560, Countess Erzsebet (Elizabeth) Bathory came from one of the wealthiest families in Hungary. Of course, all families have their secrets and Elizabeth's had more than their fair share. One uncle was allegedly a devil worshipper and an aunt was believed to be a witch. So when Elizabeth herself started acting a bit odd and suffering from violent, uncontrolled fits of rage, no one really thought much about it.

A Taste for Blood

At age 15, with no sign of her fits subsiding, Elizabeth married Ferencz Nádasdy and moved into his castle. By most accounts, the castle's dungeon gave Bathory her first opportunities to experiment with torture. With her husband gone for long periods of time, she apparently began experimenting with black magic, often inviting people to the castle to take part in strange, sadistic rituals. Legend has it that, during this time, in a fit of rage, Bathory slapped a young servant girl across the face, drawing blood. Allegedly, Bathory looked down at her hand, which was covered in the young girl's blood, and thought the blood was causing her own skin to glow. This, according to the legend, is why Bathory believed that the blood of virginal girls would keep her young forever.

In 1604, Nádasdy died, leaving Bathory alone in the castle. For a while, she traveled abroad and, by all accounts, continued her quest to fulfill her insatiable thirst for blood. But she eventually returned and purchased her own castle. Shortly thereafter, servant girls and young girls from the neighboring villages began disappearing in the middle of the night, never to be heard from again.

Ungodly Horrors

During this time period, villagers knew better than to speak out against nobility. So when people started implying that the countess was kidnapping young girls and murdering them in her castle, the villagers kept their mouths shut. Even when Bathory's carriage would ride through town late at night with young girls in the back, villagers still kept their heads down and went about their business. Villagers were often awakened in the middle of the night by the sound of piercing screams coming from Bathory's castle. However, it wasn't until young aristocratic girls began disappearing that the decision was made to investigate. By that time, though, hundreds of young girls had already gone missing.

In December 1610, King Matthias II of Hungary sent a group of men out to Bathory's castle to investigate claims that local girls were being held there against their will. Heading up the group was a man named Gyorgy Thurzo. It would be his subsequent testimony of what the group encountered that would bring the full weight of the court down on Bathory.

Thurzo later stated that when the group arrived at the castle, the things they found inside were so horrific and gruesome that he could not bring himself to write them down.

Thurzo said that inside the door they found a young girl, dead and apparently drained of blood. A short distance away, they found another girl, alive but near death. She also appeared to have lost a large amount of blood. Advancing down into the dungeon, the group encountered several young girls who were being held captive. The group released them and then began the search for Bathory herself. In the end, Bathory and four of her servants were taken into custody. The servants were taken into the village for questioning while Bathory herself was confined to her bedroom in the castle.

Unspeakable Acts

Twenty-one judges presided over the proceedings that began on January 2, 1611. Bathory remained in her castle while her four accomplices were questioned. The things these four individuals claimed took place in the castle were almost too horrific to describe. One of Bathory's employees, a dwarf named Ficzko, said that he personally knew of at least 37 girls the countess had killed. Bathory's childhood nurse, Ilona Joo, stated that she had personally helped Bathory kill somewhere in the neighborhood of 50 girls, using such horrific devices as cages filled with spikes, fire pokers, and oily sheets that were placed between victims' legs and set on fire.

As the proceedings went on, the descriptions got worse and worse: stabbings with needles and scissors, tearing off limbs, and even sewing girls' mouths shut. It was also made known that the countess enjoyed whipping and beating young girls until their bodies were swollen, at which point she would use a razor to draw blood from the swollen areas. There were even rumors that she bathed in the blood of the girls in an attempt to stay young.

In the end, the countess was found guilty of killing 80 girls. However, based on the number of bodies eventually recovered at the castle, the body count is probably as high as 650.

All four of Bathory's accomplices were put to death. But because the countess was a member of the nobility, she could not be executed for her crimes. Instead, she was moved to a series of small rooms in her castle and walled inside. All the doors and windows were sealed, with only a few small holes for air and one to allow food to pass though. The countess lived in her own private prison for three years before she died, still claiming she was innocent of all charges.

As of 2004, the town of Colma, California, boasted approximately 1,280 living residents—and 17 cemeteries, which occupy 73 percent of the town's area.

Creepy, Catchy Murder Ballads

"Mack the Knife"
Perhaps the most well-known murder ballad, "Mack the Knife" tells the tale of dashing, but murderous, highwayman Macheath as portrayed in the musical drama *The Threepenny Opera*. It was popularized by Bobby Darin in the late 1950s.

"Lizie Wan"
Taking an incestuous turn, this ballad tells the tale of poor Lizie, who is pregnant with her brother's child. He kills her, then tries to pretend the blood is from an animal, but finally confesses before setting sail on a ship, never to return.

"Nebraska"
Before he cemented his place in musical history with "Born in the U.S.A.," Bruce Springsteen put a modern spin on the murder ballad with his 1982 song "Nebraska," based on the late 1950s killing spree of Charles Starkweather.

"Frankie & Johnny"
This song is based on an 1899 murder case in which a prostitute named Frankie kills her teenage lover after finding out that he's cheating on her. Frankie was acquitted but died in a mental institution in the 1950s. The writer and origin of the song are debatable, but the tale led to a number of films, including a 1966 musical starring Elvis Presley.

"Banks of the Ohio"
Around since the 19th century, "Banks of the Ohio" tells the story of Willie, who proposes to his young love during a walk by the river. She turns him down, so he murders her. The song has been recorded by a variety of musicians, from Johnny Cash to Olivia Newton-John.

"Hey Joe"
Penned by Billy Roberts in the early 1960s, this song of love gone murderous was immensely popular among rock bands of the decade. One of the most popular versions was recorded by Jimi Hendrix and was played by the influential guitarist at the Woodstock Music Festival in 1969.

"Tom Dooley"
Based on the 1866 murder of Laura Foster, this tune tells the story of her boyfriend, Tom Dula, a former Confederate soldier from North Carolina. Dula was convicted and hanged for the girl's brutal stabbing death, but there is speculation that he had another lover named Ann Melton, who may have killed Foster in a fit of jealous rage. The story inspired a number one hit for the Kingston Trio in 1958 and a movie starring a young Michael Landon the following year.

"Lily, Rosemary and the Jack of Hearts"
Bob Dylan has performed numerous murder ballads in his career and has incorporated their musical style into his own songwriting. In 1975, he released his own take on the genre with this complex narrative song about a bank robber and the people of the town he has stumbled upon.

"Stagger Lee"
This song is based on the slaying of William Lyons by Lee Shelton, a black cab driver and pimp, on Christmas night 1895. The two men were friends, but after a night of drinking and gambling, things turned deadly. The tune became a staple of blues musicians, but the 1928 record by Mississippi John Hurt is considered the definitive version.

"Jellon Grame"
Drawing the story out over years, the song tells the tale of a man who kills his pregnant lover and removes the still living baby. He raises the child as his own, and, one day, when his son wants to know the truth about his mother, the man explains what happened and shows him the scene of the crime.

The boy kills his father on the spot. The tale is intertwined with the history of the British Isles and has been retold for generations.

"Omie Wise"
This murder ballad is based on an 1807 murder case in which Naomi Wise, an orphaned servant and field hand, became pregnant by her boyfriend, Jonathan Lewis. He drowned her but was found not guilty of the crime. In 1820, Lewis confessed to the murder on his deathbed.

"The Twa Sisters"
Stepping away from the love triangle or murderous lover scenario, this song explores "sororicide"—sister killing sister. Dating back to at least 1656, "The Twa Sisters" is thought to be the inspiration for a number of other ballads. In a strange twist, the body of the dead sister is made into a musical instrument that sings of its own murder—in some versions at the wedding of the guilty sister.

"El Paso"
Written and performed by Marty Robbins, "El Paso" tells the fictional saga of love turned deadly in Mexico and was Robbins's best-known song. The ballad relates the story of a cowboy who falls in love with a cantina dancer and kills another man defending her honor. Originally, it was thought the song would be a flop because of its nearly five-minute running time, unheard of during the late 1950s. Incidentally, the song was covered by the Grateful Dead and became one of their most popular tunes, performed live more than 380 times.

"Jack the Stripper"
A foray into the modern murder ballad, "Jack the Stripper" was a serial killer who murdered prostitutes in London in the 1960s and dumped their naked bodies around the city. Modern heavy metal and hard rock bands have performed this song about his dirty deeds.

Groomzilla: The Very Married Signor Vigliotto

💀 💀 💀 💀 💀

"Love 'em and leave 'em" could not have been a more appropriate motto for serial bigamist Giovanni Vigliotto, who wed 105 ladies without bothering to divorce any of them.

Vigliotto said "I do" in ten different countries as he traveled the world hawking tchotchkes and furniture at flea markets. Although he was short, paunchy, and something less than Romeo-esque, the raven-haired Vigliotto had no trouble attracting ladies. Starting in 1949 at age 19, Vigliotto perfected a method that brought in a bride every time.

Something Borrowed, Something Boo-hoo'd

Vigliotto began each con by choosing an alias that seemed appropriate to whichever country or neighborhood he found himself in. (He later claimed he used too many aliases to remember them all.) After he carefully selected a woman of financial means, who also appeared lonely and vulnerable, he preyed on her sympathy by confessing that he was lonely, too. A proposal soon followed, but before the ink was dry on the marriage license, he'd find some reason to convince his new bride to sell her home and move. That left him in a position to zoom off in a moving truck laden with all his bride's possessions while she trailed behind in her car. He would then sell her purloined belongings at the next flea market.

Walter Mitty of Love

It was a profitable setup, but his luck ran out in November 1981. Earlier that year, he'd abandoned wife Sharon Clark of Indiana, leaving her in Ontario, barefoot, alone, and $49,000 lighter. With all the stubborn rage of a woman not only scorned but robbed, Clark reasoned that if she went to enough flea markets, she would eventually find her runaway groom. Sure enough, she tracked him down in Florida and caught him peddling her possessions. By that time, he was wanted in Arizona for taking Patricia Ann Gardiner, wife number 105, for $36,500 worth of goods plus another $11,474 in profits from the sale of her house. He was hauled back to Phoenix, where he stood trial in early 1983. The 53-year-old Casanova spent his time before the trial researching the history of bigamy.

Vigliotto played the wounded victim in court, asking plaintively why it was so wrong of him to open doors for women and bring them flowers, insisting that most of his wives actually proposed to him. He also painted himself as a sort of Walter Mitty of love, innocently acting out fantasies of marriage. He never did admit that it was wrong to rob the ladies after he married them.

I Do...Find You Guilty!

In less than a half hour, a jury found Vigliotto guilty on 34 counts of bigamy and fraud; the judge subsequently fined him $336,000 and slapped him with 34 years in prison, the maximum.

Vigliotto served eight years in a state prison in Arizona before dying of a brain hemorrhage in early 1991. Local papers reported various grandiose schemes hatched by Vigliotto during that time, such as a made-for-TV movie based on his life and a million-dollar deal to become the poster boy for a male virility drug, but his plans invariably fizzled, ensuring that Vigliotto's legacy will remain that of a record-setting bigamist.

Come with the Lights and Sirens—I Dare You

In early 2008, a 50-year-old Florida woman was charged with three counts of aggravated assault after chasing paramedics down the street with a rolling pin.

A woman called 911 to report chest pains but told the fire department to show up quietly. Instead, they came with lights and sirens, which prompted the woman to grab her rolling pin and go on the attack. No one was injured.

Bachelor's Grove: America's Most Haunted Cemetery?

💀　💀　💀　💀　💀

Hidden away inside the Rubio Woods Forest Preserve near Midlothian, Illinois, lies Bachelor's Grove Cemetery, widely reported to be one of the most haunted cemeteries in the United States. Haunted or not, the cemetery certainly has an intriguing history that raises many questions but provides few answers.

Like almost everything associated with the cemetery, the very origins of Bachelor's Grove are surrounded in mystery. Some claim that the cemetery got its name in the early 1800s when several unmarried men built homes nearby, causing locals to nickname the area Bachelor's Grove. Others, however, believe the name was actually Batchelder's Grove, named after a family that lived in the area.

Abandoned and Vandalized

Despite its small size (about an acre), the cemetery became a popular site over the years because of its convenient location right off the Midlothian Turnpike. The quaint pond at the rear of the cemetery added to the allure, and as a result, about 200 individuals made Bachelor's Grove their final resting place.

All that changed during the 1960s when the branch of the Midlothian Turnpike that ran past the cemetery was closed, cutting it off from traffic. With the road essentially abandoned, people stopped coming to the cemetery altogether. The last burial at Bachelor's Grove took place in 1965, although there was an interment of ashes in 1989.

Without a proper road to get to the cemetery, Bachelor's Grove fell into a state of disrepair. Along with the cover of the Rubio Woods, this made the cemetery an attractive location for late-night parties, vandalism, and senseless desecration. Today, of the nearly 200 graves, only 20 or so still have tombstones. The rest have been broken or gone missing. This, combined with rumors that some graves were dug up, is why many believe that the spirits of Bachelor's Grove do not rest in peace.

Glow in the Dark

Who haunts Bachelor's Grove? For starters, the ghost of a woman dressed in white has been spotted late at night walking among the tombstones or sitting on top of them. So many people have seen her throughout the years that she is commonly known as the Madonna of Bachelor's Grove.

There are also reports of strange, flashing lights moving around the cemetery, especially near the algae-covered pond in the back. Some believe that the pond was used as an impromptu "burial ground" for Chicago-area gangsters and that the lights are the spirits of their victims. Others believe the ghost lights are related to the legend that, many years ago, a man plowing the nearby fields died when his horse became spooked and ran into the pond, drowning both man and horse.

Probably the most fascinating paranormal activity reported at Bachelor's Grove is that of the ghost house. On certain nights, a spectral house is said to appear in the distance along the abandoned road leading to the cemetery. Those who have witnessed this strange apparition say that the house slowly fades away until it disappears without a trace. Similarly, others have spotted a ghostly car barreling down the road, complete with glowing headlights.

Should you wish to visit Bachelor's Grove in the hopes of encountering some of these spirits, it is open every day but only during daylight hours. The abandoned road now serves as a well-worn path through the woods up to the cemetery. Just remember that you are visiting hallowed ground and the final resting places of men, women, and children. Be sure to treat it as such.

Jeffrey Dahmer:
The "Milwaukee Monster"

*The Oxford Apartments in Milwaukee don't exist anymore.
The seedy complex at 924 North 25th Street was torn down
in 1992 to prevent the site from becoming a ghoulish tourist
attraction. But the empty lot still attracts visitors hoping to see
a remnant of Apartment 213 and the "Milwaukee Monster."
The small one-bedroom apartment was reputed to be tidy,
clean, and home to charming serial killer Jeffrey Dahmer, his
pet fish, and his collection of dismembered corpses.*

Once Upon a Time

Dahmer was born in Milwaukee on May 21, 1960, and his
family later moved to Ohio. He attended Ohio State University
for one semester then enlisted in the army in 1979. After being
discharged for chronic drunkenness, he eventually moved back
to Wisconsin, where he lived with his grandmother.

According to his parents, Dahmer started off as a sweet boy
but became increasingly withdrawn during adolescence. They
even noticed his preoccupation with death, but they dismissed
it. Friends knew he liked to dissect roadkill. Once he even
impaled a dog's head on a stick. Another time, when his father
noticed foul smells coming from the garage, Jeffrey told his
dad he was using acid to strip the flesh from animal carcasses.
Later, his stepmother realized that he might have been cleaning human bones.

There's a First Time for Everything

Dahmer committed his first murder in June 1978, at age 18.
While still living with his parents in Ohio, he picked up a
young male hitchhiker. The two had sex, then Dahmer beat
the man to death, dismembered his body, and buried him
in the woods. Later, Dahmer exhumed the body, crushed
the bones with a mallet, and scattered them throughout the

woods. His next three victims were all men Dahmer met at gay bars and brought back to a hotel or his grandmother's house, where he seduced, drugged, and strangled them before sexually assaulting their corpses and cutting them up.

Bad Moves
In September 1988, Dahmer's grandmother kicked him out of her house because he and his friends were too loud and drank too much. The day after he moved into his own apartment, Dahmer was arrested for fondling, drugging, and propositioning a 13-year-old Laotian boy. He was sentenced to a year in prison but was released after ten months. No one knew at that point that he had already murdered four men.

After being released on probation for his assault on the underage boy, Dahmer moved back in with his grandmother. But as a stipulation of his early release, he was required to find his own apartment, so in May 1990, Dahmer moved to his now infamous residence at the Oxford Apartments.

Modus Operandi
Living on his own, Dahmer stepped up his killing spree. Between May and July of 1991, he killed an average of one person each week, until he had committed a total of 17 known murders. With few exceptions, the victims were poor, gay, non-white men. He would meet them in gay bars or bathhouses, drug them, strangle them, have sex with them, and then dismember them with an electric saw. He saved some parts to eat, and some skulls he cleaned and kept as trophies. He even experimented with creating "zombies" by drilling holes into his victims' heads and injecting acid into their brains while they were still alive. For the most part, he was unsuccessful, as only one man survived for more than a few hours.

On May 27, 1991, a 14-year-old Laotian boy escaped Dahmer's apartment and ran into the streets, half-naked, drugged, and groggy. Neighbors called the police, who escorted the boy back to Dahmer's apartment. Sweet-spoken Dahmer convinced the police that it was merely a lover's spat and that the boy was an adult. The police left without even doing a background check on Dahmer. If they had, they would have discovered that he was a convicted child molester who was still on probation. After the police left, the boy, who was the brother of the boy Dahmer had been imprisoned for molesting, became the madman's latest victim. The following week, when neighbors saw reports of a missing boy who looked suspiciously like Dahmer's "boyfriend," they contacted the police and FBI but were told that he was an adult and with his lover.

The One that Got Away

Tracy Edwards was the lucky one. On July 22, when police saw him running down the street with a handcuff dangling from his wrist, they stopped him for questioning. Edwards said a man was trying to kill him. The police followed him back to Dahmer's apartment, where they found a human head in the refrigerator, an array of skulls in the closet, a barrel of miscellaneous body parts, a pot full of hands and penises, a box of stray bones, a freezer full of entrails, and snapshots of mutilated bodies in various stages of decay arranged in sexual poses. The police arrested Dahmer on the spot, bringing his 13-year killing spree to an end.

Crazy Like a Fox

At his trial, Dahmer's lawyer tried to convince the jury that his client was insane, emphasizing the heinousness of the crimes. Nevertheless, Dahmer was found sane and guilty of all 15 charges against him and was sentenced to 936 years in prison—15 consecutive life sentences.

And So We Come to the End

Dahmer was fairly infamous when he entered the Columbia Correctional Institute in Portage, Wisconsin. He was kept out of the main prison population to protect him from other inmates. Even so, on November 28, 1994, he was assigned to a work detail with two convicted killers: Jesse Anderson and Christopher Scarver. When the guards checked in on them after a while, Anderson and Dahmer were dead; Dahmer's skull had been crushed.

Famous Feral Children

If your mother annoys you or your dad says something embarrassing in public, cut them some slack. If they didn't abandon you to wolves, keep you locked in a room, or make you live in a chicken coop, they couldn't have been that bad. You could have had it a lot worse. Check out the following stories of feral, or "wild," children, kids who were raised either with very little human contact or none at all.

Amala & Kamala
Reverend Joseph Singh, in charge of an orphanage in the northern part of India in 1920, kept hearing villagers speak of ghostly girls who ran with wolves at night. Singh camped out one evening to watch for these alleged figures and discovered the myth was reality. Two seemingly unrelated girls were found in a wolf den. Their hair was matted, their eyes were bugged out, and they walked on all fours. Singh tried to rehabilitate the girls, but being raised by wolves for the first years of their lives had an indelible effect. The girls tore off their clothes and only ate raw meat. Neither Amala nor Kamala lived very long—Amala was three when she died, Kamala somewhere between 14 and 17. Both learned a few words of English, and Kamala was able to walk on her own, though with an odd stride.

Oxana Malaya, the "Ukrainian Dog Girl"
Between the ages of three and eight, Ukrainian-born Oxana Malaya was either forced by her parents to live in a dog kennel in the backyard or neglected to the point that the doghouse became a better place for her to live. It's been reported that her alcoholic parents did allow her to come into the house occasionally, but Oxana spent most of her time with the dogs,

learning to sniff her food before she ate it, growl, and bark. When she was rescued in 1991, Oxana was put into a home for the mentally disabled and has since regained many human abilities, including speech. Now in her twenties, Oxana still resides in a home for the mentally challenged.

Victor, the Wild Child of Aveyron

Victor's story is important because he was one of the first well-known cases of feral children. In 1799, an 11-year-old boy was discovered digging for acorns in Aveyron, France. Victor couldn't speak and behaved like a wild animal. A doctor took him in and made rehabilitating Victor his life's work, though teaching the boy anything was reportedly rather difficult. Unlike many other feral kids before and after him, Victor lived a relatively long life, dying at age 40.

Sidi Mohamed

In 1935, when he was about five years old, Sidi Mohamed wandered off from his family in North Africa. After three days in the wild, he came upon an ostrich nest. Flash forward about ten years when Sidi was able to tell his story. He had been living with the birds all that time, running with them, eating grass and plants, and sleeping with them at night (two ostriches covered him with their wings while he slept.) Sidi was able to rejoin the human race with relative success.

Ivan Mishukov, "The Russian Dog Boy"

In the late 1990s, there were approximately two million kids living on the streets in Russia due to the country's collapsed economy. Four-year-old Ivan Mishukov befriended a pack of alley dogs, and in return for the scraps he could beg off passersby, the dogs provided him with protection and shelter from the frigid temperatures that could reach –25°Fahrenheit at night. Ivan reportedly lived with the dogs for two years before the police were able to separate him from his new family. He could speak, since he'd been raised by his parents for the first few years of his life before being abandoned, and he eventually went to school and adapted to a typical Russian life.

Spending Eternity on "The Rock"

Alcatraz, nicknamed "The Rock," was the ultimate American prison—a place that hardened criminals and assorted public enemies such as Al Capone called home. Surrounded by the heavy mist and rolling fog of San Francisco Bay, the damp prison on Alcatraz Island kept more than a thousand dangerous men cloistered from the rest of the world. The cold winds and chilly waters of the bay made Alcatraz one of the loneliest prisons in the world.

From 1934 to 1963, during its reign as a federal prison, Alcatraz was not a facility for rehabilitating hardened criminals; it was a place of harsh punishment and limited privilege. Those who endured their stay were fortunate to leave with their sanity or—as many believe—their souls.

The Island of Pelicans

When the Spanish first explored the area in 1775, they dubbed the island *La Isla de los Alcatraces,* or "the Island of the Pelicans." What they found was a rocky piece of land that was completely uninhabited, sparsely vegetated, and surrounded by churning water and swift currents.

The U.S. military took over Alcatraz Island in 1850. For several decades, it was the army's first long-term prison, and it quickly gained a reputation for being a tough facility. The military used the island until 1934, when high operating costs coupled with the financial constraints of the Great Depression forced their exit.

America's Devil's Island

The rise of criminal activity in the 1920s and early 1930s put a new focus on Alcatraz. Federal authorities decided to construct an imposing, escape-proof prison that would strike fear into even the hardest criminals, and Alcatraz was the chosen site. In 1934, the Federal Bureau of Prisons took control of the facility and implemented a strict set of rules and regulations.

The top guards and officers of the federal penal system were transferred to the island, and soon Alcatraz was transformed into an impregnable fortress.

Across the country, prison wardens were asked to send their worst inmates to Alcatraz. This included inmates with behavioral issues, those who had previously attempted to escape, and the most notorious criminals of the day, including Al Capone, George "Machine Gun" Kelly, Doc Barker (of the Ma Barker Gang), and Alvin "Creepy" Karpis.

Life on "The Rock" was anything but luxurious. Each cell measured five feet by nine feet and featured a fold-up bunk, desk, chair, toilet, and sink. Each day was exactly the same, from chow times to work assignments. The routine never varied and was completely methodical. Compliance was expected, and the tough guards sometimes meted out severe punishment if rules were not followed.

If prisoners broke the rules, they could be sent to a punishment cell known as "the hole." There were several of these cells, which were dreaded by the convicts. Here, men were stripped of all but their basic right to food. During the

daytime, mattresses were taken away and steel doors blocked out any natural light. Prisoners might spend as long as 19 days in "the hole" in complete isolation from other inmates. Time spent there usually meant psychological and physical abuse from the guards as well. Screams from hardened criminals could be heard echoing throughout the entire building in a stark warning to the other prisoners.

After time spent in "the hole," men often came out with pneumonia or arthritis after spending days or weeks on the cold cement floor with no clothing. Others came out devoid of their sanity. Some men never came out of "the hole" alive.

Alcatraz and "Scarface" Al Capone

Al Capone arrived at Alcatraz in August 1934. He was fairly well behaved, but life on "The Rock" was not easy for the ex-crime boss. He was involved in a number of fights during his incarceration, was once stabbed with a pair of scissors, and spent some time in isolation while at Alcatraz.

Attempts on his life, beatings, and the prison routine itself took their toll on Capone. Seeking a diversion, he played the banjo in a prison band. Some legends say that Scarface spent most of his time strumming his banjo alone, hoping to avoid other prisoners. In reality, after more than three years in Alcatraz, Capone was on the edge of total insanity. He spent the last year of his federal sentence in the hospital ward, undergoing treatment for an advanced case of syphilis.

When Capone left Alcatraz, he definitely seemed worse for the wear. It appeared that "The Rock" (and his nasty case of syphilis) had completely broken him. In January 1939, he was transferred to another prison to serve out a separate sentence. Capone was released to his family and doctors in November 1939 and became a recluse at his Florida estate. He died, broken and insane, in 1947.

Al Capone was not the only inmate to lose his grip on reality at Alcatraz. While working in the prison garage, convicted bank robber Rufe Persful picked up an ax and chopped the fingers off his left hand. Laughing maniacally, he asked another prisoner to cut off his right hand as well. An inmate named Joe Bowers sustained a superficial wound when he tried to slash his own throat with a pair of broken eyeglasses. Ed Wutke, who was at Alcatraz for murder, managed to use a pencil sharpener blade to fatally cut through his jugular vein. These were not the only suicide attempts, and many other men suffered mental breakdowns at Alcatraz.

Escapes from Alcatraz

During Alcatraz's 29 years as a federal prison, 34 different men tried to escape the island in 14 separate attempts. In almost every case, the escapees were killed or recaptured. Two escape attempts are particularly infamous.

In May 1946, six inmates captured a gun cage, obtained prison keys, and took over a cell house in less than an hour. Unfortunately for them, the only key they did not get was the one that would let them out of the cell building, which effectively grounded the escape plot. The prison break turned into a heated gunfight that led to the deaths of three of the escapees, as well as several guards. When it was over, two of the surviving escapees were sentenced to death and the third received a life sentence.

Though the 1946 incident may have been the most violent escape attempt at Alcatraz, it is not the most famous. That distinction belongs to a 1962 attempt by Frank Morris and brothers Clarence and John Anglin. Over several months, the men chipped away at the vent shafts in their cells using tools they had stolen from work sites. They also created makeshift rafts and inflatable life vests using raincoats. They even collected hair from the barbershop and made lifelike dummies to fool the guards on duty during the escape. Then, on the night of June 11, 1962, after making their way out of the prison, the trio boarded their rafts and set out into the cold waters of the bay, never to be seen again.

More than four decades later, it is still unclear whether or not the escapees survived. According to the Bureau of Prisons, the men are either missing or presumed drowned. The story of the escape was brought to the silver screen in the 1979 film *Escape from Alcatraz*, starring Clint Eastwood.

The Haunted Prison

On March 23, 1963, less than a year after this last escape attempt, Alcatraz ended its run as a federal prison, and the island remained largely abandoned until the early 1970s. Congress placed the island under the purview of the National Park Service in 1972, and Alcatraz opened to the public in 1973. It is now one of the most popular historic sites in America.

In the daytime, the former prison bustles with the activity of tour guides and visitors, but at night, the buildings play host to some unexplainable phenomena. Many believe that some of those who served time on "The Rock" linger for all eternity.

Accounts of hauntings have been widely reported since Alcatraz first shut its doors. Park service employees and visitors to Alcatraz report weird, ghostly encounters in the crumbling, old buildings. Unexplained clanging sounds, footsteps, and disembodied voices and screams are commonly heard coming from the empty corridors and long-abandoned cells. Some guides have reportedly witnessed strange events in certain areas of the prison, such as the infamous "holes," where prisoners suffered greatly.

But perhaps the most eerie sound is the faint banjo music sometimes heard in the shower room. Legend has it that Al Capone would often sit and strum his banjo in that spot rather than risk going out into the yard. Is it the broken spirit of Al Capone that creates this mournful melody on his phantom instrument? Or is it another ghostly inmate, unable to escape, even after death?

Armed Burglar Becomes Too Relaxed

Evidently it was a hard day at work for burglar Patrick Hazell, who took so many muscle relaxants that he fell asleep on the job.

Hazell was worn out after breaking into two cars and two houses in Bonifay, Florida, in late 2007, so he laid down on one homeowner's bed. Finding Hazell asleep in his bed with a pistol in his hand, the resident called 911. Deputies disarmed, awakened, and arrested the intruder.

- Napoleon wore black silk handkerchiefs regularly as part of his wardrobe and steadily won battle after battle. But in 1815, he decided to vary his attire and donned a white handkerchief before heading into battle at Waterloo, France. He was defeated, and it led to the end of his rule as emperor.

- The shoe has historically been a symbol of fertility. In some Eskimo cultures, women who can't have children wear shoes around their necks in the hope of changing their childbearing luck.

- In the Middle Ages, pointy-toed shoes were all the rage. The fad was so popular that King Edward III outlawed points that extended longer than two inches. The public didn't listen, and eventually the points were 18 inches long or more!

- Catherine de Medici popularized high heel shoes for women when she wore them for her 1533 wedding to Henri II of France, who later became king. However, several sources say that men had been wearing heels long before that to keep their feet from slipping off stirrups while horseback riding. A century later, when King Louis XIV of France wore high heels to boost his short stature, the trend became popular with the nobility.

- When Joan of Arc was burned at the stake, she was condemned for two crimes: witchcraft and wearing men's clothing.

- In the 16th century, men wore codpieces for numerous reasons. The frontal protrusions held money, documents, or whatever else they needed to carry.

Weird Web Buys

Today's consumers have no qualms about purchasing goods online. But, as it turns out, there are some truly bizarre cyber-bargains to be had at the touch of a keypad.

The Anti-Ticket Donut
Catering to the stereotype of the donut-loving cop, this product (a fake donut available in chocolate or "sprinkle") retails for $9.95, fits easily into a glove compartment, and is designed to dissuade hungry police officers from issuing traffic tickets.

Bacon Strips Adhesive Bandages
Who needs plain old pink bandages when you can dress your wounds in simulated bacon? This novelty item (you get 15 strips for about five bucks) could be seen as a key argument against unchecked capitalism, but apparently the market is there for this meat/medical supply hybrid.

Fish 'n Flush
The family john can be an ugly piece of porcelain. So why not arrange to have a fully functioning tropical fish tank built into the back of it? As an added benefit, goldfish funerals will be remarkably convenient.

Flatulence Filters
The "TooT TrappeR" is a charcoal filter shaped like a seat cushion that's designed to silence and deodorize unwanted outbursts. It comes in gray or black and makes a rather awkward Christmas gift.

Garden Gnomes in Compromising Positions
Not the normal garden variety of gnome, these lewd lawn statues depict one gnome burying another, a gnome "dropping a moon," and other assorted indecencies—and you thought all they did was hold shovels and wheelbarrows!

Ghost in a Jar

One of eBay's zaniest offerings was an alleged spirit trapped inside a glass jar. Fourteen bids were registered by people hoping to have their very own pet poltergeist.

Gourmet Oxygen

Although it's likely intended to be a novelty item, "Big Ox" brand oxygen, which comes in flavors such as Tropical Breeze, Mountain Mint, Citrus Blast, and Polar Rush, may provide a sinister glimpse of future consumer goods in a world with depleted natural resources.

Mint-Flavored Golf Tees

It's important to have fresh breath when you're out on the links, and these tees will help—as long as you don't mind sucking on sharpened sticks of wood. A word of caution: Only use them once, or the dirt gets in the way of the mint flavor.

Shoot the Poop

Sick of carrying around a plastic bag when walking your pooch? Try shooting your dog's poop with Poop-Freeze, which forms a "white crusty film" over the droppings and solidifies them for easy pick up for proper disposal or safekeeping in your prized pet's baby book.

Stainless-Steel Lollipops

The Zilopop is a German product that promotes fresh breath through the frequent licking of a cold steel circle. After a two- to four-minute suck on this lollipop look-alike, mouth odors are neutralized. And it's reusable! Unlike the Tootsie Pop, no amount of licking will ever get you to the center of a Zilopop.

Virgin Mary Grilled Cheese Sandwich

This decade-old lunchtime miracle sold for $28,000 on eBay. Diane Duyser of Florida was one bite into her sandwich when she noticed a radiant face staring out at her from the top slice of toast. Grace is indeed everywhere!

Holy Guano, Batman!

The location of the Bat Cave was always one of Batman's best-kept secrets, but the Caped Crusader would need extra superhero powers to enter the real bat cave near Fredericksburg, Texas. The ammonia fumes produced by the guano of the millions of bats who live there (normally around two million; more than three million in July and August) can be deadly for humans. The smell alone is certainly enough to keep most mortals at bay.

Batman would likely be annoyed by the hordes of tourists who flock to this abandoned railroad tunnel each evening to witness one of nature's most awe-inspiring spectacles. One plus, though: The place is virtually insect-free.

Like Clockwork
Natural phenomena are often difficult to predict, making it hard for the average person to schedule a time to experience them firsthand, but not so with the Fredericksburg bats. Although they'll return separately throughout the night, they emerge, more or less en masse, each and every evening about an hour before or after sundown.

First, two or three small black specks can be spotted circling the tunnel's mouth. Perhaps these harbingers are sent to check things out, for in less than a minute the entire sky fills with a flapping frenzy of wings from more than two million furry, pointy-eared, Mexican free-tailed bats. The bats circle the surrounding area, gaining momentum and consuming any insects that may be lingering, before flying off into the deepening twilight sky in search of more fertile feasting grounds. Because each bat consumes its own weight in insects nightly, it's no wonder they need to go out in search of food.

Nothing to Fear
It takes about an hour from the emergence of the first sentries before the last stragglers join the night's hunt, but for that

short time observers are treated to one of the most bizarre and awe-inspiring sights they are ever likely to behold. Of course, some folks might be a bit timid about being in such close proximity to so many bats. In reality, the bat-phobic have nothing to worry about. The old wives' tales about bats getting caught in people's hair are just that—tales. True, bats can't see well with their eyes, but their radar systems are so finely tuned that they can pick up matter as fine as a single strand of hair, so there's no way they would purposely entangle themselves. Park rangers confirm that the bats want to avoid contact with people as much as people want to avoid contact with bats. That same extraordinary radar also prevents bats from ever colliding with each other, even within the cramped quarters of the tunnel, and allows a mother bat to immediately find her baby among all the other bats living in the abandoned tunnel tenement.

A Sight to Behold

Visitors stand on viewing areas that are far enough away from the tunnel's entrance to avoid the full force of the pungent aromas emanating from inside. Although its unpleasant stench might indicate otherwise, the guano is actually a good thing. Regularly mined for use as fertilizer, bat guano serves as its own little ecosystem, supporting a variety of life forms. The park rangers here are happy to wax poetic on the gory but fascinating details of all the species that survive and thrive in guano—but be warned, they're not for the squeamish.

Folks in the nearby capital of Austin can also view bats, albeit a mere 1.5 million of them, that emerge each evening from under the city's Congress Avenue Bridge.

Sweet-Smelling Cops

In 2007, plans were underway in Ahmadabad, India, to have police officers smelling like roses...or lemons. The police department was working with a team of designers to provide 8,000 officers with new uniforms specially made of lightweight scented fabric designed to keep officers smelling clean and sweat free.

Delectable Dinners
Throughout History

Throughout culinary history, people have eaten some mighty strange things. Although various odd foods probably seemed like good ideas at the time, believe it or not, they have fallen out of favor with most modern diners.

Peacock
A popular food served in ancient Greece, peacock also appeared at the court of Henry VIII. The whole roasted bird was often presented with a gold leaf-gilded beak and adorned in an ornate cloak of its own feathers, which were removed and then replaced after cooking.

Roasted Locusts
John the Baptist ate this protein-rich insect in the desert, and the Book of Leviticus specifically mentions four species of locust that are permitted as food for Jews.

Grilled Beavers' Tails
Medieval Christians especially enjoyed beaver tails on the days when it was forbidden to eat meat. Because beavers live in water, they were conveniently classified as fish.

Sea Mammals
Seals and porpoises were eaten in England during the Middle Ages, along with boiled or roasted whale, a particularly economical choice because a single animal could feed hundreds of people. Plus, like beavers, the sea-dwelling animals were considered fish.

Swan

Swan consumption can be traced to the ancient Romans. Whole swans were also served by early English royalty for special occasions, often presented with a crown upon the roasted bird's head.

Raw Duck or Quail

Salted, without the heat of cooking, was a popular way for ancient Egyptians to enjoy duck and quail.

Cock Ale

Imbibers in 17th-century England could down a pint of this concoction made by boiling a whole rooster until it was jellified, then crushing it along with raisins and spices. The resulting fruity meat paste was then mixed with ale.

Ox Cheeks

Folks in merry ole England enjoyed ox in many forms. The cheeks were an especially popular and economical cut of meat and were served baked, boiled, or encased in a pie.

Dormouse

People from the ancient Romans through the Middle Ages enjoyed these rodents sauced, stuffed, or as a savory pastry or pie filling.

Rat, Dog, Elephant, et al

While Paris was under siege by the Prussians between 1870 and 1871, folks pretty much ate anything that moved—including creatures from the Paris Zoo. Culinary delights of the time include rat, dog, cat, horse, feral sheep, and even elephant, all prepared with Parisian flair, of course.

The cruise liner Queen Elizabeth II *moves only six inches for each gallon of diesel fuel that it burns.*

The Black Dahlia Murder Mystery

*One of the most baffling murder mysteries in U.S. history
began innocently enough on the morning of January 15, 1947.
Betty Bersinger was walking with her young daughter in
the Leimert Park area of Los Angeles, when she spotted
something lying in a vacant lot that caused her blood to
run cold. She ran to a nearby house and called the police.
Officers Wayne Fitzgerald and Frank Perkins arrived
on the scene shortly after 11:00 A.M.*

A Grisly Discovery

Lying only several feet from the road, in plain sight, was the
naked body of a young woman. Her body had numerous cuts
and abrasions, including a knife wound from ear to ear that
resembled a ghoulish grin. Even more horrific was that her
body had been completely severed at the midsection, and the
two halves had been placed as if they were part of some morbid display. That's what disturbed officers the most: The killer
appeared to have carefully posed the victim close to the street
because he wanted people to find his grotesque handiwork.

Something else that troubled the officers was that even
though the body had been brutally violated and desecrated,
there was very little blood found at the scene. The only blood
evidence recovered was a possible bloody footprint and an
empty cement package with a spot of blood on it. In fact, the
body was so clean that it appeared to have just been washed.

Shortly before removing the body, officers scoured the
area for a possible murder weapon, but none was recovered.
A coroner later determined that the cause of death was from
hemorrhage and shock due to a concussion of the brain and
lacerations of the face, probably from a very large knife.

Positive Identification

After a brief investigation, police were able to identify the
deceased as Elizabeth Short, who was born in Hyde Park,

Massachusetts, on July 29, 1924. At age 19, Short had moved to California to live with her father, but she moved out and spent the next few years moving back and forth between California, Florida, and Massachusetts. In July 1946, Short returned to California to see Lt. Gordon Fickling, a former boyfriend, who was stationed in Long Beach. For the last six months of her life, Short lived in an assortment of hotels, rooming houses, and private homes. She was last seen a week before her body was found, which made police very interested in finding out where and with whom she spent her final days.

The Black Dahlia Is Born

As police continued their investigation, reporters jumped all over the story and began referring to the unknown killer by names such as "sex-crazed maniac" and even "werewolf." Short herself was also given a nickname: the Black Dahlia. Reporters said it was a name friends had called her as a play on the movie *The Blue Dahlia*, which had recently been released. However, others contend Short was never called the Black Dahlia while she was alive; it was just something reporters made up for a better story. Either way, it wasn't long before newspapers around the globe were splashing front-page headlines about the horrific murder of the Black Dahlia.

The Killer Is Still Out There

As time wore on, hundreds of police officers were assigned to the Black Dahlia investigation. They combed the streets, interviewing people and following leads. Although police interviewed thousands of potential suspects—and dozens even confessed to the murder—to this day, no one has ever officially been charged with the crime. More than 60 years and several books and movies after the crime, the Elizabeth Short murder case is still listed as "open." We are no closer to knowing who killed Short or why than when her body was first discovered.

There is one bright note to this story. In February 1947, perhaps as a result of the Black Dahlia case, the state of California became the first state to pass a law requiring all convicted sex offenders to register themselves.

Unidentified Submerged Objects

💀   💀   💀   💀   💀

*Much like their flying brethren, unidentified submerged objects
captivate and mystify. But instead of vanishing into the skies,
USOs, such as the following, plunge underwater.*

Sighting at Puerto Rico Trench

In 1963, while conducting exercises off the coast of Puerto
Rico, U.S. Navy submarines encountered something extraordinary. The incident began when a sonar operator aboard
an accompanying destroyer reported a strange occurrence.
According to the seaman, one of the subs traveling with the
armada broke free from the pack to chase a USO. This quarry
would be unlike anything the submariners had ever pursued.

Underwater technology in the early 1960s was advancing
rapidly. Still, vessels had their limitations. The U.S.S. *Nautilus*,
though faster than any submarine that preceded it, was still
limited to about 20 knots (23 miles per hour). The bathyscaphe
Trieste, a deep-sea submersible, could exceed 30,000 feet in
depth, but the descent took as long as five hours. Once there,
the vessel could not be maneuvered side to side.

Knowing this, the submariners were stunned by what they
witnessed. The USO was moving at 150 knots (170 miles per
hour) and hitting depths greater than 20,000 feet! No underwater vehicles on Earth were capable of such fantastic numbers. Even today, modern nuclear subs have top speeds of
about 25 knots (29 miles per hour) and can operate at around
800-plus feet below the surface.

Thirteen separate crafts witnessed the USO as it criss-
crossed the Atlantic Ocean over a four-day period. At its
deepest, the mystery vehicle reached 27,000 feet. To this day,
there's been no earthly explanation offered for the occurrence.

USO with a Bus Pass

In 1964, London bus driver Bob Fall witnessed one of the
strangest USO sightings. While transporting a full contingent

of passengers, the driver and his fares reported seeing a silver, cigar-shape object dive into the nearby waters of the River Lea. The police attributed the phenomenon to a flight of ducks, despite the obvious incongruence. Severed telephone lines and a large gouge on the river's embankment suggested something far different.

Shag Harbour Incident

The fishing village of Shag Harbour lies on Canada's East Coast. This unassuming hamlet is to USOs what Roswell, New Mexico, is to UFOs. Simply put, it played host to the most famous occurrence of a USO ever recorded.

On the evening of October 4, 1967, the Royal Canadian Mounted Police (RCMP) were barraged by reports of a UFO that had crashed into the bay at Shag Harbour. Laurie Wickens and four friends witnessed a large object (approximately 60 feet in diameter) falling into the water just after 11:00 P.M. Floating approximately 1,000 feet off the coast they could clearly detect a yellow light on top of the object.

The RCMP promptly contacted the Rescue Coordination Center in Halifax to ask if any aircraft were missing. None were. Shortly thereafter, the object sank into the depths of the water and disappeared from view.

When local fishing boats went to the USO crash site, they encountered yellow foam on the water's surface and detected an odd sulfuric smell. No survivors or bodies were ever found. The Royal Canadian Air Force officially labeled the occurrence a UFO, but because the object was last seen under water, such events are now described as USOs.

Pascagoula Incident

On November 6, 1973, at approximately 8:00 P.M., a USO was sighted by at least nine fishermen anchored off the coast of Pascagoula, Mississippi. They witnessed an underwater object an estimated five feet in diameter that emitted a strange amber light.

First to spot the USO was Rayme Ryan. He repeatedly poked at the light-emitting object with an oar. Each time he made contact with the strange object, its light would dim and it would move a few feet away, then brighten once again.

Fascinated by the ethereal quality of this submerged question mark, Ryan summoned the others. For the next half hour, the cat-and-mouse game played out in front of the fishermen until Ryan struck the object with a particularly forceful blow. With this action, the USO disappeared from view.

The anglers moved about a half mile away and continued fishing. After about 30 minutes, they returned to their earlier location and were astounded to find that the USO had returned. At this point, they decided to alert the Coast Guard.

After interviewing the witnesses, investigators from the Naval Ship Research and Development Laboratory in Panama City, Florida, submitted their findings: At least nine persons had witnessed an undetermined light source whose characteristics and actions were inconsistent with those of known marine organisms or with an uncontrolled human-made object. Their final report was inconclusive, stating that the object could not be positively identified.

STRANGE STATS

- Residents of Andorra, a small country located in the mountains between France and Spain, have the highest life expectancy at birth, living 5.5 years longer than Americans, who rank 45th.

- The Panama Hat actually originated in Ecuador. In the 1880s, when Americans were building the Panama Canal, they erroneously named it, thinking it was a local creation.

- One out of every 2,000 babies is born with a tooth.

- The heart produces enough pressure to squirt blood more than 30 feet.

- The smallest frog hails from Cuba and measures less than a half inch when fully grown.

Weird Ways to Attract True Love

💀   💀   💀   💀   💀

It's likely that you or one of your single friends spends a good deal of time complaining about how difficult it is to meet people worth dating. Problem solved! These strange customs from all over the world give single people inventive ways to find true love. Go get an apple and we'll show you.

An Apple a Day...

In Elizabethan times, it was desirable for a girl to peel an apple and stick it under her armpit until it was saturated with sweat. The girl would then give it to her potential beau so that he could inhale her heavenly scent. We figure most men would prefer a hanky scented with Chanel N°5, but whatever works.

Eat Your Greens

Ladies, a few directions: Go to Ireland. Find a shamrock. Eat said shamrock while thinking of your true love. Wait for the gentleman to arrive, fully in love with you. In certain parts of Ireland, this custom is said to work like a (lucky) charm.

Backyard Safari

It takes a little preplanning, but if you can spare the time on Valentine's Day, go on a little wildlife adventure to determine your future with love and help your selection process. According to old European folktales, the types of animals you see on February 14 foretell the person you'll marry. Squirrels mean you'll find a cheapskate; goldfinch sightings point to a millionaire; a robin means you'll marry a crime fighter. And if you should find a glove that day, the owner of the other glove is your true love.

Pillaging, Etc.

If you're a warrior or male tribal member who happens to be looking for love, why not try the ancient custom of a hostile takeover? They're always dramatic and you don't have to worry about a curfew. But beware: If your new bride's family comes looking for her, you have to hide out with her for as long as it takes the moon to go through a full cycle.

Spooning
Dating back to 17th-century Wales, men carved spoons when they had a crush on a woman. Much like the secret codes in flower-giving (i.e., red roses=love, daisies=loyalty, etc.), the spoons were carved with various embellishments that let the girl know the man's intentions. Vines meant that feelings continued to grow, for example, and a circle inside a square signified a desire for children.

Victorian Dating Bureaucracy
If you think the politics of dating are weird today, you don't know how good we have it. In the Victorian age, dating among the elite was more complicated than filing taxes. First of all, nothing happened without a chaperone, and everything usually took place in full view of the entire family/town. Before a man could even speak to a woman, he had to be formally introduced. After that, he gave her his card. If the young lady was interested, he might be able to take her out for a stroll. Many "bodice-ripping" books and films are set in the Victorian era—nothing makes for a good story like repressed erotic love.

Sniffin' for Love
A study at the University of New Mexico found that when some women are ovulating, their sense of smell is seriously elevated, allowing them to evaluate how attracted a man is to them just by sniffing his worn shirts. Ladies, if the guy questions your sniffing, just tell him "it's a pheromone thing."

You cannot tickle yourself because your brain knows it is you and will not react in the same way as if it were someone else doing the tickling.

FREAKY FACTS: FROGS

Kermit, Jeremiah the Bullfrog, Prince Charming—frogs are clearly special creatures with many talents. They're also sort of gross. Check out these freaky frog facts that are sure to delight and disgust.

- *At about four weeks old, tadpoles get a bunch of very tiny teeth, which help them turn their food into mushy, oxygenated particles.*

- *Horned lizards are often called horny toads, though they're not actually amphibians. Horny toads can squirt blood from their eyeballs to attack predators. This only happens in extreme cases, but they can shoot it up to three feet, so watch out.*

- *The Goliath frog of West Africa is the largest frog in the world. When fully stretched out, this sucker is often more than 2.5 feet long!*

- *When frogs aren't near water, they will often secrete mucus to keep their skin moist.*

- *Frogs typically eat their old skin once it's been shed.*

- *One European common toad lived to be 40 years old, making it the oldest known toad on record.*

- *While swallowing, a frog's eyeballs retreat into its head, applying pressure that helps push food down its throat.*

- *A frog's ear is connected to its lungs. When a frog's eardrum vibrates, its lungs do, too. This special pressure system keeps frogs from hurting themselves when they blast their seriously loud mating calls.*

- *The earliest known frog fossils were found in Arizona and are thought to be about 190 million years old.*

Odd Sporting Events

☻ ☻ ☻ ☻ ☻

Because many modern sports have become mundane, main-stream activities, it's refreshing to discover pursuits that fall well outside those confines. Here are a few of those "untamed" sports.

Roach Racing

At least two U.S. venues offer roach racing, a sport that's definitely not meant for the squeamish. New Berlin, Wisconsin, joins in the fun with an annual contest held by Batzner Pest Management, and they do it with style. The contestants at this event are boisterous and ever-so-huge Madagascar hissing cockroaches. At the seventh annual event in 2007, a competitor named Rocky went the distance, thus ensuring that a local charity would become $200 richer. During the Roachingham 500, held each year at Bugfest in Raleigh, North Carolina, cockroaches race in front of huge crowds that have come to see this and other bug-related events.

Segway Polo

Why play ordinary polo on the back of an outdated, analog horse, when you can play on a Segway, a two-wheeled electric vehicle that is ridden while standing? This unique scooter was first put into polo-playing use during a Minnesota

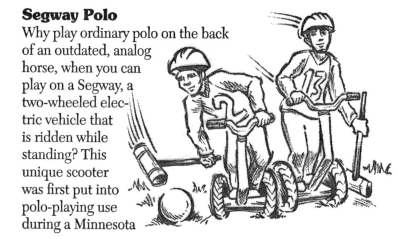

Vikings halftime show in 2003. Since then, this funky sport has attracted many people, and organized groups have popped up. Segway polo's greatest advantage over regular polo is that there's nothing to shovel off the field when the game is over.

Underwater Hockey

Aside from the obvious differences in playing surfaces, another major distinction between ice hockey and underwater hockey is the uniforms. Ice hockey players layer up with heavy padding and clothing, but underwater hockey players must don a swimsuit, fins, a snorkel, and a mask, and then submerge themselves in water. Invented in 1954 by Alan Blake of England, underwater hockey has evolved into an international sport. Forty-four teams from 17 countries competed at the 2006 World Championships held in the United Kingdom. Rules are similar to traditional hockey, but the equipment varies greatly between the two sports, most notably the sticks and pucks. Since underwater hockey requires that its participants push the puck along the bottom of a pool, the disc is suitably hefty, weighing about three pounds. On the other hand, the stick is a wimpy device, approximately one foot long.

Ferret Legging

Ferret legging is a bizarre English sport with roots tracing back to the 1970s. It encourages interplay between humans and ferrets and has many critics up in arms, citing animal cruelty.

The premise is straightforward: Two ferrets are dropped into a competitor's trousers after the bottoms have been tied off. This precludes an easy escape and forces the wily critters to feverishly climb the competitor's legs in search of an exit. Yet, the shrewd contestants also tightly cinch their belts, just for added fun. As the ferrets become panicked, they begin to bite, a behavior that the elongated critters indulge in with alarming ferocity. And did we mention that participants must compete *sans* underwear? The winner is the player who ends up "keepin' 'em down" the longest, to use the sport's jargon. For many years, the ferret-legging record stood at just under one minute, but the current record stands at more than five hours!

Grew-some Gluttons

*When truly great eaters strap on the feedbag, their gastric
achievements seem boundless. Here are a few grand masters
who lived mostly to eat, and one amateur who ate solely to live.*

Diamond Jim Brady

Railroad magnate Diamond Jim Brady could make quick work
out of almost any meal placed before him. Cheekily described
as "my best 25 customers" by the owner of Charles Rector's,
a Manhattan bistro and a favorite Brady haunt, the gilded-age
gourmet devoured enormous quantities of food there. This
included two to three dozen oysters, a half dozen crabs, a few
servings of green turtle soup, two ducks, six to seven lobsters, a
sirloin steak, two servings of terrapin, and assorted vegetables.
Dessert consisted of a platter of pastries and a two-pound box
of candy. After his death, Diamond Jim's prodigious belly was
discovered to be six times that of the average person!

Henry VIII

When England's King Henry VIII (1491–1547) sat to dine, it
wasn't the size of his meal that was so unusual but the outrageous items that he devoured, such as dolphin. For an appetizer, the King might nosh on pies stuffed with delectable
songbirds. Since he loved to hunt, all manner of prey was
considered fair game and most would find their way down his
gullet. Dessert? Perhaps a dish of gelatin made from deer antlers or stained with children's urine. Mmm, mmm, good!

King Farouk

The gastronomic prowess of Egypt's King Farouk (1920–1965)
is typically not well known. Given to excess in most every
aspect of his life, the rotund king also appreciated healthy
portions at mealtime. Staples of his diet consisted of numerous
tablespoons of caviar, slabs of roast lamb, dozens of oysters,
beans, lobster thermador, pounds of chocolate, assorted cakes

and fruit, and copious quantities of champagne and coffee. Not surprisingly, King Farouk, sporting some 300 pounds of well-earned heft, allegedly died from a heart attack at age 45.

Vitellius

Roman Emperor Aulus Vitellius (A.D. 15–69) was known for his prodigious appetite and "gags." In a gut-wrenching twist compared to ordinary tales of gluttony, this iron-handed ruler swallowed agents to induce vomiting after each course, then bellied-up to the feeding trough for another round. He divided his feasts into four sessions including breakfast, brunch, lunch, and dinner, then capped them off with an evening drinking bout—always taken to excess. His cuisine typically included tongues of flamingos, brains of peacocks and pheasants, and the entrails of lampreys. One formal dinner for himself and his guests included 2,000 fish and 7,000 birds—bountiful victuals by even the most extreme standards. Vitellius's food obsession was best illustrated whenever he left his court. While roaming the countryside, the compulsive eater couldn't resist snatching bits of meat and pie from inns, including half-eaten portions left over from the previous day. Some might have gagged at the thought of eating such leftovers, but it likely aided Vitellius in his "process."

George Fordyce

As a noted 18th-century physician and chemist, Dr. George Fordyce (1736–1802) likely knew that gluttony was an unhealthy process. Nevertheless, the good doctor regularly fed his compulsion by downing a super-size meal large enough to choke a horse. Arriving at his favorite restaurant around 4:00 P.M. each day, the doctor would first sip from a huge tankard of ale to prepare his palate. Next, he would down an entire bottle of port. Not quite juiced yet, Fordyce would then swallow a half-pint of brandy. When his main course arrived, it was generally a 1.5-pound steak accompanied by a broiled chicken, vegetables, and to top it all off, a tart. When Fordyce famously quipped, "One meal a day is enough for a lion, and it ought to be for a man," he was speaking from personal experience.

Nicholas Wood

Deemed the "Great Eater of Kent" in the early 1600s, England's Nicholas Wood was a veritable eating sensation. His consumptive exploits trump many of the world's most voracious gluttons, past and present, and feature a number of bizarre dishes. Items devoured in individual sittings reportedly included the following: 360 pigeons, 84 rabbits, 60 pounds of cherries, one whole hog, and an entire sheep in its raw, uncooked state. A celebrated breakfast consisted of a leg of mutton, 60 eggs, 3 large pies, and a bowl of pudding. After this waist-splitting meal (so excessive that it reportedly left the restaurant's cupboards bare), the glutton was reportedly still hungry. To remedy the situation, Wood's waiter fetched a large duck from a nearby pond and brought it to him. It is unclear if the bird arrived at his table alive or dead. With purposeful determination, the great masticator tore into it, leaving only its beak and feathers as proof of its earthly existence.

Donald Snyder

Though we often associate gluttony with eating oneself to death, we rarely, if ever, hear of times when it is used to accomplish the opposite. For Donald Snyder, gluttony represented sweet life. In the 1950s, Snyder was a 150-pound convicted murderer awaiting electrocution at New York's Sing Sing Prison. He reasoned that if he couldn't physically fit into "Old Sparky"—the whimsical name bestowed upon Sing Sing's electric chair—his would-be executioners would have one less convict to fry. How and where he secured his immense quantities of food is unclear, but nevertheless, he did manage to bulk up to more than 300 pounds. He was likely smiling when he took his final walk toward the chair. One can only imagine how quickly that smile faded when he discovered that "Old Sparky" fit him like a glove.

When babies are born, they have 300 bones, but by the time they reach adulthood, their smaller bones have fused together, leaving them with only 206.

Silly Classified Ads

- **Job Wanted—Man,** honest. Will take anything.

- **Sale**—Stock up and save. Limit one.

- **Used Cars**—Why go elsewhere to be cheated? Come here first!

- **Explosives Worker**—Man wanted to work in dynamite factory. Must be willing to travel.

- **Christmas Tag Sale**—Handmade gifts for the hard-to-find person.

- **Furniture**—Sofas. Only $299! For rest or fore play.

- **Teacher**—Three-year-old teacher needed for pre-school. Experience preferred.

- **For Sale**—Antique desk suitable for lady with thick legs and large drawers.

- **Grand Opening**—The Superstore—unequaled in size, unmatched in variety, unrivaled inconvenience.

- **For Sale**—Mixing bowl set designed to please a cook with round bottom for efficient beating.

- **Expertise**—We do not tear your clothing with machinery. We do it carefully by hand.

- **Helper**—Tired of cleaning yourself? Let me do it.

- **Auto Repair Service**—Free pick-up and delivery. Try us once, you'll never go anywhere again.

- **For Sale**—Amana washer $100. Owned by clean bachelor who seldom washed.

- **Free Puppies**—Half cocker spaniel, half sneaky neighbor's dog.

America's Most Haunted Lighthouse

Built in 1830, the historic Point Lookout Lighthouse is located in St. Mary's County, Maryland, where the Potomac River meets Chesapeake Bay. It is a beautiful setting for hiking, boating, fishing, camping, and ghost-hunting.

The Most Ghosts

Point Lookout Lighthouse has been called America's most haunted lighthouse, perhaps because it was built on what later became the largest camp for Confederate prisoners of war.

Marshy surroundings, tent housing, and close quarters were a dangerous combination, and smallpox, scurvy, and dysentery ran rampant. The camp held more than 50,000 soldiers, and between 3,000 and 8,000 died there.

Park rangers and visitors to the lighthouse report hearing snoring and footsteps, having a sense of being watched, and feeling the floors shake and the air move as crowds of invisible beings pass by. A photograph of a former caretaker shows the misty figure of a young soldier leaning against the wall behind her, although no one noticed him when the photo was taken during a séance at the lighthouse. And a bedroom reportedly smelled like rotting flesh at night until the odor was publicly attributed to the spirits of the war prisoners.

The Lost Ghost

In December 1977, Ranger Gerald Sword was sitting in the lighthouse's kitchen on a stormy night when a man's face appeared at the back door. The man was young, with a floppy cap and a long coat, and peered into the bright room. Given the awful weather, Sword opened the door to let him in, but the young man floated backward until he vanished entirely. Later, after a bit of research, Sword realized he had been face-to-face with Joseph Haney, a young officer whose body had washed ashore after the steamboat he was on sank during a similar storm in 1878.

The Host Ghost
One of Point Lookout's most frequent visitors is the apparition of a woman dressed in a long blue skirt and a white blouse who appears at the top of the stairs. She is believed to be Ann Davis, the wife of the first lighthouse keeper. Although her husband died shortly after he took the post, Ann remained as the keeper for the next 30 years, and, according to inspection reports, was known for clean and well-kept grounds. Caretakers claim to hear her sighing heavily.

Who Said That?
Point Lookout's reputation drew Hans Holzer, Ph.D., a renowned parapsychologist, who tried to capture evidence of ghostly activity. Holzer and his team claimed to have recorded 24 different voices in all, both male and female, talking, laughing, and singing. Among their recordings, the group heard male voices saying "fire if they get too close," "going home," and more than a few obscenities.

Take Care, Caretaker
One former caretaker reported waking in the middle of the night to see a ring of lights dancing above her head. She smelled smoke and raced downstairs to find a space heater on fire. She believes that the lights were trying to protect her and the lighthouse from being consumed by flames.

A Full House
The lighthouse was decommissioned in 1966, after 135 years of service. In 2002, the state of Maryland purchased it, and it is now open for tours and paranormal investigations. The Point Lookout Lighthouse continues to have a steady stream of visitors—even those who are no longer among the living.

Curious Displays and Museums

From a museum that "digs up the dirt," to another that "plants" people six feet into it, these showcases feature anything but the expected as they celebrate the wacky and wild.

Burlingame Museum of Pez

Who can resist the quirky little candies that are ejected from a whimsical dispenser? Certainly not Gary Doss. In 1995, he opened the Burlingame Museum of Pez in California to showcase his collection of more than 500 Pez dispensers. Favorites include Mickey Mouse, Tweety Bird, and Bugs Bunny, but offerings such as Uncle Sam, a wounded soldier, and a stewardess are also on display.

The name "Pez" comes from *pfefferminz,* the German word for peppermint. The candy was originally introduced in Austria in 1927 to aid smokers trying to kick the habit. The first dispensers, utilitarian in design, appeared around 1950. By 1952, cartoon heads and fruit-flavored candies had made the scene. The popularity of the dispensers has turned them into highly collectible items. Doss's collection features a Mr. Potato Head version that, due to its small parts, was deemed a hazard to children and was yanked from store shelves in 1973. Today, the dispenser is valued at around $5,000.

Leila's Hair Museum

If you walk into Leila's Hair Museum in Independence, Missouri, expecting to find curlers, dryers, and similar hair-styling implements, you'll be sorely disappointed. If, however, you go ape for jewelry, wreaths, chains, broaches, hat pins, postcards, and a host of other intriguing things made *from* hair, you'll feel like a veritable Lady Godiva at this shrine to follicles. With more than 2,000 pieces of hair jewelry and 150 hair wreaths at which to gawk, a visitor could grow out of their haircut if they stayed to scrutinize each one.

Created by Leila Cohoon in 1990, the museum was originally a place to store her burgeoning hair-wreath collection. Cohoon continually increases her hair collection by visiting garage sales, antique dealers, auctions, and other sources. She even has a hair wreath donated by comedian Phyllis Diller, who is noted for her kooky hairdos.

Museum of Dirt

Here's a dirty little secret: Boston's Museum of Dirt isn't just about dirt. Oh sure, you can find the brown, gritty, and cruddy stuff there, but the museum also contains such filthy offshoots as a ball of lint, crumpled leaves, and rocks. (In case you're wondering, the ball of lint came to the museum compliments of humorist Dave Barry, and the crumpled leaves are straight from Martha Stewart's yard.)

Glenn Johanson started his collection when he dug up some dirt as a souvenir from the Liberace Museum in Las Vegas. With this offbeat memento acting as impetus, the soil-buff dug up more dirt and things simply got filthier from there.

Much of the museum's dirt collection has been donated by people from around the world. But visitors will also find granules scraped from Gianna Versace's front step, as well as dirt lifted from Eartha Kitt's star on the Hollywood Walk of Fame. Some morbid pieces are also on display, such as a rock retrieved from the grounds of the Alfred P. Murrah Federal Building in Oklahoma City after it was blown up by terrorists in 1995, and pieces of thatching taken from the estate of O. J. Simpson, where Nicole Brown Simpson and Ron Goldman were murdered.

Hoover Historical Center

The Hoover Historical Center, aka the Vacuum Cleaner Museum, in North Canton, Ohio, is one of the few places where the statement "this thing really sucks" means something good. The name Hoover is synonymous with vacuum cleaners, so it comes as no surprise that, in 1978, the boyhood home of the company's founder, William H. "Boss" Hoover (who popularized the machine but did not invent it), became a showcase for great "suckers" of the past.

Visitors to the dirt-removal museum will find antique cleaning devices and manual machines dating from the late 1800s. The 1908 portable "Model 0" (the first electric Hoover vacuum, which was invented by janitor James Murray Spangler in 1907) is featured at the museum beside such thoroughly odd pieces as the 1910 Kotten suction cleaner. This piece of ingenuity required the user to stand on a platform and rock side-to-side to create suction. Not too practical by today's standards.

Another interesting piece found at the Hoover Historical Center is a 1923 Hoover Model 541. Made of super-sleek, die-cast aluminum, it's easy to imagine a 1920s-era flapper pushing the device to and fro as she sashayed her dirt away.

National Museum of Funeral History

We all have to go sometime, but if Robert L. Waltrip has his way, it won't be until we've visited his National Museum of Funeral History in Houston, Texas. With more than 20,000 square feet, this museum is packed to the rafters with caskets, coffins, hearses, and other items related to dying.

Opened in 1992 as a way to honor "one of our most important cultural rituals," the scope of the operation is impressive, as are some of its more unusual exhibits. A real crowd pleaser is a 1916 Packard funeral bus. This bizarre vehicle seems to ask, "Why deal with long funeral processions when this baby can do it all?" Designed to carry a coffin, pallbearers, and up to 20 mourners, the bus was retired after it tipped over during a funeral in San Francisco in the 1950s, ejecting mourners and the deceased onto the street.

Another interesting item is the "casket for three." Built for a heartbroken couple bent on suicide after their baby passed away, it ended up at the museum after they dashed their plan.

A playful sign in the museum reads, "Any day above ground is a good one." True, but after checking out the museum's ultra-cool fantasy coffins, designed to resemble objects such as a car, an airplane, or a fish, six-feet under doesn't seem so bad.

Museum of Questionable Medical Devices

Can you imagine zapping a case of arthritis with a "Cosmos Bag" (a 1920s-era cloth bag stuffed with low-grade radioactive ore) or curing a case of constipation with a painfully large "Recto Rotor," the anal answer to a plumber's mechanical snake? Imagine no more.

In the early 1980s, founder Bob McCoy opened the Museum of Questionable Medical Devices in St. Anthony, Minnesota. But since 2002, the operation has been located at the Science Museum of Minnesota in St. Paul. Visitors gawk at a collection of the most dubious medical instruments ever devised by humankind, such as a prostate gland warmer, a "phrenology" machine (designed to measure human head bumps to determine personality), a foot-operated breast enlarger, "electropathy" machines (to electrically treat diseases and conditions), radium cures, a violet-ray generator (to cure everything from heart disease to writer's cramp), and hundreds of others. There's even a Contemporary Quackery section that proves that such nuttiness lives on.

Museum of Bad Art

Some would consider a velvet Elvis or *Dogs Playing Poker* too atrocious for an art collection, but the Museum of Bad Art, located in Dedham, Massachusetts, is dedicated to the acquisition and exhibition of such rarely revered works.

The museum began where only such an institution could: in the garbage. That's where, in 1992, Boston antiques dealer Scott Wilson spotted the serendipitous work that's now cherished as the museum's *Mona Lisa,* a subtly disturbing painting he's dubbed *Lucy in the Field with Flowers,* which depicts a gray-haired matriarch sitting among a field of lilies that undulate beneath a fluorescent yellow-green sky. The old lady's lawn chair hovers nearby.

Since then the collection has grown to about 250 pieces that are, as their motto states, simply "too bad to be ignored." Twenty-five of those are on display at any given time on the lower floor of the Dedham Community Theater, just outside the men's room.

Robert Ripley: Master of Weird

In the world of the weird and unusual, there are few names more widely known than Robert Ripley. If you've ever read a *Ripley's Believe It or Not!* book or magazine, been to a Ripley's Odditorium, or watched episodes of the old TV show, you know that his enterprise was a cultural zeitgeist for much of the 20th century.

Though some of his contemporaries were less than compassionate regarding their bizarre subjects, Ripley was known for his intelligence as well as his reverence for the wondrous sights he brought to the masses for more than 30 years.

Believe It or Not Beginnings

Ripley was born in Santa Rosa, California in 1890. He dropped out of high school to support his family, but as a gifted artist, he discovered at age 16 that his cartoons were good enough to sell. In the early 1900s, while pursuing a brief stint as a semi-pro baseball player, Ripley sold cartoons to several San Francisco papers. By 1913, he was living in New York City, drawing cartoons for *The New York Globe,* and sending money home.

It was at the *Globe* in 1918 that Ripley drew his first "Believe It or Not!" cartoon, which portrayed oddities from the world of sports. The response was incredible. In the days before the Internet and flights to far-flung locales, the masses were hungry for news of the weird, and they definitely got their fix with the bizarre stuff featured in Ripley's drawings.

Ripley married in 1919 and began traveling the world a few years later. He knew that the more places he explored, the better his stories would be. In 1925, he published a travel journal as well as a how-to book about handball. In 1926, he became the handball champion of New York City—believe it or not.

The Most Popular Man in America

The *New York Evening Post* bought Ripley's wildly popular cartoon in 1923, then, in 1929, sold it to publishing magnate

William Randolph Hearst for syndication. This brought Ripley immense fame—it's estimated that at its peak, 80 million people across the United States read his cartoon series every day.

In the 1930s, Ripley broadened his base when his radio show went on the air. He took a tape recorder with him on his world travels and reported from the road, much to the delight of his listeners. Shortly after the radio program launched, Ripley did several film reels for Vitaphone Pictures. Then, at the Chicago World's Fair in 1933, he opened his first Odditorium—a museum that housed collections (both authentic and replicated) of the strange and unusual things he saw in his travels, such as mummified cats, sideshow performers, and scale models of sharks. By 1940, there were Odditoriums in New York, San Francisco, Cleveland, Dallas, and San Diego.

Ripley's radio show stayed on the air for more than 18 years, dazzling home audiences with extraordinary tales from inside caves, deep under water, and odd foreign locales. When television arrived, Ripley recognized the need to change formats, and the radio show ended. In 1949, the first broadcast of the *Believe It or Not!* television show aired with Ripley as host. However, he only filmed 13 episodes due to his deteriorating health, and he died of a heart attack on May 27 at age 58.

All-Around Decent Guy

People in the early part of the 20th century—caught up in spiritualism and often overwhelmed by the industrial advances lurching the country forward—clamored for news of the odd and impossible. Ripley could have manipulated such a naive public, but he swore that he never made anything up and was willing to prove every statement he made. Norbert Pearlroth, his assistant of more than 25 years, worked tirelessly in the New York Public Library to verify his boss' wild reports.

Today, Ripley's Believe It or Not! museums and attractions around the world bring in more than 13 million visitors each year. Sure, curious folks can search online for images of body-modification artists or an anaconda swallowing a deer, but they still appreciate the spin that Robert Ripley had on the wild world he explored.

The Real Hound
of the Baskervilles

In March 1901, Sir Arthur Conan Doyle believed that he was going on a relaxing golf holiday. At the time, he also thought that he was finished writing Sherlock Holmes stories. But he was wrong on both counts. His experiences at England's Royal Links Hotel in the town of Cromer led to the most famous Holmes adventure ever, and it all began with the story of a shaggy dog.

Soon after he arrived at the Royal Links Hotel, the famous author heard an amazing tale. A huge, sinister, ghostly dog was said to haunt the nearby coast, and the animal could be seen from the hotel on stormy nights. Supposedly, the black dog was the size of a calf and had glowing red eyes and an odor like brimstone. In Conan Doyle's words, it was "a spectral hound, black, silent, and monstrous." The author immediately began searching for this extraordinary beast.

England's Black Shuck

Throughout most of England, this type of terrifying hound is called a "black shuck." Some people describe it as an unusually large black wolfhound; others say it is a hound from hell. Shucks have been reported for hundreds of years, including some late 20th-century encounters with the police.

Most shuck sightings occur along England's picturesque southeastern coast. The town of Cromer, where Conan Doyle vacationed, is at the heart of this area. During the daytime, Cromer is a deceptively quaint and peaceful town, but on stormy nights, the town has a much darker reputation. In his 1901 book, *Highways and Byways of East Anglia,* author William Dutt described Cromer's black shuck. "He takes the form of a huge black dog, and prowls along dark lanes and lonesome field footpaths, where, although his howling makes the hearer's blood run cold, his footfalls make no sound."

Neither an Officer nor a Gentleman

Squire Richard Cabell—the basis of Arthur Conan Doyle's villain, Hugo Baskerville—may have been the first person killed by a black shuck. Cabell was born around 1620 and grew up in Brook Manor near what is now England's eerie Dartmoor National Park. Like his father, Cabell supported the Royalists, who taxed peasants rather than landowners. This made the Cabell family unpopular with their neighbors, and some people claimed that Richard Cabell had sold his soul to the devil.

The Black Shuck's Revenge

When the Royalists were defeated in the English Civil War, Cabell hastily married Elizabeth Fowell, the daughter of the local tax collector. According to local lore, Cabell resented his wife and was also insanely jealous and abusive toward her. One night, Elizabeth and her dog attempted to flee across the moor as Squire Cabell chased after them.

When Cabell caught up with his wife and began to beat her, the dog increased in size and its skin stretched over its expanding frame, giving the hound a skeletal appearance. Then, his eyes began to glow with rage, or perhaps the fires of hell. The dog ripped Cabell's throat out and then disappeared across the moor, leaving the corpse at Elizabeth's feet. From that moment on, similar hounds have been sighted around Dartmoor as well as along Norfolk's coastline.

The Devil Claims His Own

Soon after Richard Cabell was interred in the Holy Trinity Church graveyard, people began reporting strange occurrences at the cemetery. Some claimed they'd seen Cabell on stormy nights, rising from his grave and leading a pack of phantom hounds on a hunt across the moor, possibly searching for Elizabeth. According to legend, the squire's eyes glowed red with rage, and he would attack anyone who crossed his path.

Allegedly for protection, the town placed a heavy stone slab over Cabell's grave. Still, the reports of his ghost continued, along with sightings of the black shuck. Later, a huge stone building—referred to as "the sepulchre"—was constructed around the grave. A heavy wooden door was added, along with metal bars on the windows, to keep Cabell's spirit inside.

To this day, people report an ominous red glow emanating from inside the building. According to local lore, if you run around the crypt seven times and reach through the window, either Cabell or the devil will lick or bite your fingertips.

Cabell's Revenge

Whether these stories of Cabell's afterlife prison are true or not, the graveyard and the church next to it have been the victims of extraordinarily bad luck since the 1800s.

First, the cemetery became a target for body snatchers in the 1820s. Then the church caught fire several times, including a blaze in 1849 that was attributed to arson. Later, around 1885, the church was struck by lightning. Some years after that, the stained-glass windows shattered and had to be replaced. The church was plagued by problems like these until 1992, when a fire started under the altar. The flames were so intense that the church's ancient Norman font exploded from the heat. Area residents, weary of such calamities, decided not to repair the church. Today, Holy Trinity Church is an empty shell and perhaps a monument to the Cabell curse.

The Real Baskerville

Sir Arthur Conan Doyle's novel *The Hound of the Baskervilles* matches many of the chilling details of the Richard Cabell legend. He describes the fictional Hugo Baskerville as "a most wild, profane, and godless man" with "a certain wanton and cruel humour." In the novel, Baskerville kidnaps the lovely daughter of a nearby landowner and holds her captive until she marries him. After mistreating his wife, Baskerville is attacked and killed by a vicious, phantom hound.

Conan Doyle intended *The Hound of the Baskervilles* to be fiction, so he did not choose to call his villain Richard Cabell. Instead, the author whimsically used the surname of William Henry "Harry" Baskerville, the coachman who drove him around Devon during his research. Interestingly, Harry was a distant relative of Elizabeth Fowell, whose storied flight from Richard Cabell was the inspiration for the legend of Dartmoor's black shucks.

The Shucks Still Roam

On stormy days and damp nights, many believe that black shucks can still be seen throughout England. Some also think that a black shuck left scratches and burn marks on the door at Blythburgh's Holy Trinity Church, also called the Cathedral of the Marshes. Throughout the 20th century, shuck sightings continued to be reported. Shuck Lane in the coastal Norfolk town of Overstrand was given that name because the beast is said to frequently appear there.

According to paranormal researchers, the best place to find a black shuck is at Coltishall Bridge just north of Norwich. If you walk that bridge at night, you may sense or hear the beast. If you are especially unlucky, you may actually see it. But close your eyes if you think a black shuck is nearby, for—as William Dutt reported in his book—"to meet him is to be warned that your death will occur by the end of the year."

Military Intelligence?

In 2007, the U.S. Department of Defense realized that it had been conned. A Pentagon investigation discovered that a small firm based in South Carolina had fraudulently collected $20.5 million in shipping charges from the department over a period of six years. In one particularly embarrassing instance, an invoice totaling $999,798 was issued to send two washers (valued at 19 cents apiece) to a base in Texas. According to a Bloomberg News report, the swindle was easy because the department maintains a policy of automatically—without question—paying shipping bills labeled "priority."

What's in the Closet?

Often fans will acquire an item that their favorite star once owned. Here are a few of the more outrageous examples.

What Gall
Barton Lidicé Beneš, noted celebrity-relic collector, was a fan of J. R. Ewing (Larry Hagman)—the cutthroat yet charming baron from the television series *Dallas.* Demonstrating his continued devotion, Beneš had one of Hagman's gallstones placed in a setting, creating a handsome ring.

Enterprising Barber
Elvis Presley's personal hair stylist, Homer Gilleland, so loved the King that he saved a fist-size ball of Presley's hair clippings. He later gave them away to an industrious friend who put them up for auction. Starting bid? $10,000!

Prime Sucker
If you prefer presidential memorabilia, a half-sucked throat lozenge from President Bill Clinton might fit the bill.

Heads, You Lose
Following Sir Walter Raleigh's beheading in 1618, his wife was presented with his embalmed head. She kept it for 29 years, and upon her death, the rotting heirloom was inherited by the couple's son Carew. The head was buried with Carew in 1666.

Einstein's "Computer"
Albert Einstein was one smart cookie. So it comes as no surprise that after his death in 1955, his brain was retained for examination to see what made it so far above average. Sliced into 240 sections for distribution, Einstein's gray matter was compared against other brains and found to be some 15 percent wider than the norm. Today, the bulk of Einstein's brain rests at Princeton Hospital in New Jersey.

Pretentious Pee

In November 1996, a souvenir-hunting art dealer saw a grand opportunity. While dining at a celebrity-filled Los Angeles bistro, the man happened upon Sylvester Stallone in the men's room. Noticing that the muscular star had neglected to flush his urinal, the man leaped into action. He hastily emptied a pill bottle and scooped out a few ounces of Sly's "essence."

A Leg Up on the Competition

Some people save their own body parts as souvenirs. Such was the case with Union General Daniel Sickles. After having his right leg amputated after the Battle of Gettysburg, the unfazed warrior donated the limb to the National Museum of Health and Medicine in Washington, D.C. Reportedly, the enterprising officer escorted lady friends to see the relic, regaling them with tales of his bravery.

Pint-Sized Phallus

Although the cause of Napoleon Bonaparte's May 1821 death is still open to debate, a certain part of his anatomy is thought to have been removed during his autopsy. Yes, *that* part! A priest by the name of Ange Vignali is said to have taken home the souvenir.

In 1916, Vignali's heirs sold the item. The pint-sized appendage (approximately one inch in length) has since gotten around—perhaps even more than during the famed general's life—and it currently resides with an American urologist.

Proud Appendage

The "Mad Monk" Rasputin is said to have left behind more than his legacy after being murdered in 1916. Tales of his castration have circulated since his death, and his surviving body part is purported to be of uncommon size. In 2004, the Russian mystic's alleged organ was placed on display at a St. Petersburg museum. "We can stop envying America, where Napoleon Bonaparte's is now kept," bragged the museum about their massive find. "Napoleon's is but a small 'pod'; it cannot stand comparison to our organ of 30 centimeters (11.8 inches)."

Entertainment or Exploitation?

Nobody would choose to be born with a disability or disfigurement. But if you were born that way before 1940 or so, chances were good that you'd be labeled a "freak" and go straight into a sideshow—and you could bet there wouldn't be any handicapped parking spaces reserved for you when you got there.

During the vaudeville and circus sideshow era, many of these famous "freaks" were put on display for the masses. For better or worse, the following individuals made such an impression on the public that their names are hard to forget.

Eng and Chang—Siamese Twins

The term "Siamese twins" started with Eng and Chang Bunker, conjoined twins born in Siam (modern day Thailand) in 1811. A sideshow act discovered the twins when they were about 18 and took them all over the world, which later led them to tour with P. T. Barnum. Eventually, the twins settled down, became farmers, married sisters, and fathered 21 children between them. In January 1874, Chang died, possibly from a cerebral clot following a severe case of bronchitis. Eng followed just a couple of hours later.

Grace McDaniels—The Mule-Faced Woman

A degenerative, genetic condition known as Sturge–Weber syndrome was likely to blame for Grace McDaniels's lot in life. Born in 1888, Grace's face grew and twisted into an alarming balloonlike mass of tissue and discolored skin as she got older. She joined F. W. Miller's freak show in 1935 after winning an "ugly woman" contest, though she much preferred to be known as "The Mule-Faced Woman."

General Tom Thumb

Charles S. Stratton was born in Connecticut in 1838 weighing a hearty 9.2 pounds. But by age six, he had stopped growing at only about two feet tall. P. T. Barnum discovered Stratton in 1843 when he was just five years old, nicknamed him General Tom Thumb, and took him on the road. General Tom Thumb became one of the biggest celebrities of the 19th century. He met queens, kings, and politicians, and when he married his wife Lavinia (she was slightly taller at around 33 inches), congressmen and millionaires were in attendance.

Grady Stiles, Jr.—Lobster Boy

For several generations, the Stiles family has suffered from a disfiguring condition known as ectrodactyly, which shapes hands and feet into claws or pincherlike stumps. This is why Grady came to be known as "Lobster Boy." Born in 1937, Grady did his share of exhibition shows and interviews because of his disfigurement, but his name would make the news many years later for a more sinister reason. An abusive, aggressive man, Grady shot and killed his daughter's boyfriend. He was convicted, but because the prison system wasn't equipped to deal with his physical challenges, he got off with 15 years of probation. In November 1992, in a tragic twist of fate, Grady was murdered by a hitman hired by his wife, Maria.

Simon Metz—aka Schlitzie the Pinhead

Microcephalus is a condition that causes a person's cranium to be abnormally small and pointed. People born with this condition used to be called "pinheads," and Simon Metz was the most famous of them all. Born in the Bronx in 1901 and sold by his parents to a show a few years later, Simon was billed as a female because he often wore a dress due to his incontinence. His condition affected his mental capacity and speech, but that didn't keep Metz—known for his childlike attitude and ever-present smile—from working with some of the biggest names in the business, including circuses in America and abroad. Metz was steadily employed until he retired in the 1960s. He passed away at a nursing home in 1971.

Prince Randian—The Human Caterpillar
In 1871, a deformed baby was born in British Guyana to servant parents. The baby, whose real name is lost to history, arrived with no arms or legs, although he possessed a fully developed head that sat atop a healthy torso. Named "Prince Randian" by P. T. Barnum's scouts, the boy was put on the sideshow circuit in 1889 when he was around 18 and performed incredible feats such as writing, painting, and rolling and lighting a cigarette using the dexterity of his lips and tongue. Randian and his wife, Sarah, had several children and retired to New Jersey, where he lived until his death in 1934.

Robert Wadlow—The World's Tallest Man
Born in Alton, Illinois, in 1918, Robert Wadlow appeared to be a normal, healthy boy. Then he started growing—and he didn't stop. Wadlow's excessive growth stemmed from a hormone abnormality, which resulted in gigantism. At age eight, he was over six feet tall. At age sixteen, he was seven feet tall. By the time he was in his early twenties, Wadlow weighed almost 450 pounds and was nearly nine feet tall. His astonishing size garnered him a lot of publicity and a tour with the Ringling Brothers Circus. Unfortunately, the abnormality that made him a celebrity came at a price. In 1940, Wadlow needed braces to walk, which caused blisters. When one of the blisters became infected, the world's tallest man required a blood transfusion, which failed. More than 40,000 people attended Wadlow's funeral—12 pallbearers were needed to carry the casket.

Captain Fred Walters
Born in England in 1855, Captain Fred Walters wasn't always sad, but he was definitely blue. The Captain suffered from a neural condition known as locomotor ataxia, but that's not what gave his skin its distinct blue-gray hue. The Captain was given silver compounds as a treatment for his disease. The silver turned his skin blue, so Walters decided to profit from it. He took as much silver as he could to remain as blue as can be, receiving much attention and publicity for it. Unfortunately, the silver poisoned him, and his heart gave out when he was 68.

Saartjee Baartman—The Hottentot Venus

Saartjee, or "Sara," Baartman, a young woman from South Africa, was taken from her homeland and exhibited as a freak in sideshows across Britain. Her voluptuous body earned her the title of the "Hottentot Venus" and laid the foundation for the disparaging attitudes toward the sexuality of women of African descent.

But Baartman's body wasn't actually "disfigured." For 19th-century Europeans, her dark skin, full figure, and native dress were enough for them to label her a sideshow spectacle. Later studied by French anatomists, Baartman's private parts and skeleton were exhibited in Paris until 1985.

Jo-Jo the Dog-Faced Boy

Like his father, Fedor Jefticheiv was born with a medical condition called generalized hypertrichosis—excessive, full-body hair growth. By the time Fedor hit puberty, hair covered his entire face and much of his body. Spotted by a P. T. Barnum talent scout in 1884, Fedor was dubbed "Jo-Jo the Dog-Faced Boy" and was one of the most astonishing attractions of the show. Audience members would pull "Jo-Jo's" beard, stroke his head, and basically taunt him mercilessly, which caused Jo-Jo to snarl occasionally, reinforcing the dog moniker. In 1904, Fedor died of pneumonia at age 35.

Joseph Merrick—The Elephant Man

Perhaps the most famous of the "freaks," Joseph Merrick was the subject of many books, films, and medical research during his lifetime and since his death in 1890. Today, doctors believe that Merrick suffered from Proteus syndrome, an incredibly rare disease characterized by abnormal, excessive, debilitating, and often disfiguring overgrowth of both tissues and bones. Victorian Britain was fascinated by the hideously disfigured Merrick, who in the face of such extremely trying circumstances was still the picture of decorum. Merrick died at age 27 in the care of doctors who rescued him from abusive sideshow producers and often cruel public treatment.

No Humans Allowed

💀 💀 💀 💀 💀

Every dog has its day. But when your dog's day has passed, or your cat has used up all of its nine lives, if you live near L.A., you might take your departed friend to the Pet Memorial Park.

Originally named the Los Angeles Pet Cemetery, these ten acres of land in Calabasas, California, have served as the final resting place for cats, dogs, horses, and virtually every other kind of pet imaginable since 1928, making it one of the oldest pet cemeteries on the West Coast. It's now the final resting place of several famous animals, including Petey from *The Little Rascals,* Rudolph Valentino's dog, Kabar, and Hopalong Cassidy's horse, Topper.

Saving the Cemetery

In 1973, the entire property was donated to the Los Angeles Society for the Prevention of Cruelty to Animals (LASPCA). In the early 1980s, when word spread that the LASPCA was considering selling the cemetary to developers, pet lovers throughout Los Angeles decided something had to be done to save it. Several individuals banded together to create S.O.P.H.I.E. (Save Our Pets' History In Eternity), a nonprofit organization to save the Los Angeles Pet Cemetery.

Through a series of fund-raisers, S.O.P.H.I.E. was able to purchase the entire property, and, in September 1986, the cemetery was reopened as the Los Angeles Pet Memorial Park. The facility is now a fully operational animal funeral home, complete with a crematory and an area with couches and chairs where owners can spend a few minutes saying their final goodbyes to their faithful, furry friends.

Teacher's Pet

Visitors to the Los Angeles Pet Cemetery often find it hard to locate specific monuments because upright markers are not allowed. Of course, rules were made to be broken. In this case, they were broken for a special cat named Room Eight.

Shortly after the 1952 school year kicked off, one of the students in Room 8 at Elysian Heights Elementary School in Los Angeles noticed a black-and-white cat sneaking into the classroom through an open window. For the rest of the school year, the cat, which the students named Room Eight, visited the classroom. At the end of the school year, as the students were filing out for summer vacation, Room Eight jumped out the window and scampered off as if he had summer plans, too.

Everyone thought that was the last they would see of Room Eight, until the start of school the following year, when a familiar black-and-white tomcat popped through the window. Once again, Room Eight stayed the entire school year and then took off for parts unknown for summer break, only to return again in September.

Year after year, students, faculty, and even reporters, waited eagerly to see if and when Room Eight would show up again. For the next 16 years, Room Eight returned to the school. Sadly, he passed away in 1968. Following his death, an upright monument was placed over his grave in the Los Angeles Pet Memorial Park. Hundreds of students and faculty members from Elysian Heights Elementary School attended the beloved cat's funeral and burial.

Brevity Is a Virtue

In October 2007, Reverend Robert Shields of Dayton, Washington, passed away. He left behind 91 boxes filled with diary entries totaling some 37 million words—an introspective opus composed over a 25-year period. The journal included such earth-shattering entries as, "July 25, 1993, 7 A.M.: I cleaned out the tub and scraped my feet with my fingernails to remove layers of dead skin; 7:05 A.M.: Passed a large, firm stool, and a pint of urine. Used 5 sheets of paper."

Weird Hotels

*What makes a hotel weird? It isn't the ugly curtains, the funny
smell in the carpet, or the wagon-wheel coffee tables in the
lobby. To earn a spot on this list of unusual hotels, a hotel has
to be in a weird place, be made out of weird materials, or
otherwise completely embody a weird ethos.*

Icehotel, Jukkasjärvi, Sweden
At this hotel, guests sit on chairs made out of ice, drink from
ice cups, and sleep on ice beds. With an average indoor temperature of 23°Fahrenheit, it's just like any other hotel—only
much colder. Guests can book a night in one of the ice rooms
or ice-sculpture-filled suites, get married in the exquisite ice
chapel, and meet friends at the ice bar. But make your reser-
vation early—this hotel is only open from December through
April, when it melts, then it is rebuilt the next year.

Jules's Undersea Lodge, Key Largo, Florida
To enter this former research laboratory, guests must dive
21 feet under water to reach the entrance. Built five feet above
the ocean floor, this two-bedroom hotel has a view like no other
as guests are greeted by tropical fish peering in at them through
the windows. Guests can cook their own meals in the fully
stocked kitchen, have meals prepared by a "mer-chef," or even
enjoy a local pizza delivered by a diver. With plenty to do and
see, guests can remain underwater for days at a time.

Das Park Hotel, Linz, Austria
What would you pay to spend a night in a sewer pipe? Due to
the strange nature and limited amenities of this hotel, guests
are asked to "pay as you wish." Between May and October,

guests can stay in three bedrooms made from concrete drain-pipes and outfitted with double beds and electricity. For luxuries such as restrooms, restaurants, and showers, guests must use the facilities at the public park surrounding the hotel.

The Old Jail, Mount Gambier, Australia
This hotel/dorm/hostel operated as the South Australian State Prison from 1866 to 1995. Now, it offers cheap beds in a gorgeous landscape, complete with gun turrets and razor wire. Guests sleep tight behind bars in the original cells, shower in communal baths in the former women's cellblock, and can play soccer in the enclosed recreation yard.

Capsule Inn, Akihabara, Tokyo, Japan
Designed to be economical and space saving, the concept of the capsule hotel is catching on in Japan and other parts of the world. For approximately $40 per night, guests get an 18-square-foot metal cubby (3 feet wide, 3 feet tall, 6 feet long)—just big enough for a body to get in and lie down. The room comes with a mattress, a pillow, a TV, a radio, an alarm clock, lights, curtains, and a control panel similar to an airplane's, and everything is accessible from a prone position.

Dog Bark Park Inn, Cottonwood, Idaho
A bed-and-breakfast isn't complete without a friendly dog, but what about a B & B that *looks* like a dog? This hotel was created by chain saw artists whose carved wooden dogs are featured on the bedposts and in the gift shop. Up to four guests can sleep in Sweet Willy, currently the world's largest beagle at 30 feet tall, while the world's second largest beagle, Toby, (12 feet tall) looks on.

Woodlyn Park, Otorohanga, New Zealand
Would you rather sleep in a 1950s train car, 1950s cargo plane, World War II patrol boat, or the "world's first hobbit motel"? At Woodlyn Park, you can try them all out. Guests can also enjoy nearby glowworm caves or a Kiwi Culture show that includes sheep shearing, log sawing, and a dancing pig.

Harbour Crane Hotel, Harlingen, Netherlands
This one-room hotel sits on a dock overlooking the Wadden Sea. Used as a crane until 1996, guests can still slip into the cabin to control the crane itself for panoramic views of the harbor from more than 50 feet above ground. Two elevators take guests and (very small) bags to the former machine room, where a minibar, a plasma TV, a rooftop patio, ultramodern decor, and a two-person shower with a light show await.

Controversy Tram Hotel, Hoogwoud, Netherlands
The strange brainchild of Frank and Irma Appel, this hotel consists of two tram cars and a luxury train car. The two trams can sleep four couples and contain bathrooms and common rooms; the luxury train car also includes a whirlpool tub and can sleep four. A UFO-styled library floats nearby, overlooked by a MIG fighter jet. The hosts' house is built around a French van and a double-decker bus. Their pet donkeys sleep in the bus, but the cat prefers the roof of a Lamborghini.

Ariau Amazon Towers Hotel, Manaus, Brazil
This eco-resort is built entirely at the level of the rainforest canopy. With seven towers linked by more than four miles of catwalks, this treehouse hotel offers eye-level views of monkeys, birds, and sloths, while piranhas circle below. Although it might seem well suited to Tarzan's tastes, it promises a glimpse of the Amazon that is usually off-limits to tourists.

Wigwam Village Motel, Various Locations
Frank Redford built the first of several Wigwam Village motels in 1933 near popular tourist spot Mammoth Cave in Kentucky. Seven more were built in the southern and southwestern United States by the early 1950s. Each wigwam features a guest room that is naturally suited to the southwestern stretch of Route 66. The Holbrook, Arizona; Rialto, California; and Cave City, Kentucky, locations are still in business, with the marquee in front of the Holbrook location posing the question: "Have you slept in a wigwam lately?"

Fresno's Underground Gardens

Italians have always had a knack for ingenuity, and Baldassare Forestiere was no exception, handcrafting a complex network of underground gardens when he realized his plot of land couldn't grow wine grapes.

No Vino

In 1905, Baldassare Forestiere and his brother arrived in California's San Joaquin Valley. They had come to "the land of opportunity" to seek their fortune by growing fruit trees.

Unfortunately, the land they bought was a lemon—but not the kind you can harvest and sell. Instead of giving up after buying land that was totally unfit to grow much of anything, Forestiere combined his knowledge of farming with his fascination with Roman architecture and decided to go underground.

Dig It, Baby!

The cool cellarlike tunnels Forestiere dug provided naturally air-conditioned rooms to beat the oppressive Fresno heat. And with access to groundwater and enough sunlight, he figured he might actually be able to grow something underground.

Forestiere first built a home that provided shelter from Fresno's hot summers, and for the next 40 years, he kept on digging. Shovel by shovel, he and his brother carved their worthless farmland into a maze of underground caverns where their dreams of plant cultivation were realized.

By 1923, they had carved out more than ten acres of tunnels, rooms, patios, and grottos in the rocky soil—all by hand. They dug bed niches, bath alcoves, peepholes, stairways, grape arboretums, gardens, and holes that reached up through the bedrock so that trees growing beneath could get sunlight. Forestiere's underground home even had a parlor with a fireplace.

Visitors can still tour Forestiere's underground universe. The (under)grounds welcome visitors and are taken care of by Forestiere's relatives.

The Legend and Lore of Ohio's Most Haunted House

💀 💀 💀 💀 💀

Cleveland's Franklin Castle, a foreboding stone building, has earned the dubious distinction of being Ohio's most haunted house. Frightening tales have been told of doors flying off their hinges, light fixtures spinning on their own, ghostly babies crying, and a woman dressed in black peering from a window. But what could have caused this house to become so haunted?

Myths, Mysteries, and Murder at Franklin Castle

Truth and legend are easily confused at Franklin Castle. However, it is known that in 1866, a German immigrant named Hannes Tiedemann, his wife, Luise, and their children moved to the spot where the mansion would later be built.

In January 1881, the Tiedemanns' daughter Emma died, and shortly after, Hannes's elderly mother also passed away. Legend has it that within the next few years, the Tiedemanns lost three more children. In the face of such events, real or imagined, rumors began to spread that the family was cursed.

Possibly to distract his wife from the tragic family events, Tiedemann hired a renowned architectural firm to design a grand mansion for the family. He spared no expense and incorporated turrets, gargoyles, and steep gables into the design, adding to the four-story castle's gothic appearance. The 26-room mansion also included moving panels, concealed doors, hidden passageways, secret rooms, and five fireplaces.

When Luise died in 1895, rumors once again began to spread about the numerous unfortunate deaths in the Tiedemann family. A few years later, Hannes sold the castle to the Mullhauser family, who were in the brewing business. By the time Tiedemann died in 1908, his entire family was gone, and he was left without an heir.

Even with Tiedemann gone, stories and speculation about the man and strange events in his former home continued.

Rumors circulated that he had been an unfaithful husband and had illicit encounters within the vast mansion. Eventually, this speculation led to stories of murder. One grisly tale alleged that Hannes killed his niece by hanging her in a secret hallway connected to the castle's ballroom. Apparently, Tiedemann murdered the girl because he believed she was insane and he wanted to end her suffering.

According to legend, Hannes also killed a servant girl named Rachel after she rejected his advances. In another incarnation of the story, Rachel was actually Tiedemann's mistress, and she suffocated when he bound and gagged her after discovering her plan to marry someone else. Could it be that Rachel's spirit is the castle's "woman in black" who appears in the mansion's windows? Some past residents believe they've heard a woman choking in that part of the house. Others have even claimed to feel that they themselves were being choked while visiting the room.

The stories of murder and foul play in the house do not end with Tiedemann. In 1913, the Mullhauser family sold the house to the German Socialist Party, who used the house only for meetings and gatherings—or so they claimed. Legend has it that the new residents were actually German spies and that an underground group of Nazis executed a large group of people in one of the secret passageways. Whatever might have happened, the group sold the house in the late 1960s.

Perhaps the most gruesome secret uncovered in the house was in one of the hidden rooms, where, in the 1970s, the skeletons of a dozen babies were found. It was suggested that perhaps they were the victims of a doctor's botched experiments or even medical specimens, but no one knows for sure. A medical examiner was only able to determine that they were old bones.

The Haunted Castle

James Romano, along with his wife and children, moved into Franklin Castle in January 1968. On the day they moved in, the children came down from playing upstairs to ask if they could take a cookie to their new friend, a little girl who was crying. When Mrs. Romano accompanied the children upstairs, the sad little girl was gone. After this happened several times, the Romanos began to wonder if they were getting ghostly visits from the Tiedemann children.

While living in the house, Mrs. Romano also believed she heard footsteps moving through the hallways and organ music playing, despite the fact that there was no organ in the house. On the third floor, she heard voices and glasses clinking, even though she was alone in the house. Eventually, the Romanos consulted a priest about the strange events in their home. But the priest refused to perform an exorcism, stating that he felt an evil presence and that the family should move.

By 1974, fed up with their strange home, the Romanos sold the castle to Sam Muscatello who, after finding out about the mansion's ghoulish history, began providing guided tours. Some of his visitors reported hearing odd sounds and encountering the mysterious woman in black.

Interest in the house's checkered past caused Muscatello to begin looking for the hidden doors and passageways. During his search, he made a ghastly find when he discovered a skeleton hidden behind a panel in the tower room, where, according to legend, a bloody ax murder once took place. The Cleveland coroner's office examined the bones and judged that they belonged to someone who had been dead for a very long time. Muscatello was never able to convert the place into a successful tourist attraction, and he eventually sold it.

The End of the Haunting?

Franklin Castle was sold and resold several times until being purchased in April 1999. The interior of the house sustained damage in November of that year when a vagrant set fire to it. As of late 2007, restoration seems to be at a standstill. Has the alleged bloody past of the house left a ghostly mark on the building? Are the tragic events of days gone by being repeated in the present? Do the ghosts of yesterday still wander the corridors of this gothic house? We may never know for certain, but some claim that strange experiences still occur in the daunting mansion.

You Live Where???: Some Silly City Names

Angels Camp, California
Angel Fire, New Mexico
Bear, Delaware
Benevolence, Georgia
Black River, New York
Blue Earth, Minnesota
Boring, Maryland
Bread Loaf, Vermont
Bumble Bee, Arizona
Busti, New York
Buttermilk, Kansas
Buttzville, New Jersey
Cheddar, South Carolina
Chipmunk, New York
Church, Iowa
Climax, Georgia
Conception, Missouri
Convent, Louisiana
Deadman Crossing, Ohio
Devil Town, Ohio
Devils Den, California
Devil's Slide, Utah
Ding Dong, Texas
Energy, Illinois
Fanny, West Virginia
Frogtown, Virginia
Gold Hill, Nevada
Gray Mule, Texas
Gray Summit, Missouri
Green Pond, New Jersey
Half Hell, North Carolina
Hell, Michigan
Hooker, Oklahoma

Horneytown, North Carolina
Hot Coffee, Mississippi
Hygiene, Colorado
Intercourse, Pennsylvania
Jackass Flats, Nevada
Lizard Lick, North Carolina
Monkeys Eyebrow, Kentucky
Mosquitoville, Vermont
Nirvana, Michigan
Oatmeal, Texas
Ordinary, Virginia
Pie, West Virginia
Pray, Montana
Rainbow City, Alabama
Red Devil, Alaska
Sandwich, Massachusetts
Santa Claus, Indiana
Silver Creek, Washington
Spider, Kentucky
Success, Missouri
Suck-Egg Hollow, Tennessee
Tea, South Dakota
Ticktown, Virginia
Tightwad, Missouri
Toad Suck, Arkansas
Toast, North Carolina
Turkey Foot, Florida
Waterproof, Louisiana
White Marsh, Maryland
Why, Arizona
Vixen, Louisiana
Yellow Bluff, Alabama
Yum Yum, Tennessee

True Tales of Being Buried Alive

Generally, burial is something that happens after death.
Whether by accident, intent, or diabolical design, there are
some who settled down for a "dirt nap" a little prematurely.

David Blaine

On April 5, 1999, before an estimated crowd of 75,000 on
Manhattan's Upper West Side, magician David Blaine undertook his "Buried Alive" stunt, voluntarily going six feet under,
albeit with a small air tube. Placed inside a transparent plastic
coffin with a mere six inches of headroom and two inches on
either side, the illusionist was lowered into his burial pit. Next,
a three-ton water-filled tank was lowered on top of his tomb.
The magician ate nothing during his stunt and reportedly only
sipped two to three tablespoons of water per day—a fasting
schedule likely designed to keep bodily wastes to a minimum.
After seven days of self-entombment, Blaine popped out,
none the worse for wear. Many believed that the magician had
somehow left his tomb and returned only when it was time to
emerge. However, these naysayers couldn't explain why he'd
been visible the entire time and how witnesses saw him move
on a number of occasions. Blaine called it a "test of endurance
of…the human body and mind…." Even famous debunker
and fellow magic man James Randi praised him.

Barbara Jane Mackle

Could there be anything more horrifying than a forced burial?
Emory University student Barbara Jane Mackle suffered
through such an ordeal and miraculously lived to tell the tale.
Abducted from a motel room on December 17, 1968, the
20-year-old daughter of business mogul Robert Mackle was
whisked off to a remote location and buried under 18 inches
of earth. Her coffinlike box was sparsely equipped with food,
water, a pair of vent tubes, and a light. After receiving their

$500,000 ransom, the kidnappers informed the FBI of the girl's location. Some 80 hours after Mackle entered her underground prison, she was discovered in a wooded area roughly 20 miles northeast of Atlanta. Her light source had failed just a few hours after her burial, and she was severely dehydrated, but otherwise the young woman was in good condition. Both kidnappers were eventually apprehended.

School Bus Kidnapping and Live Burial

A notably bizarre burial occurred in 1976 when an entire school bus filled with children was hijacked in Chowchilla, California. The driver and 26 children were removed from the bus, placed into vans, and driven a hundred miles to a quarry in the town of Livermore. There they were forced into a moving van buried several feet below ground. Limited survival supplies and minimal air vents welcomed them into a pitch-black, claustrophobic hell. After 12 long hours, the students feverishly started looking for ways out. Fashioning a crude ladder out of old mattresses, the bus driver and a group of boys climbed to the top of the moving van where they had originally entered. Using a wooden beam, they were able to slowly pry off the heavy, metal lid that separated them from sweet freedom. After 16 hours below ground, they emerged. Despite their harrowing experience, all survived. A ransom note was eventually traced back to Frederick Woods, the quarry owner's son. He and accomplices Richard and James Schoenfeld were convicted and sentenced to life in prison.

Toltecs

The Toltecs, a pre-Columbian Native American people, practiced a ceremony called "Burial of the Warrior." During this rite of passage, a young man would enter a forest and bury himself in a shallow grave for a full day. In a modern-day incarnation of the ritualistic practice, people voluntarily go underground claiming that burial beneath Mother Earth is a way of returning to the womb. Breathing strategies and duration of burial are left unknown until the moment of truth.

Celebrity Haunts

It's not surprising that so many celebrity ghosts hang out near Hollywood. What other town could inspire such dreams and passions, highs and lows?

Marilyn Monroe

Hollywood's Roosevelt Hotel, home of the first ever Academy Awards in 1929, eternally hosts at least two celebrity spooks (along with a handful of other less famous specters). The ghostly reflection of silver-screen goddess Marilyn Monroe has often been seen in a wood-framed mirror that used to hang in the room where she frequently stayed. Today, visitors can simply visit the lower level, just outside the elevators, to get a glimpse of the mirror. Being a restless sort, Monroe's ghost has also been reported hovering near her tomb in the Westwood Memorial Cemetery and at San Diego's Hotel del Coronado.

Montgomery Clift

Marilyn Monroe isn't lonely at the Roosevelt. Her good friend, four-time Oscar nominee Montgomery Clift, has also never left the hotel that served as his home for more than three months in 1952 while filming *From Here to Eternity.* To commune with Clift, reserve Room 928, where he is said to leave the phone off the hook, pace the floor, and cause inexplicable loud noises. One guest even reported feeling an unseen hand tap her on the shoulder.

Rudolph Valentino

The ghost of romantic hero Rudolph Valentino has been spotted all over Hollywood, including near his tomb at the

Hollywood Forever Memorial Park, floating over the costume department at Paramount Studios, and at his former Beverly Hills mansion. Throughout the years, owners of his former home have reported seeing "The Sheik" roaming the hallways, hanging out in his former bedroom, and visiting the stables (now turned into private residences). Others report seeing his specter enjoying the view of Los Angeles from the second-floor windows of the main house.

Ozzie Nelson

Bandleader and television star Ozzie Nelson can't seem to leave the Hollywood Hills home he shared with Harriet, David, and Ricky for more than 25 years. Reports of Nelson's ghost started circulating in Tinseltown soon after Harriet sold the house in 1980. Subsequent residents of the house have reported seeing doors open and close by unseen hands and lights and faucets turning on and off by themselves. One female homeowner even reported that the ghost pulled down the bed covers and got amorous with her.

Orson Welles

One of Hollywood's most respected writers, actors, and directors, Orson Welles still reportedly spends time at his favorite Hollywood bakery. Known as a man with gourmet tastes, it's no wonder Welles's spirit lingers at Melrose Avenue's Sweet Lady Jane, legendary for their extraordinary desserts. Tales of Welles's apparition have circulated among staff and guests of the restaurant for years. Visions of him seated at his favorite table are often accompanied by the scent of his favorite cigar and brandy.

John Wayne

Drive down the coast about an hour or so from Los Angeles, and you'll come to Newport Beach, home of the *Wild Goose*. The vessel served as a minesweeper for the Canadian Navy during World War II before actor John Wayne purchased her in 1965 and converted her into a luxury yacht. The ship was said to be "Duke's" favorite possession, and he put her to good use during countless family vacations, star-studded parties, and poker sessions with buddies such as Dean Martin, Bob Hope, and Sammy Davis, Jr. Shortly after Wayne's death in 1979, new owners claimed to see a tall smiling man in various places on the yacht. Sightings of John Wayne's ghost on the *Wild Goose* have continued ever since. Those who want to try to see Duke's ghost for themselves can charter the *Wild Goose* for private events. But be prepared to bring your wallet—prices to charter the haunted boat start at $1,450 per hour.

Benjamin "Bugsy" Siegel

One ghost who can't seem to decide where to haunt is gangster Bugsy Siegel. Some stories claim that Siegel's ghost haunts the Beverly Hills home that once belonged to his girlfriend Virginia Hill, where he was gunned down in 1947. But the most prevalent Siegel sightings occur at the Flamingo Hotel in Las Vegas. Though the hotel has changed completely since Siegel opened it in the early 1940s, his ghost is said to still linger around the pool, as well as the statue and memorial to him in the hotel's gardens. Guests in the hotel's presidential suite have been sharing their lodgings with Siegel's spirit for years. He seems to favor spending time near the pool table when he's not in the bathroom.

Elvis Presley

Apparently, Elvis has NOT left the building, or so claim stagehands at the Las Vegas Hilton, formerly the International Hotel. Presley made his big comeback there and continued to draw sellout crowds in the hotel's showroom until his death in 1977. The most common place to spot the King's sequined jumpsuit-clad ghost is backstage near the elevators. Elvis is also known to haunt his Memphis home, Graceland.

Beware of Cries from the Bridge

Bridges provide us with a way to get from one place to another. But when that other place is the afterlife, a crybaby bridge is born. Located throughout the United States, crybaby bridges are said to mark locations where a baby died. And, according to legend, if you're brave enough to wait patiently on the bridge, you'll actually hear the baby cry. Here are some of the most popular crybaby bridges across the United States.

Middletown, New Jersey
Cooper Road is a lonely stretch of road that wanders through the backwoods of Middletown. Stay on this road long enough and you will eventually come to the crybaby bridge under which a baby is said to have drowned. If you want to hear the baby cry, just position your vehicle in the middle of the bridge and wait. But make sure you don't turn your car off or you won't be able to start it again.

Monmouth, Illinois
It's a case of "the more the scarier" for this crybaby bridge in western Illinois. According to legend, an entire busload of small children drove off the bridge when the driver lost control. It is said that if you go to the bridge at night, turn off your car's engine, and put your vehicle in neutral, you'll hear cries from the dead children. Shortly thereafter, ghostly hands will push your car across the bridge and back onto the road, leaving tiny handprints on the back of your car.

Concord, North Carolina
Just outside of Concord is a bridge on Poplar Tent Road that locals refer to as Sally's Bridge. According to local lore, a young

woman named Sally was driving home with her baby when she lost control of her car, skidded across the bridge, and crashed. The baby was ejected from the vehicle and fell into the water. Panic-stricken, Sally dove into the water to try to save her child, but sadly both mother and child drowned.

Today, legend has it that Sally's ghost will bang on your car, desperately trying to find someone to help save her dying child.

Upper Marlboro, Maryland

The story associated with this crybaby bridge says that a young, single woman became pregnant. Embarrassed and afraid of being disowned, she somehow managed to conceal her pregnancy from her family and friends. When the baby was born, the woman waited until nightfall, walked out to the bridge, then threw the baby from the bridge into the water below. Legend has it that if you go out to the bridge at night, you'll hear the baby crying.

Cable, Ohio

Far and away, Ohio harbors the most crybaby bridges, each with its own unique spin on the classic crybaby bridge story. For example, legend has it that on a cold November night in the tiny town of Cable, a deeply depressed woman bundled up her newborn baby and walked onto a bridge that crossed over some railroad tracks. She waited patiently until she heard the sound of a distant train whistle. With the baby still in her arms, the woman jumped in front of the oncoming train just as it reached the bridge. Both were killed instantly.

If you visit this bridge, be forewarned—especially when it's close to midnight. Unlucky travelers crossing the bridge at that time have reported that their cars suddenly stalled. When they tried to restart the engines, they heard the sound of a distant train whistle, which seemed to signal the start of a bizarre and ghostly flashback. As the whistle got closer, motorists reported hearing a baby crying. Then, just when it sounded as though the train was right next to the bridge, they heard a woman scream...and then everything went silent. Only then were they able to start their cars again.

Enrico Caruso:
The Superstitious Songster

☠ ☠ ☠ ☠ ☠

One of the most famous tenors of all time, Italian opera singer Enrico Caruso played many unusual roles in his day, but none were as eccentric as Caruso himself.

Details of Caruso's birth in Naples on February 25, 1873, vary widely, but sources say he was the 18th of 21 children in a family that included 19 brothers and one lone sister; most of his siblings died in infancy. Because his mother was too ill, Enrico was nursed by Signora Rosa Baretti. He believed her milk caused him to be different from the rest of his family.

The Caruso family was quite poor—Enrico's father was a mechanic and he encouraged his son to become one as well. Instead, Enrico began singing in churches and cafés at age 16 to help support himself and his family. It may have been his impoverished youth or his need for order that led to his habit of obsessively recording even the most minor purchases in carefully tended books. And yet Caruso was extremely generous, dispensing handouts to almost everyone who asked. He also saved every newspaper clipping about his performances in large scrapbooks.

Caruso moved to the United States after making a big splash at New York's Metropolitan Opera in *Rigoletto* in 1903. Later, while touring with the Met, he found himself smack in the middle of the 1906 San Francisco earthquake. Although he escaped unscathed, the experience incited him to vow never to return. Upon his departure from the city, he is famously known to have shouted, "Give me Vesuvius!" (the explosive volcano of his native Italy that had erupted two weeks earlier).

The Weird Tenor's Tenets
Caruso regulated his life with a rigid set of curious and unexplained superstitions. In her account of Caruso's life, his wife, Dorothy Park Benjamin, revealed that he considered it bad luck to wear a new suit on a Friday, and he shunned the

phrase, "Good luck!" for fear it would produce the opposite effect. For reasons unknown, he also refused to start any new undertakings on either a Tuesday or a Friday.

Like many artistic geniuses, he was germ-phobic and bathed twice daily, often changing all of his clothes many times a day. As might be expected, some of Caruso's strongest and most peculiar beliefs were related to his magnificent voice. Before going on stage, he performed the following ritual:

1. Smoked a cigarette in a holder so as not to dirty his hands

2. Gargled with salt water to clean his throat

3. Sniffed a small amount of snuff

4. Sipped a cup of water

5. Ate precisely one quarter of an apple

6. Asked his deceased mother to help him sing

Caruso also believed he could enhance his vocal prowess by wearing anchovies around his neck and smoking two packs of cigarettes a day.

The Final Crazy Curtain

Enrico Caruso died in 1921 from complications of bronchial pneumonia. After his death, the Naples Museum in Italy claimed he had left them his throat for examination, and newspapers in Rome printed a diagram of what was supposedly the singer's internal sound system. According to *The New York Times*, doctors said Caruso had vocal cords twice as long as normal, a supersized epiglottis, and the lung power of a "superman." But the *Times* also printed his wife's denial that any organs had been removed from her husband.

Despite the strange circumstances of his life, Caruso left an almost superhuman legacy to the world of music. With nearly 500 recordings of his stupendous voice, he remains one of the top-selling artists of record company RCA more than 80 years after his death.

Unexplained Phenomena

If a phenomenon can't be readily explained, does that make it any less true to those who witnessed it?

The Philadelphia Experiment

The Philadelphia Experiment (aka Project Rainbow) is one for the "too strange not to be true" file. Allegedly, on October 28, 1943, a supersecret experiment was being conducted at the Philadelphia Naval Shipyard. Its objective? To make the USS *Eldridge* and all of its inhabitants disappear! That day, some reported that the *Eldridge* became almost entirely invisible amidst a flash of blue light. Inexplicably, it had not only vanished but also tele-transported—at the same instant, it was witnessed some 375 miles away at the U.S. Naval Base in Norfolk, Virginia. Legend has it that most sailors involved in the experiment became violently ill afterward. They were the lucky ones. Others were supposedly fused to the ship's deck or completely vaporized and were never seen again. Justifiably horrified by these results, the navy is said to have pulled the plug on future experiments and employed brainwashing techniques to help the affected seamen forget what happened.

Moodus Noises

The Moodus Noises are thunderlike sounds that emanate from caves near East Haddam, Connecticut, where the Salmon and Moodus Rivers meet. The name itself is derived from the Native American word *machemoodus,* which means "place of noises." When European settlers filtered into the area in the late 1600s, the Wangunk tribe warned them about the odd, supernatural sounds. Whether or not anything otherworldly exists there is open to debate. In 1979, seismologists showed that the noises were always accompanied by small earthquakes (some measuring as low as magnitude 2 on the Richter scale) spread over a small area some 5,000 feet deep by 800 feet wide. But this doesn't explain the fact that no known faultline exists at Moodus. Nor does it describe how small tremors—producing 100 times less ground motion than is detectable by human beings—can generate big, bellowing booms. The mystery and the booms continue.

Rock Concert

Visitors looking to entertain themselves at Pennsylvania's Ringing Rocks Park often show up toting hammers. Seems odd, but they're necessary for the proper tone. Ringing Rocks is a seven-acre boulder field that runs about ten feet deep. For reasons that are still unexplained, some of these rocks ring like bells when struck lightly by a hammer or other object. Because igneous diabase rocks don't usually do this, the boulder field has caused quite a stir through the years. In 1890, Dr. J. J. Ott held what may have been the world's first "rock concert" at the park. He assembled rocks of different pitches, enlisted the aid of a brass band for accompaniment, and went to town.

Cry Me a Red River

Tales of "crying" statues have become almost commonplace. Sometimes they're revealed as hoaxes, but other times they can truly confound the senses. The Mother Mary statue that cries "tears of blood" at the Vietnamese Catholic Martyrs Church in Sacramento apparently began crying in November 2005 when parishioners discovered a dark reddish substance flowing from her left eye. A priest wiped it away only to see it miraculously reappear a moment later. News of the incident spread like…well, like news of a crying Mother Mary statue. Soon, hordes of the faithful made a pilgrimage to witness the miracle. Skeptics say that black paint used as eyeliner on the statue is the true culprit and that her "tears" are closer to this color than red. The faithful think the nonbelievers are blinded by anything but the light because the tears continually reappear even after the excess substance is wiped away.

Lingering Spirits of the *Eastland* Disaster

The city of Chicago has a dark history of disaster and death, with devastating fires, horrific accidents, and catastrophic events. One of the most tragic took place on July 24, 1915. On that overcast, summer afternoon, hundreds of people died in the Chicago River when the Eastland *capsized just a few feet from the dock. This calamity left a ghostly impression on the Windy City that is still felt today.*

Company Picnic Turns Tragic

July 24 was going to be a special day for thousands of Chicagoans. It was reserved for the annual summer picnic for employees of the Western Electric Company, which was to be held across Lake Michigan in Michigan City, Indiana. And although officials at the utility company had encouraged workers to bring along friends and relatives, they were surprised when more than 7,000 people arrived to be ferried across the lake on the five excursion boats chartered for the day. Three of the steamers—the *Theodore Roosevelt,* the *Petoskey,* and the *Eastland*—were docked on the Chicago River near Clark Street.

On this fateful morning, the *Eastland,* a steamer owned by the St. Joseph–Chicago Steamship Company, was filled to its limit. The boat had a reputation for top-heaviness and instability, and the new federal Seaman's Act, which was passed in 1915 as a result of the RMS *Titanic* disaster, required more lifeboats than previous regulations did. All of this resulted in the ship being even more unstable than it already was. In essence, it was a recipe for disaster.

Death and the *Eastland*

As passengers boarded the *Eastland,* she began listing back and forth. This had happened on the ship before, so the crew emptied the ballast compartments to provide more stability. As the boat was preparing to depart, some passengers went below

deck, hoping to warm up on the cool, cloudy morning, but many on the overcrowded steamer jammed their way onto the deck to wave to onlookers on shore. The *Eastland* tilted once again, but this time more severely, and passengers began to panic. Moments later, the *Eastland* rolled to her side, coming to rest at the bottom of the river, only 18 feet below the surface. One side of the boat's hull was actually above the water's surface in some spots.

Passengers on deck were tossed into the river, splashing about in a mass of bodies. The overturned ship created a current that pulled some of the floundering swimmers to their doom, while many of the women's long dresses were snagged on the ship, tugging them down to the bottom.

Those inside were thrown to one side of the ship when it capsized. The heavy furniture onboard crushed some passengers, and those who were not killed instantly drowned a few moments later when water rushed inside. A few managed to escape, but most of them didn't. Their bodies were later found trapped in a tangled heap on the lowest side of the *Eastland.*

Firefighters, rescue workers, and volunteers soon arrived and tried to help people escape through portholes. They also cut holes in the portion of the ship's hull that was above the water line. Approximately 1,660 passengers survived the disaster, but they still ended up in the river, and many courageous people from the wharf jumped in or threw life preservers as well as lines, boxes, and anything that floated into the water to the panicked and drowning passengers.

In the end, 844 people died, many of them young women and children. Officially, no clear explanation was given for why the vessel capsized, and the St. Joseph–Chicago Steamship Company was not held accountable for the disaster.

The bodies of those who perished in the tragedy were wrapped in sheets and placed on the *Theodore Roosevelt* or lined up along the docks. Marshall Field's and other large stores sent wagons to carry the dead to hospitals, funeral homes, and makeshift morgues, such as the Second Regiment Armory, where more than 200 bodies were sent.

After the ship was removed from the river, it was sold and later became a U.S. warship as the gunboat U.S.S. *Wilmette*. The ship never saw any action but was used as a training ship during World War II. After the war, it was decommissioned and eventually scrapped in 1947.

The *Eastland* may be gone, but its story and ghosts continue to linger nearly a century later.

Hauntings at Harpo Studios

At the time of the *Eastland* disaster, the only public building large enough to be used as a temporary morgue was the Second Regiment Armory, located on Chicago's near west side. The dead were laid out on the floor of the armory and assigned identification numbers. Chicagoans whose loved ones had perished in the disaster filed through the rows of bodies, searching for familiar faces, but in 22 cases, there was no one left to identify them. Those families were completely wiped out. The names of these victims were learned from neighbors who came searching for their friends. The weeping, crying, and moaning of the bereaved echoed off the walls of the armory for days.

The last body to be identified was Willie Novotny, a seven-year-old boy whose parents and older sister had also perished on the *Eastland*. When extended family members identified the boy nearly a week after the disaster took place, a chapter was closed on one of Chicago's most horrific events.

As years passed, the armory building went through several incarnations, including a stable and a bowling alley, before Harpo Studios, the production company owned by talk-show maven Oprah Winfrey, purchased it. A number of *The Oprah Show*'s staff members, security guards, and maintenance workers claim that the studio is haunted by the spirits of those who tragically lost their lives on the *Eastland.* Many employees have experienced unexplained phenomena, including the sighting of a woman in a long gray dress who walks the corridors and then mysteriously vanishes into the wall. Some believe she is the spirit of a mourner who came to the armory looking for her family and left a bit of herself behind at a place where she felt her greatest sense of loss.

The woman in gray may not be alone in her spectral travels through the old armory. Staff members have also witnessed doors opening and closing on their own and heard people sobbing, whispering, and moaning, as well as phantom footsteps on the lobby's staircase. Those who have experienced these strange events believe that the tragedy of yesterday is still manifesting itself in the old armory building's present state.

Chicago River Ghosts

In the same way that the former armory seems to have been impressed with a ghostly recording of past events, the Chicago River seems haunted, too. For years, people walking on the Clark Street bridge have heard crying, moaning, and pleas for help coming from the river. Some have even witnessed the apparitions of victims helplessly splashing in the water. On several occasions, some witnesses have called the police for help. One man even jumped into the river to save what he thought was an actual person drowning. When he returned to the surface, he discovered that he was in the water alone. He had no explanation for what he'd seen, other than to admit that it might have been a ghost.

So it seems that the horror of the *Eastland* disaster has left an imprint on this spot and continues to replay itself over and over again, ensuring that the unfortunate victims from the *Eastland* will never truly be forgotten.

A Feast for the Fearless: The World's Most Revolting Foods

Turning our attention briefly to some of the most curious delicacies of the world, from maggot-infested cheese to mouse-flavored liquor, we present the following culinary adventures.

Baby Mice Wine

Those brave men and women who enjoy eating the worm from the bottom of a tequila bottle and want to advance to spirit-soaked vertebrates might be interested in baby mice wine, which is made by preserving newborn mice in a bottle of rice wine. This traditional health tonic from Korea and China is said to aid the rejuvenation of one's vital organs. Anecdotal evidence, however, suggests that the sight of dead baby mice floating helplessly in liquor is more likely to break your heart than rejuvenate it.

Balut

Balut are eaten in the Philippines, Cambodia, Vietnam, and China. They are duck eggs that have been incubated for 15 to 20 days (a duckling takes 28 days to hatch) and then boiled. The egg is then consumed—both the runny yolk and the beaky, feathery, and veiny duck fetus. Balut are usually sold on the streets for the equivalent of about 25 cents each; one can have them with coarse salt or vinegar, or just plain. Those who are trying balut for the first time are strongly advised to keep their eyes tightly closed.

Casu Marzu

The Sardinian delicacy *casu marzu* is a hard sheep's milk cheese infested with *Piophila casei*, the "cheese fly." The larvae eat the cheese and release an enzyme that triggers a fermentation process, causing their abode to putrefy. The cheese is not considered true casu marzu until it becomes a caustic, viscous gluey mass that burns your mouth and wriggles on your tongue when you eat it. *Nota bene*: The cheese fly is also called "the cheese skipper," because its larvae have the amazing ability to leap up to six inches in the air when disturbed. Since the larvae rightfully consider it disturbing to be eaten, it is suggested that consumers of casu marzu make use of protective eye gear during the repast.

Cobra Heart

This Vietnamese delicacy delivers precisely what it promises: a beating cobra heart, sometimes accompanied by a cobra kidney and chased by a slug of cobra blood. Preparations involve a large blade and a live cobra. If you find yourself in the uncomfortable situation where the snake has already been served but you feel your courage failing, ask for a glass of rice wine and drop the heart into it. Bottoms up!

Escamoles

Escamoles are the eggs, or larvae, of the giant venomous black *Liometopum* ant. This savory Mexican chow, which supposedly has the consistency of cottage cheese and a surprisingly buttery and nutty flavor, can be found both in rural markets and in multi-star restaurants in Mexico City. A popular way to eat escamoles is in a taco with a dollop of guacamole, but it is said that they are also quite delicious fried with black butter or with onions and garlic.

Hákarl

Hákarl, an Icelandic dish dating back to the Vikings, is putrefied shark meat. Traditionally, it has been prepared by burying a side of shark in gravel for three months or more; nowadays, it might be boiled in several changes of water or soaked in a large vat filled with brine and then cured in the open air for two months. This is done to purge the shark meat of urine and trimethylamine oxide. Sharks have an extra concentration of both to maintain essential body fluid levels, but the combination makes the meat toxic. Since rancid shark meat is not considered all that tasty, native wisdom prescribes washing it down with a hearty dose of liquor.

Lutefisk

If the idea of rotten shark meat does not appeal, consider lutefisk, or "lye fish"—possibly the furthest from rotten that food can get. This traditional Scandinavian dish is made by steeping pieces of cod in lye solution. The result is translucent and gelatinous, stinks to the high heavens, and corrodes metal kitchenware. Enjoy it covered with pork drippings, white sauce, or melted butter, with potatoes and Norwegian flatbread on the side. (As a side note: The annual lutefisk-eating contest in Madison, Minnesota, is scheduled right before an event called the Outhouse Race. This might not be entirely a coincidence.)

Pacha

This dish can be found everywhere sheep can be found, especially in the Middle East. To put it simply, *pacha,* which is the Iraqi name for it, is a sheep's head stewed, boiled, or otherwise slow-cooked for five to six hours together with the sheep's intestines, stomach, and feet. Other meats might also be added to the broth. Something to keep in mind: If you are served this dish in Turkmenistan, where it is called *kelle-bashayak,* this means two things—one, you're the guest of honor at the gathering, and two, you will be expected to help consume the head or else risk offending the hosts.

Spiders

Spiders are popular fare in parts of Cambodia, especially in the town of Skuon; however, they are not part of the traditional cuisine and were not widely eaten until the horror years of the bloody Khmer Rouge regime in the late 1970s, when food became scarce. After the country was rebuilt, the villagers' taste for spiders did not recede entirely. Today, tarantulas are sold on the streets for about ten cents per spider and are said to be very good fried with salt, pepper, and garlic.

Every minute, a human's skin sheds 50,000 cells.

New Uses for Cold War Relics

In response to the Cold War, the U.S. government began constructing secret nuclear missile complexes throughout the country. Each one housed a fully operational, locked-and-loaded nuclear missile that could be fired at will once the launch sequence was activated. But as the Cold War ended, the complexes were no longer needed. And by 1965, most of them were abandoned, leading to an interesting question: Just what does one do with a multimillion-dollar abandoned missile silo? More than you might think!

School's a Blast!

In 1969, the Holton, Kansas, school district paid $1 million to the federal government for land that had housed a nuclear missile base until 1964. As ground broke on the Jackson Heights High School, many wondered what would be done with the abandoned silo. The answer was simple: Incorporate it into the school. And that's exactly what they did. They turned the silo's command center into a classroom, then they sealed off the missile bay doors and turned the bay into a bus garage.

The Ultimate Bachelor (Launch) Pad

Late one night in 1985, Bruce Townsley was watching *The Tonight Show* as Johnny Carson talked about people turning old missile silos into homes. From that point on, Townsley was obsessed. His dream finally came true in 1997, when he moved from Chicago to Oplin, Texas, and bought his very own silo.

Townsley has spent years working on the silo, which was originally one of several missile bases operated by Dyess Air Force Base. However, he still hasn't figured out what to do with the 185-foot-deep chamber that used to house the missile.

Nuclear Scuba

Because the silos were made to launch missiles, you might assume that visitors to one would spend their time looking up into the sky. Not so in Midland, Texas, where a silo has been converted into the world's largest indoor deep-diving training facility. Dive Valhalla, now part of Family Scuba Center, is an old ICBM (intercontinental ballistic missile) silo filled with water up to ground level. Divers gear up in the silo's old control room before moving on to where the missile was housed. From there, divers enter the water, where they can descend to depths of more than 120 feet, exploring the old silo as they go.

Titan Missile Museum

Because old missile silos have quite an allure, you don't need to do much to attract people to them. Case in point: the Titan Missile Museum in Sahuarita, Arizona. Declared a national historic landmark in 1994, the museum represents the only Titan II missile site in the United States that is open to the general public. Most of the silo has been preserved just as it was when it was operational in the 1960s, from the three-ton blast doors to the 103-foot Titan II ICBM in the launch duct. (Don't worry—the active warhead has been removed!) If you're looking to get a taste of doomsday, tours offer visitors the chance to sit through a simulated missile-launch sequence.

A Safe Place to Park Your Plane

If you're looking for a spacious silo to call your own, head to the Adirondack State Park in upstate New York, where in 2007 "the world's most unique luxury home" went on the market. Above ground, you'll get 2,000 square feet of living space, complete with a master suite and fireplace. If you'd like to spread out, just follow the 125-foot stairwell down to the silo and the launch control center, which offers an additional 2,300 square feet of luxurious living space, including marble floors and a whirlpool. If all of that isn't enough of a selling point, consider this: The silo/house even comes with its own private FAA/DOT-approved runway!

Conjuring Up Spirits

Can someone believe in a ghost so much that one actually appears? A 1972 study in Toronto, Canada, suggests just that.

Eight people invented a ghost named Philip and met weekly in Toronto to make contact with him via séance. None of the group members claimed to have had any previous psychic experience. They simply wanted to see what would happen if they created a ghost and then summoned him.

The group made up a whole story about Philip: He was a wealthy British aristocrat living in the mid-1600s, who supported the king of England during the English Civil War. But when his beloved mistress, Margo, was convicted of witchcraft and burned at the stake, Philip committed suicide. It was a romantic story that included real locations and events, but Philip, his wife, and his mistress were entirely fictional.

When it came time for the group to put its theory to the test, members took turns acting as a medium to contact Philip. But after a full year, nothing had happened.

The Imaginary Ghost Speaks

After many failed attempts at otherworldly contact, the group reviewed a 1960 study conducted by several paranormal researchers, who supposedly made a table weighing nearly 40 pounds rise from the floor—without touching it.

Inspired by the 1960 group, the Toronto group modified its approach. Instead of sitting quietly around a table in dim lighting, they talked normally and used regular light levels, and within three or four meetings, Philip began to manifest. First, he vibrated the table gently, then he rapped on the table loud enough for everyone to hear it.

Using table raps—one for yes and two for no—the group learned to communicate with Philip. They learned more about Philip by asking him questions, and soon the eerie phenomena increased. The table began to slide around the floor during part of each session, and sometimes the table creaked loudly. At other times, lights flickered in response to questions.

The Dancing Table
In later meetings, the Toronto group reportedly used a new, sturdier table that was made entirely of wood, and it behaved even more strangely. At first, the table made rapping noises and slid gently around the room. Then, it rose and stood on one leg. It danced across the room, and at other times, it chased group members. When a new guest arrived, the table would rush over as if to greet the person.

This continued for months. In November 1973, both the ghostly Philip and the table continued to produce phenomena, even while being filmed by the Canadian Broadcasting Company for a talk show. This was followed by a January 1974 documentary, *Philip, The Imaginary Ghost.* On a TV show soon afterward, the table rocked back and forth and climbed three stairs, one at a time. The studio audience gasped in amazement as cameras filmed the strange event.

Beyond Philip
Following the success of the Philip experiment, the Toronto group started a second study with a newly invented ghost named Lilith. As with the first experiment, the group made up a story about Lilith, a fictional woman who, as a member of the French Resistance during World War II, had been captured and shot as a spy.

Lilith also manifested as Philip had. Like Philip, when she told her story during séances, every detail matched the group's made-up tale. The group concluded that "inventing" a ghost is a learned skill, and any group can repeat this experiment.

Later studies, including the Skippy Experiment in Sydney, Australia, and the research of Dr. Michael A. Persinger of Canada's Laurentian University, have demonstrated that ghosts—or the appearance of ghostly phenomena—can be created simply by believing. So, if you believe in ghosts—or want to—be careful what you wish for. You just might have a terrifying encounter with "the other side."

The Boneyard:
Where Military Aircraft Go to Die

💀   💀   💀   💀   💀

Many call it "The Boneyard," but Davis–Monthan Air Force Base in Tucson, Arizona, could be called "The Aerospace Hospice" or "Aerospace Death Row." The U.S. Air Force's 309th Aerospace Maintenance and Regeneration Center (AMARC) handles aircraft retired from active service. A few will fly again; most will not. Either way, "The Boneyard" is a surreal place.

Why Tucson?

Let's suppose that you need somewhere to stash hundreds of old warplanes long enough to find a use for them. Maybe a Third World dictator or a parts dealer will come shopping; perhaps a tech zillionaire always wanted his own jet fighter. Rain or humidity would mean corrosion, which is no good. And unless you want to pour thousands of acres of pavement, you'll need dry, compact soil. Otherwise, the heavy bombers and stratotankers would sink into the earth. And you'd look incompetent if the Tanzania People's Defence Force bought some used fighter planes and you had to tell them that they could have them as soon as they shoveled them out of the mud.

So, what's your best option? A blistering hot desert no one else wants. The Army Air Corps searched for such a spot after World War II, and they settled on Tucson.

What Lives There?

What sleeps at "The Boneyard" has a value of many billions of dollars—probably equal to several years of defense budgets adjusted for inflation. In fact, Davis–Monthan pastures most of the U.S. military's retired aircraft from the last 50 years.

For example, you could find enough F-4 Phantom fighters to equip an air force, enough F-14s to shoot down that air force, and enough A-4 Skyhawks to wipe out the air force on the ground. Add to that enough naval strike and anti-sub aircraft to outfit several aircraft carriers and sink a main battle fleet, and enough KC-135 aerial tankers to refuel them all in flight. Other treasures include an old NASA "Vomit Comet" astronaut training plane; artifacts such as B-57 Canberras and B-58 Hustlers, remembered only by aircraft geeks and the air force itself; and Death Row— dozens of B-52 intercontinental bombers scrapped, or awaiting scrapping, by a huge guillotine.

Airplane Guillotine and Ghost Planes

When U.S. warplanes leave active service or Uncle Sam promises other countries that he'll destroy their airplanes, pilots fly them to Davis– Monthan and land them in the desert where crews render them inoperative or dismember them using a huge mobile guillotine with a six-ton blade. For the B-52 fleet (being destroyed in compliance with the 1991 Strategic Arms Reduction Treaty, better known as START I), that means slicing off each bomber's wings, nose, and tail. The wreckage lies there so the Russians can verify the destruction by satellite photo.

Another Davis–Monthan oddity is the ghost A-10s. Perhaps to deceive against possible enemy attacks, on one runway, the Air Force has painted several A-10 shapes visible from the air.

Diamonds in the Rough

"The Boneyard" really shines when someone needs spare parts. Salvaging engine guts from old aircraft is cheaper than ordering new ones from Boeing, so the AMARC crew extracts the necessary parts and sends them where they're needed.

There are other U.S. aircraft graveyards, mainly in the Southwest, but Davis–Monthan is the largest and most interesting for one reason: If all the aircraft at AMARC took to the air with trained pilots, they could easily whip the vast majority of the world's air forces.

The Year Without a Summer

"The Year Without a Summer" may sound like Armegeddon, but these words describe an actual year in human history—the year 1816, which Americans nicknamed "eighteen-hundred-and-froze-to-death." It was a year of floods, droughts, and unparalleled summertime frosts that destroyed crops, spread diseases, incited riots, and otherwise wrought havoc upon the world. The culprit of this global meteorological mayhem was the eruption of Tambora, a volcano on the Indonesian island of Sumbawa—the largest explosive eruption in recorded history.

Monster Eruption

Tambora was considered inactive until 1812, when a dense cloud of smoke was seen rising above its summit. But neither the smoke, which grew denser and denser over the next three years, nor the occasional rumbles heard from the mountain, could prepare the islanders for what was to come.

When Tambora exploded in April 1815, the blast was heard 1,700 miles away and so much ash was ejected into the atmosphere that islands 250 miles away experienced complete darkness. Only a couple thousand of the island's 12,000 inhabitants survived the fiery three-day cataclysm. Altogether, the eruption and its after-effects killed more than 90,000 people throughout Indonesia, mostly through disease, pollution of drinking water, and famine. Ash rains destroyed crops on every island within hundreds of miles.

Global Cooling

Along with about 140 gigatons of magma, Tambora expelled hundreds of millions of tons of fine ash, which was spread worldwide through winds and weather systems. It is this ash that scientists now blame for the subsequent "Year Without a Summer." The sulfate aerosol particles contained in it remained in the atmosphere for years and reflected back solar radiation, cooling the globe. The effect was aggravated by the activity of other volcanoes: Soufrière St. Vincent in the West Indies (1812), Mount Mayon in the Philippines (1814), and Suwanose–Jima in Japan, which erupted continuously from 1813 to 1814. To make matters worse, all this took place during an extended period of low solar energy output called the Dalton Minimum, which lasted from about 1795 to the 1820s.

Spring of 1816 in the New World

Although the last three months of 1815 and February 1816 were all warmer than usual, the mild winter hesitated to turn into spring. Under the influence of the hot ash winds from the equator, the low-pressure system usually sitting over Iceland at this time of year shifted south toward the British Isles, and America was penetrated by polar air masses. By March, weather was becoming erratic.

On Sunday, March 17, Richmond, Virginia, was treated to summerlike temperatures; however, the next day, there was hail and sleet, and on Tuesday morning, the flowers of apricot and peach trees were covered with icicles. At the end of May, there were still frosts and snowfall from Ohio to Connecticut.

June 1816

The first days of June were deceptively warm, with 70s, 80s, and even low 90s in the northeastern United States. But on June 6, temperatures suddenly dropped into the 40s and it began to rain. Within hours, rain turned into snow, birds dropped dead in the streets, and some trees began shedding their still unexpanded leaves. This distemper of nature continued through June 11, when the wind shifted and the cold spell was over…or so people thought.

But strange weather continued to vex the population. Gales and violent hailstorms pummeled crops. On June 27, West Chester, Pennsylvania, reportedly experienced a torrential storm where hailstones the size of walnuts fell from the sky.

July 1816

Just as the farmers were beginning to think that the damage to their crops might be minimal, another cold spell checked their hopes. On July 6, a strong northwestern wind set in, and for the next four days, winter descended upon New England and the Mid-Atlantic states once more as temperatures again dropped to the 30s and 40s. The outlook for a successful harvest was looking bleaker day by freezing day; what vegetation remained intact in New England was flavorless and languid.

August 1816

The folk wisdom that bad things come in threes proved itself before the end of the summer. On August 20, another wave of frost and snow finished off the fruit, vegetables, vines, and meager remains of the corn and bean crops. The fields were said to be "as empty and white as October." For many farmers, that spelled ruin. Even though wheat and rye yielded enough to carry the country through to the next season without mass starvation, panic and speculation drove the price of flour from $3 to nearly $20 per barrel. Animal feed became so expensive that cattle had to be slaughtered en masse. Many New England farmers, unable to cope with the disastrous season, loaded up their belongings and headed west.

Summer Overseas

Meanwhile, Europe was faring no better. Snow fell in several countries in June. Alpine glaciers advanced, threatening to engulf villages and dam rivers. In France, grapes were not ripe enough to be harvested until November, and the wine made from them was undrinkable. Wheat yields in Europe reportedly fell by 20 to 40 percent, both because of cold and water damage and because rains delayed and hampered harvesting.

Famine hit Switzerland especially hard. People began eating moss, sorrel, and cats, and official assistance had to be given to the populace to help them distinguish poisonous and nonpoisonous plants. In Rhineland, people reportedly dug through the fields for rotten remains of the previous year's potato harvest. Wheat, oats, and potatoes failed in Britain and Ireland, and a typhus epidemic swept the British Isles, killing tens of thousands. Grain prices doubled on average; in west-central Europe, they rose between three and seven times their normal price. This was a disaster for the masses of poor people, whose average expenditures for bread totaled between one-quarter and one-half of their total income.

Dearth led to hunger, and high prices led to increased poverty, which led to mass vagrancy and begging. People looted grain storages and pillaged large farms. There was a wave of emigrations to America. The European economy was still unsteady from the aftermath of the Napoleonic wars, and the crisis of 1816 led to a massive retreat from liberal ideas. By 1820, Europe was in the grip of political and economic conservatism—thanks in no small part to a volcanic eruption in Indonesia.

Who's to Blame?
Theories for why summer failed to come in 1816 abound. Many lay the blame directly on the sun. Due to volcanic particles in the air, the solar disk had been dimmed all year, which made large sunspots visible to the naked eye. Others believed that the ice persisting in the Atlantic and the Great Lakes was absorbing great quantities of heat from the atmosphere.

Silver Lining
In 1816, Geneva, Switzerland, had experienced the coldest summer it would face between 1753 and 1960. It was this bad weather that kept Mary Wollstonecraft Godwin, Percy Shelley, and Lord Byron indoors at the Villa Diodati on the shores of Lake Geneva in June 1816. As they listened to the wind howl and watched the awesome thunderstorms rage over the lake, they recited poetry and told each other ghost stories, which they vowed to record on paper.

His mood very much under the weather, Byron penned his lengthy poem *Darkness,* a vivid imagination of the Apocalypse, which the weather made seem altogether at hand. ("Morn came and went, and came, and brought no day....") And Mary Wollstonecraft Godwin, who would later become Mary Shelley, Percy's wife, began work on a masterpiece that would eventually bear the title *Frankenstein or the Modern Prometheus.*

Wacky Jelly Belly Flavors

There was a time when root beer was considered an exotic flavor for a jelly bean. With locations based in California and southern Wisconsin, the Jelly Belly candy makers have raised the bar for strange flavors, especially with some of their most recent selections.

- Pickle
- Black Pepper
- Booger
- Dirt
- Earthworm
- Earwax
- Sausage
- Rotten Egg
- Soap
- Vomit
- Sardine
- Grass
- Skunk Spray
- Bacon
- Baby Wipes

- Pencil Shavings
- Toothpaste
- Moldy Cheese
- Buttered Popcorn
- Dr. Pepper
- Jalapeño
- Margarita
- Spinach
- Cappuccino
- Peanut Butter
- Café Latte
- 7UP
- Pomegranate
- Baked Beans

Bonnie and Clyde's Final Showdown

From the time Bonnie Parker met Clyde Barrow back in 1930, it seemed as though they were always running from the law. At first, the press and general public had looked upon this unlikely couple with something resembling starstruck eyes. True, they were outlaws. But they were also desperately in love with each other, which made for a rather twisted romantic tale.

But in January 1934, Clyde made a fatal mistake while carrying out what he called the Eastham Breakout. The plan was to help two Barrow Gang members, Raymond Hamilton and Henry Methvin, break out of jail. The plan worked, but during the escape, a police officer was shot and killed. As a result, an official posse, headed by Frank Hamer, was formed with the sole intent of tracking down Bonnie and Clyde.

Wanted: Dead or Alive

In the month after the Eastham Breakout, Hamer studied Bonnie and Clyde's movements. He discovered that the pair kept to a fairly regular pattern that involved traveling back and forth across the Midwest. Hamer also learned that Bonnie and Clyde used specific locations to meet in the event they were ever separated from the rest of the Barrow Gang. Upon hearing that the pair had recently split off from other gang members during a chase, Hamer checked his maps for the couple's nearest rendezvous point, which turned out to be the Louisiana home of Methvin's father, Ivy. Hamer quickly held a meeting and told the posse they were heading south.

By mid-May, the posse had arrived in the tiny town of Gibsland, Louisiana. Finding that Bonnie and Clyde hadn't arrived yet, Hamer decided to set up an ambush along Highway 154, the only road into Gibsland. The posse picked a wooded location along the road and began unpacking the dozens of guns and hundreds of rounds of ammunition they had brought with them, which included armor-piercing bullets. The only thing left to figure out was how to get Bonnie and Clyde to stop their car so arrests could be made (or a clear shot could be had if they attempted to run).

Setting the Trap

Hamer came up with a solution: Ivy Methvin's truck was placed on one side of the road as if it had broken down, directly opposite from where the posse was hiding in the trees. Hamer hoped that Bonnie and Clyde would recognize the truck and stop to help Ivy. This would put the pair only a few feet away from the posse's hiding place. As for Methvin's role in all this, some say he willingly helped the posse in exchange for his son getting a pardon. Others claim the posse tied Methvin to a tree and gagged him before stealing his truck. Either way, the truck was put in place, and the posse took its position in the trees along the road on the evening of May 21.

Working in shifts, the posse waited all night and the following day with no sign of Bonnie and Clyde. They were about ready to leave on the morning of May 23 when, at approximately 9:00 A.M., they heard Clyde's stolen car approaching. At that point, Hamer and the other five men present—Texas ranger Manny Gault, Dallas deputy sheriffs Bob Alcorn and Ted Hinton, and Louisiana officers Henderson Jordan and Prentiss Oakley—took cover in the trees.

So Much for a Peaceful Surrender

The official report said that Clyde, with Bonnie in the passenger seat, slowed the car as it neared Methvin's truck. At that point, standard procedure would have been for the posse to make an announcement and give the couple a chance to surrender peacefully. Hamer, however, gave the order to simply fire at will.

The first shot was fired by Oakley, which, by all accounts, fatally wounded Clyde in the head. The rest of the posse members weren't taking any chances, though, and they all fired at the car with their automatic rifles, using up all their rounds before the car even came to a complete stop. The posse members then emptied their shotguns into the car, which had rolled past them and had come to a stop in a ditch. Finally, all of the men fired their pistols at the car until all weapons were empty. In all, approximately 130 rounds were fired.

When it was all over, Bonnie and Clyde were both dead. Upon examination, it was reported that the bodies each contained 25 bullet wounds, though some reports put that number as high as 50. Unlike Clyde, who died almost instantly, it is believed that Bonnie endured an excruciating amount of pain, and several members of the posse reported hearing her scream as the bullets ripped into her. For this reason, many people to this day question the actions of the posse members and wonder why they never gave the pair a chance to surrender.

The Aftermath

Afterward, members of the posse removed most of the items from Bonnie and Clyde's car, including guns, clothing, and even a saxophone. Later, they supposedly allowed bystanders to go up to the car and take everything from shell casings and broken glass to bloody pieces of Bonnie and Clyde's clothing and locks of their hair. There are even reports that two different people had to be stopped when they attempted to remove parts of Clyde's body (his ear and his finger) as grisly souvenirs.

Despite Bonnie and Clyde's wish to be buried alongside each other, Bonnie's parents chose to bury her alone in the Crown Hill Memorial Park in Dallas. Clyde Barrow is interred at another Dallas cemetery, Western Heights.

Even though it's been more than 70 years since Bonnie and Clyde left this earth, they are still as popular as ever. Every May, the town of Gibsland holds its annual Bonnie and Clyde Festival, the highlight of which is a reenactment of the shootout, complete with fake blood. If you're looking for something even more morbid, Bonnie and Clyde's bullet-riddled car and the shirt Clyde wore on that fateful day are both currently part of a display at the Primm Valley Resort and Casino in Nevada.

Like fingerprints, all tongue prints are unique.

Keeping the Flame: The Loyal Keeper of the White River Light

💀 💀 💀 💀 💀

Are you dedicated enough to your job to perform your duties until the day you die? What about the day after?

Let There Be Light

In the late 1850s, local mill owners and merchants became concerned about frequent shipwrecks occurring where the White River emptied into Lake Michigan near Whitehall, Michigan. The narrow river connected the lumber mills of White Lake (an area called "The Lumber Queen of the World") and the Great Lakes shipping channels. The state legislature responded by approving the construction of and funding for a lighthouse; however, the White River Light would not be built for another 12 years.

In 1872, a beacon light was set up at the area's South Pier, and shipping captain William Robinson was granted the position of light keeper. In 1875, the White River Light Station was built, and Robinson and his beloved wife, Sarah, moved into the keeper's residence, where they happily raised their 11 children. Robinson often said he was so happy there that he would stay until his dying day. That happiness was marred by Sarah's unexpected death in 1891. Robinson, who had expected to live with her at the lighthouse until his retirement, was inconsolable. Grief-stricken, he poured all of his attention into tending the lighthouse.

Like (Grand)father, Like (Grand)son

As Robinson grew older, the Lighthouse Board began to consider his replacement, finally awarding the post to his grandson (and assistant keeper), Captain William Bush, in

1915. Although the board expected Bush to immediately take over Robinson's duties, he kindly allowed his grandfather to continue as keeper and remain in the keeper's residence for several years.

In 1919, after 47 years of loyal service, the board demanded that Robinson vacate the premises, but he refused. The board allegedly met and agreed to take legal action against Robinson if he didn't leave, but they never got the chance. Two weeks later, on the day before the deadline, Robinson died in his sleep. Bush moved into the residence, and the board was satisfied with their new man. But Captain Robinson stayed on, apparently still refusing to budge.

Thump, Thump, Tap

The lighthouse was decommissioned in 1960 and was turned into a museum in 1970. Today, museum staff and visitors believe that Robinson still occupies the building and continues his duties as lighthouse keeper. Curator Karen McDonnell lives in the lighthouse and reports hearing footsteps on the circular staircase in the middle of the night. She attributes this to Robinson, rather than natural causes, because of the unmistakable sound of his walking cane on the stairs.

McDonnell believes Robinson may have also gotten his wish—to stay in the lighthouse with his wife—because Sarah seems to have returned to the lighthouse as well. She helps with dusting and light housework, leaving display cases cleaner than they were before. Museum visitors often talk about feeling warm and safe inside the building and feeling a sense of love and peace. One tourist felt the presence of a smitten young couple, sitting in one of the window nooks.

We'll Leave the Light on for You

Visitors are welcome to explore the museum, which is open from June through October, and learn more about the shipping history of the Great Lakes. Perhaps you could even get a guided tour from the light's first and most loyal keeper—William Robinson, a man devoted to his wife and his job, who saw no reason why death should interfere with either.

Going Underground in Indiana

In the late 1970s, Vic Cook was busy working as a high school music teacher and musician in Indiana. Unlike many of us, however, he was also busy dreaming of living a Walden-like existence in a low-cost, energy-efficient home in the woods.

While giving a guitar lesson one day, Cook told his student that he wanted to build a monument to nature but feared that the state's building codes would prevent it from happening. The student mentioned that his sister was trying to sell some wooded land in Pendleton, Indiana. Two weeks later, Cook purchased the land and had a site for his dream house. When he found an 1890s stove at a yard sale, he was on his way. Then he started digging.

Digging Deep

Cook eventually dug 22 feet down into the earth. He erected the walls of his house, each made from six inches of solid wood, which would also act as natural insulation for the house with the heat of the earth doing the rest. The result was that the house stays around 68 degrees year-round, although a small kerosene heater is needed on rare occasions.

When it came to the roof and the structure that would be visible above ground, Cook wanted to make sure they were aesthetically pleasing and, more importantly, blended well with the natural environment. The roof, which includes solar panels, was designed to be aerodynamic, making it able to withstand winds of 200 miles per hour. The panels use sunlight to power six solar batteries, which are capable of storing up to a month's supply of electricity for the entire house. A generator is kept on hand, though, just in case the sun decides not to make an appearance for several days.

All the Comforts of Home

Cook found his makeshift refrigerator one day when he came across a log in the woods. For the next six weeks, he worked on the refrigerator, hollowing it out, lining it with insulation, and adding a solar battery to it. The battery supposedly helps pull cool air out of the earth and into the log. Cook even added a freezer, which uses nothing more than a microchip to cool down the earth's air.

The next comfort of home that Cook added to his house was running water. Obviously, he wasn't going to be able to get city water out in the woods and he wasn't keen on digging a well. Instead, he designed special tanks for the roof that could catch rainwater. Gravity is all it takes to give Cook running water in the kitchen and bathroom. In keeping with the theme of the house being one with nature, Cook opted to go the composting route with his bathroom.

The most amazing thing of all is that Cook spends only about $30 each month on utilities, and because the house has no utility hookups, his property taxes are extremely low.

The Giant

Considering that the house has literally become one with the earth, Cook decided to name his labor of love the Earthship. Over the years, though, the house has acquired a nickname— the Giant—after Neil Armstrong's famous line about his "one giant leap for mankind." The line also reflects Cook's leap of faith into a one-man home-building project with a budget of less than $8,000.

All in all, Cook has spent more than a decade and 26,000 hours building his dream home. And he's always happy to show it off. Beginning each spring, Cook offers tours of the Earthship, welcoming the chance to inspire people to follow their dreams and to try to make a difference in the world.

When is a four-point buck not a four-point buck? When it's a four-point doe! In 2002, a hunter from Washington began dressing the 250-pound whitetail he'd shot, only to discover that the buck stopped at the antlers, prompting local newspapers to joke about the cross-dressing deer.

Strange Structures

Humans have the capacity to achieve great things, conquer the seemingly impossible, and invent wonders that make our world a better place. However, sometimes they just like to build things that are big, tall, or strange.

Personal Vanity Gets Etched in Stone

South Dakota has Mount Rushmore, but nestled in the Catskill Mountains is the town of Prattsville, New York, which features Pratt Rocks—a set of relief carvings begun 84 years before its famous western counterpart. Zadock Pratt, who founded the world's largest tannery in the 1830s, commissioned a local sculptor to immortalize his visage high up on a mountainside. The numerous stone carvings include a coat of arms, Pratt's own bust, his business milestones, and even his personal accomplishments, such as his two terms in the U.S. House of Representatives. Carvings also include a shrine to Pratt's son George, who was killed during the Civil War. But the strangest bit found at this site is a recessed tomb that was intended to house Pratt's decaying corpse for eternity. It leaked, Pratt balked, and the chamber remains empty.

Mega-Megaliths

The offbeat dream of Bill Cohea, Jr., and Frederick Lindkvist, two highly spiritual fellows, Columcille was designed to resemble an ancient Scottish religious retreat located on the Isle of Iona. More than 80 oblong stones are "planted" in a Bangor, Pennsylvania, field to approximate the ancient site, a place where some say "the veil is thin between worlds." In addition to the megaliths, Columcille has enchanting chapels, altars, bell towers, cairns, and gates—enough features to lure Harry

Potter fans into an entire day of exploration. Cohea and Lindkvist began their ever-evolving project as a spiritual retreat in 1978. They encourage everyone to visit their nondenominational mystical park. Their request? Simply "be."

Stacked Really High

It's quite surprising to encounter a 1,216-foot-tall smokestack, especially when that chimney is located in a rural town deep in western Pennsylvania. Homer City Generating Station produces electricity by burning coal. But the process has one troubling side effect: Its effluence can be toxic in certain quantities. The super-tall smokestack's purpose is to harmlessly disperse this undesirable by-product, thereby rendering it safe. It does this by releasing the agents high up in the atmosphere where they (theoretically) have ample time to dilute before falling back to Earth. At present, this soaring chunk of steel-reinforced concrete ranks as the third tallest in the world, just behind a 1,250-foot-tall smokestack located in Canada and a 1,377-foot-tall monster over in Kazakhstan.

Fee! Fie! Foe! Fum!

A drive through Staunton, Virginia, may leave some wondering if they've mistakenly entered the land of the giants. After all, an 18-foot-tall watering can and a six-foot-tall flowerpot are displayed on the main boulevard. But fear not. It's no giant who dwells in this hamlet but rather an average-size gent named Willie Ferguson. A large concentration of this metal fabricator's giant works can be seen on the grounds of his sculpture studio. At this metal "imaginarium," visitors will find a six-foot-long dagger, a ten-foot-long set of crutches, a six-foot-tall work boot—everything, it seems, but the proverbial beanstalk.

Cross with Caution

If you've crossed Vermont's Brookfield Floating Bridge by car, you're aware of its treachery. If you tried it on a motorcycle, you probably took an unplanned swim. That's because the lake that the bridge is supposed to cross occasionally crosses *it.* The 320-foot-long all-wooden Brookfield Bridge rests on 380 tarred, oaken barrels that were designed to adjust to the level of Sunset Lake and keep the bridge deck high and dry. But more often than not, they allow the bridge to sink several inches below the surface. Why does this bridge float in the first place? Sunset Lake is too deep to support a traditional, pillared span, so since 1820, impromptu "water ballet" maneuvers have been taking place as vehicles amble across.

Tower City

As drivers creep along I-76 just west of Philadelphia, they witness a stand of super-tall broadcasting masts towering over a suburban neighborhood. The Roxborough Antenna Farm is to broadcasting towers what New York City is to skyscrapers. In the land of broadcasting, height equals might, so the higher the tower, the better the signal strength. With eight TV/FM masts jutting above the 1,000-foot mark (the tallest stretches to 1,276 feet), the array easily outclasses most skyscrapers in height. The reason these big sticks exist in such a concentrated area? Location, location, location. The Roxborough site is a unique setting that features geographical height, proper zoning clearances, and favorable proximity to the city—a trifecta by industry standards.

Rock On

In the summer of 2007, the Swedish government's employment service granted Roger Tullgren a supplemental income based on his struggles with addiction—to heavy-metal music. Tullgren claims he attends around 300 concerts a year and has been addicted for ten years. The rocker procured three psychologists to officially call his condition a disability.

FREAKY FACTS: ANIMALS

- *Most fish have voices that get deeper with age.*

- *A cockroach can regrow its wings, legs, and antennae, and can live without a head for up to a week.*

- *A polar bear's fur is actually transparent rather than white; it merely appears white due to the way it reflects light.*

- *In bright sunlight, walnut shells tan.*

- *Just as humans favor their right or left hand, elephants favor their right or left tusk.*

- *Zebras are black with white stripes (not white with black stripes) and have black skin.*

- *Hummingbirds consume fewer than ten calories per day.*

- *Howler monkeys are the loudest land animals; their calls can be heard up to three miles away.*

- *The dark purple color of a giraffe's tongue protects it from getting sunburned while the animal eats leaves from tall trees.*

- *A billion years ago, a month on Earth lasted only 20 days and a day was only 18 hours long.*

- *The fastest (non-storm) wind ever recorded was 231 miles per hour at Mount Washington, New Hampshire, on April 12, 1934.*

- *Louisiana loses 30 square miles of land each year to erosion and sinking.*

- *Mosquito Bay in Puerto Rico is filled with bioluminescent organisms (720,000 per gallon) that glow when the water is disturbed.*

The Champion of American Lake Monsters

💀   💀   💀   💀   💀

In 1609, French explorer Samuel de Champlain was astonished to see a thick, eight- to ten-foot-tall creature in the waters between present-day Vermont and New York. His subsequent report set in motion the legend of Champ, the "monster" in Lake Champlain.

Eerie Encounters

Even before Champlain's visit, Champ was known to Native Americans as *Chaousarou*. Over time, Champ has become one of North America's most famous lake monsters. News stories of its existence were frequent enough that in 1873, showman P. T. Barnum offered $50,000 for the creature, dead or alive. That same year, Champ almost sank a steamboat, and in the 1880s, a number of people, including a sheriff, glimpsed it splashing playfully offshore. It is generally described as dark in color (olive green, gray, or brown) with a serpentlike body.

Sightings have continued into modern times, and witnesses

have compiled some film evidence that is difficult to ignore. In 1977, a woman named Sandra Mansi photographed a long-necked creature poking its head out of the water near St. Albans, Vermont, close to the Canadian border. She estimated the animal was 10 to 15 feet long and told an investigator that its skin looked "slimy" and similar to that of an eel. Mansi presented her photo and story at a 1981 conference held at Lake Champlain. Although she had misplaced the negative by then, subsequent analyses of the photo have generally failed to find any evidence that it was manipulated.

In September 2002, a researcher named Dennis Hall, who headed a lake monster investigation group known as Champ Quest, videotaped what looked like three creatures undulating through the water near Ferrisburgh, Vermont. Hall claimed that he saw unidentifiable animals in Lake Champlain on 19 separate occasions.

In 2006, two fishermen captured digital video footage of what appeared to be parts of a very large animal swimming in the lake. The images were thoroughly examined under the direction of ABC News technicians, and though the creature on the video could not be proved to be Champ, the team could find nothing to disprove it, either.

Champ or Chump?

As the sixth-largest freshwater lake in the United States (and stretching about six miles into Quebec, Canada), Lake Champlain provides ample habitat and nourishment for a good-size water cryptic, or unknown animal. The lake plunges as deep as 400 feet in spots and covers 490 square miles.

Skeptics offer the usual explanations for Champ sightings: large sturgeons, floating logs or water plants, otters, or an optical illusion caused by sunlight and shadow. Others think Champ could be a remnant of a species of primitive whale called a zeuglodon or an ancient marine reptile known as a plesiosaur, both believed by biologists to be long extinct. But until uncontestable images of the creature's entire body are produced, this argument will undoubtedly continue.

Champ does claim one rare, official nod to the probability of its existence: Legislation by both the states of New York and Vermont proclaim that Champ is a protected—though unknown—species and make it illegal to harm the creature in any way.

Abandoned Amusement Parks

💀 💀 💀 💀 💀

From crumbling midways to rusting and rotting rides, there's something creepy yet intriguing about an abandoned amusement park. Here's a sampling of defunct venues that currently await their uncertain fate and others that have completely disappeared.

Six Flags New Orleans

Though an abandoned amusement park is a sad spectacle in itself, Six Flags New Orleans bears stark, physical reminders of Hurricane Katrina. When the hurricane blew through in August 2005, it forever altered the landscape and robbed citizens of far more than their summer amusements. Squeals of delight were once plentiful at Six Flags. Now, howling winds are all that whistle past rides such as the classic wooden coaster, Mega Zeph. Ninety percent of the park was under water during the catastrophe, and now any hope of rebuilding the operation has been lost to time.

Perhaps it's just as well. Six Flags is situated well away from the French Quarter and other popular tourist areas. As a result, it had always been an under-performer by the company's lofty standards. A sign reading, "Have a Great Day…" still welcomes urban explorers and curiosity seekers to the grounds, which are now officially cordoned off. A dingy mark of the flood-line rises halfway up the sign, serving as a reminder of how quickly laughter can be replaced by despair.

Pripyat Amusement Park, Ukraine

Though some abandoned amusement parks were once able to bring joy, there is one that never had the chance to do so. Pripyat Amusement Park never sold a puffy plume of cotton candy, or cranked a white-knuckled rider up the steep hill of a roller coaster, because this park had the misfortune of being located within the "hot zone" of Chernobyl, Ukraine.

The brand-new amusement complex at Pripyat was scheduled to open May 1, 1986. But that happy moment never came. Just days before, on April 26, an explosion at the nearby Chernobyl Nuclear Power Plant flooded the atmosphere with deadly radioactive particles, resulting in scores of deaths in the months and years that followed. Effects continue to this day. The notorious event is regarded as the world's worst nuclear disaster.

Viewed from a distance, Pripyat's amusement park seems relatively normal. A large yellow Ferris wheel stands motionless beside a bank of high-rise apartment buildings, suggesting that the operation has simply closed for the day. But closer scrutiny reveals that the giant wheel's frame has decayed to a point of instability, and its round cars have dropped to the ground. Swings located adjacent to the wheel are rotting, rusting hulks, no longer whimsical conveyances of mirth and merriment. And everywhere, an oppressive stillness permeates.

No one will ever ride the park's amusements, test their skill on the carnival games, or walk the midway. Once a vibrant city of about 50,000, Pripyat is now a radiation-tainted cast-off from the nuclear era. And it will remain as such until levels of Caesium-137 and Strontium-90 reach a point safe for human habitation, which could take many generations.

Palisades Amusement Park

Say the word *palisades* to most anyone in the New York metropolitan area, and they'll likely envision an amusement park, not a line of cliffs overlooking New York City. Northeastern New Jersey's Palisades Amusement Park ranked as one of America's most famous parks for much of its existence between 1898 and 1971. With rides like the Cyclone (a classic wooden roller coaster) and the Lake Placid Bobsled (a ride so intimidating that its lift hill was enclosed to prevent riders from looking down), Palisades packed them in like sardines. Throw in the world's largest outdoor saltwater pool and free entertainment from the likes of Diana Ross and the Supremes, Tony Bennett, the Jackson 5, and a host of others, and it's easy to see why.

Despite its success, Palisades Amusement Park was demolished in 1971. Ironically, this occurred because the park had become *too* popular and was causing congestion and noise problems in the surrounding suburban area. Today, high-rise condominiums stand where people once let loose their cares and worries, and a monument marks the spot where the park once stood. It reads: "Here we were happy, here we grew!"

Old Chicago

In 1975, an amusement park with a twist opened 30 miles southwest of Chicago in Bolingbrook, Illinois. Old Chicago featured two roller coasters and a Ferris wheel, but it did so under a roof and surrounded by a shopping mall. Despite the uniqueness of the operation and its early success, Old Chicago was plagued with troubles.

The cavernous building, which contained the 73-foot-tall "Chicago Loop" coaster, was the victim of cost overruns that nearly flattened the operation. Then, adding insult to injury, another theme park—Marriott's Great America—opened in 1976 in Gurnee, 40 miles north of the Windy City, funneling a significant number of visitors away from Old Chicago.

But in the end, it was a lack of popular anchor stores that stopped the crowds from coming. The amusement park portion of Old Chicago closed in 1980, and its rides were sold off to other parks. The shopping center closed soon after in 1981. Nevertheless, its central idea lived on. Eventually, the vast West Edmonton Mall in Alberta, Canada (the world's largest mall), would feature a successful indoor amusement park, as would Minnesota's huge Mall of America. Today, a car auction lot sits where the unique amusement park once stood.

Cascade Park

Opened in May 1897 for the New Castle Traction Company trolley line, Cascade Park was named for the picturesque waterfall that tumbled beside it. In many ways, the New Castle, Pennsylvania, park typified the contemporary amusement ventures that would endure well into the 20th century. It featured a picnic grove, a wooden roller coaster (the Comet), a merry-go-round, a dance pavilion, and an assortment of eateries and concession stands. It also offered a 15-acre lake for swimming and a tourist camp that could accommodate more than 2,000 campers.

The park was turned over to the city of New Castle in 1934, and became a public recreation area. Attendance waned when trolley service to the park was discontinued in the 1940s, but picnickers continued to support the park. Nevertheless, by the mid-1980s, the rides were removed and a chapter in amusement park history was closed.

Nostalgia seekers can still find numerous reminders of past glory at the old site. The carousel building, dance pavilion, and refreshment stands are all intact, as are the loading stations for the Tumble Bug ride and the park's train. Concrete footings that once supported the Comet roller coaster can also be found. Annual community events are now held at the park.

Circus World

Circus World lived a strange life as far as amusement parks go. Opened as the Circus World Showcase in Haines City, Florida, in 1974, the park was originally envisioned as a museum to document the history of the circus industry. But the venture faced stiff competition from two nearby theme parks: the mega-popular Disney World in Orlando and the formidable Busch Gardens in Tampa. To better compete, the operation added full-scale amusements, such as the Zoomerang (a steel looping coaster) and the Roaring Tiger (a wooden colossus known for its prodigious "airtime").

But by 1986, the circus-themed park had not lived up to expectations and was sold. It reopened in 1987 as Boardwalk and Baseball, a turn-of-the-century styled oceanfront boardwalk coupled with baseball memorabilia. Despite being a first-class effort, this too floundered and finally closed in 1990. By 2003, all traces of the park were gone. Today, visitors will find condos, hotels, and offices standing where a quirky amusement park once entertained wide-eyed children and adults alike. The circus, as they say, has left town.

Presidential Peculiarities

- **George Washington (1789–1797)** When he was elected, America's first president had only one tooth and wore dentures made from hippopotamus and elephant ivory, not wood as commonly thought.

- **John Adams (1797–1801)** After a long feud with Thomas Jefferson, the two former presidents finally called a truce and developed a friendship that lasted the rest of their lives. Both men died on July 4, 1826—the 50th anniversary of the adoption of the Declaration of Independence.

- **James Madison (1809–1817)** Madison was the smallest president, weighing only 100 pounds and standing just 5′4″.

- **Andrew Jackson (1829–1837)** In 1791, Jackson married Rachel Donelson, believing that her former husband had applied for a divorce. A few years later, they were informed that no divorce had ever been sought, and the couple was being charged with adultery. Once the situation was remedied, Donelson and Jackson quietly remarried.

- **Martin Van Buren (1837–1841)** Van Buren was characterized as a "dandy" and was known to have a weakness for rich foods, fine wine, and clothing.

- **William Henry Harrison (1841)** Harrison was the first president to die in office. During his lengthy inaugural speech, which was more than two hours long, he contracted a cold that quickly developed into pneumonia.

- **John Tyler (1841–1845)** Two decades after leaving the White House, Tyler joined the Confederacy and became the only president named a sworn enemy of the United States.

- **Franklin Pierce (1853–1857)** During his presidency, Pierce allegedly ran over a woman with his horse. He was arrested, but the case was dropped due to lack of evidence.

- **Abraham Lincoln (1861–1865)** Lincoln was the only president to receive a patent; it was for a device designed to lift boats over shoals.

- **Andrew Johnson (1865–1869)** Johnson never received any formal schooling; he credited his wife with teaching him to read and write.

- **Ulysses S. Grant (1869–1877)** The war hero and president was once cast in the role of Desdemona in an all-soldier production of *Othello* during the Mexican–American War.

- **Chester A. Arthur (1881–1885)** After his election, Arthur sold more than two dozen wagons full of White House furniture. Some of the items dated back to the John Adams administration. Arthur commissioned Louis Comfort Tiffany as designer for his White House makeover.

- **Grover Cleveland (1885–1889, 1893–1897)** In his earlier days, Cleveland served as a New York sheriff and carried out at least two hangings, refusing to delegate the unpleasant task to others. After being diagnosed with mouth cancer in 1893, he had a secret operation on a yacht to remove part of his upper jaw. A few weeks later, he was fitted with a rubber prosthesis to fill the hole.

- **Benjamin Harrison (1889–1893)** He was the first president to use electricity in the White House, but after getting an electrical shock, he refused to touch light switches, and he and his family would often leave the lights on all night.

- **Theodore Roosevelt (1901–1909)** Though it was after his term in office, Roosevelt was the first president to ride in an airplane. In 1910, he flew for three minutes and twenty seconds in a plane built by the Wright Brothers. The pilot of that flight, Arch Hoxsey, crashed and died two months later.

- **William H. Taft (1909–1913)** As president, Taft had a series of firsts. In 1910, he was the first president to throw the first baseball of a season and the first president to own a car while in office. In 1930, his funeral was also the first presidential funeral to be broadcast on the radio.

- **Woodrow Wilson (1913–1921)** Wilson played golf as a source of exercise, even in winter. He had his golf balls painted red so he could see them in the snow.

- **Warren G. Harding (1921–1923)** Harding suffered his first nervous breakdown at age 24 and spent time in a sanitarium run by J. H. Kellogg of breakfast cereal fame.

- **Herbert Hoover (1929–1933)** Having never held an elected office before becoming president, Hoover was the first self-made millionaire to reside in the White House after earning his fortune in the mining industry.

- **Franklin D. Roosevelt (1933–1945)** Roosevelt was very well connected. He was related by either blood or marriage to 11 other presidents and was a fifth cousin once removed to his wife Eleanor.

- **Harry Truman (1945–1953)** Truman suffered from bad eyesight, which kept him from attending West Point. When World War I broke out, he passed his vision test by secretly memorizing the eye chart.

- **John F. Kennedy (1961–1963)** Not only was Kennedy the first Catholic president, he was also the first president to have been a Boy Scout.

- **Lyndon B. Johnson (1963–1969)** Johnson and his wife, Lady Bird, were married with a $2.50 wedding ring bought at Sears the day after he proposed to her.

- **Richard M. Nixon (1969–1974)** Though Nixon's mother wanted her son to become a Quaker missionary, his true desire was to be an FBI agent. He applied to the Bureau but wasn't accepted.

- **Gerald R. Ford (1974–1977)** Ford played football for the University of Michigan from 1931 to 1934, and was offered tryouts by both the Detroit Lions and Green Bay Packers.

- **Jimmy Carter (1977–1981)** Carter is a speed-reader, and has been recorded reading 2,000 words per minute.

- **Ronald W. Reagan (1981–1989)** Reagan was the only president to have worn a Nazi uniform. He donned it as an actor in the 1942 film *Desperate Journey*.

- **George H. W. Bush (1989–1993)** At age 19, Bush became the youngest pilot in the U.S. Navy's history. He went on to fly 58 combat missions during World War II and was shot down in 1944.

- **William J. Clinton (1993–2001)** Early in his presidency, Clinton suffered from a series of allergies including cat dander, beef, milk, mold spores, and weed and grass pollens. He took injections to control the allergies, which allowed him to partake in a favorite food at the time—cheeseburgers.

- **George W. Bush (2001–2009)** Bush had some of the highest and lowest approval ratings ever recorded for a president. In October 2001, he held an 88 percent positive rating—the highest in the Harris Poll's 40-year history. However, he also had one of the lowest positive ratings, 28 percent in April 2007, with only Jimmy Carter (22 percent in 1980) and Richard Nixon (26 percent in 1974) ever scoring lower.

Everyone Wants to Be a Millionaire

In South Carolina, in 2007, a man attempted to open a bank account with a $1 million bill. These, of course, do not exist. The savvy teller refused the transaction and alerted police while the agitated man cursed up a storm. Alexander Smith, 31, of Augusta, Georgia, was subsequently charged with forgery and disorderly conduct. His bail was set at a paltry $257 dollars—loose change to any millionaire.

Murder in the Heartland

☠ ☠ ☠ ☠ ☠

If you ever find yourself in northwestern Kansas looking for the village of Holcomb, don't blink or you'll miss it. It's the kind of place where nothing ever seems to happen. And yet, back in 1959, Holcomb became one of the most notorious locations in the history of American crime.

"Everyone Loved the Clutters..."

In the 1940s, successful businessman Herb Clutter built a house on the outskirts of town and started raising a family with his wife, Bonnie. The Clutters quickly became one of the most popular families in the small village, due largely to their friendly nature. People would be hard-pressed to find some-one who had a bad word to say about them.

On the morning of Sunday, November 15, 1959, Clarence Ewalt drove his daughter Nancy to the Clutter house so she could go to church with the family as she did every week. She was a good friend of the Clutters' teenage daughter, who was also named Nancy. Nancy Ewalt knocked on the door several times but got no response. She went around to a side door, looked around and called out, but no one answered. At that point, Mr. Ewalt drove his daughter to the Kidwell house nearby and picked up Susan Kidwell, another friend. Susan tried phoning the Clutters, but no one answered. So the three drove back to the Clutter house. The two girls entered the house through the kitchen door and went to Nancy Clutter's room, where they discovered her dead body.

Unspeakable Acts

Sheriff Robinson was the first officer to respond. He entered the house with another officer and a neighbor, Larry Hendricks. According to Nancy Ewalt, the three men went first to Nancy Clutter's room, where they found the teenager dead of an apparent gunshot wound to the back of the head. She was lying on her bed facing the wall with her hands and ankles bound. Down the hallway in the master bedroom, the body of Bonnie Clutter was discovered. Like her daughter, Bonnie's hands and feet were also bound, and she appeared to have been shot point-blank in the head.

In the basement of the Clutter home, police found the bodies of Herb Clutter and his 15-year-old son, Kenyon. Like his mother and sister, Kenyon had been shot in the head; his body was tied to a sofa.

As atrocious as the other three murders were, Herb Clutter appeared to have suffered the most. Like the others, he had been shot in the head, but there were slash marks on his throat, and his mouth had been taped shut. And although his body was lying on the floor of the basement, there was a rope hanging from the ceiling suggesting that, at some point, he may have been hung from the rope.

Dewey's Task Force

Alvin A. Dewey of the Kansas City Bureau of Investigation (KBI) was put in charge of the investigation. Even though Dewey was a police veteran and had seen his fair share of violent murders, the Clutter murders hit him hard. Herb Clutter was a friend, and their families had attended church together.

At his first press conference after the bodies were discovered, Dewey announced that he was heading up a 19-man task force that would not rest until they found the person or persons responsible for the horrific murders. But he knew it was going to be a tough case. For one, the amount of blood and gore at the scene suggested that revenge might have been the motive. But the Clutters were upstanding members of the community and loved by all, as evidenced by the nearly 600 mourners who showed up for the family's funeral service. The idea that the murders were the result of a robbery gone bad was also being pursued, but Dewey had his doubts about that, as well. For him, it just didn't fit that the entire Clutter family would have walked in on a robbery and then been killed the way they had. For that reason, Dewey began to believe that there had been more than one killer.

A Secret Clue

There was not a lot of evidence left behind at the crime scene. Not only was the murder weapon missing, but whoever pulled the trigger had taken the time to pick up the spent shells. However, Dewey did have an ace up his sleeve, and it was something not even the press was made aware of. Herb Clutter's body had been found lying on a piece of cardboard. On that cardboard were impressions from a man's boot. Both of the victims found in the basement, Herb and Kenyon Clutter, were barefoot, which meant the boots may have belonged to the killer. It wasn't much to go on, but for Dewey, it was a start. Still, as Christmas 1959 crept closer, the case was starting to come to a standstill. Then, finally, a big break came from an unlikely place: Lansing Prison.

A Break in the Case

The man who would break the case wide open was Lansing Prison inmate Floyd Wells. Earlier in the year, Wells had been sentenced to Lansing for breaking and entering. His cellmate was a man named Richard Hickock. One night, the two men were talking, and Hickock mentioned that even though he was going to be released from prison soon, he had nowhere to go. Wells told him that back in the late 1940s, he had been out looking for work and stumbled across a kind, rich man named Clutter who would often hire people to work around his farm. Once he mentioned Herb Clutter, Hickock seemed obsessed with the man. He wouldn't stop asking Wells to tell him everything he knew about Clutter. How old was he? Was he strong? How many others lived in the house with him?

One night, Hickock calmly stated that when he was released, he and his friend Perry Smith were going to rob the Clutters and murder anyone in the house. Wells said that Hickock even went so far as to explain exactly how he would tie everyone up and shoot them one at a time. Wells further stated that he never believed Hickock was serious until he heard the news that the Clutters had been murdered in exactly the way Hickock had described.

Captures and Confessions

On December 30, after attempting to cash a series of bad checks, Hickock and Smith were arrested in Las Vegas. Among the items seized from the stolen car they were driving was a pair of boots belonging to Hickock. When confronted with the fact that his boots matched the imprint at the crime scene, Hickock broke down and admitted he had been there during the murders. However, he swore that Perry Smith had killed the whole family and that he had tried to stop him.

When Smith was informed that his partner was putting all the blame on him, he decided it was in his best interest to explain his side. Smith gave a very detailed version of how Hickock had devised a plan to steal the contents of a safe in Herb Clutter's home office. The pair had arrived under cover of darkness at approximately 12:30 A.M. Finding no safe in the office, the pair went up into the master bedroom, where they surprised Herb Clutter, who was sleeping alone in bed. When told they had come for the contents of the safe, Herb told them to take whatever they wanted, but he said there was no safe in the house. Not convinced, Smith and Hickock rounded up the family and tied them up, hoping to get one of them to reveal the location of the safe. When that failed, Smith and Hickock prepared to leave. But when Hickock started bragging about how he had been ready to kill the entire family, Smith called his bluff, and an argument ensued. At that point, Smith said he snapped and stabbed Herb Clutter in the throat. Seeing the man in such pain, Smith said he then shot him to end his suffering. Smith then turned the gun on Kenyon. Smith ended his statement by saying that he'd made Hickock shoot and kill the two women.

The Verdict

The murder trial of Richard Hickock and Perry Smith began on March 23, 1960, at Finney County Courthouse. Five days later, the case was handed over to the jury, who needed only 40 minutes to reach their verdict: Both men were guilty of all charges. They recommended that Hickock and Smith be hanged for their crimes.

Sitting in the front row when the verdicts were read was Truman Capote, who had been writing a series of articles about the murders for *The New Yorker.* Those articles would later inspire his best-selling novel *In Cold Blood.*

After several appeals, both men were executed at Lansing Prison, one right after the other, on April 14, 1965. Richard Hickock was the first to be hanged, with Perry Smith going to the same gallows roughly 30 minutes later. Agent Alvin Dewey was present for both executions.

Several years after the murders, in an attempt to heal the community, a stained-glass window at the First Methodist Church in Garden City, Kansas, was posthumously dedicated to the memory of the Clutter family. Despite an initial impulse to bulldoze the Clutter house, it was left standing and today is a private residence.

Socking It to the Car Wash

Twice in late 2007, J. L. Walker was caught on surveillance cameras with socks on his hands burglarizing the Sunshine Car Wash in Clearwater, Florida. Evidently drawn to the establishment, he later dropped off an employment application there. The manager recognized Walker from the video footage and reported him to the police. Officers arrested him at home—his address was on the application—and charged him with burglary and theft.

FREAKY FACTS: INSECTS

- *Caddisfly larvae construct little houses in ponds to live in until they reach their winged stage. Some species build little structures from bits of leaves to achieve dome or turret shapes, some stack up small pebbles and shells, and one is able to exactly reproduce the shape of a snail shell by binding sand with a silky extrusion.*

- *Earwigs, once widely (and wrongly) reputed to crawl inside human ears to lay their eggs, actually feed mostly on caterpillars, slugs, and already dead flesh. They still look creepy due to the large, pincerlike claws protruding from their rear ends that are used to grab prey.*

- *The crafty ant lion digs a sand pit by scooting itself backward and using its head as a shovel. It then hides itself in the pit with only its giant mouth sticking out and waits for an ant to tumble down into the pit.*

- *Whirligig beetles, which live in ponds and streams, have eyes that are divided into two sections: one part suited for underwater viewing and the other for ogling the atmosphere.*

- *Froghoppers are small insects that look a bit like frogs. Young froghoppers clamp onto plant stems and drain them of juice while excreting a whitish foam from their abdomens until they are completely covered in a bubble bath of their own making, resembling blobs of spittle.*

- *Tree crickets sing in exact mathematic ratio to the temperature of the air. No need for a thermometer on a summer night—just count the number of chirps a cricket makes in 15 seconds, add 40, and the result will be the current temperature in degrees Fahrenheit.*

- *The female praying mantis is a pitiless lover. Her mate is also her dinner, and she often eats his head as an appetizer while he is still in the act of fertilizing her eggs.*

Liberace: Predestined to Play

*Like his singing counterpart Elvis Presley, Liberace entered
the world with a stillborn twin. But Liberace, christened
Wladziu Valentino Liberace and usually called "Lee" or
"Walter," was born with part of the birth sac over his head.
Throughout the ages, the birth sac (or caul) has been seen as a
mystical portent of special talents or powers, and in this case,
the old wives' tale got it right: Few human beings have
possessed Liberace's magical power to enthrall a crowd.*

Born to Beguile

Born in 1919, in West Allis, Wisconsin, young Walter was a
sickly boy. He spoke with an odd accent that he later compared to Lawrence Welk's, although it may have come from
seven years of childhood speech therapy. Nevertheless, he
could joyously pound out accurate piano tunes by the time
he was three, and, at age seven, he won a scholarship to the
Wisconsin School of Music.

As a teen, Liberace soloed with the Chicago Symphony, as
he originally wanted to be a classical concert pianist. He also
hammered the ivories in silent-movie houses in the Milwaukee
area. In 1939, he had a revelation after being

asked to play a popular
song, "Three Little
Fishes," at the end of
a classical concert in
LaCrosse, Wiscon-
sin. When the crowd
went wild over the
way he hammed up
the song, he real-
ized his destiny lay
in entertaining the
masses with humor
and glitz.

By the early 1950s, Liberace was playing Carnegie Hall and Madison Square Garden. On May 26, 1954, he grossed a record $138,000 at the Garden. He was also a hit on TV with *The Liberace Show.* He received many awards—two Emmy awards, six gold albums, Entertainer of the Year, and two stars on the Hollywood Walk of Fame (one for music and one for television). He was over-the-top, and people loved him for it.

The Gatherer of Glitz

Liberace began wearing flashy clothing so he could easily be seen in huge auditoriums. He soon discovered that the glitzier he became, the more audiences loved him. His wardrobe progressed from a simple gold lamé jacket to such unparalleled items as a blue fox cape that cost $300,000 and trailed 16 feet behind him, a sequined red-white-and-blue drum major suit that substituted hot pants for trousers, a sparkly silver cape garnished with mounds of pink feathers, and a black mink cape lined with rhinestones. One of his most outrageous getups was a King Neptune costume that weighed 200 pounds.

Liberace loved to surround himself with luxurious symbols of his music. The best-known example was his piano-shape pool. He loaded his house with diamond- and crystal-studded candelabras and other objects—lamps, planters, bookends—fashioned in the shape of a baby grand. Today, much of his fabulous collection can be seen at the Liberace Museum in Las Vegas. The massive stash includes 18 pianos, such as the famed concert grand completely surfaced with tiny squares of mirror, and a Baldwin glittering with rhinestones.

Liberace's legendary wardrobe is there, too, along with his famous jewelry. He often wore five or six huge rings on each hand while performing, such as the behemoth adornment shaped like a candelabra, with diamond flames dancing over platinum candlesticks. Many of his jewelry pieces were shaped like pianos, including his wristwatch, which was studded with diamonds, rubies, sapphires, and emeralds.

Even his automobiles were decorated Liberace-style: He had a Roadster slathered in Austrian rhinestones and a Rolls-Royce covered in mirror tiles.

The Liberace Museum also includes a re-created version of Liberace's lavish bedroom from his Palm Springs home. It features examples of his collection of exclusive Czech Moser crystal and a desk once owned by Russian Czar Nicholas II.

Nunsense?

Despite his great wealth (the *Guinness Book of World Records* once listed him as the highest-paid musician and pianist), Liberace was often prone to illness. In November 1963, he was near death from kidney failure caused by breathing toxic fumes from his costumes. He was calling relatives and friends to his hospital bed so he could say goodbye and give away his earthly goods, when he was suddenly and inexplicably cured. His explanation for the miracle was that a mysterious white-robed nun had come into his room and told him to pray to St. Anthony, patron saint of missing things and lost persons, then she touched his arm and left. Liberace never discovered who the nun was or where she came from, but he did recover.

Although raised Catholic, Liberace was very superstitious and was a great believer in numerology and fate. He insisted that his success was due to his favorite book, *The Magic of Believing*.

He Who Plays in Vegas, Stays in Vegas

Liberace eventually found a perfect venue for his talents in Las Vegas, where he bought a supper club just off the Strip called Carluccio's Tivoli Gardens. With its piano-shape bar and lavish decor, it was pure Liberace.

After Liberace's death from complications of AIDS on February 4, 1987, at least two psychics claimed that his spirit remained at the restaurant. Staff reported floating capes, doors mysteriously opening and closing, and unexplained electrical disturbances. A magazine reporter, who accompanied investigators on a ghost hunt at Carluccio's almost two decades after "Mr. Showmanship's" death, wrote in a February 2005 article that the pair snapped a photo of a restaurant employee that revealed a ghostly form standing next to her. If ever there was a chance for one last photo op, Liberace would certainly find it very hard to resist showing his big smile for the camera.

America's Haunted Hotels

💀 💀 💀 💀 💀

Looking for ghosts can be a tiring experience, and sometimes, while on the road, even the most intrepid ghost hunter needs a good night's sleep. But if a peaceful night is what you're looking for, you may want to go elsewhere. In these places, no one rests in peace!

Admiral Fell Inn (Baltimore, Maryland)

The Admiral Fell Inn, located just steps away from the harbor on historic Fell's Point in Baltimore, was named for a shipping family who immigrated from England in the 18th century. With parts of the inn dating back to the 1700s, it's a charming place with stately rooms, an intimate pub, and wonderful service. It is also reportedly home to a number of spirits.

The ghosts at the Admiral Fell Inn include a young boy who died from cholera, a woman in white who haunts Room 218, and a man who died in Room 413. Staff members claim this room is always chilly and has strange, moving cold spots.

In 2003, during Hurricane Isabel, the hotel's guests were evacuated to safety, but several of the hotel managers stayed behind. At one point in the night, they reported the sounds of music, laughter, and dancing from the floor above the lobby. When they checked to see what was going on, they discovered no one else in the building.

Blennerhassett Hotel (Parkersburg, West Virginia)

The Blennerhassett Hotel was designed and built in 1889 by William Chancellor, a prominent businessman. The hotel was a grand showplace and has been restored to its original condition in recent years. These renovations have reportedly stirred the ghosts who reside there into action.

There are several ghosts associated with the hotel, including a man in gray who has been seen walking around on the second floor and the infamous "Four O'Clock Knocker," who likes to pound on guest room doors at 4:00 A.M. There is also a ghost who likes to ride the elevators, often stopping on floors where the button has not been pushed. But the most famous resident spirit is that of hotel builder William Chancellor. Guests and employees have reported seeing clouds of cigar smoke in the hallways, wafting through doorways, and circling a portrait of Chancellor that hangs in the library.

Stanley Hotel (Estes Park, Colorado)

The Stanley Hotel has gained quite a reputation over the years, not only as a magnificent hotel with a breathtaking view but also as the haunted hotel that provided the inspiration for Stephen King's book *The Shining*.

In 1909, when Freelan Stanley opened his grand hotel, it immediately began to attract famous visitors from all over the country. Today, it attracts a number of ghostly guests as well.

The hotel's most notable ghost is Stanley himself; his apparition is often seen in the lobby and the billiard room. Legend has it that Stanley's wife, Flora, still entertains guests by playing her piano in the ballroom. Many people have reportedly seen the keys moving on the piano as music plays, but if they try to get close to it, the music stops. Another resident ghost seems especially fond of Room 407, where he turns lights on and off and rattles the occupants with inexplicable noises.

The Lodge (Cloudcroft, New Mexico)

Opened in the early 1900s, The Lodge has attracted famous visitors such as Pancho Villa, Judy Garland, and Clark Gable. And since 1901, every New Mexico governor has stayed in the spacious Governor's Suite.

The Lodge is reportedly haunted by the ghost of a beautiful young chambermaid named Rebecca, who was murdered by her lumberjack boyfriend when he caught her cheating on him. Her apparition has frequently been spotted in the hallways, and her playful, mischievous spirit has bedeviled guests in the rooms. She is now accepted as part of the hotel's history, and there is even a stained-glass window with her likeness prominently displayed at The Lodge.

The hotel's Red Dog Saloon is reputedly one of Rebecca's favorite spots. There she makes her presence known by turning lights on and off, causing alcohol to disappear, moving objects around, and playing music long after the tavern has closed. Several bartenders claim to have seen the reflection of a pretty, red-haired woman in the bar's mirror, but when they turn around to talk to her, she disappears.

Hollywood Roosevelt Hotel (Hollywood, California)

Hollywood boasts a number of haunted hotels, but the Hollywood Roosevelt, which opened in 1927, is the most famous. Since 1984, when the hotel underwent renovations, the ghosts have been putting in frequent appearances.

One of the hotel's famous ghosts is Marilyn Monroe. Her image is sometimes seen in a mirror that hangs near the elevators. The specter of Montgomery Clift, who stayed at the hotel in 1952 while filming *From Here to Eternity,* has been seen pacing restlessly in the corridor outside of Room 928, where he appears to be rehearsing his lines and learning to play the bugle, which was required for his role in the movie.

Staff members and guests have frequently reported other unexplained phenomena, such as loud voices in empty rooms and hallways; lights being turned on in empty, locked rooms; a typewriter that began typing on its own in a dark, locked office; phantom guests that disappeared when approached; and beds that make and unmake themselves. Those Hollywood ghosts can be so demanding!

The Kecksburg Incident

*Did visitors from outer space once land in a western
Pennsylvania thicket?*

Dropping in for a Visit

On December 9, 1965, an unidentified flying object (UFO)
streaked through the late-afternoon sky and landed in
Kecksburg—a rural Pennsylvania community about 40 miles
southeast of Pittsburgh. This much is not disputed. However, specific accounts vary widely from person to person.
Even after closely examining the facts, many people remain
undecided about exactly what happened. "Roswell" type incidents—ultra-mysterious in nature and reeking of a govern-
mental cover-up—have an uncanny way of causing confusion.

Trajectory-Interruptus

A meteor on a collision course with Earth will generally
"bounce" as it enters the atmosphere. This occurs due to
friction, which forcefully slows the average space rock from
6 to 45 miles per second to a few hundred miles per hour, the
speed at which it strikes Earth and officially becomes a meteorite. According to the official explanation offered by the U.S.
Air Force, it was a meteorite that landed in Kecksburg. However, witnesses reported that the object completed back and
forth maneuvers before landing at a very low speed—moves
that an un-powered chunk of earthbound rock simply cannot
perform. Strike one against the meteor theory.

An Acorn-Shape Meteorite?

When a meteor manages to pierce Earth's atmosphere, it
has the physical properties of exactly what it is: a space rock.
That is to say, it will generally be unevenly shaped, rough,
and darkish in color, much like rocks found on Earth. But at
Kecksburg, eyewitnesses reported seeing something far, far
different. The unusual object they described was bronze to

golden in color, acorn-shape, and as large as a Volkswagen Beetle automobile. Unless the universe has started to produce uniformly shaped and colored meteorites, the official explanation seems highly unlikely. Strike two for the meteor theory.

Markedly Different

Then there's the baffling issue of markings. A meteorite can be chock-full of holes, cracks, and other such surface imperfec-

tions. It can also vary somewhat in color. But it should never, *ever* have markings that seem intelligently designed. Witnesses at Kecksburg describe intricate writings similar to Egyptian hieroglyphics located near the base of the object. A cursory examination of space rocks at any natural history museum reveals that such a thing doesn't occur naturally. Strike three for the meteor theory. Logically following such a trail, could an unnatural force have been responsible for the item witnessed at Kecksburg? At least one man thought so.

Reportis Rigor Mortis

Just after the Kecksburg UFO landed, reporter John Murphy arrived at the scene. Like any seasoned pro, the newsman immediately snapped photos and gathered eyewitness accounts of the event. Strangely, FBI agents arrived, cordoned off the area, and confiscated all but one roll of his film. Undaunted, Murphy assembled a radio documentary entitled *Object in the Woods* to describe his experience. Just before the special was to air, the reporter received an unexpected visit by two men.

According to a fellow employee, a dark-suited pair identified themselves as government agents and subsequently confiscated a portion of Murphy's audiotapes. A week later, a clearly perturbed Murphy aired a watered-down version of his documentary. In it, he claimed that certain interviewees requested their accounts be removed for fear of retribution at the hands of police, military, and government officials. In 1969, John Murphy was struck dead by an unidentified car while crossing the street.

Resurrected by Robert Stack

In all likelihood the Kecksburg incident would have remained dormant and under-explored had it not been for the television show *Unsolved Mysteries*. In a 1990 segment, narrator Robert Stack took an in-depth look at what occurred in Kecksburg, feeding a firestorm of interest that eventually brought forth two new witnesses. The first, a U.S. Air Force officer stationed at Lockbourne AFB (near Columbus, Ohio), claimed to have seen a flatbed truck carrying a mysterious object as it arrived on base on December 10, 1965. The military man told of a tarpaulin-covered conical object that he couldn't identify and a "shoot to kill" order given to him for anyone who ventured too close. He was told that the truck was bound for Wright–Patterson AFB in Dayton, Ohio, an installation that's alleged to contain downed flying saucers. The other witness was a building contractor who claimed to have delivered 6,500 special bricks to a hanger inside Wright–Patterson AFB on December 12, 1965. Curious, he peeked inside the hanger and saw a "bell-shaped" device, 12-feet high, surrounded by several men wearing anti-radiation style suits. Upon leaving, he was told that he had just witnessed an object that would become "common knowledge" in the next 20 years.

Will We Ever Know the Truth?

Like Roswell before it, we will probably never know for certain what occurred in western Pennsylvania back in 1965. The more that's learned about the case, the more confusing and contradictory it becomes. For instance, the official 1965 meteorite explanation contains more holes than Bonnie and Clyde's death car, and other explanations, such as orbiting space debris (from past U.S. and Russian missions) reentering Earth's atmosphere, seem equally preposterous. In 2005, as the result of a new investigation launched by the Sci-Fi Television Network, NASA asserted that the object was a Russian satellite. According to a NASA spokesperson, documents of this investigation were somehow misplaced in the 1990s. Mysteriously, this finding directly contradicts the official air force version that nothing at all was found at the Kecksburg site. It also runs counter to a 2003 report made by NASA's own Nicholas L. Johnson, Chief Scientist for Orbital Debris. That document shows no missing satellites at the time of the incident. This includes a missing Russian Venus Probe (since accounted for)—the very item that was once considered a prime crash candidate.

Brave New World

These days, visitors to Kecksburg will be hard-pressed to find any trace of the encounter—perhaps that's how it should be. Since speculation comes to an abrupt halt whenever a concrete answer is provided, Kecksburg's reputation as "Roswell of the East" looks secure, at least for the foreseeable future. But if one longs for proof that something mysterious occurred there, they need look no further than the backyard of the Kecksburg Volunteer Fire Department. There, in all of its acorn-shape glory, stands an full-scale mock-up of the spacecraft reportedly found in this peaceful town on December 9, 1965. There too rests the mystery, intrigue, and romance that have accompanied this alleged space traveler for more than 40 years.

Egyptians, always seeming to be ahead of the fashion curve, were the earliest people known to have worn gloves as decorative accessories. King Tutankhamun's tomb contained linen gloves woven with colored threads.

Beyond Recognition: Coping with the Destructiveness of War

War has disfigured people since the first warring human bashed in another's cheekbone with a club, then spared his life. These days, humans have become remarkably efficient killers— yet we were less so during World War I. With the advent of battlefield medicine and popular photography, World War I let the mutilated vets live—but then forced them to face a society that might not have been ready to face them.

Blast, Fire, and Beyond

World War I was the first war to use some of the technology of the era, such as airplanes, tanks, and wireless communication. Great adventure and glory beckoned. Each side stood convinced of righteousness in a noble, manly struggle. The soldiers looked so young and proud.

But they were headed off to squalor, mutilation, and pestilence. They were as likely to die from unglamorous war-related dangers like disease as from something that sounds good in a folk song—such as a bullet piercing a proud young heart. World War I dragged on with aerial bombings, blindness from chlorine and mustard attacks, observation balloons bursting into balls of flame, brutal machine-gun mow downs, slow deaths while trying to cut barbed wire, trenches lined with a biohazardous mud-blood-urine sludge, and armored monsters belching steel, cordite, and death.

Those civilians who had deluded themselves with visions of war as a gallant pageant could deny the sordid reality no longer. The contrary evidence had just returned from the army hospital, and to look upon it frightened them.

"I Can't Even Face Myself"

By 1918, everyone was tired of war, and none were wearier than those veterans who had lost jaws, eyes, noses, or cheeks—

sometimes all of the above. Modern medicine did all it could, more than ever before in history, but doctors proved better at saving lives than salvaging smiles. On Armistice Day, thousands of disfigured Allied soldiers—known as *mutilés* in France—had relatively little reason to cheer. That is, assuming they could still hear cheers or see revelers.

When doctors could reconstruct features, they did so, inventing and refining plastic surgery as they went. Yet all was not quite lost for the grenadier who had sacrificed himself on the war's bloody altar. What if someone could make customized masks to cover and resemble the victims' missing parts? The alternative was to have them wear veils or hoods, hiding their ruined visages from the eyes of the public—an unfair if understandable solution. Near-normal looks might mean near-normal lives. Children might not hide from them; adults might not stare. Here was born the new discipline of anaplastology—making artificial versions of lost or deformed body parts.

Welcome to the Tin Noses Shop

In Sidcup, England, in 1916, Francis Derwent Wood founded the Masks for Facial Disfigurement Department, or the Tin Noses Shop, as wounded soldiers facetiously called it. Wood's mission was to sculpt a small mask of copper and paint it to resemble the victim's prewar look. When possible, a mask was shaped using a detailed plaster cast of the unmarred side of the face; when impossible, a prewar photo provided the artist with a basis for painting. Glasses held the masks in place.

The vast majority of the artists were supposedly female, and they faced special creative challenges. They needed to match the flesh tone yet compensate for different types of sunlight. Often the mask was painted while being worn to best match the veteran's skin tone. The artists even had to match eyes and the looks of eyes. If the soldier had a mustache or an eyebrow that needed to be re-created, the victim's real hair was harvested and applied, or silver wire was used. The artist had to be part nurse, part sculptor, and part painter.

The most prominent artist helping French and American wounded was Anna Coleman Ladd, the wife of a Boston physician, who went to France to open a Red Cross anaplastology studio. When she heard of Wood's work with British soldiers, she did in France what the Tin Noses Shop's founder had done in Britain. Reports from the period describe her work as perhaps the finest in the field. In 1932, a grateful French Republic invested Ladd with the Legion of Honor in the Grade of Chevalière (knight).

Whither the Prostheses?

The manufacture of these masks stopped around 1920, and sadly, few survive. They wore out after a few years—enamel paint on soft, thin metal doesn't hold up well in day-to-day life. Perhaps some were repainted, but many owners were vulnerable to infection and other health problems related to their wounds, and thus didn't often survive long.

One theory as to why so few of the hundreds of masks so carefully made have survived is that they were buried with their owners. But we do have black-and-white photos to show us how the men looked wearing their metal masks. It was the best that could be done for them at the time.

Lending a Helping Hand

Although India has the world's largest railway system, its trains can always use a helping hand. This was taken literally in 2007 when passengers were asked to help push a stalled train to the next electrical pole so the engine could be restarted. Indian railroads transport more than 14 million passengers daily but often face severe maintenance problems.

Funky Flavors of Jones Soda

For Seattle-based Jones Soda Co., if it's not innovative, it's not worth drinking. At least, that's how it seems when you take a gander at some of the flavors they've created over the years. Go on—try a Roadkill-flavored soda! Dare ya!

- Antacid
- Bananaberry
- Black cat licorice
- Broccoli casserole
- Brussels sprout with prosciutto
- Bug juice
- Candy corn
- Christmas ham
- Christmas tree
- Dirt
- Fruit cake
- Green bean casserole
- Invisible
- Jelly doughnut
- Latke
- Lemon meringue pie
- Mashed potatoes and butter
- Natural field turf
- Pecan pie
- Perspiration
- Pumpkin pie
- Roadkill
- Salmon pâté
- Sugar plum
- Turkey and gravy
- Wild herb stuffing

Howard Hughes:
The Paragon of Paranoia

The sad condition of reclusive mogul Howard Hughes in his last years is well known—he became a bearded, emaciated, germophobe hiding in his Las Vegas hotel room. But the actual details of Hughes's strange life are even more shocking.

A Golden Youth

Born in Houston, Texas, in 1905, to an overprotective mother and an entrepreneur father who made a fortune from inventing a special drill bit, Howard Hughes moved to California shortly after his mother died when he was 17. There he was exposed to the Hollywood film industry through his screenwriter uncle, Rupert Hughes. When his father died two years later, Howard inherited nearly a million dollars while still in his teens. Through shrewd investments he managed to parlay that into a serious fortune, which gave him the means to pursue his interest in films that had been ignited by Uncle Rupert.

Hughes became the darling of Hollywood beauty queens. He produced several successful films, including *Scarface* and *Hell's Angels* (which cost him nearly $4 million of his own money). Next, he turned his imaginative talents to aviation. He formed his own aircraft company, built many planes himself, and broke a variety of world records. He even won a Congressional Gold Medal in 1939 for his achievements in aviation.

But his life took a drastic turn in 1946, when he suffered injuries in a plane crash that led to a lifelong addiction to painkillers. He also downed several seaplanes and was involved in a few auto accidents—perhaps these mishaps planted the idea that the world was out to get him.

Evolving into a Hermit

Hughes married movie starlet Jean Peters in 1957, but they spent little time together and later divorced. He eventually moved to Las Vegas and bought the Desert Inn so he could turn its penthouse into his personal safe house.

In 1968, *Fortune* magazine named Howard Hughes the richest man in America, with an estimated wealth of $1 billion. But his personal eccentricities mounted almost as quickly as his fortune. Hughes was afraid of outside contamination of all sorts, from unseen bacteria to city water systems to entire ethnic groups. He was even afraid of children. He also burned his clothes if he found out that someone he knew had an illness.

Dangerously Decrepit

Biographer Michael Drosnin provided shocking details about Hughes's lifestyle: He spent most of his time naked, his matted hair hanging shoulder-length and his nails so long they curled over. Hughes even stored his own urine in glass jars. His home was choked with old newspapers and used tissues, and he sometimes wore empty tissue boxes as shoes. Hughes was obsessive, however, about organizing the memos that he scribbled on hundreds of yellow pads.

Hughes usually ate just one meal per day, and he sometimes subsisted on dessert alone. His dental hygiene was abysmal—his teeth literally rotted in his mouth. When he finally died from heart failure in 1976, the formerly robust, 6′4″ man weighed only 90 pounds. He had grown too weak to handle his codeine syringe and had turned himself into a human pincushion, with five broken hypodermic needles embedded in his arms.

He Couldn't Take It with Him

Howard Hughes died without a will, although he had kept his aides in line for nearly two decades by dangling the promise of a fat windfall upon his death. In the end, his giant estate was inherited by some cousins.

Hughes left another legacy—his long list of achievements. He built the first communication satellite—the kind used today to link the far corners of the world. His Hughes Aircraft Company greatly advanced modern aviation. And he produced award-winning movies. However, the full extent of his influence on the world will probably never be known.

The Lizzie Borden Murder Mystery

Most people know the rhyme that begins, "Lizzie Borden took an axe and gave her mother 40 whacks…" In reality, approximately 20 hatchet chops cut down Abby Borden, but no matter the number, Lizzie's stepmother was very much dead on that sultry August morning in 1892. Lizzie's father, Andrew, was killed about an hour later. His life was cut short by about a dozen hatchet chops to the head.

No one knows who was guilty of these murders, but Lizzie has always carried the burden of suspicion.

Andrew Borden, an American "Scrooge"

Andrew Jackson Borden had been one of the richest men in Fall River, Massachusetts, with a net worth of nearly half a million dollars. In 1892, that was enormous wealth. Andrew was a shrewd businessman: At the time of his death, he was the president of the Union Savings Bank and director of another bank plus several profitable cotton mills.

Despite his wealth, Andrew was miserly. Though some of his neighbors' homes had running hot water, the three-story Borden home had just two cold-water taps, and there was no water available above the first floor. The Bordens' only latrine was in the cellar, so they generally used chamber pots that were either dumped onto the lawn behind the house or emptied into the cellar toilet. And, although most wealthy people used gas lighting, the Bordens lit their house with inexpensive kerosene lamps.

Worst of all, for many years, Andrew was an undertaker who offered some of the lowest prices in town. He worked on the bodies in the basement of the Borden home, and allegedly, he bent the knees of the deceased—and in some cases, cut off their feet—to fit the bodies into smaller, less expensive coffins in order to increase his business.

So, despite the brutality of Andrew's murder, it seems few people mourned his loss. The question wasn't why he was killed, but who did it.

Lizzie vs. William

In 1997, when psychic Jane Doherty visited the murder site, she uncovered several clues about the Lizzie Borden case. Doherty felt that the real murderer was someone named "Willie." There is no real evidence to support this claim, but some say Andrew had an illegitimate son named William, who may have spent time as an inmate in an insane asylum. His constant companion was reportedly his hatchet, which he talked to as though it were a friend. Also, at least one witness reportedly saw William at the Borden house on the day of the murders. William was supposedly there to challenge Andrew about his new will.

Was William the killer? A few years after the murders, William took poison and then hung himself in the woods. Near his swinging body, he'd reportedly left his hatchet on the ground. So with William dead and Lizzie already acquitted, the Borden murder case was put to rest.

Lizzie's Forbidden Romance

One of the most curious explanations for the murder involves the Bordens' servant Bridget Sullivan. Her participation has always raised questions. Like the other members of the Borden household, Bridget had suffered from apparent food poisoning the night before the murders. She claimed to have been ill in the backyard of the Borden home.

During the time Abby was being murdered, Bridget was apparently washing windows in the back of the house. Later, when Andrew was killed, Bridget was resting in her room upstairs. Why didn't she hear two people being butchered?

According to some theories, Lizzie and Bridget had been romantically involved. In this version of the story, their relationship was discovered shortly before the murders. Around this same time, Andrew was reportedly rewriting his will. His wife was now "Mrs. Borden," to Lizzie, not "Mother," as Lizzie had called her stepmother for many years. The reason for the estrangement was never clear.

Lizzie also had a strange relationship with her father and had given him her high school ring, as though he were her sweetheart. He wore the ring on his pinky finger and was buried with it.

Just a day before the murders, Lizzie had been attempting to purchase prussic acid—a deadly poison—and the family came down with "food poisoning" that night. Some speculate that Bridget was Lizzie's accomplice in the murders and helped clean up the blood afterward.

This theory was bolstered when, a few years after the murders, Lizzie became involved with actress Nance O'Neil. For two years, Lizzie and the statuesque actress were inseparable. This prompted Emma Borden, Lizzie's sister, to move out of their home.

At the time, the rift between the sisters sparked rumors that either Lizzie or Emma might reveal more about the other's role in the 1892 murders. However, neither of them said anything new about the killings.

Whodunit?

Most people believe that Lizzie was the killer. She was the only one accused of the crime, with good reason. Lizzie appeared to be the only one in the house at the time, other than Bridget. She showed no signs of grief when the murders were discovered. During questioning, Lizzie changed her story several times. The evidence was entirely circumstantial, but it was compelling enough to go to trial.

Ultimately, the jury accepted her attorney's closing argument, that the murders were "morally and physically impossible for this young woman defendant." In other words, Lizzie had to be innocent because she was petite and well bred. In 19th-century New England, that seemed like a logical and persuasive defense. Lizzie went free, and no one else was charged with the crimes.

But Lizzie wasn't the only one with motive, means, and opportunity. The most likely suspects were family members, working alone or with other relatives. Only a few had solid alibis, and—like Lizzie—many changed their stories during police questioning. But there was never enough evidence to officially accuse anyone other than Lizzie.

So whether or not Lizzie Borden "took an ax" and killed her parents, she's the one best remembered for the crime.

Lizzie Borden Bed & Breakfast

The Borden house has been sold several times over the years, but today it is a bed-and-breakfast—the main draw, of course, being the building's macabre history. The Victorian residence has been restored to reflect the details of the Borden home at the time of the murders, including the couch on which Andrew lay, his skull hideously smashed.

As a guest, you can stay in one of six rooms, even the one in which Abby was murdered. Then, after a good night's sleep, you'll be treated to a breakfast reminiscent of the one the Bordens had on their final morning in 1892. That is, if you got to sleep at all. (They say the place is haunted.)

As with all good morbid attractions, the proprietors at the Lizzie Borden B&B don't take themselves too seriously. Before you leave, you can stop by the gift shop and pick up a pair of hatchet earrings, an "I Survived the Night at the Lizzie Borden Bed & Breakfast" T-shirt, or an ax-wielding Lizzie Borden bobble-head doll.

Woman Shoplifts, Flees with Puppy in Shirt

All ended well for a Chihuahua puppy stolen from a pet store in Plantation, Florida. In January 2008, surveillance cameras caught a 26-year-old woman stuffing the dog into her shirt and fleeing the store without paying. She soon brought the tiny dog back and turned herself in to police.

The woman was taken into custody, but had she remained at large, the outlook was not promising—the $1,600 dog had a tracking microchip.

Male Impersonators

A young girl nowadays has a lot more freedom to choose what she wants to be when she grows up. This hasn't always been the case, but the women on this list didn't let that stop them: These fearless females did what they wanted to do, even if that meant masquerading as men for most of their lives.

Charley Parkhurst

Times were rough for ladies in the Wild West, so this cracker-jack stagecoach driver decided to live most of her life as a man. Born in 1812, Parkhurst lived well into her sixties, though how she managed to do it is the stuff of miracles. She is remembered to have been a hard-drinking, tobacco-chewing, one-eyed brute with a taste for adventure. Parkhurst gave birth at one point, but the child died. She lived out the rest of her life pursuing her stagecoach career until she died in December 1879. It was then that her true identity was revealed, much to the surprise of her friends.

Dr. James Barry

The life of James Barry, M.D., is proof positive that truth is often stranger than fiction. A vegetarian, teetotaler, and gifted doctor with skills ahead of his time (he performed one of the first successful cesarean sections while serving as a military surgeon), Dr. Barry was also quite possibly a female. If you lived in 19th-century Britain and happened to be a girl, you could kiss your dreams of being a surgeon goodbye. Barry, whose real name may have been Miranda, allegedly assumed a male identity to become an army physician. Barry's voice was high and he reportedly challenged those who made fun of it to a duel on the spot. When Barry died in 1865, the woman who was preparing the body for burial was said to be the first to discover his secret.

Billy Tipton

Born in Oklahoma in 1914, Dorothy Lucille Tipton was a gifted musician from the start. Her love of the saxophone and the piano was bittersweet, as the school she was attending wouldn't let girls play in the band. After escaping high school, Tipton decided to do whatever it took to pursue her passion. She started going by "Billy," wore suits, and bound her chest with tape to create the illusion that she was one of the guys. It worked, and Tipton's musical career was on its way. Tipton performed with some of the era's jazz greats and even recorded an album with The Billy Tipton Trio. Tipton married a woman, adopted three sons, and was reportedly a good father. Tipton died in 1989, and it was then that Tipton's sons learned of their father's true identity.

Pope Joan

Long held as a hero for feminists and anti-Catholics alike, Pope Joan's story is a debatable one. Even if the story is purely fictional, it's a good one nonetheless. "John Anglicus" was an Englishman in the ninth century who traveled to Rome where his fame as a lecturer led to his becoming a cardinal in the church. According to the story, when Pope Leo IV died in A.D. 855, Anglicus was unanimously elected Pope. Legend has it that during a citywide processional, the Pope stopped by the side of the road complaining of a stomachache and suddenly gave birth to a child. The jig was up: Pope John was actually a woman. Was it true? The Catholic Church denies that any "John Anglicus" was ever pope—according to their documents, Benedict III succeeded Leo IV.

John Taylor

Mary Anne Talbot was a troublemaker, but she was also a brave soldier, a hard worker, and a true talent in the art of male impersonation. Born in Britain in 1778, Talbot was orphaned when her mother died during childbirth. She was the mistress of a naval officer and accompanied him on trips across the Atlantic by posing as his footboy. When the naval officer died in battle in 1793, she had no choice but to continue posing as a man—John Taylor. She was wounded in the leg in 1794 and suffered from complications from the injury for the rest of her life. During her life, Talbot was a prisoner of war in France, an officer aboard an American merchant vessel, a highway worker, a London pensioner, a jewelry maker, an actor, and a nurse.

William Cathay

Born in Missouri in the midst of slavery, Cathay Williams served as a house slave until Union soldiers freed her during the Civil War. The soldiers employed her after that, and she worked for them for a while before wanting to see more action firsthand. Since women weren't allowed in the army, Williams dressed as a man in order to enlist. Of the approximately 5,000 black infantrymen and cavalry who served in the frontier army, "William Cathay" was the only woman to serve as a Buffalo Soldier (the nickname given to members of the U.S. 10th Cavalry Regiment of the U.S. Army, which now often refers to soldiers in any of the six black regiments that served in the war.) Williams was examined by an army surgeon in 1868 who discovered her true identity. She was discharged and retired to New Mexico where she passed away at age 82.

Joan of Arc

Born in France in 1412, 17-year-old Jeanne d'Arc disguised herself as a page when journeying through enemy territory so as to go unnoticed by soldiers. Before she was burned at the stake for being a heretic, Joan allegedly claimed that she was "doing a man's work" and therefore had to dress the part. The Catholic Church finally took back all the nasty things it said about Joan and recognized her as a saint in 1920.

Wacky Sports Injuries

- **Ryan Klesko**—In 2004, this San Diego Padre was in the middle of pregame stretches when he jumped up for the singing of the national anthem and pulled an oblique/rib-cage muscle, which sidelined him for more than a week.

- **Freddie Fitzsimmons**—In 1927, New York Giants pitcher "Fat Freddie" Fitzsimmons was napping in a rocking chair when his pitching hand got caught under the chair and was crushed by his substantial girth. Surprisingly, he only missed three weeks of the season.

- **Clarence "Climax" Blethen**—Blethen wore false teeth, but he believed he looked more intimidating without them. During a 1923 game, the Red Sox pitcher had the teeth in his back pocket when he slid into second base. The chompers bit his backside and he had to be taken out of the game.

- **Chris Hanson**—During a publicity stunt for the Jacksonville Jaguars in 2003, a tree stump and ax were placed in the locker room to remind players to "keep chopping wood," or give it their all. Punter Chris Hanson took a swing and missed the stump, sinking the ax into his non-kicking foot. He missed the remainder of the season.

- **Lionel Simmons**—As a rookie for the Sacramento Kings, Simmons devoted hours to playing his Nintendo Game Boy. In fact, he spent so much time playing the video game system that he missed a series of games during the 1991 season due to tendonitis in his right wrist.

- **Jaromir Jagr**—During a 2006 playoff game, New York Ranger Jagr threw a punch at an opposing player. Jagr missed, his fist slicing through the air so hard that he dislocated his shoulder. After the Rangers were eliminated from the playoffs, Jagr underwent surgery and continued his therapy during the next season.

- **Paulo Diogo**—After assisting on a goal in a 2004 match, newlywed soccer player Diogo celebrated by jumping up on a perimeter fence, accidentally catching his wedding ring on the wire. When he jumped down he tore off his finger. To make matters worse, the referee issued him a violation for excessive celebration.

- **Clint Barmes**—Rookie shortstop Barmes was sidelined from the Colorado Rockies lineup for nearly three months in 2005 after he broke his collarbone when he fell carrying a slab of deer meat.

- **Darren Barnard**—In the late 1990s, professional British soccer player Barnard was sidelined for five months with knee ligament damage after he slipped in a puddle of his puppy's pee on the kitchen floor. The incident earned him the unfortunate nickname "Whiz Kid."

- **Marty Cordova**—A fan of the bronzed look, Cordova was a frequent user of tanning beds. However, he once fell asleep while catching some rays, resulting in major burns to his face and body that forced him to miss several games with the Baltimore Orioles.

- **Gus Frerotte**—In 1997, Washington Redskins quarterback Frerotte had to be taken to the hospital and treated for a concussion after he spiked the football and slammed his head into a foam-covered concrete wall while celebrating a touchdown.

- **Jamie Ainscough**—A rough and ready rugby player from Australia, Ainscough's arm became infected in 2002, and doctors feared they might need to amputate. But after closer inspection, physicians found the source of the infection—the tooth of a rugby opponent had become lodged under his skin, unbeknownst to Ainscough who had continued to play for weeks after the injury.

- **Sammy Sosa**—In May 2004, Sosa sneezed so hard that he injured his back, sidelining the Chicago Cubs all-star outfielder and precipitating one of the worst hitting slumps of his career.

Beer, Wine, and Spirits: The Haunted Lemp Mansion

☠ ☠ ☠ ☠ ☠

There is no other place in St. Louis, Missouri, with a ghostly history quite like the Lemp Mansion. It has served as many things over the years—stately home, boarding house, restaurant, bed-and-breakfast—but it has never lost the notoriety of being the most haunted place in the city. In fact, in 1980, *Life* magazine called the Lemp Mansion "one of the ten most haunted places in America."

The Lemp brewery, and the Lemp family itself, gained recognition during the mid-1800s. Although they were credited with making one of the first lager beers in the United States and once rivaled the annual sales of Anheuser–Busch, few people remember much about the Lemps today—most people in St. Louis can barely even recall that the Lemps once made beer. They are now more familiar with the family's mansion on the city's south side than with the decaying brewery that stands two blocks away. The Lemps have been gone for years, but their old house stands as a reminder of their wealth and the tragedies that plagued them. Perhaps that's why there's still an aura of sadness looming over the place.

During the day, the house is a bustling restaurant, filled with people and activity, but at night, many people believe the old mansion is haunted. Are its ghosts the restless spirits of the Lemps wandering the corridors of their former home? It seems possible, given the enormous number of tragedies that struck the prominent family.

The Lemp Empire Begins

Adam Lemp left Germany in 1836, and by 1838 had settled in St. Louis. He had learned the brewer's trade as a young man, and he soon introduced the city to one of the first American lagers, a crisp, clean beer that required months of storage in a cool, dark place to obtain its unique flavor. This new beer quickly became a regional favorite.

Business prospered, and by the 1850s, thanks to the demand for lager, Lemp's Western Brewing Company was one of the largest in the city. When Adam Lemp died in 1862, his son William took the reins, and the company entered its period of greatest prominence.

After the death of his father, William began a major expansion of the brewery. He purchased more land and constructed a new brewery—the largest in St. Louis. In 1899, the Lemps introduced their famous Falstaff beer, which became a favorite across the country. Lemp was the first brewery to establish coast-to-coast distribution of its beer, and the company grew so large that as many as 100 horses were needed to pull the delivery wagons in St. Louis alone.

In 1876, during the time of his company's greatest success, William purchased a home for his family a short distance away from the brewery. He immediately began renovating and expanding the house, which had been built in the early 1860s, decorating it with original artwork, hand-carved wood decor, and ornately painted ceilings. The mansion featured a tunnel that traveled from the basement of the house along a quarried shaft and exited at the brewery. Ironically, it was in the midst of all this success that the Lemp family's troubles began.

Death Comes Calling

The first death in the family was that of Frederick Lemp, William's favorite son and heir to the Lemp empire. As the most ambitious and hardworking of the Lemp children, he'd been groomed to take over the family business. He was well liked and happily married but spent countless hours at the brewery working to improve the company's future. In 1901, his health began to fail, and, in December of that year, he died at age 28. Many believe that he worked himself to death.

Frederick's death devastated his parents, especially his father. William's friends and coworkers said he was never the same afterward. He was rarely seen in public and walked to the brewery using the tunnel beneath the house.

On January 1, 1904, William suffered another crushing blow with the death of his closest friend, fellow brewer Frederick

Pabst. This tragedy left William nervous and unsettled, and his physical and mental health began to deteriorate. On February 13, 1904, his suffering became unbearable. After breakfast, he went upstairs to his bedroom and shot himself with a revolver. No suicide note was ever found.

In November 1904, William, Jr., became president of the William J. Lemp Brewing Company. With his inheritance, he filled the house with servants, built country houses, and spent huge sums on carriages, clothing, and art.

Will's wife, Lillian, nicknamed the "Lavender Lady" because of her fondness for that color, was soon spending the Lemp fortune as quickly as her husband. They eventually divorced in 1906, causing a scandal throughout St. Louis. When it was all over, the Lavender Lady went into seclusion.

Less Drinking, More Death

In 1919, the 18th Amendment was passed, prohibiting the manufacture, transportation, and sale of alcohol in the United States. This signaled the end for many brewers, including the Lemps. Many hoped that Congress would repeal the amendment, but Will decided not to wait. He closed down the plant without notice, thus closing the door on the Lemp empire.

Will sold the famous Lemp "Falstaff" logo to brewer Joseph Griesedieck for $25,000. In 1922, he sold the brewery to the International Shoe Co. for a fraction of its estimated worth ($7 million before Prohibition).

With Prohibition destroying the brewery, the 1920s looked to be a dismal decade for the Lemp family. And it began on a tragic note, with the suicide of Elsa Lemp Wright in 1920. The second member of the family to commit suicide, Elsa was the wealthiest woman in St. Louis after inheriting her share of her father's estate. After a stormy marriage to wealthy industrialist Thomas Wright between 1910 and 1918, the couple divorced but then remarried in March 1920. Shortly after, Elsa inexplicably shot herself. No letter was ever found.

Will and his brother Edwin rushed to Elsa's house when they heard of their sister's suicide. Will had only one comment: "That's the Lemp family for you."

Will's own death came a short time later. While sitting in his office in the mansion, Will shot himself in the chest. His secretary found him lying in a pool of blood, and he died before a doctor could be summoned. As with his father and sister before him, Will had left no indication as to why he had ended his life.

Oddly, Will seemed to have had no intention of killing himself. After the sale of the brewery, he had discussed selling off the rest of his assets and said he wanted to rest and travel. He and his second wife were even planning a trip to Europe. Friends were baffled by his sudden death.

With William, Jr., gone and his brothers, Charles and Edwin, involved with their own endeavors, it seemed that the days of the Lemp empire had come to an end. But the days of Lemp tragedy were not yet over.

Charles was never very involved with the Lemp Brewery. His work had mostly been in the banking and financial industries, and he sometimes dabbled in politics as well. In the 1920s, Charles moved back into the Lemp Mansion.

Charles was a mysterious figure who became odd and reclusive with age. A lifelong bachelor, he lived alone in the rambling old house, and by age 77, he was arthritic and ill. He had grown quite eccentric and developed a morbid attachment to the Lemp family home. Because of the history of the place, his brother Edwin often encouraged Charles to move out, but he refused. Finally, when he could stand it no more, he became the fourth member of the Lemp family to take his own life.

On May 10, 1949, one of the staff members found Charles dead in his second-floor bedroom. He had shot himself at some point during the night. He was the only member of the family to leave a suicide note behind. He wrote: "In case I am found dead, blame it on no one but me."

The Lemp family, once so large and prosperous, had been nearly destroyed in less than a century. Only Edwin Lemp remained, and he had long avoided the life that had turned so tragic for the rest of his family. He was known as a quiet, reclusive man who lived a peaceful life on his secluded estate. In 1970, Edwin, the last of the Lemps, passed away quietly of natural causes at age 90.

Lemp Mansion Hauntings

After the death of Charles Lemp, the grand family mansion was sold and turned into a boarding house. It soon fell on hard times and began to deteriorate along with the neighborhood. In later years, stories emerged that residents of the boarding house often complained of ghostly knocks and phantom footsteps inside. As these tales spread, it became increasingly hard to find tenants to occupy the rooms, so the old Lemp Mansion was rarely filled.

The decline of the house continued until 1975, when Dick Pointer and his family purchased it. The Pointers began remodeling and renovating the place, working for years to turn it into a restaurant and inn. But the Pointers soon realized they were not alone in the house. Workers told of ghostly events occurring, such as strange sounds, tools that vanished and appeared again in other places, and an overwhelming feeling that they were being watched.

After the restaurant opened, staff members began to report their own odd experiences. Glasses were seen lifting off the bar and flying through the air, inexplicable sounds were heard, and some people even glimpsed actual apparitions. Visitors to the house reported that doors locked and unlocked on their own, voices and sounds came from nowhere, and even the Lavender Lady was spotted on occasion.

These strange events continue today, so it is no surprise that the inn attracts ghost hunters from around the country. Many spend the night in the house and report their own bizarre happenings, from eerie sounds to strange photographs. One woman awoke to see the specter of a lady standing next to her bed. The ghost raised a finger to her lips, as if asking the woman not to scream, and then vanished.

Paul Pointer manages the business today, along with his sisters, Mary and Patty. They all accept the ghosts as part of the ambience of the historic old home. As Paul once said, "People come here expecting to experience weird things, and fortunately for us, they are rarely disappointed."

Very Odd Jobs

From weed farmers to barnyard masturbators, our world is teeming with offbeat jobs that rarely, if ever, find ink in newspaper classifieds. Here are a few that might make you look at your job title in an entirely different way.

Ant Catcher

Remember when you were a kid and got down on your hands and knees to search for ants? Well, imagine being a grown-up that gets paid to do so. Ant catchers collect the little critters to populate colonies in toy ant farms.

Barnyard Masturbator

The "BM's" job is to collect sperm from a bull for fertility studies or artificial insemination. To do this, he or she must step in at the most intense moment of bovine arousal, replace the living, breathing female with an artificial one, and grab the bull by the "horns," so to speak. A thankless job, but someone has to do it.

Boner

In days past, the term *boner* meant a blunder or an error. Today, although it could mean an activity not remotely fit for this book, a boner is also a textile worker who inserts stays into women's corsets and brassieres.

Brain Picker

Here's another job that is not as seems. A brain picker does *not* extract information from geniuses in a think tank. He or she *does* split the skulls of slaughterhouse animals for the sole intent of picking out their brains, thereby rendering them more palatable to fussy human beings.

Chicken Sexers

A person with this job gets to distinguish between male and female chicks. This is necessary in the poultry industry so that egg-laying females are separated from their male counterparts. In some cases, the gender of specially bred hatchlings can be determined by their feathers. But in most cases, poultry sleuthing requires that feces be squeezed from the chick in order to obtain an inside view of its reproductive organs. If a small bump (not unlike that found on a "Ken" doll) is discovered, the chick is deemed male.

Circus Elephant Tender

Visitors to a circus have seen these workers and likely sympathized with their plight. Their job is to follow elephants around and pick up after them. With a gritty air of determination and an ever-present shovel, these unsung heroes unceremoniously perform their duties. The downside includes poop inhalation and the risk of being trampled to death should Dumbo get rambunctious.

Citrus Fruit Colorer

The next time you marvel at the vibrant color of an orange or tangerine, you should know that a Citrus Fruit Colorer had as much to do with this agreeable veneer as nature—maybe more. Because citrus fruit is generally picked *before* it is fully ripe, a squad of "artists," aided by steam and chemicals, steps in to help things along.

Furniture Tester

When and where is the statement: "Get off your lazy butt and get back to work!" almost never heard? At a facility that employs furniture testers, of course! Part of the tester's job requires sitting and/or lying down on the pieces being tested, so it's probably the furniture tester's favorite part of the day.

Hooker Inspector

If this misleading job were advertised in the classifieds, perhaps a thousand men would apply. Despite its suggestive name, however, the men would not be checking out painted ladies at a bordello. Instead, they'd find themselves in a drab textile mill twisting skeins—yarn or thread wound around reels—on a hooking machine. The device is so named because it "hooks" each end of the skein to clasps on the machine. Get your mind out of the gutter!

Hot Walker
Though the term *hot walker* conjures up images of a super-model sashaying seductively along a beach, its real meaning is a bit more mundane. In reality, a hot walker walks racehorses just after a competition or workout to aid the four-leggers in the cooling-down process. As off the mark as its name sounds, it's a highly necessary duty. If this task is not performed, the horse could suffer kidney damage.

Weed Farmer
The trend of misleading job titles continues with weed farmer, a job that sounds like something straight out of a Cheech & Chong movie. Its true meaning, of course, is far less intoxicating and far more legal. A weed farmer merely grows weeds that will later be sold to chemical companies and universities for herbicide research, *not* for turning on, tuning in, and dropping out.

Wrinkle Chaser
Unfortunately, a wrinkle chaser does not provide transportation to the fountain of youth. Nor does he or she she perform at-home facials. This worker simply irons away wrinkles in footwear that have emerged during the production process so that shoes are smooth as silk when they arrive at stores for sale.

Male lions do very little other than mate—approximately every 20 minutes. Scientists observed one lion doing it 157 times in 55 hours.

Monster on the Chesapeake

Chesapeake Bay, a 200-mile intrusion of the Atlantic Ocean into Virginia and Maryland, is 12 miles wide at its mouth, allowing plenty of room for strange saltwater creatures to slither on in. Encounters with giant, serpentine beasts up and down the Eastern seaboard were reported during the 1800s, but sightings of Chessie, a huge, snakelike creature with a football-shape head and flippers began to escalate in the 1960s. Former CIA employee Donald Kyker and some neighbors saw not one, but four unidentified water creatures swimming near shore in 1978.

Then in 1980, the creature was spotted just off Love Point, sparking a media frenzy. Two years later, Maryland resident Robert Frew was entertaining dinner guests with his wife, Karen, when the whole party noticed a giant water creature about 200 yards from shore swimming toward a group of people frolicking nearby in the surf. They watched the creature, which they estimated to be about 30 feet in length, as it dove underneath the unsuspecting humans, emerged on the other side, and swam away.

Frew recorded several minutes of the creature's antics, and the Smithsonian Museum of Natural History reviewed his film. Although they could not identify the animal, they did concede that it was "animate," or living.

The Chessie Challenge

Some believe Chessie is a manatee, but they usually swim in much warmer waters and are only about ten feet long. Also, the fact that Chessie is often seen with several "humps" breaking the water behind its head leads other investigators to conclude that it could be either a giant sea snake or a large seal.

One Maryland resident has compiled a list of 78 different sightings over the years. And a tour boat operator offers sea-monster tours in hopes of repeating the events of 1980 when 25 passengers on several charter boats all spotted Chessie cavorting in the waves.

Winchester Mystery House

By the time she was 22, Sarah Pardee was seriously popular—she spoke four languages, played the piano, and was exceedingly pretty. Nicknamed the "Belle of New Haven," she had her pick of suitors.

She chose a young man named William W. Winchester, the only son of Oliver Winchester, a stockholder with the successful New Haven Arms Company. When Sarah and William married in 1862, William had plans to expand the business by buying out some of his competition and introducing the repeating rifle, so named because its lever action allowed a gunman to fire many shots in succession. The gun became known as "The Gun that Won the West," and the now fabulously wealthy Winchester name was woven into the fabric of American history.

Can't Buy Me Love

In the summer of 1866, Sarah gave birth to a daughter, but the joy of a new baby was brief. The child was born sickly, diagnosed with marasmus, a protein deficiency that typically afflicts infants in third-world countries. The baby was unable to gain weight and succumbed to the disease in just a few weeks.

Sarah and William were both bereft, but Sarah took it the hardest. She sank into a serious depression from which she would never totally recover.

Fifteen years later, when Oliver Winchester passed away, William stepped into his dad's shoes at the family business. However, he had only held the job for a few months when he lost a battle with tuberculosis and died in 1881.

Sarah was now 41 years old and without the family she had built her life around. She was also extremely wealthy. In the late 1880s, the average family income hovered around $500 per year. Sarah was pulling in about $1,000 per day! Because her husband left her everything, she had more than 700 shares of stock in addition to income from current sales. Sarah was up to her eyeballs in money. When William's mother died in 1898, Sarah inherited 2,000 more shares, which meant that she owned about 50 percent of the business. Sarah Winchester was all dressed up and had absolutely nowhere to go—even if she did have someplace, there was no one with whom she could share it.

"I See Dead People"
Today, most people regard psychics with more than a little suspicion and skepticism, but in the late 19th century, psychics had grabbed much of the public's attention and trust. The period after the Civil War and the onslaught of new industry had left so much destruction and created so much change for people that many were looking for answers in a confusing world. With claims that they could commune with the "Great Beyond," psychics were consulted by thousands hoping for some insight.

Sarah was not doing well after the death of her husband. Losing her child had been a debilitating blow, but after her husband's passing, she was barely able to function. Fearing for her life, one of Sarah's close friends suggested she visit a psychic to see if she could contact her husband or daughter or both.

Sarah agreed to visit a Boston medium named Adam Coons, who wasted no time in telling her that William was trying to communicate with her, and the message wasn't good.

Apparently, William was desperate to tell Sarah that the family was cursed as a result of the invention of the repeating rifle. Native Americans, settlers, and soldiers all over the world were dead, largely due to the Winchester family. The spirits of these people were out for Sarah next, said William through the medium. The only way for her to prolong her life was to "head toward the setting sun," which meant, "move to California." The medium told her that once she got there, she would have to build a house where all those spirits could live happily together—but the house had to be built big and built often. Sarah was told that construction on the house could never cease, or the spirits would claim her and she would die. So Sarah packed up and left New Haven for California in 1884.

Now That's a House!

Sarah bought an eight-room farmhouse on the outskirts of the burgeoning town of San Jose, on the southern end of San Francisco Bay. Legend has it that she hired more than 20 workmen and a foreman and kept them working 24 hours a day, 365 days a year. To ensure that they would keep quiet about what they were doing—and not leave because the house was more than a little weird—she paid them a whopping $3 per day—more than twice the going rate of the time.

The workmen took the money and built as their client wished, though it made no sense whatsoever. Sarah was not an architect, but she gave the orders for the house's design. Sarah's odd requests, the constant construction, and an endless stream of money resulted in a rather unusual abode—stairs lead to ceilings, windows open into brick walls, and some rooms have no doors. There are also Tiffany windows all over the place, many containing the number 13, with which Sarah was obsessed. There are spiderweb-paned windows, which, although lovely, didn't do much to dispel rumors that Sarah was preoccupied with death and the occult.

The house kept on growing, all because the spirits were supposedly "advising" Sarah. Chimneys were built and never used. There were so many rooms that counting them was pointless. Reportedly, one stairway in the house went up seven steps and down eleven, and one of the linen closets is bigger than most three-bedroom apartments.

Very few people ever saw the lady of the house. When she shopped in town, merchants came to her car, as she rarely stepped out. Rumors were rampant in San Jose: Who was this crazy lady? Was the house haunted by spirits or just the energy of the aggrieved widow who lived there? Would the hammers *ever* stop banging? The workers knew how weird the house was, but no one knew for sure what went on inside Sarah's head.

Still, Sarah was generous in the community. She donated to the poor, occasionally socialized, and, in the early days, even threw a party every once in a while. She had a maid she was quite fond of and was exceedingly kind to any children she encountered. But as the house grew and the years passed, the rumors became more prevalent and the increasingly private Winchester retreated further into her bizarre hermitage.

The End
In 1922, Sarah Winchester died in her sleep, and the construction finally ceased after 38 years. In her will, Sarah left huge chunks of her estate to nieces, nephews, and loyal employees. The will was divided into exactly 13 parts and was signed 13 times. Her belongings, everything from ornate furniture to chandeliers to silver dinner services, were auctioned off. It took six weeks to remove everything.

And as for the house itself, it wasn't going to find a buyer any time soon: The structure at the time of Sarah's passing covered several acres and had more than 10,000 window panes, 160 rooms, 467 doorways, 47 fireplaces, 40 stairways, and 6 kitchens. A group of investors bought the house in hopes of turning it into a tourist attraction, which they did. What they didn't do was employ guides or security, however, so for a small fee, thousands of curious people came from all over the country to traipse through the house, scribbling graffiti on the walls and stealing bits of wallpaper. It wasn't until the house was purchased in the 1970s and renamed the Winchester Mystery House that it was restored to its original state. Millions of people have visited the house, which continues to be one of the top tourist attractions in California.

The Footnote
With so many people going in and out of the house over the years, it's not surprising that there are tales of "strange happenings" in the Winchester mansion. People have claimed that they've heard and seen banging doors, mysterious voices, cold spots, moving lights, doorknobs that turn by themselves, and more than a few say that Sarah herself still roams the many rooms. Psychics who have visited the house solemnly swear that it is indeed haunted.

This can't be proven, of course, but it doesn't stop the claims, and it didn't stop the lady of the house from undertaking one of the world's most incredible construction projects.

A Realtor's Worst Nightmare

*It seems every town in the world has a local haunted house—
the one house that animals and locals avoid like the plague.
But when it comes to haunted houses that can chill your bones
with just one glance and give you nightmares for weeks, nothing can hold a ghostly candle to a foreboding Dutch Colonial
in Amityville, New York, which once glared down at passersby
with windows that seemed to resemble demonic eyes.*

Brutal Beginnings

Most hauntings begin with tragic circumstances, and the house
at 112 Ocean Avenue is no exception. In the early morning
hours of November 13, 1974, someone fatally shot six of the
seven members of the DeFeo family—father Ronald, Sr., his
wife, Louise, and four of their children: Mark, John, Allison,
and Dawn. The only one to escape the massacre was 23-year-
old Ronnie "Butch" DeFeo, who was subsequently arrested
and charged with all six murders. He eventually confessed and
was sentenced to 25 years to life in prison. During the trial,
there were rumors that demonic
voices had directed
DeFeo to commit the
murders, although pros-
ecutors claimed he was
only trying to col-
lect the family's
$200,000 insur-
ance policy.

The DeFeo
house stood
alone and aban-
doned until
December 1975,
when new own-
ers came calling.

The Horror Begins

George and Kathy Lutz knew they had a bargain on their hands when their realtor showed them 112 Ocean Avenue. The house had six bedrooms, a pool, and even a boathouse, all for the unbelievable price of $80,000. Of course, an entire family had been murdered in the house, and some of their belongings were still inside, but after a family meeting, the Lutzes decided it was too good a deal to pass up. So George and Kathy moved in with their three young children: Daniel, Christopher, and Missy. Shortly thereafter, the nightmare began. To the Lutzes, it quickly became obvious that there were demonic forces at work inside the house. Some of the paranormal experiences that allegedly took place in the home include:

- George had trouble sleeping and would continually wake up at exactly 3:15 A.M., believed to be the time the DeFeo murders took place.

- Daughter Missy began talking to an imaginary friend: a girl named Jodie who sometimes appeared as a pig. Standing outside the house one night, George looked up and saw a giant pig with glowing red eyes staring back at him from Missy's room. Later, cloven hoofprints were found in the snow outside the house.

- Even though it was the middle of winter, certain rooms in the house, especially the sewing room, were constantly infested with flies.

- A small room painted blood red was found hidden behind shelving in the basement. Dubbed the Red Room, the entire family felt there was something evil in the room. Even the family dog, Harry, refused to go near it.

- During an attempt to bless the house, a priest suddenly became violently ill and heard an inhuman voice yell at him to "Get out!" When George and Kathy attempted to bless the house on their own, they heard voices screaming, "Will you stop?"

- Green slime oozed out of the toilets and dripped from the walls.

- George began (unintentionally) taking on the mannerisms of Ronald DeFeo, Jr., and even grew out his beard, causing him to resemble DeFeo. Apparently the likeness was so uncanny that when Lutz walked into a bar DeFeo used to frequent, patrons thought he was DeFeo.

On January 14, 1976, unable to cope with the unseen forces at work in the house, George and Kathy Lutz gathered up their children and their dog and fled the house in the middle of the night. The following day, George sent movers out to gather up all their belongings. The Lutzes themselves never again set foot inside 112 Ocean Avenue.

Searching for Evil

In an attempt to understand exactly what happened to his family inside the house, George brought in demonologists Ed and Lorraine Warren, who arrived at the house with a local news crew on March 6, 1976. Lorraine said that she sensed a very strong evil presence in the house. Several years later, a series of time-lapse infrared photographs were released that appeared to show a ghostly boy with glowing eyes standing near one of the staircases.

Jay Anson's book *The Amityville Horror—A True Story* was released in September 1977. The book, which chronicled the Lutz family's harrowing ordeal, was compiled from more than 40 hours of tape-recorded interviews with George and Kathy and became a best seller almost immediately. With that, everyone started taking a closer look into what really happened at 112 Ocean Avenue.

Controversy Begins

Once people started looking at the specifics in Anson's book, things didn't seem to add up. For one, a check of weather conditions showed there was no snow on the ground when George claimed to have found the strange cloven footprints in the snow. Likewise, windows and doors that ghostly forces had supposedly broken or demolished in the book were found to still be intact. Reporters interviewing neighbors along Ocean Avenue found that not a single person could remember ever seeing or hearing anything strange going on at the house. And despite the book mentioning numerous visits by local police to investigate strange noises at the Lutz house, the Amityville Police Department publicly stated that during the whole time the Lutzes lived at 112 Ocean Avenue, they never visited the home or received a single phone call from the family.

The Lawsuits
In May 1977, George and Kathy Lutz filed a series of law-suits against numerous magazines and individuals who had either investigated 112 Ocean Avenue or had written about the reported hauntings. They alleged that these people had invaded their privacy and caused their family mental distress. There was one other name in the lawsuit that raised more than a few eyebrows: William Weber, Ronald DeFeo, Jr.'s defense lawyer. Even more surprising was that Weber filed a counter-suit for $2 million for breach of contract.

Weber contended that he had met with the Lutzes and that "over many bottles of wine" the three made up the story of the house being haunted. When Weber found out that the Lutzes had taken their story to Jay Anson and essentially cut him out of the deal, he sued. In September 1979, U.S. District Court judge Jack B. Weinstein dismissed all of the Lutzes' claims and also made some telling remarks in his ruling, including that he felt the book was basically a work of fiction that relied heavily upon Weber's suggestions. Weber's countersuit was later set-tled out of court for an undisclosed amount.

What Really Happened?
Even though it's been more than 30 years since the Lutzes occupied the house at 112 Ocean Avenue, many questions still remain unanswered. A series of books and movies all bearing the name *The Amityville Horror* were released, which con-tinued to blur the lines between what really happened in

the home and what was a fabrication. In 2005, a remake of *The Amityville Horror* movie was released that added many new elements to the story that have yet to be substantiated, including a link between the house in Amityville and a mythical figure, John Ketcham, who was reportedly involved with witchcraft in Salem, Massachusetts.

Kathy Lutz died of emphysema in August 2004. George Lutz passed away from complications of heart disease in May 2006. Both went to their graves still proclaiming that what happened to them inside 112 Ocean Avenue did indeed occur and was not a hoax.

The house itself is still standing. You would think that with a building as famous (or infamous) and well known as the Amityville Horror house is, it would be easy to find. Not so. In order to stop the onslaught of trespassing thrill seekers, the address has been changed, so 112 Ocean Avenue technically no longer exists. The famous quarter-moon windows have also been removed and replaced with ordinary square ones.

Since the Lutz family moved out, the property has changed hands several times, but none of the owners have ever reported anything paranormal taking place there. They did acknowledge being frightened from time to time but that was usually from being startled by the occasional trespasser peering into their windows trying to get a glimpse of the inside of this allegedly haunted house.

Amazing Journey

There are stories of dogs and cats finding their way home over long distances, but this is different: In January 2008, a Texas man was unpacking from a trip when a kitten popped out of his suitcase. The cat had gotten through security and survived the journey without a scratch. Realizing that he'd picked up the wrong suitcase, he contacted the owners, who were reunited with their worldly kitty a few days later.

Son of a Gun

In November 1874, an article in *The American Medical Weekly* told a fantastic tale. According to Dr. LeGrand G. Capers, the article's author and firsthand witness, a bullet struck a Confederate soldier at the Battle of Raymond in Mississippi, ricocheted, then struck a young woman at a nearby farmhouse. Both survived. Had this been the end of the story, it would read like countless tales from the Civil War. But this one was different.

Capers noted that the "Minnie ball" (a soft lead bullet) first passed through the soldier's scrotum before it ricocheted, striking the unlucky woman in her abdominal cavity. Nine months later, she gave birth to an eight-pound son.

With social dictates of the period acting as a driving force, Capers was called upon to explain how the virginal girl could have become impregnated.

Three weeks later the doctor was again summoned, this time by the young woman's grandmother, who asked the physician to examine the newborn's scrotum, which had become dangerously enlarged. The doctor immediately saw that something was wrong and decided to operate. To his utter amazement, Capers found a Minnie ball embedded in the child. He reasoned that the bullet had passed through the soldier's scrotum and collected sperm cells while on its way into the woman's reproductive system, thereby impregnating her. It then worked its way into the flesh of the fetus where it now lay.

According to Capers, the soldier was notified of the bizarre occurrence and he and the young woman met, eventually married, and produced two more children by the conventional method.

Though the story was published by *The American Medical Weekly* and reprinted elsewhere, it was found to be completely false. Dr. Capers had concocted the tale as a way to lampoon fictitious Civil War stories then making the rounds.

Strange and Unusual Talents

Rubberboy: Daniel Browning Smith

Nicknamed "Rubberboy," Daniel is unique, even among his peers. Most contortionists are either forward benders or backward benders, but rarely both. Daniel, who is able to contort and dislocate his 5'8" body into almost any formation, is that rare exception, so much so that he holds three Guinness World Records. Daniel's opening and closing acts are especially awe-inspiring—he emerges from a tiny 19.5"×13.5"×16" box to begin and manages to fold himself back into the box before being carried off stage at the finale.

The Ayala Sisters

When Michelle, Andrea, and Alexis Ayala enter the circus ring, the petite sisters juggle fire, twirl, and spin—all while hanging by their long locks. Traditional hair suspension acts go up and down more than the stock market, never leaving the performer suspended for more than a half minute. But the Ayala sisters, like their mother before them, remain aloft for nearly six minutes, only coming back to the circus floor long enough to gain momentum for their final dizzying, high-speed spin.

The Wolf Boy

Take one look at Danny Gomez and you'll realize there's something different about him. Born with a condition called hypertrichosis, his entire body, including his face, is covered with thick black hair. But Danny is about much more than his unusual physical appearance. He's been performing since he was a small child—more than 20 years—and his amazing skills include juggling, trampoline, trapeze, and even daredevil motorcycle stunts. Danny's warm personality and quirky sense of humor make him a favorite with audiences, especially children. Danny and his older brother, Larry, who is also afflicted with hypertrichosis, frequently performed together as the Wolf Brothers until recently when Larry retired from showbiz.

Tim "Zamora the Torture King" Cridland

Audience members may cringe while watching Zamora perform, but they never forget him. Using martial arts techniques combined with Eastern teaching, hypnosis, and an extensive knowledge of anatomy, Zamora astounds and shocks his fans with feats of mind over matter—jumping on and eating glass, sword swallowing, electrocution, and body skewering—only to emerge intact and unscathed. That can't always be said for the more squeamish members of the crowd.

George "The Giant" McArthur

At 7′3″, George McArthur stands out among performers but not just because of his imposing size. This multitalented gentle giant holds a Guinness World Record for having the most weight—1,387 pounds from slabs of cement—broken on his body while lying on a bed of nails. George started in the circus business as a fire-eater, a skill he learned while determined to rid himself of a fear of flames. Since then he's added sword swallowing, walking on broken glass, and straight jacket escapes to his performing repertoire.

Mighty Mike Murga

A supermarket of unique talent, "little person" Mighty Mike Murga works as a strong man, fire-eater, unicycle rider, and juggler. Though these might seem like typical circus skills, at 4′3″, Mike has to work harder to overcome the challenges of his size and low center of gravity to perfect the skills his taller peers take for granted. Recently, Mike completed a tour with Mötley Crüe, whose heavy metal fans immediately fell in love with the diminutive star.

Griping in Tune:
Complaint Choirs

💀   💀   💀   💀   💀

People spend a whole lot of time and energy complaining about almost everything. Whether it's work, relationships, family, or the weather, a good percentage of our days are spent complaining or listening to someone else complain. Look out, disgruntled world—complaint choirs are popping up across the globe and are giving complaints a sonic facelift.

A Disgruntled Dream

In 2005, Finnish artist Oliver Kochta-Kalleinen and his wife became interested in the Finnish expression *valituskuoro,* which, literally translated, means "complaints choir." The couple wanted to take a positive approach to complaining, so they took the literal meaning of valituskuoro to heart and set out to create the world's first complaint choir.

They approached several different venues with their idea and got some interest, but it wasn't until the Springhill Institute—an international artist-in-residence program in Birmingham, England—expressed interest that the first complaint choir formed.

Birmingham residents had a lot to complain about—the economy wasn't very good, the public transit system left a lot to be desired, and the social scene was less than robust—so the idea of airing grievances in song was met with enthusiasm. Local composer Mike Hurley turned the complaints that had been gathered into lyrics for a chamber choir type of song, and participants gathered to rehearse.

Lights, Camera, Complain!

The Birmingham singers practiced for a few weeks before their first performance, which they filmed and posted on YouTube. Word started to spread, and soon the interest in complaint choirs snowballed. Before long, the Kalleinens were helping form a choir in their hometown of Helsinki. This large group of Finnish singers performed in public places such as train stations and parks. Crowds cheered when they heard the dulcet tones of the choir sing lines like, "Old forests are cut down and turned into toilet paper, and still the toilets are always out of paper," and truly bleak lines such as, "My dreams are boring." In fact, one of the most distinguishing characteristics of the work of every complaint choir is the nature of the complaints. There is rarely any profanity, and most of the complaints have a decidedly humorous tone. One complaint from a Norwegian choir bemoans: "There's never enough time to polish all my nails—today I just polished my thumb."

Complaint choirs formed in Hamburg, St. Petersburg, Pennsylvania, Alaska, and even in Jerusalem. The Budapest choir is an especially active group, performing in huge numbers on rooftops, on trams, and in the middle of the street. Most of these choirs have videotaped their "concerts," which can be viewed online.

Hey, I Have Complaints, Too!

If you'd like to get something off your chest, you can join a complaint choir or start your own. Instructions can be found online for those with a desire to sing their grievances to the world and use their griping to create a piece of music.

Calling in Heartsick

A Tokyo-based marketing company is now granting "heartache leave" for employees. If you get dumped or your relationship ends, you can take one to three days off to nurse your broken heart, depending on your age. Women in their early twenties get just one day off, but women who are older get more because, according to the CEO, it's harder to find love when you're older.

Giant Frogman Spotted in Ohio!

For the most part, frogs are rather unintimidating—unless they're more than four feet tall and standing along a dark road in the middle of the night.

The First Encounter

On March 3, 1972, police officer Ray Shockey was driving his patrol car along Riverside Road toward the small town of Loveland, Ohio. At approximately 1:00 A.M., Shockey saw what he thought was a dog lying alongside the road, but as he got closer, the creature suddenly stood up on two feet. Amazed, Shockey stopped his car and watched the creature climb over a guardrail and scamper down the ditch toward the Little Miami River. Shockey drove back to the police station and described what he'd seen to fellow officer Mark Matthews. Shockey said the creature was approximately four feet tall and weighed between 50 to 75 pounds. It stood on two legs and had webbed feet, clawed hands, and the head of a frog.

After hearing his story, Matthews accompanied Shockey back to the site of the encounter. The pair could not locate the frogman, but they did find strange scratch marks along the section of guardrail the creature had climbed over.

Frogman Returns

On the night of March 17, Matthews was on the outskirts of town when he saw an animal lying in the middle of the road. Thinking that the animal had been hit by a car, Matthews stopped his squad car. But when the animal suddenly stood up on two legs, Matthews realized that it was the same creature that Shockey had encountered. Just as before, the creature walked to the side of the road and climbed over a guardrail. Matthews simply watched, although some reports say he shot at the animal. Either way, the creature moved down the embankment toward the river and vanished.

The Aftermath

When news spread of a second Frogman sighting, the town of Loveland was inundated with calls from reporters across the country. Obviously, reports of four-foot-tall froglike creatures are rarely considered newsworthy, but two witnesses had seen the creature on different nights, and both were police officers.

In the beginning, Shockey and Matthews stuck to their stories and even had sketches made of the creature they'd encountered. But over time, the public turned on the officers, accusing them of fabricating the whole thing. In recent years, the officers now claim that what they encountered was merely an iguana. Most seem happy with that explanation. But it doesn't explain how an iguana stood up on two legs and walked across the road. Or why their sketches looked nothing like an iguana.

So Where Is the Frog Today?

A local farmer also claimed he saw the Frogman lumbering through his field one evening, but there have been no other sightings since the 1970s. Those who believe in the Loveland Frogman claim that after Matthews allegedly shot at it, it became frightened and moved to a more isolated area. Others think that Matthews's shot killed the creature. Of course, there are some who believe that the Loveland Frogman is still out there and has merely become more elusive. Just something to consider should you ever find yourself driving alongside the Little Miami River near Loveland on a dark, moonless night.

Circle Marks the Spot:
The Mystery of Crop Circles

The result of cyclonic winds? Attempted alien communication? Evidence of hungry cows with serious OCD? There are many theories as to how crop circles, or grain stalks flattened in recognizable patterns, have come to exist. Most people dismiss them as pranks, but there are more than a few who believe there's something otherworldly going on.

Ye Ole Crop Circle

Some experts believe the first crop circles date back to the late 1600s, but there isn't much evidence to support them. Other experts cite evidence of more than 400 simple circles 6 to 20 feet in diameter that appeared worldwide hundreds of years ago. The kinds of circles they refer to are still being found today, usually after huge, cyclonic thunderstorms pass over a large expanse of agricultural land. These circles are much smaller and not nearly as precise as the geometric, mathematically complex circles that started cropping up in the second half of the 20th century. Still, drawings and writings about these smaller circles lend weight to the claims of believers that the crop circle phenomenon isn't a new thing.

The International Crop Circle Database reports stories of "UFO nests" in British papers during the 1960s. About a decade or so later, crop circles fully captured the attention (and the imagination) of the masses.

No, Virginia, There Aren't Any Aliens

In 1991, two men from Southampton, England, came forward with a confession. Doug Bower and Dave Chorley admitted that they were responsible for the majority of the crop circles found in England during the preceding two decades.

Inspired by stories of "UFO nests" in the 1960s, the two decided to add a little excitement to their sleepy town. With boards, string, and a few simple navigational tools, the men worked through the night to create complex patterns in fields that could be seen from the road. It worked, and before long, much of the Western world was caught up in crop circle fever. Some claimed it was irrefutable proof that UFOs were landing on Earth. Others said God was trying to communicate with humans "through the language of mathematics." For believers, there was no doubt that supernatural or extraterrestrial forces were at work. But skeptics were thrilled to hear the confession from Bower and Chorley, since they never believed the circles to be anything but a prank in the first place.

Before the men came forward, more crop circles appeared throughout the 1980s and '90s, many of them not made by Bower and Chorley. Circles "mysteriously" occurred in Australia, Canada, the United States, Argentina, India, and even Afghanistan. In 1995, more than 200 cases of crop circles were reported worldwide. In 2001, a formation that appeared in Wiltshire, England, contained 409 circles and covered more than 12 acres.

Many were baffled that anyone could believe these large and admittedly rather intricate motifs were anything but human-made. Plus, the more media coverage crop circles garnered, the more new crop circles appeared. Other people came forward, admitting that they were the "strange and unexplained power" behind the circles. Even then, die-hard believers dismissed the hoaxers, vehemently suggesting that they were either players in a government cover-up, captives of aliens forced to throw everyone off track, or just average Joes looking for 15 minutes of fame by claiming to have made something that was clearly the work of nonhumans.

Scientists were deployed to ascertain the facts. In 1999, a well-funded team of experts was assembled to examine numerous crop circles in the UK. The verdict? At least 80 percent of the circles were, beyond a shadow of a doubt, created by humans. Footprints, abandoned tools, and video of a group of hoaxers caught in the act all debunked the theory that crop circles were created by aliens.

But Still...

So if crop circles are nothing more than hoaxers having fun or artists playing with a unique medium, why are we still so interested? Movies such as *Signs* in 2002 capitalized on the public's fascination with the phenomenon, and crop circles still capture headlines. Skeptics will scoff, but from time to time, there is a circle that doesn't quite fit the profile of a human-made prank.

There have been claims that fully functional cell phones cease to work once the caller steps inside certain crop circles. Could it be caused by some funky ion-scramble emitted by an extraterrestrial force? Some researchers have tried to re-create the circles and succeeded, but only with the use of high-tech tools and equipment that wouldn't be available to the average prankster. If all of these circles were made by humans, why are so few people busted for trespassing in the middle of the night? And where are all the footprints?

Eyewitness accounts of UFOs rising from fields can hardly be considered irrefutable evidence, but there are several reports from folks who swear they saw ships, lights, and movement in the sky just before crop circles were discovered.

STRANGE STATS

- *Elephants can run up to 30 miles per hour and kill approximately 500 people each year.*

- *The Limax redii slug has a penis seven times the length of its body...33 inches long!*

- *The muntjak, a small deer of Asia, is also known as the barking deer because its loud bleat sounds like a dog's bark. But stranger still is that male muntjaks grow long upper canine teeth that hang down like tusks and, even weirder, can be wiggled to create a rattling sound.*

- *The youngest mother on record was a five-year-old Peruvian girl named Lina Medina. In 1939, she gave birth to a six-pound son by cesarean section.*

History's Maddest Rulers

💀   💀   💀   💀   💀

We all complain about our nation's leadership from time to time, but check out these crazy rulers and their devilish deeds.

Vlad the Impaler
Everyone has heard of the infamous Count Dracula. Half man, half bat, this beastly hybrid lived to drink human blood. But not everyone knows that novelist Bram Stoker's inspiration for the evil madman came from an actual person who was much worse than he's been portrayed. Vlad III Dracula (1431–1476) governed Wallachia, a Hungarian principality that later merged with neighbors Transylvania and Moldavia to form Romania. To say that Dracula ruled with an iron fist barely scratches the surface—an "iron stake" is more accurate. During his six-year reign of terror, it is believed that Dracula murdered as many as 40,000 people whom he considered enemies. Most of these unfortunates met their end by impalement, hence Dracula's ominous moniker. With a sharpened stake as wide as a man's arm, his victims were often pierced from the anus to the mouth, not through the heart as Hollywood legend implies. The madman often blinded, strangled, decapitated, hanged, boiled, burned, or skinned his victims. Once, a concubine hoping to spare her life claimed that she was carrying Dracula's child. When he discovered she was lying, he had her womb cut open and remarked, "Let the world see where I have been."

Idi Amin Dada
To the eye, Ugandan president Idi Amin Dada (1925–2003) was a deceptive contradiction. Viewed as a cartoonlike character by the press (*Time* dubbed him a "killer and clown, big-hearted buffoon and strutting martinet"), the former

major general nevertheless found a way to kill an estimated 300,000 people while in power. Many of his victims were killed to squelch the ruler's paranoid fears of being overthrown. Others were eliminated simply for his own ghoulish pleasure. Known as the "butcher of Uganda," Dada reportedly kept severed heads in his refrigerator and may have eaten some of his victims. And allegedly, when Dada learned that his second wife was pregnant with another man's child, he had her dismembered. After the atrocity, he ordered her remains stitched together so he could show her corpse to their children.

Justin II

In the final days of his reign, Byzantine Emperor Justin II (c. 520–578) descended into an overwhelming insanity that was only briefly punctuated by moments of lucidity. Accounts tell of a daft ruler who went mad after a nervous breakdown. Monitored closely by attendants, the emperor sometimes needed to be restrained lest he commit undue harm upon himself or others. The crazed ruler would often lunge at his attendants in an attempt to bite them, and reports suggest that he actually devoured a number of his faithful servants during his reign.

King George III

Great Britain's King George III (1738–1820) suffered recurring bouts of dementia during his reign. Believed to be suffering the ill effects of porphyria, a blood disorder that can produce psychotic symptoms, the king often acted in an outlandish manner. Fits of gloom and melancholy often alternated with excited periods where the king would talk incessantly and act strangely. During one such bout, George III reportedly spoke nonsense for a period lasting some 58 hours. But whether or not the king was insane, his "caregivers" were a bit suspect as well, at least by today's standards. Doctors often tried bleeding him to remove bad substances. When this failed, another doctor decided to draw the poison out of his brain by cutting small holes in his forehead. The king was also confined to a straightjacket, denied heat in the winter, and fed chemical agents that did nothing more than make him vomit.

King George III eventually went blind and died in a back room of Windsor Castle. Such a tale begs the obvious question: Who was really mad here?

Vitellius

If an unquenchable bloodlust is the hallmark of a true madman, Roman emperor Aulus Vitellius Germanicus Augustus (A.D. 15–69) ranks near the top. Simply known as Vitellius, he took perverse joy in watching his victims squirm. His actions sound like something lifted from a Stephen King novel, yet they are reportedly true. Consider this: On impulse, and purely for his own amusement, Vitellius would summon personal friends and acquaintances to his court, then order them killed, or do the deed himself. On one occasion, two sons begging for their father's life were executed beside him. At another time, Vitellius gave a glass of poisoned water to a thirsty man stricken with fever and watched in utter glee as it took effect. Psychological tortures also factored heavily into this madman's repertoire. The ruler once issued a reprieve to a subject who was to be executed. As the man praised the emperor for his mercy, Vitellius ordered him killed in his presence saying that he wished to "feast [on] his eyes." His motives for such loathing are shrouded in mystery, but in the end, Vitellius was tortured, killed, and thrown in the Tigris River by the leader of an opposing faction.

Caligula

The famed Caligula (Gaius Caesar Augustus Germanicus) (A.D. 12–41) served as emperor of Rome from A.D. 37 until his death. During that time, he reputedly engaged in long-term incestuous trysts with his sisters; forced losers of an oratory competition to erase their wax tablets with their tongues; ordered men's heads shaved (due to his own insecurity over his baldness); bestowed a consulship and priesthood upon his favorite horse; and ordered spectators to fight lions and tigers to the death during a shortage of criminals. In A.D. 41, Caligula was stabbed to death by his own Praetorian guards. Live by the sword; die by the sword.

Deadly Bling?:
The Curse of the Hope Diamond

☠ ☠ ☠ ☠ ☠

Diamonds are a girl's best friend, a jeweler's meal ticket, and serious status symbols for those who can afford them. But there's one famous diamond whose brilliant color comes with a cloudy history. The Hope Diamond is one of the world's most beautiful gemstones—and one that some say causes death and suffering to those who possess it. So is the Hope Diamond really cursed? There's a lot of evidence that says "no," but there have been some really strange coincidences.

The Origin of Hope

It's believed that this shockingly large, blue-hued diamond came from India several centuries ago. At the time, the exceptional diamond was slightly more than 112 carats, which is enormous. (On average, a diamond in an engagement ring ranges from a quarter to a full carat.) According to legend, a thief stole the diamond from the eye of a Hindu statue, but scholars don't think the shape would have been right to sit in the face of a statue. Nevertheless, the story states that the young thief was torn apart by wild dogs soon after he sold the diamond, making this the first life claimed by the jewel.

Courts, Carats, and Carnage

In the mid-1600s, a French jeweler named Tavernier purchased the diamond in India and kept it for several years without incident before selling it to King Louis XIV in 1668, along with several other jewels. The king recut the diamond in 1673, taking it down to 67 carats. This new cut emphasized the jewel's clarity, and Louis liked to wear the "Blue Diamond of the Crown" around his neck on special occasions. He, too, owned the gemstone without much trouble.

More than a hundred years later, France's King Louis XVI possessed the stone. In 1791, when the royal family tried to flee the country, the crown jewels were hidden for safekeeping, but they were stolen the following year. Some were eventually returned, but the blue diamond was not.

King Louis XVI and his wife Marie Antoinette died by guillotine in 1793. Those who believe in the curse are eager to include these two romantic figures in the list of cursed owners, but their deaths probably had more to do with the angry mobs of the French Revolution than a piece of jewelry.

Right this Way, Mr. Hope

It is unknown what happened to the big blue diamond from the time it was stolen in France until it appeared in England nearly 50 years later. When the diamond reappeared, it wasn't the same size as before—it was now only about 45 carats. Had it been cut again to disguise its identity? Or was this a new diamond altogether? Because the blue diamond was so unique in color and size, it was believed to be the diamond in question.

In the 1830s, wealthy banker Henry Philip Hope purchased the diamond, henceforth known as the Hope Diamond. When he died (of natural causes) in 1839, he bequeathed the gem to his oldest nephew, and it eventually ended up with the nephew's grandson, Francis Hope.

Francis Hope is the next person supposedly cursed by the diamond. Francis was a notorious gambler and was generally bad with money. Though he owned the diamond, he was not allowed to sell it without his family's permission, which he finally got in 1901 when he announced he was bankrupt. It's doubtful that the diamond had anything to do with Francis's bad luck, though that's what some believers suggest.

Coming to America

Joseph Frankel and Sons of New York purchased the diamond from Francis, and by 1909, after a few trades between the world's most notable jewelers, the Hope Diamond found itself in the hands of famous French jeweler Pierre Cartier. That's where rumors of a curse may have actually originated.

Allegedly, Cartier came up with the curse concept in order to sell the diamond to Evalyn Walsh McLean, a rich socialite who claimed that bad luck charms always turned into good luck charms in her hands. Cartier may have embellished the terrible things that had befallen previous owners of his special diamond so that McLean would purchase it—which she did. Cartier even inserted a clause in the sales contract, which stated that if any fatality occurred in the family within six months, the Hope Diamond could be exchanged for jewelry valued at the $180,000 McLean paid for the stone. Nevertheless, McLean wore the diamond on a chain around her neck constantly, and the spookiness surrounding the gem started picking up steam.

Whether or not anything can be blamed on the jewel, it certainly can't be denied that McLean had a pretty miserable life starting around the time she purchased the diamond. Her eldest son died at age nine in a fiery car crash. Years later, her 25-year-old daughter killed herself. Not long after that, her husband was declared insane and was committed to a mental institution for the rest of his life. With rumors swirling about the Hope Diamond's curse, everyone pointed to the necklace when these terrible events took place.

In 1947, when McLean died (while wearing the diamond) at age 60, the Hope Diamond and most of her other treasures were sold to pay off debts. American jeweler Harry Winston forked over the $1 million asking price for McLean's entire jewelry collection.

Hope on Display

If Harry Winston was scared of the alleged curse, he didn't show it. Winston had long wanted to start a collection of gemstones to display for the general public, so in 1958, when the Smithsonian Institute started one in Washington, D.C., he sent the Hope Diamond to them as a centerpiece. These days, it's kept under glass as a central figure for the National Gem Collection at the National Museum of Natural History. So far, no one's dropped dead from checking it out.

Per capita, the United States ranks fifth in the world in deaths from rat bites.

FREAKY FACTS: ANIMAL MATING

- *The funnel-web spider knocks his mate unconscious with pheromones before mating.*

- *The male Argyrodes zonatus spider secretes a drug that intoxicates the female, which is good because otherwise she would devour him.*

- *Harlequin bass and hamlet fish take turns being male and female, including releasing sperm and eggs during the mating process.*

- *Male North American fireflies flash their light every 5.8 seconds while females flash every 2 seconds, so there isn't any confusion.*

- *An albatross can spend weeks courting, and their relationships can last for decades. However, the actual act of mating lasts less than a minute.*

- *Fruit flies perform an elaborate seven-step dance before mating. If any part is not completed perfectly, there will be no copulation.*

- *Male mites mate with their sisters before they are born. After birth, the females rush off in search of food and their brothers are left to die.*

- *Mayflies live for one day, during which they do nothing but mate.*

- *The rattlesnake has two penises, while that of the echidnas has four heads and a pig's is shaped like a corkscrew.*

- *The male swamp antechinus, a mouselike marsupial in Australia, has sex until he dies, often from starvation. Sometimes he's simply too weak after mating to escape predators and is eaten.*

Preposterous Ways to
Pop the Question

Getting down on one knee—are you kidding? That's so old-fashioned. Lovers who want to pop the question in a memorable way might be inspired by the following people who refused to be conventional when it was time to take the plunge.

Ready for Prime Time

Proposals on the big screen at sporting events are a dime a dozen. So in 2006, Rand Fishkin decided to propose to his girlfriend via a TV ad on Superbowl Sunday…until he found out it was going to set him back $2.5 million. Fishkin spread the word online, which garnered attention from several media outlets, but he could only raise $85,000. However, CBS wouldn't lower their price, so for just $3,000, Rand purchased a local ad that ran during his girlfriend's favorite show. She saw the commercial, said yes, and the rest of the money was donated to charity.

Baby, Light My Fire

In 2005, Todd Grannis of Grants Pass, Oregon, lit himself on fire, jumped into a swimming pool, and then swam over to his girlfriend, Malissa, to ask for her hand in marriage. This stunt, which nobody should ever try at home, was overseen by a stuntman and was executed while paramedics and a safety crew were standing by. Grannis was shown how to wrap his body in protective garments before igniting for a few seconds. After recovering from the horror she must have felt when she saw her boyfriend go up in flames, Malissa said yes.

Zero Gravity, Lots of Heart

In 2007, a Manhattan couple boarded a specially designed Boeing 727 aircraft that created the experience of weightlessness that astronauts feel in orbit. The 90-minute trip (which cost $3,500 per person) was a birthday gift from Alexander Loucopoulos to his girlfriend, a "space enthusiast," who wanted to experience weightlessness for four to five minutes as the plane flew up and down between 24,000 and 35,000 feet. While floating through the plane's cabin, Loucopoulos popped the question, though he was worried the ring "would float really far away." It worked out, and the couple hope to spend their tenth wedding anniversary in space.

From Crush to Crash

In 2006, Adam Sutton had it all planned out. He would take his girlfriend, Erika Brussee, up in a chartered plane and ask her to look out the window, high above Rome, Georgia, where family members would be holding a large sign with his proposal written on it. But instead, she saw flames just before the plane crashed onto the runway. No one was seriously injured, and Brussee did say yes, but the ring was lost in the rubble.

STRANGE STATS

- *Many typewriter companies started out making ammunition, including Remington and Smith-Corona.*

- *Seawater contains enough gold that if it were mined, every person on Earth would receive nine pounds.*

- *The average price of a McDonald's Big Mac in Iceland is $6.67 but only $0.68 in Qatar.*

- *Forty-one percent of American men wear briefs, and only 4 percent wear thongs.*

- *According to the Catholic Church, bad driving and speeding are sins.*

The Mysterious Area 51

Who killed JFK? Did Americans really land on the moon? Conspiracy theorists have been debating these questions for years. But they all agree on one thing—these conspiracies pale in comparison to the mother of all conspiracies: Area 51.

Alien autopsies. Covert military operations. Tests on bizarre aircraft. These are all things rumored to be going on inside Area 51—a top secret location inside the Nevada Test and Training Range (NTTR) about an hour northwest of Las Vegas. Though shrouded in secrecy, some of the history of Area 51 is known. For instance, this desert area was used as a bombing test site during World War II, but no facility existed on the site until 1955. At that time, the area was chosen as the perfect location to develop and test the U-2 spy plane. Originally known as Watertown, it came to be called Area 51 in 1958 when 38,000 acres were designated for military use. The entire area was simply marked "Area 51" on military maps. Today, the facility is rumored to contain approximately 575 square miles. But you won't find it on a map because, officially, it doesn't exist.

An Impenetrable Fortress

Getting a clear idea of the size of Area 51, or even a glimpse of the place, is next to impossible. Years ago, curiosity seekers could get a good view of the facility by hiking to the top of two nearby mountain peaks known as White Sides and Freedom Ridge. But government officials soon grew weary of people climbing up there and snapping pictures, so in 1995, they seized control of both. Currently, the only way to legally catch a glimpse of the base is to scale 7,913-foot-tall Tikaboo Peak. Even if you make it that far, you're still not guaranteed to see anything because the facility is more than 25 miles away and is only visible on clear days with no haze.

The main entrance to Area 51 is along Groom Lake Road. Those brave (or foolhardy) souls who have ventured down the road to investigate quickly realize they are being watched. Video cameras and motion sensors are hidden along the road, and signs alert the curious that if they continue any further, they will be entering a military installation, which is illegal "without the written permission of the installation commander." If that's not enough to get unwanted guests to turn around, one sign clearly states: "Use of deadly force authorized." Simply put, take one step over that imaginary line in the dirt, and they *will* get you.

Camo Dudes
And just exactly who are "they"? They are the "Camo Dudes," mysterious figures watching trespassers from nearby hillsides and jeeps. If they spot something suspicious, they might call for backup—Blackhawk helicopters that will come in for a closer look. All things considered, it would probably be best to just turn around and go back home. And lest you think about hiring someone to fly you over Area 51, the entire area is considered restricted air space, meaning that unauthorized aircraft are not permitted to fly over, or even near, the facility.

Who Works There?
Most employees are general contractors who work for companies in the area. But rather than allow these workers to commute individually, the facility has them ushered in secretly and en masse in one of two ways. The first is a mysterious white bus with tinted windows that picks up employees at several unmarked stops before whisking them through the front gates of the facility. Every evening, the bus leaves the facility and drops the employees off.

The second mode of commuter transport, an even more secretive way, is JANET, the code name given to the secret planes that carry workers back and forth from Area 51 and Las Vegas McCarran Airport. JANET has its own terminal, which is located at the far end of the airport behind fences with special security gates. It even has its own private parking lot. Several times a day, planes from the JANET fleet take off and land at the airport.

Bob Lazar

The most famous Area 51 employee is someone who may or may not have actually worked there. In the late 1980s, Bob Lazar claimed that he'd worked at the secret facility he referred to as S-4. In addition, Lazar said that he was assigned the task of reverse engineering a recovered spaceship in order to determine how it worked. Lazar had only been at the facility for a short time, but he and his team had progressed to the point where they were test flying the alien spaceship. That's when Lazar made a big mistake. He decided to bring some friends out to Groom Lake Road when he knew the alien craft was being flown. He was caught and subsequently fired.

During his initial interviews with a local TV station, Lazar seemed credible and quite knowledgeable as to the inner workings of Area 51. But when people started trying to verify the information Lazar was giving, not only was it next to impossible to confirm most of his story, his education and employment history could not be verified either. Skeptics immediately proclaimed that Lazar was a fraud. To this day, Lazar contends that everything he said was factual and that the government deleted all his records in order to set him up and make him look like a fake. Whether or not he's telling the truth, Lazar will be remembered as the man who first brought up the idea that alien spaceships were being experimented on at Area 51.

What's Really Going On?

So what really goes on inside Area 51? One thing we do know is that they work on and test aircraft. Whether they are alien spacecraft or not is still open to debate. Some of the planes worked on and tested at Area 51 include the SR-71 Blackbird and the F-117 Nighthawk stealth fighter. Currently, there are rumors that a craft known only by the codename Aurora is being worked on at the facility.

If you want to try and catch a glimpse of some of these strange craft being tested, you'll need to hang out at the "Black Mailbox" along Highway 375, also known as the Extraterrestrial Highway. It's really nothing more than a mailbox along the side of the road. But as with most things associated with Area 51, nothing is as it sounds, so it should come as no surprise that the "Black Mailbox" is actually white. It belongs to a rancher, who owns the property nearby. Still, this is the spot where people have been known to camp out all night just for a chance to see something strange floating in the night sky.

The Lawsuit

In 1994, a landmark lawsuit was filed against the U.S. Air Force by five unnamed contractors and the widows of two others. The suit claimed that the contractors had been present at Area 51 when large quantities of "unknown chemicals" were burned in trenches and pits. As a result of coming into contact with the fumes of the chemicals, the suit alleged that two of the contractors died, and the five survivors suffered respiratory problems and skin sores. Reporters worldwide jumped on the story, not only because it proved that Area 51 existed but also because the suit was asking for many classified documents to be entered as evidence. Would some of those documents refer to alien beings or spacecraft? The world would never know because in September 1995, while petitions for the case were still going on, President Bill Clinton signed Presidential Determination No. 95–45, which basically stated that Area 51 was exempt from federal, state, local, and interstate hazardous and solid waste laws. Shortly thereafter, the lawsuit was dismissed due to a lack of evidence, and all attempts at appeals were rejected. In 2002, President George W. Bush renewed Area 51's exemptions, ensuring once and for all that what goes on inside Area 51 stays inside Area 51.

So at the end of the day, we're still left scratching our heads about Area 51. We know it exists and we have some idea of what goes on there, but there is still so much more we don't know. More than likely, we never will know everything, but then again, what fun is a mystery if you know all the answers?

Spirits in Chains

Peering out over miles of farmland is one of southern Illinois's most haunted locations. When it was completed in 1838, the large home known as Hickory Hill was a horrific place to the men and women who were brought there in chains. Thanks to this part of its history, Hickory Hill has been nicknamed the "Old Slave House."

Since the early 1900s, people have come from all over the country to see this strange and ominous place. The atrocities that occurred there were revealed years ago, but many stories claim that the dead of Hickory Hill do not rest in peace.

Working in the Salt Mines

Hickory Hill was built by John Hart Crenshaw, a descendant of an old American family with ties to the founding of the country. He was born in November 1797, on the border of North and South Carolina, but his family moved west and settled in New Madrid, Missouri, only to have their home destroyed by the earthquake of 1811. A short time later, they moved to southern Illinois and started a farm.

By the time he was in his mid-thirties, Crenshaw had amassed such a fortune in the salt industry that, at one point, he paid one-seventh of all the taxes collected in the state. But Crenshaw is best remembered for Hickory Hill and his ties to the kidnapping and illegal trafficking of slaves. Although Illinois was a free state, it allowed slaves to be leased for work in the salt mines of southern Illinois. Work in the salt mines was backbreaking, hot, and brutal and attracted only the most desperate workers. Because of this, slavery became essential to the success of the salt-mining operations.

Slaves had no protection under the law and free blacks had very little. And few officials interfered with the men who seized black people and carried them south for sale at auction.

Perhaps those most guilty of this practice were the "night riders" of the 1830s and 1840s—bands of men who posted riders along the Ohio River at night to capture escaped slaves and return them for a reward. They also kidnapped free black men and their children and sold them in the South. The night riders were the opposite of the Underground Railroad, sending escaped slaves back to the southern plantations rather than to the northern cities and freedom.

Allegedly, Crenshaw, who leased slaves to work the salt mines, kept a number of night riders in his employ. He used this as a profitable sideline to his legitimate businesses. Rather than collecting any rewards, Crenshaw realized that he could make much more money by working the captured slaves or by selling them back into the southern market.

Most people viewed Crenshaw as an upstanding businessman and community leader who was active in his church. No one knew that he was holding illegal slaves or that he was suspected of kidnapping black families and selling them into slavery. They would have been even more surprised to learn that the slaves were being held captive in the barred chambers of the attic of Hickory Hill. The men were often subjected to cruelty and the women to the "breeding chamber," which made even more money for Crenshaw. A pregnant slave on the southern market was worth much more than a female with no child. The practice turned a handsome profit and kept Crenshaw supplied with workers.

The Old Slave House

Crenshaw built Hickory Hill, his classic Greek plantation house, on a hill overlooking the Saline River. The house was certainly grand, but it had some unusual and less visible additions. Legend says there was once a tunnel connecting the basement to the banks of the Saline River to load and unload slaves at night. Another large passageway at the rear of the house allowed wagons to enter the house so that slaves could be unloaded where they would not be seen from the outside.

Located on the third floor of Hickory Hill were the infamous confines of the attic and proof that Crenshaw had something sinister in mind when he had the house built. The attic can still be reached today by a flight of narrow, well-worn stairs that end at a wide hallway containing about a dozen cell-like rooms with flat, wooden bunks facing the narrow corridor that runs between them. The slaves spent their time in these cells chained to the walls. Barred windows at either end provided the only light and the only ventilation. During the summer, the heat in the attic was unbearable.

In 1842, Crenshaw was indicted on criminal charges. It was reported that he had engineered the kidnapping of a free black woman and her children. He allegedly had them taken from their home and carried by wagon out of state. Unfortunately, the prosecutor couldn't prove this, and Crenshaw went free.

But soon, rumors began to spread about Crenshaw's business activities. These rumblings, combined with the earlier indictment, started to upset a lot of people in the area. In March 1842, a steam mill that Crenshaw owned was burned to the ground. It is believed that the fire was started by a group of free black men, angry over Crenshaw's actions.

In 1846, Crenshaw's business holdings began to decline. In addition to several civil court actions against him, demand fell for Illinois salt. Even worse, Crenshaw was attacked by one of his workers, resulting in the loss of a leg. After that, he sold off his slaves and closed down most of his salt operations. During the Civil War, he sold Hickory Hill, but when he died in December 1871, he was buried in Hickory Hill Cemetery, a lonely piece of ground just northeast of his former home.

Ghosts in the Attic

John Crenshaw has been in his grave for more than a century, but according to local legend, many of the slaves that he once kept chained in his attic do not rest in peace. These stories, which come from southern Illinois folklore and scholarly works alike, maintain that eerie voices are sometimes heard in the attic of the house as they moan, cry, and whisper of the horrific things that were done to them in centuries past.

George Sisk, a former owner of the Old Slave House, insisted that the place was haunted, and many visitors to the house agree. The old slave quarters are often hot and cramped and at other times are inexplicably cold.

In the 1920s, Sisk opened the house to tourists. Soon after, visitors began complaining of weird happenings in the house, such as inexplicable sounds in the attic, especially crying, moaning, whimpering, and even the rattling of chains. A number of people told of uncomfortable feelings in the slave quarters, such as sensations of intense fear, sadness, and of being watched. Others felt as if they'd been touched by invisible hands or had unseen figures brush by them.

Other legends soon became attached to Hickory Hill, such as a story that arose in the 1920s, which claimed that no one could spend the night in the attic of the house and survive. Many would-be thrill seekers tried, but no one managed to make it to daybreak in the attic of Hickory Hill until 1978, when a reporter from Harrisburg, Illinois, managed to make it through the night, beating out more than 150 previous challengers. The reporter felt pretty good afterward but confessed that he didn't want to make it an annual event.

Still Haunted?

People still claim to feel cold chills and hear voices in the house, but for most visitors, a visit to Hickory Hill is not so bizarre. Many experience nothing, while others say they feel unsettled, frightened, or overwrought with emotion in the attic. Perhaps this is not a sign of the supernatural, but the attic is certainly an eerie place with a great deal of odd energy.

The Old Slave House closed down in 1996 but was purchased by the state of Illinois a few years later. Eventually, the house will reopen as a historic site. Whether or not the ghosts will be a part of the new attraction is uncertain. At the very least, visitors should take a moment to remember those unfortunate souls who once suffered in the house and pray that they have finally found peace on the other side.

Taste buds need 24 hours to regain full sensitivity after being exposed to cigarette smoke, spicy foods, or alcohol.

Strange But True Inventions

Pierced Glasses

Tired of your glasses slipping down your nose? Try pierced glasses—spectacles that connect to a piercing surgically implanted into the nose. Invented by James Sooy in 2004, these glasses should appeal to body modification artists.

The Bulletproof Bed

Are you consumed with fearful thoughts when you go to bed? Perhaps you'll rest more peacefully in a bulletproof bed. The Quantum Sleeper's coffinlike design protects from attacks, fires, and natural disasters with its airtight and waterproof interior. The bed features an air filtration system and can be fitted with DVD screens, a refrigerator, and even a microwave!

The Portable Crosswalk

There never seems to be a crosswalk when you need one, and nobody wants to break the law by jaywalking. Instead, use a portable crosswalk, a vinyl sheet that can be spread across a busy street to ensure your safety as you make your way through traffic. Though its legality may be in question, it will certainly stop traffic…we hope.

Sauce-Dispensing Chopsticks

Need to shave time from your daily schedule? Try sauce-dispensing chopsticks for the sushi eater in a rush. No longer do you have to waste valuable seconds dipping your food into the soy sauce—just squeeze the end of the stick and the liquid flows right onto your food! The utensils cost about $20, but can you really put a price on time-saving of this magnitude?

The Drymobile

In this day and age, everyone is looking for ways to save time and energy. Now you can do both with the Japanese Drymobile. Hang your clothes from a rack that fits on top of your car and your clothes will be dry in no time as you run your daily errands…unless, of course, it starts to rain.

One-Cut Nail Clippers

Staying well groomed can be quite time-consuming. But now one task can be shortened with one-cut nail clippers. A series of five clippers are positioned over the toes or fingernails, allowing the user to cut all five nails at once.

The Gas Grabber

Sometimes you just can't blame the dog. For those occasions, turn to the Gas Grabber, a charcoal filter that slips into your underwear to cover up those social faux pas. The filter was originally developed by the British to guard against nerve agents.

The Grin Grabber

Some people just don't smile enough, so it's the Grin Grabber to the rescue! Attach a hook to each side of your mouth, grasp the string, and yank. The pulley system will lift the corners and soon you'll be beaming from ear to ear!

The Snot Sucker

No tissue? No problem! The WIVA-VAC Nasal Aspirator uses vacuum power to clean up a runny nose. Perfect for children on the go, just slip the tapered end into a nostril and suck the snot right out of 'em!

The Daddy Nurser

Since the beginning of time, men have been accused of not pulling their weight in the baby department. Now men can truly experience the joy of motherhood with the Daddy Nurser, a pair of milk-filled orbs that connect to a man's chest to mimic the act of breast-feeding. Now if they could only invent a way for men to give birth!

A Superior Haunting:
The *Edmund Fitzgerald*

💀   💀   💀   💀   💀

Many ships have been lost to the dangers of the Great Lakes, but few incidents have fascinated the world like the sinking of the Edmund Fitzgerald off the shores of northern Michigan on November 10, 1975. The mysterious circumstances of the tragedy, which took 29 lives, and lingering tales of a haunting—all memorialized in a 1976 song by Gordon Lightfoot—have kept the horrific story fresh for more than three decades.

Least Likely to Sink

Lake Superior is well known among sailors for its treachery, especially when the unusually strong autumn winds sailors call the "Witch of November" roil the waves. But the 729-foot-long *Edmund Fitzgerald* was considered as unsinkable as any steamer ever launched, and its cost of $8.4 million made it the most expensive freighter in history at the time.

At its christening in June 1958, it was the Great Lakes' largest freighter, built with state-of-the-art technology, comfortable crew quarters, and elegant staterooms for guests. Its name honored Edmund Fitzgerald, the son of a sea captain and the president of Northwestern Mutual Insurance Company, who had commissioned the boat.

During the christening, a few incidents occurred that some saw as bad omens from the get-go. As a crowd of more than 10,000 watched, it took Mrs. Fitzgerald three tries to shatter the bottle of champagne. Then, when the ship was released into the water, it hit the surface at the wrong angle and kicked up a wave that splattered the entire ceremonial area with lake water, and knocked the ship into a nearby dock. If that weren't enough, one spectator died on the spot of a heart attack.

The Last Launch

The weather was unseasonably pleasant the morning of November 9, 1975, so much so that the crew of 29 men who set sail from Superior, Wisconsin, that day were unlikely to have been concerned about their routine trip to Zug Island on the Detroit River. But the captain, Ernest McSorley, knew a storm was in the forecast.

McSorley was a 44-year veteran of the lakes, had captained the *Fitzgerald* since 1972, and was thought to have been planning his retirement for the following year. He paid close attention to the gale warnings issued that afternoon, but no one suspected they would turn into what weather-watchers called a "once in a lifetime storm." However, when the weather report was upgraded to a full storm warning, McSorley changed course to follow a route safer than the normal shipping lanes, instead chugging closer to the Canadian shore.

Following the *Fitzgerald* in a sort of "buddy" system was another freighter, the *Arthur Anderson*. The two captains stayed in contact as they traveled together through winds measuring up to 50 knots (about 58 miles per hour) with waves splashing 12 feet or higher. Around 1:00 P.M., McSorley advised Captain Cooper of the *Anderson* that the *Fitzgerald* was "rolling." By about 2:45 P.M., as the *Anderson* moved to avoid a dangerous shoal near Caribou Island, a crewman sighted the *Fitzgerald* about 16 miles ahead, closer to the shoal than Cooper thought safe.

About 3:30 P.M., McSorley reported to Cooper that the *Fitzgerald* had sustained some minor damage and was beginning to list, or roll to one side. The ships were still 16–17 miles apart. At 4:10 P.M., with waves now lashing 18 feet high, McSorley radioed that his ship had lost radar capability. The two ships stayed in radio contact until about 7:00 P.M. when the *Fitzgerald* crew told the *Anderson* they were "holding [their] own." After that, radio contact was lost and the *Fitzgerald* dropped off the radar. Around 8:30 P.M., Cooper told the Coast Guard at Sault Ste. Marie that the *Fitzgerald* appeared to be missing. The search was on.

Evidently, the *Fitzgerald* sank sometime after 7:10 P.M. on November 10, just 17 miles from the shore of Whitefish Point, Michigan. Despite a massive search effort, it wasn't until November 14 that a navy flyer detected a magnetic anomaly that turned out to be the wreck of the *Fitzgerald.* The only other evidence of the disaster to surface was a handful of lifeboats, life jackets, and some oars, tools, and propane tanks. A robotic vehicle was used to thoroughly photograph the wreck in May 1976.

One Mysterious Body

One troubling aspect of the *Fitzgerald* tragedy was that no bodies were found. In most lakes or temperate waters, corpses rise to the surface as decomposition causes gases to form, which makes bodies float. But the Great Lakes are so cold that decomposition and the formation of these gases is inhibited, causing bodies to remain on the lake bottom. One explanation

was that the crew had been contained in the ship's enclosed areas. The wildest speculation surmised that the ship was destroyed by a UFO and the men were abducted by aliens.

In 1994, a Michigan businessman named Frederick Shannon took a tugboat and a 16-foot submarine equipped with a full array of modern surveillance equipment to the site, hoping to produce a documentary about the ship. But his crew was surprised when they discovered a body near the bow of the wreck, which had settled into the lake bottom. The remains were covered by cork sections of a deteriorated canvas life vest and were photographed but not retrieved. However, there was nothing to conclusively prove that this body was associated with the *Fitzgerald.* Two French vessels were lost in the same region in 1918, and none of those bodies had been recovered either. A sailor lost from one of them could have been preserved by the lake's frigid water and heavy pressure.

Many have pondered whether the men of the *Edmund Fitzgerald* might have been saved had they had better disaster equipment, but survival time in such cold water is only minutes. Most of the life jackets later floated to the surface, indicating that the crewmen never put them on. The seas were much too rough to launch wooden lifeboats, and there was probably no time to find and inflate rubber life rafts.

What Sank the Mighty *Fitz*?

She went down fast, that much was evident. Three different organizations filed official reports on the ship's sinking without coming to any common conclusions. It was thought impossible for such a large, well-built, and relatively "young" ship, only in its 18th year, to break up and sink so quickly, particularly in this age of modern navigation and communication equipment.

One popular theory is that the *Fitzgerald* ventured too close to the dangerous Six-Fathom Shoal near Caribou Island and scraped over it, damaging the hull. Another is that the ship's hatch covers were either faulty or improperly clamped, which allowed water infiltration. Wave height may also have played its part, with the storm producing a series of gargantuan swells known as the "Three Sisters"—a trio of lightning-fast waves that pound a vessel with a 1–2–3 punch—the first washes over the deck, the second hits the deck again so fast that the first has not had time to clear itself, and the third quickly adds another heavy wash, piling thousands of gallons of water on the ship at once. Few ships have the ability to remain afloat under such an onslaught.

In addition, the ship was about 200 feet longer than the 530-feet-deep water where it floundered. If the waves pushed the ship bowfirst down into the water, it would have hit bottom and stuck (which is what appears to have happened), snapping the long midsection in two as a result of continuing wave action and exploding steam boilers. The ship's 26,000-pound cargo of iron ore pellets shifted as the ship twisted and sank, adding to the devastation.

Some fingers pointed to the ship's prior damages. The *Fitzgerald* had been knocked around a bit during its career on the lakes: In 1969, it crunched ground near the locks at Sault Ste. Marie, Michigan, and less than a year later, in April 1970, it sustained a minor collision with the S.S. *Hochelaga.* In September of that year, the *Fitzgerald* slammed a lock wall for a total of three damaging hits within the span of 12 months. It's possible that these impacts inflicted more structural problems than were realized or that they were not repaired properly.

Spirits of the Lake

Author Hugh E. Bishop says that since the mighty *Fitz* went down, sailors have claimed to see a ghostly ship in the vicinity of the sinking. The captain of a Coast Guard cutter, the *Woodrush,* was on duty near the *Fitzgerald* site in 1976 and spent a night stuck in shifting ice masses directly over the wreckage. All throughout the night, the captain's normally carefree black Labrador whined and cowered, avoiding certain spots on the ship as if some invisible presence existed.

Bishop also noted that on October 21, 1975, a San Antonio psychic named J. Nickie Jackson recorded in her diary a dream she'd had that foretold the *Fitzgerald*'s doom. In her dream, she saw the freighter struggling to stay afloat in giant waves before it finally plunged straight down into the depths. The real-life event occurred just three weeks later. Jackson was familiar with the *Edmund Fitzgerald* because she had previously lived in Superior but was surprised to dream about it in her new life in Texas.

For Whom the Bell Tolls...

On July 4, 1995, a year after the lone body was documented, the bell of the *Edmund Fitzgerald* was retrieved from the wreckage and laid to rest in the Great Lakes Shipwreck Historical Museum in Whitefish Bay, Michigan. With the wreckage, the diving crew left a replica of the bell, which symbolizes the ship's "spirit." Every year on November 10, during a memorial service, the original, 200-pound, bronze bell is now rung 29 times—once for each crew member who perished on the *Edmund Fitzgerald.*

Gone Without a Trace

*While we all watch in amazement as magicians make every-
thing from small coins to giant buildings disappear, in our
hearts, we all know it's a trick. Things don't just disappear,
especially not people. Or do they?*

Louis Le Prince

The name Louis Aimé Augustin Le Prince doesn't mean much
to most people, but some believe he was the first person to
record moving images on film, a good seven years before
Thomas Edison. Whether or not he did so is open to debate,
as is what happened to him on September 16, 1890. On that
day, Le Prince's brother accompanied him to the train station
in Dijon, France, where he was scheduled to take the express
train to Paris. When the train reached Paris, however, Le
Prince and his luggage were nowhere to be found. The train
was searched, as were the tracks between Dijon and Paris,
but no sign of Le Prince or his luggage was ever found. Theories about his disappearance range from his being murdered
for trying to fight Edison over the patent of the first motion
picture to his family forcing him to go into hiding to keep
him safe from people who wanted his patents for themselves.
Others believe that Le Prince took his own life because he was
nearly bankrupt.

Jimmy Hoffa

On the afternoon of July 30, 1975, Jimmy Hoffa, former president of the International Brotherhood of Teamsters, stepped
onto the parking lot of the Manchus Red Fox Restaurant near
Detroit and into history. Scheduled to meet with known mob-
sters from New Jersey and New York, Hoffa vanished and was

never seen or heard from again. Since that day, wild theories involving mob hits and political assassinations have run rampant. But despite hundreds of anonymous tips, confessions from mob hitmen, and even the wife of a former mobster accusing her husband of the hit, it is still unknown what happened to Hoffa or where he's buried, and the case officially remains open. As recently as May 2006, FBI agents were still following leads and digging up yards in Michigan trying to find out what happened to Hoffa.

Dorothy Arnold

After spending most of December 12, 1910, shopping in Manhattan, American socialite Dorothy Arnold told a friend she was planning to walk home through Central Park. She never made it. Fearing their daughter had eloped with her one-time boyfriend George Griscom, Jr., the Arnolds immediately hired the Pinkerton Detective Agency, although they did not report her missing to police until almost a month later. Once the press heard the news, theories spread like wildfire, most of them pointing the finger at Griscom. Some believed he had murdered Arnold, but others thought she had died as the result of a botched abortion. Still others felt her family had banished her to Switzerland and then used her disappearance as a cover-up. No evidence was ever found to formally charge Griscom, and Arnold's disappearance remains unsolved.

D. B. Cooper

On the evening of November 24, 1971, a man calling himself Dan Cooper (later known as D. B. Cooper) hijacked an airplane, and demanded $200,000 and four parachutes, which he received when the plane landed in Seattle. Cooper allowed the plane's passengers to disembark but then ordered the pilot to fly to Mexico. Once the plane had gained enough altitude, somewhere over the Cascade Mountains near Woodland, Washington, Cooper jumped from the plane and fell into history. Despite a massive manhunt, no trace of him has ever been found. In 1980, an eight-year-old boy found nearly $6,000 in rotting $20 bills lying along the banks of the Columbia River. A check of their serial numbers found that they were part of the ransom money given to Cooper, but what became of the rest of the money, and Cooper, is a mystery to this day.

Frederick Valentich

To vanish without a trace is rather unusual. But to vanish in an airplane while chasing a UFO—now that's unique. Yet that's exactly what happened to 20-year-old pilot Frederick Valentich on the night of October 21, 1978. Shortly after 7:00 P.M., while flying a Cessna 182L to King Island, Australia, Valentich radioed that an "unidentified craft" was hovering over his plane. For the next several minutes, he attempted to describe the object, which had blinking lights and was "not an aircraft." At approximately 7:12 P.M., Valentich stated that he was having engine trouble. Immediately after that, the flight tower picked up 17 seconds of "metallic, scraping sounds." Then all was silent. A search began immediately, but no trace of Valentich or his plane was ever found. Strangely enough, the evening Valentich disappeared, there were numerous reports of UFOs seen all over the skies of Australia.

Frank Morris, John Anglin, and Clarence Anglin

Officially, records show that there was never a successful escape from Alcatraz Prison while it was in operation. Of course, those records leave out the part that three men *might* have made it, but they disappeared in the process.

After spending two years planning their escape, inmates Frank Morris and brothers Clarence and John Anglin placed homemade dummies in their bunks, crawled through hand-dug tunnels, and made their way to the prison roof. Then they apparently climbed down, hopped aboard homemade rafts, and made their way out into San Francisco Bay.

The next day, one of the largest manhunts in history began. Pieces of a raft and a life preserver were found floating in the bay, as well as a bag containing personal items from the escapees, but that was all. The official report stated that in all likelihood, the men drowned. However, a 2003 episode of *Mythbusters* determined that the men may have survived.

Real-Life Superheroes in Michigan

Crime-fighting men in tights, masked ladies in catsuits, and superheroes making the world safer one step at a time—these are not only the stuff of comic books. The town of Jackson, Michigan, has its own prowling super man, woman, and girl: Captain Jackson, the Queen of Hearts, and Crimefighter Girl.

Birth of a Superhero

In 1999, when a Detroit man in his early forties moved to the city of Jackson for a new job, he became concerned that local police were not visible enough to deter crime in the city's aging downtown streets. The brand-new maximum-security prison on the outskirts of town seemed to be admitting all too many native sons. As he pondered the problem, it occurred to him that perhaps all it might take to turn things around was someone to serve as a middleman between law enforcement agencies and the town's citizens. He nominated himself for the position and phoned a local radio talk show to let them know that Captain Jackson had just arrived to save the city.

Custom Costumes

Captain Jackson, a man of average size who prefers to remain anonymous, devised his own costume, using Batman as a rough model. He dons a black hood and eye mask, a gray shirt and briefs, and of course, black tights. A round chest logo and flowing purple cape complete his dashing look.

But Jackson wasn't the only would-be caped crusader shopping for spandex. When his daughter began joining him on his rounds as Crimefighter Girl, she chose a yellow mask and cape to cover her black leotard and tights.

Then one evening in downtown Jackson, a woman with long blonde hair, a red heart on her chest, and a gold metallic belt showed up and introduced herself as the Queen of Hearts. Together, the three call themselves the Crimefighter Corps.

Here They Come to Save the Day

Once Captain Jackson had properly costumed himself, he began walking the city's streets every evening, stopping in taverns and other businesses to make sure things were running smoothly. Reactions ranged from amusement to relief that someone was keeping an eye on things. But the new "caped crusader" was careful not to overstep his bounds. Captain Jackson quickly developed a working relationship with the police and fire departments, and in 2005, Jackson's chief of police said the once crime-ridden downtown area patrolled by the Captain had become the most crime-free part of the city.

In addition to making downtown Jackson a safer place, the Captain hopes to inspire people in other places to take back their streets. The Queen of Hearts, a martial arts expert, aspires to help mend broken hearts by fighting domestic violence.

Unmasked

In the comics, Clark Kent and Peter Parker live in fear that their alter egos (Superman and Spider-Man, respectively) will be unmasked and their true identities revealed. Captain Jackson is no different in his desire for privacy, but in 2005, his name was revealed to the public when, off-duty, his alter ego was arrested for impaired driving. Jackson police had always known the Captain's identity but operated under an agreement to keep their ally's name a secret. Captain Jackson showed true superhero fortitude in riding out the worldwide flurry of publicity and continued making his nightly rounds.

Future-Man

Although Crimefighter Girl is going off to college after logging thousands of public service hours, Captain Jackson plans to go right on checking the back doors of downtown businesses and discouraging panhandlers for as long as he is able. An Australian filmmaker has visited Michigan to showcase the Captain going about his duties, and he continues to make news as one of the few "superheroes" that actually do crime-fighting work. And as Captain Jackson said in a recent interview, "Time flies when you're saving the world."

Strange Catastrophes

💀   💀   💀   💀   💀

Life is full of surprises, some less pleasant than others. From beer floods to raining frogs to exploding whales, headlines continually prove that truth is sometimes stranger than fiction.

The London Beer Flood

In 1814, a vat of beer erupted in a London brewery. Within minutes, the explosion had split open several other vats, and more than 320,000 gallons of beer flooded the streets of a nearby slum. People rushed to save as much of the beer as they could, collecting it in pots, cans, and cups. Others scooped the beer up in their hands and drank it as quickly as they could. Nine people died in the flood—eight from drowning and one from alcohol poisoning.

The Great Siberian Explosion

Around 7:00 A.M. on June 30, 1908, 60 million trees in remote Siberia were flattened by a mysterious 15-megaton explosion. The huge blast, which occurred about five miles above the surface of the earth, traveled around the world twice and triggered a strong, four-hour magnetic storm. Magnetic storms occur about once every hundred years, and can create radiation similar to a nuclear explosion. These storms start in space and are typically accompanied by solar flares.

The 1908 explosion may have started with a comet of ice, which melted and exploded as it entered Earth's atmosphere. Or, it may have been an unusual airburst from an asteroid. Others believe that the source was a nuclear-powered spacecraft from another planet. However, no physical evidence of the cause has ever been found.

The Boston Molasses Disaster

On an unusually warm January day in 1919, a molasses tank burst near downtown Boston, sending more than two million gallons of the sticky sweetener flowing through the city's North End at an estimated 35 miles per hour. The force of the molasses wave was so intense that it lifted a train off its tracks and crushed several buildings in its path. When the flood finally came to a halt, molasses was two to three feet deep in the streets, 21 people and several horses had died, and more than 150 people were injured. Nearly 90 years later, people in Boston can still smell molasses during sultry summer days.

It's Raining...Frogs

On September 7, 1953, clouds formed over Leicester, Massachusetts—a peaceful little town near the middle of the state. Within a few hours, a downpour began, but it wasn't rain falling from the sky—thousands of frogs and toads dropped out of the air. Children collected them in buckets as if it was a game. Town officials insisted that the creatures had simply escaped from a nearby pond, but many of them landed on roofs and in gutters, which seemed to dispute this theory. It is still unclear why the frogs appeared in Leicester or why the same thing happened almost 20 years later in Brignoles, France.

Oregon's Exploding Whale

When an eight-ton sperm whale beaches itself in your town, what do you do? That's a question residents of Florence, Oregon, faced in November 1970. After consulting with the U.S. Navy, town officials decided to blow up the carcass with a half ton of dynamite. Spectators and news crews gathered to watch but were horrified when they were engulfed in a sandy, reddish mist and slapped by flying pieces of whale blubber. A quarter mile away, a car was crushed when a gigantic chunk of whale flesh landed on it. No one was seriously hurt in the incident, but when the air cleared, most of the whale was still on the beach. The highway department hauled the rest of it away.

Ghosts of the *Queen Mary*

Once considered a grand jewel of the ocean, the decks of the
Queen Mary *played host to such rich and famous guests as*
Clark Gable, Charlie Chaplin, Laurel and Hardy, and Eliza-
beth Taylor. Today, the Queen Mary *is permanently docked,*
but she still hosts some mysterious, ghostly passengers!

The *Queen Mary* Goes to War

The *Queen Mary* took her maiden voyage in May 1936, but
a change came in 1940 when the British government pressed
the ocean liner into military service. She was given a coat of
gray paint and was turned into a troop transport vessel. The
majestic dining salons became mess halls and the cocktail bars,
cabins, and staterooms were filled with bunks. Even the swimming pools were boarded over and crowded with cots for the
men. The ship was so useful to the Allies that Hitler offered
a $250,000 reward and hero status to the U-Boat commander
who could sink her. None of them did.

Although the *Queen Mary* avoided enemy torpedoes during
the war, she was unable to avoid tragedy. On October 2, 1942,
escorted by the cruiser HMS *Curacoa* and several destroyers,
the *Queen Mary* was sailing on the choppy North Atlantic near
Ireland. She was carrying about 15,000 American soldiers.

Danger from German vessels was always present, but things
were quiet until suddenly, before anyone could act, the *Queen
Mary*'s massive bow smashed into the *Curacoa*. There was no
way to slow down, no time for warning, and no distress calls to
the men onboard. They had only seconds to react before their
ship was sliced in two. Within minutes, both sections of the
ship plunged below the surface of the icy water, carrying the
crew with them. Of the *Curacoa*'s 439-man crew, 338 of them
perished on that fateful day. The *Queen Mary* suffered only
minor damage and there were no injuries to her crew.

After that, the *Queen Mary* served unscathed for the
remainder of the war. Following the surrender of Germany,

she was used to carry American troops and GI war brides to the United States and Canada, before returning to England for conversion back to a luxury liner.

Last Days of an Ocean Liner

After the war, the *Queen Mary* and her sister ship, the *Queen Elizabeth,* were the preferred method of transatlantic travel for the rich and famous. But by the 1960s, airplane travel was faster and cheaper, and so, in late 1967, the *Queen Mary* steamed away from England for the last time. Her decks and staterooms were filled with curiosity seekers and wealthy patrons who wanted to be part of the ship's final voyage. She ended her 39-day journey in Long Beach, California, where she was permanently docked as a floating hotel, convention center, museum, and restaurant. She is now listed on the National Register of Historic Places and is open to visitors year-round.

The Haunted *Queen Mary*

The *Queen Mary* has seen much tragedy and death, so it's no surprise that the ship plays host to a number of ghosts. Because of the sheer number of passengers who have walked her decks, accidents were bound to happen. One such mishap occurred on July 10, 1966, when John Pedder, an engine room worker, was crushed to death when an automatic door closed on him.

There have been other reported deaths onboard, as well. For instance, during the war, when the ship was used for troop transport, a brawl broke out in one of the galleys and a cook was allegedly shoved into a hot oven, where he burned to death. There are also reports of a woman drowning in the ship's swimming pool and stories of passengers falling overboard.

Another strange death onboard was that of Senior Second Officer William Stark, whose ghost has often been spotted on deck and in his former quarters. Stark died after drinking lime juice mixed with cleaning solution, which he mistook for gin. He realized his error, and while he joked about it, he called the ship's doctor. Unfortunately, though, Stark soon felt the effects of the poison. As the young officer's condition worsened, he lapsed into a coma and died on September 22, 1949.

Witnesses have also encountered a spectral man in gray overalls who has been seen below deck. He has dark hair and a long beard and is believed to be a mechanic or maintenance worker from the 1930s.

Another friendly spirit, dubbed "Miss Turner," is believed to have been a switchboard operator on the ship. A ghostly woman known as "Mrs. Kilburn" wears a gray uniform with starched white cuffs. She was once in charge of the stewardesses and bellboys, and she's still watching over the comings and goings on the ship. And although it is unknown who the ship's "Lady in White" might be, she haunts the Queen's Salon and is normally seen wearing a white, backless evening gown. Witnesses say she dances alone near the grand piano as if listening to music only she can hear, then vanishes.

Security guards, staff members, and visitors have also reported doors unlocking, opening, and closing on their own, often triggering security alarms. Other unexplained occurrences include phantom voices and footsteps, banging and hammerings sounds, cold spots, inexplicable winds that blow through closed-off areas, and lights that turn on and off.

During a tour of the ship, one guest felt someone tugging on her purse and sweater and stroking her hair. Cold chills crept down her spine when she realized there was no one near her at the time!

In 1967, some 25 years after the tragic accident with the *Curacoa,* a marine engineer working inside the ship heard the terrible sound of two ships colliding. He even heard screams and shredding steel. Did the terrible events of 1942 somehow leave an impression on the atmosphere of this grand old ship? Or worse, is the crew of the *Curacoa* still doomed to relive that fateful October afternoon for eternity?

Echoing the Present

The stories of mysterious encounters and strange events go on and on. It seems almost certain that the events of the past have left an indelible impression on the decks, corridors, and cabins of the *Queen Mary,* creating a haunting that is rivaled by few others in the annals of the supernatural.

The Watseka Wonder

💀   💀   💀   💀   💀

The story of the "Watseka Wonder," a phenomenon that occurred in a small town in Illinois in the late 1800s, still stands as one of the most authentic cases of spirit possession in history. It has been investigated, dissected, and ridiculed, but to this day, no clear explanation has ever been offered.

An Otherworldly Connection

Beginning on July 11, 1877, 13-year-old Watseka resident Lurancy Vennum started falling into strange trances that sometimes lasted for hours. During these trances, she claimed to speak with spirits and visit heaven. But when she awoke, she could not recall what had occurred during the spell.

Doctors diagnosed Lurancy as mentally ill and recommended that she be sent to the state insane asylum. But in January 1878, a man named Asa Roff, who also lived in Watseka, visited the Vennums. He told them that his daughter Mary had displayed the same behavior as Lurancy nearly 13 years before, and he advised the family to keep Lurancy out of the asylum.

Roff explained that on July 5, 1865, his 19-year-old daughter Mary had died in the state insane asylum. In the beginning, strange voices filled her head. Then she fell into long trances where she spoke as though possessed by the spirits of the dead. She later developed an obsession with bloodletting, poking herself with pins, applying leeches to her body, and cutting herself with a razor. Finally, her parents took her to the asylum, where she died a short time later.

The Strange Case of Lurancy Vennum

At the time of Mary Roff's death, Lurancy Vennum was barely a year old. Born on April 16, 1864, Lurancy moved with her family to Watseka a few years after Mary Roff's death and knew nothing of the girl or her family. When Lurancy's attacks began in July 1877, her family had no idea that she was suffering from the same type of illness that Mary had.

On the morning of her first trance, Lurancy collapsed and fell into a deep sleep that lasted more than five hours. When she awoke, she seemed fine. But the spell returned again the next day, and this time, while Lurancy was unconscious, she spoke of seeing angels and walking in heaven. She told her family that she had talked to her brother, who had died three years before.

As rumors of Lurancy's affliction spread around town, Asa Roff realized how closely her symptoms mirrored those of his own daughter, and he was convinced that the illnesses were the same. Roff kept quiet, but when it was suggested that Lurancy be institutionalized, he knew he had to speak up.

When Roff contacted the Vennum family on January 31, 1878, they were skeptical, but they allowed him to bring Dr. E. Winchester Stevens to meet with Lurancy. Like Roff, Dr. Stevens was a spiritualist. They felt that Lurancy was not insane but was possessed by spirits of the dead.

When Dr. Stevens arrived, Lurancy began speaking in another voice, claiming that she was a woman named Katrina Hogan. A few moments later, her voice changed again, and she said that she was Willie Canning, a boy who had killed himself many years before. Willie spoke for more than an hour. Then, just as Dr. Stevens and Asa Roff prepared to leave, Lurancy threw her arms into the air and fell on the floor stiff as a board. After Dr. Stevens calmed her down, Lurancy claimed she was in heaven and that spirits, some good and some bad, were controlling her body. She said the good spirit who most wanted to control her was a young woman named Mary Roff.

The Return of Mary Roff

After about a week of being possessed by the spirit of Mary Roff, Lurancy insisted on leaving the Vennum house, which was unfamiliar to her, and going "home" to the Roff house. When Mrs. Roff heard what was going on, she rushed over to the Vennum house with her daughter Minerva. As Lurancy watched the two women hurry up the sidewalk, she cried out, "There comes my ma and my sister Nervie!" "Nervie" had been Mary's pet name for her sister.

To those involved, it seemed evident that Mary's spirit had taken over Lurancy's body. She looked the same, but she knew nothing of the Vennum family or of her life as Lurancy. Instead, she had intimate knowledge of the Roffs and acted as though they were her family. Although Lurancy treated the Vennums politely, they were strangers to her.

On February 11, realizing that it was best for Lurancy, the Vennums allowed their daughter to go stay with the Roffs— although Lurancy told the Roffs that she would only be with them until "sometime in May."

On their way home, as the Roffs and Lurancy traveled past the house where they'd lived when Mary died, Lurancy wanted to know why they weren't stopping. The Roffs explained that they'd moved to a new home a few years back, which was something that Lurancy/Mary would not have known.

Within a short time, Lurancy began to exhibit signs that she knew more about the Roffs and their habits than she could have possibly known if she was only pretending to be Mary. She knew of incidents and experiences that were private and had taken place long before she was even born.

As promised, Lurancy stayed with the Roff family until early May. When it was time for Mary to leave Lurancy's body, she was deeply saddened, but she seemed to understand that it was time to go. On May 21, Lurancy returned to the Vennums. She showed no signs of her earlier illness, and her parents and the Roffs believed that she had been cured of her affliction by the possession of Mary's spirit.

Lurancy grew into a happy young woman and exhibited no ill effects from the possession. She married and had 13 children.

An Unsolved Mystery

Although Lurancy had no memories of being possessed by Mary, she felt a closeness to the Roffs that she could never explain. She stayed in touch with the Roff family even after they moved away from Watseka in 1879. Each year, when they returned, Lurancy would allow Mary's spirit to possess her, and things were just as they were for a time in 1878.

Wacky Weight-Loss Fads

The U.S. weight-loss industry brings in more than $50 billion a year as people try new ways to slim down. We've all heard that the key to losing weight is to burn more calories than you consume, but most people don't want to work that hard to lose weight. Instead, they'll try some pretty odd diets and contraptions in the hopes of shedding unwanted pounds.

Electric Ab Exercisers
Countless versions of the same machine have been unleashed on the flabby public with the same results: none whatsoever. These machines claim to send an electric current to abdominal muscles via plates, electrodes, or bands, causing the muscles to contract and release and therefore burn belly fat. All the machines actually do is leave red marks on the stomach and a dent in the wallet.

The "7–7–7 Diet"
On this diet, which circulated online a few years ago, dieters get to eat seven eggs throughout the day. Seven eggs *only*. On day two, it's seven oranges; on day three, seven bananas. According to believers, on the fourth day you'll wake up seven pounds lighter. And very, very hungry.

The JumpSnap
It's a jump rope…without the rope! This invention gets people jumping as if they were using a jump rope but eliminates the pesky rope that usually trips them up. A snapping sound emanates from two battery-powered handles, and a voice tells you how and when to jump. Another option: Save the cash, and just jump up and down.

The Breathing Diet
Overweight? Just breathe! For the low, low price of around $19.95, this diet claims to teach overeaters how to lose weight simply by learning how to breathe correctly.

The Vacunaut
The Vacunaut exercise system involves donning a rubbery neoprene suit attached to some vacuum hoses. As you run, the vacuum pressure is said to increase blood flow in the fatty tissue around the stomach and waist, whittling you down to that svelte god/goddess you've always wanted to be.

HandyTrim Light Pocket Gym
Step one: Take string out of pocket. Step two: Twirl. Step three: Watch those pounds melt off! The makers of this weight-loss gadget don't promise to turn you into a strapping hunk overnight, but with continued use, they swear the Pocket Gym will make a difference in your upper body. And since it's small and portable, you can exercise anywhere. Finally, a way to make those boring meetings productive!

The Cabbage Soup Diet
The supporters of this diet claim you can lose up to ten pounds in one week by eating little more than a super-green soup made largely from cabbage. Those who promote the diet claim that it's not a long-term thing—it just provides a kick-start when embarking on a more moderate diet. We imagine that anyone who actually likes cabbage at the beginning of the week will probably hate it by week's end.

The Dumbbell Phone
The Japanese have a word for the art of "unuseless" inventions: *chindogu.* What better problem than weight loss to inspire a thousand unuseless inventions? The dumbbell phone is a free-weight attachment for the telephone that purportedly helps build muscle every time you pick up the handset. This works best if you have a lot of short conversations and, thus, are lifting the phone and setting it down every minute or so. (Perfect for telemarketers, perhaps?)

Mike the Headless Chicken

💀   💀   💀   💀   💀

Chickens are known not for their intelligence but for their pecking, their much-emulated dance, and, in one special case, a chicken named Mike was known for losing his head.

A Slip of the Knife

On a fall day in 1945, on a farm in Fruita, Colorado, chickens were meeting their maker. It was nothing out of the ordinary; Lloyd and Clara Olsen slaughtered chickens on their farm all the time. But this particular day was fortuitous for Lloyd and one of his chickens. As Lloyd brought down his knife on the neck of a future meal, the head came off, clean as a whistle. The decapitated chicken flapped and danced around, which is what normally happens when a chicken loses its head.

But this chicken didn't *stop* flapping and dancing around. Most headless chickens only live a few minutes before going to that big chicken coop in the sky, but this particular bird was alive and well several hours (and then several months) after it had lost its, er, mind.

Open Mike

Lloyd was fascinated by this chicken that had somehow cheated death. The chicken continued to behave exactly like the other chickens on the farm—he just didn't have a head. Mike, as he was named, even attempted to cluck, although it sounded more like a gurgle since it came out of a hole in his neck.

Lloyd was starting to see the entrepreneurial possibilities that Mike had created—a living, breathing headless chicken was sure to be a goldmine. But Lloyd knew he had to devise a way for Mike to get nutrients or he would die. Using an eyedropper, a mixture of ground-up grain and water was sent down Mike's open esophagus, and little bits of gravel were dropped down his throat to help his gizzard grind up food.

That'll Be a Quarter
Mike the Headless Chicken was not some magical beast with the ability to cheat death; he was just an ordinary chicken that got lucky. Scientists who examined Mike determined that Lloyd had done a shoddy job of butchering him. Most of his head was actually gone, but the slice had missed Mike's jugular vein, and a blood clot prevented him from bleeding to death. Most of a chicken's reflex actions originate in the brain stem, and Mike's was pretty much untouched.

None of this mattered to the general public. When Mike went on a national sideshow tour in 1945, people lined up to see this wonder chicken and paid a quarter for the privilege. At his most popular, Mike was drawing in about $4,500 per month, which is equivalent to about $50,000 today. He was insured for $10,000 and featured in *Life* magazine.

What became of Mike's head is a mystery. Most photos show a chicken head alongside Mike, either at his feet or pickled in a jar. But rumor has it that the Olsens' cat ate the original head, and Lloyd used another chicken's head as a stand-in.

A Moment of Silence, Please
It's wasn't the lack of a head that was toughest on Mike—he had a problem with choking on his own mucus. The Olsens employed a syringe to suck the mucus out of Mike's neck, but one fateful night, Mike was traveling back home to Fruita, roosting with the Olsens in their motel room. Lloyd and Clara heard Mike choking in the middle of the night and reached for the syringe. Alas, they discovered they had left it in the last town where Mike had appeared. Mike finally succumbed to death that night in Phoenix in 1947.

These days, Fruita holds an annual Mike the Headless Chicken Day every third weekend in May in honor of their most famous resident.

Brainless Bad Guys

Even crime has its dimmest moments. Here's a collection of crime-related gaffes that put the "dumb" in dumbfound.

Digitized Dummy

They say a picture is worth a thousand words. Sometimes it's worth even more. In 2003, when a Wal-Mart in Long Island, New York, discovered that $2,000 worth of digital cameras had been lifted from their store, they went straight to the videotape. There they found images of a male and female suspect but couldn't identify either due to the tape's grainy nature. Then they spotted something of interest: At one point during the heist, the female accomplice had taken pictures with a demonstration camera. Her subject? Her partner in crime, of course. When the digital information was fed into a printer, out popped a high-quality color image of a balding man with a mustache. The 36-year-old crook was subsequently identified through a tip line and charged with grand larceny. Like Narcissus, the love of his own image brought him down.

Leave Only Footsteps

Sometimes, ambition can impede the job at hand. According to prosecutors, in 2005, a 23-year-old man filled out a job application while waiting for a pie at a Las Vegas pizza parlor. Then, out of nowhere, the man flashed a gun and demanded that the cashier give him all the money inside her cash drawer. He fled the scene $200 richer. A witness recorded his license plate, and the robber was arrested at home shortly thereafter. But this lucky break wasn't really necessary because he'd jotted down his *real* name and address on the job application.

Statute of Style Limitations
A security guard working at Neiman Marcus in White Plains, New York, apprehended a young woman in 2007 for shoplifting. He caught up with the 19-year-old outside of the store and accused her of stealing a pair of $250 jeans. While he waited for police to arrive, the accused railed bitterly against the guard. According to the police report, she was convinced that she was immune from prosecution based on a legal technicality, stating triumphantly, "It's too late. I already left the store!"

Big-Time Loser
Some criminals don't know when to stop. In 2007, a New York man was pulled over for a traffic stop and racked up a bunch of criminal infractions in the process. He was intoxicated; not wearing a seat belt; driving toward oncoming traffic lanes with an open beer container by his side; driving with an expired inspection sticker and with license plates from another car; operating an uninsured vehicle; and transporting his two-year-old daughter without benefit of a car seat or a fastened seat belt.

Indiscriminate Crook
In 2007, an ex-con pulled a fake handgun on two victims and demanded their cash. The only problem was, they were two *uniformed* New York City police officers. The officers responded by drawing their real weapons, and the mugger surrendered after a brief, but tense, standoff.

Crime Doesn't Pay
In 2007, a thief entered a Fairfield, Connecticut, Dunkin' Donuts. Intent on snaring the contents of its cash register, the would-be crook handed the clerk a note stating that he was carrying a gun and a bomb, and he would use both if he didn't receive cash. With that, the robber grabbed the entire machine from the counter and made his getaway. But there was one significant problem: The hapless criminal had made off with an adding machine instead of the cash register.

Who Wants to Be a Billionaire?

According to legend, more than $2 billion in gold may be hidden on Oak Island in Mahone Bay, about 45 minutes from Halifax, Nova Scotia. For more than 200 years, treasure hunters have scoured the island, looking for the bounty, but the pirates who buried the treasure hid it well...and left booby traps, too.

Folklore Leads to Fact

Since 1720, people have claimed that pirate treasure was buried on Oak Island. Then, in the fall of 1795, young Daniel McGinnis went hunting on the island and found evidence that those stories might be true. But he found something rather odd: An oak tree had been used with a hoist to lift something very heavy. When McGinnis dug at that spot, he found loose sand indicating a pit about 12 feet in diameter.

He returned the next day with two friends and some digging tools. When the boys had dug ten feet down, they encountered a wooden platform—beneath it was more dirt. Ten feet further down, they reached another wooden platform with more dirt beneath it. At that point, the boys had to give up. They needed better tools and engineering expertise to continue their search.

They didn't get the help they needed, but one thing was certain: Something important had been buried on Oak Island. Soon, more people visited the island hoping to strike it rich.

An Encouraging Message

In the early 1800s, a Nova Scotia company began excavating the pit. The slow process took many years, and every ten feet, they found another wooden platform and sometimes layers of charcoal, putty, or coconut fiber.

About 90 feet down, the treasure hunters found an oily stone about three feet wide. It bore a coded inscription that read, "Forty feet below, two million pounds lie buried." (Gold worth two million pounds in 1795 would be worth approximately $2 billion today.)

However, as they dug past that 90-foot level, water began rushing into the hole. A few days later, the pit was almost full of seawater. No matter how much the team bailed, the water maintained its new level, so the company dug a second shaft, parallel to the first and 110 feet deep. But when they dug across to the original tunnel, water quickly filled the new shaft as well. The team abandoned the project, but others were eager to try their luck.

More Digging, More Encouragement, More Water

Since then, several companies have excavated deeper in the original shaft. Most treasure hunters—including a team organized by Franklin D. Roosevelt—have found additional proof that something valuable is buried there. For example, at 126 feet—nearly "forty feet below" the 90-foot marker—engineers found oak and iron. Farther down, they also reached a large cement chamber, from which they brought up a tiny piece of parchment, which encouraged them to dig deeper.

A narrow shaft dug in 1971 allowed researchers to use special cameras to study the pit. The team thought they saw several chests, some tools, and a disembodied hand floating in the water, but the shaft collapsed before they could explore further.

` Since then, flooding has continued to hamper research efforts, and at least six people have been killed in their quests to find buried treasure. Nevertheless, the digging continues.

As of late 2007, the 1971 shaft had been redug to a depth of 181 feet. It offers the greatest promise for success. But just in case, investors and engineers plan to continue digging.

A Vacation Worth a Fortune?

But the digging isn't limited to professionals. Oak Island has become a unique vacation spot for people who like adventure and the chance to go home with a fortune. Canadian law says any treasure hunter can keep 90 percent of his or her findings.

Some vacationers dig at nearby islands, believing that the Oak Island site may be an elaborate, 18th-century "red herring." There are more than 100 other lovely islands in Mahone Bay. Perhaps the treasure is actually buried on one of them?

Freaky Foods from Around the World

☠ ☠ ☠ ☠ ☠

*People around the globe eat many things that seem bizarre
and distasteful to American palates. And we're not just talking
about snails, raw herring, and spices so hot they nearly melt
your mouth. These foods are downright strange!*

Balut

A favorite in some parts of Southeast Asia, balut consists of a
fertilized duck egg that's been steamed at the brink of hatch-
ing. Diners, who usually pick up one from a street vendor on
the way home from a night of imbibing, chow down on the
entire contents of the egg: the head, beak, feet, and innards.
Only the eggshell is discarded.

Bird's Nest Soup

The key ingredient of this famous Chinese dish is the saliva-
rich nest of the cave swiftlet, a swallow that lives on cave walls
in Southeast Asia. This delicacy is so popular that it has endan-
gered the bird's population. Some enterprising suppliers have
started farming nests by providing birds with houses in which
to build. Still, wild nests remain the most highly prized.

Century Eggs

When Sam I Am was expressing his disgust for green eggs in
Dr. Seuss's classic book, he was probably talking about the
Chinese specialty known as century eggs, also called thousand
year eggs or preserved eggs. To make the dish, chicken, duck,
or goose eggs are preserved in a mixture of salt, lime, clay,
ash, and rice husks or tea leaves, then allowed to ferment for

several weeks or months. The process turns the egg whites into gelatinous, transparent dark-brown masses, while the yolks become pungent yet intensely flavored orbs of variegated shades of green. What's not to like?

Cobra's Blood Cocktails
Those looking for an exotic drink in Indonesia can quench their thirst with a fresh cocktail of cobra's blood, served either straight or mixed with liquor. Depending on the establishment, consumers can choose between different types of cobras to supply the blood, with the King Cobra being the most prized and expensive.

Fugu/Pufferfish
Diners must have the utmost confidence in the chef preparing this Japanese dish because eating improperly prepared puffer-fish can result in sudden death. As such, Japan requires extensive training and apprenticeship, as well as special licensing, for the chefs preparing this highly sought-after delicacy.

Kopi Luwak Coffee
Java junkies may need to save up to indulge in this exotic Indonesian coffee. What makes it so special? For kopi luwak coffee, only the sweetest, tastiest coffee beans are picked by experts—not human experts, but rather wild civets who live in Indonesia's coffee-producing forests. The animals nibble on the fruity exterior before swallowing the hard inner beans. During the digestive process, their gastric juices remove some of the proteins that ordinarily make coffee bitter. Humans don't intervene in the coffee-making process until it's time to separate the undigested beans from the civet dung. Experts claim the result is an exceptionally smooth and balanced cup of Joe.

Seal Flipper Pie
A specialty of Newfoundland, this maritime favorite is made from the chewy cartilage-rich flippers of seals, usually cooked in fatback with root vegetables and sealed in a flaky pastry crust or topped with dumplings.

Michael Jackson: Falling Star

💀 💀 💀 💀 💀

A boy from the Midwest rises to astronomical fame and fortune only to fall from grace years later, as an increasingly eccentric man embroiled in scandal and controversy. Is Michael Jackson a tortured-but-gifted artist or simply a famous-person-turned-freak? Either way, he's a strange yet fascinating man.

Boy Wonder

Michael Jackson was born on August 29, 1958, the seventh of nine kids. From the outside, the Jacksons looked like a typical working-class family from Gary, Indiana. But in 1964, patriarch Joe Jackson organized his sons into a singing group, and it was clear that the Jackson boys were anything but average.

The group, which Joe named the Jackson 5, was comprised of brothers Jermaine, Jackie, Tito, Marlon, and Michael. With segregation still firmly in place in the early 1960s, the group performed on the "urban music circuit." Venues such as Harlem's famous Apollo Theater and Chicago's Regal Theater gave black performers a place to perform and be seen by industry professionals. Show by show, the Jackson 5 garnered attention with their catchy songs and slick dance moves.

Of all the boys, Michael was clearly the most talented—the consensus among biographers is that the youngest Jackson was a bona fide prodigy. His eye-popping dance moves were matched by his charismatic personality and his innate ability to nail vocals. The more the boys performed, the clearer it became: Michael was in every way a star.

Before long, the Jackson 5 had a deal with Motown Records, and they quickly charted hit after hit, including "I'll Be There," "ABC," and "I Want You Back." American audiences (black *and* white) embraced the cute singing sensations, and record sales soared. As the group became more successful, Michael received the most attention. He was the unofficial front man of the group, and he was also penning most of their hits. People wanted more Michael, and record producers took note.

Look Ma, No Brothers!

In 1979, Michael teamed up with hit-maker Quincy Jones on a solo album. (The Jackson 5 didn't officially disband until 1984.) *Off the Wall* featured hits such as "Rock With You" and "Don't Stop 'Til You Get Enough" and eventually sold more than seven million copies. The album's disco-inspired sounds were embraced by the boogie-crazed masses, and collaborations with the likes of Paul McCartney and Stevie Wonder gave the album depth. Honors and acclamations followed, including American Music Awards and a Grammy. All this solidified Jackson as a solo star, but nothing could prepare the world for what came next.

Michael Mania Dominates the World

On December 1, 1982, *Thriller* hit with the force of a tsunami. The album shot to number one on *Billboard* charts and stayed there for 37 weeks. Never before or since has one album sold as well as *Thriller*—it went platinum 27 times, selling more than 50 million copies worldwide. Even after it relinquished the top spot on the charts, it continued to chart for two more years. Total and complete Michael Jackson mania took over the world. He quickly earned the undisputed title "The King of Pop."

One of the reasons for this astonishing success was Michael's ingenious use of the new cable television channel MTV. The burgeoning station was the perfect medium for visually savvy artists like Michael Jackson, Madonna, Prince, and others to catch the attention of Generation X. Videos for singles such as "Billie Jean" and "Beat It" instantly became classic visuals. But it was the video for "Thriller" that became a "cultural zeitgeist." The video premiered with intense hype on MTV, is still ranked number one on MTV's list of "Greatest Music Videos Ever Made," and was the highest-selling VHS tape ever sold after it was packaged with the documentary *The Making of Michael Jackson's "Thriller."*

At the Grammy Awards in 1984, Michael and *Thriller* were nominated for 12 awards and won a record-breaking 8. The press was touting him as a legend at age 25, and sales of *Thriller* contributed to one of the best years the music industry had ever seen. Fans were wearing Michael's trademark white glove;

doing his iconic dance, "the moonwalk"; and paying big bucks to see him perform in concert. No one could dispute it: Michael Jackson was one of the biggest stars the world had ever seen.

Other successful records followed during the 1980s. Michael spearheaded the "We Are the World" charity project and worked with George Lucas and Francis Ford Coppola for the 3-D film *Captain EO*. His next solo album, *Bad,* was released in 1987 and launched another string of hits, including "Man in the Mirror," "The Way You Make Me Feel," and the title track.

What Goes Up...

His accomplishments were astounding, but that doesn't mean Jackson was happy—or that the good times would last. In 1993, two years after his *Dangerous* album was released, Michael was hit with a stunning lawsuit. It was known that the star allowed children to hang out at the home he called Neverland Ranch. The suit alleged that, not only did the kids play in the amusement park and pet the animals at the zoo on Jackson's property, but they also slept over in Michael's own bedroom. The media went crazy over the allegations. Michael was appalled by the accusations and claimed that he was completely innocent of any wrongdoing. The first accuser settled out of court for a reported $20 million. Michael said he did it to avoid a courtroom media circus, but some claimed it was an admission of guilt.

Ten years later, Michael was again charged with child molestation, as well as using intoxicating substances for that purpose and conspiring to hold a boy and his family captive at Neverland Ranch. Two years later, Michael was acquitted of all charges, but further ruin had been done to his reputation. The tremendous amount of negative publicity had a devastating effect on Michael's music, and some say it's what led Michael to become even more reclusive and eccentric.

Leave Me Alone

When someone says "Michael Jackson" these days, it's hard not to immediately think of his appearance. A medium skin-toned African American as a child, Michael's skin is now pale. In 1993, rumors that he bleached his skin were denied in a television interview between Jackson and Oprah Winfrey. He claimed he suffered from a skin disease that caused his skin to lighten. Michael also wrote in his 1988 autobiography, *Moon Walk,* that he had undergone "very little" plastic surgery, claiming only two nose jobs. It was hard to believe, because Michael's entire facial structure (including his lips, nose, and chin) seemed totally different when compared to photos of him as a younger man.

As the years passed, Michael's appearance became even more bizarre. He rarely took off his sunglasses, his complexion paled to a vampirish shade, and his nose became even smaller. Along with the changes in his look, his behavior was truly baffling. A marriage to Lisa Marie Presley seemed to be a publicity stunt to battle rumors that the star was gay or attracted to children. A kiss between the couple at an awards show in 1994 was universally critiqued as being stiff and awkward. The marriage lasted less than two years.

In 1996, Michael married again and fathered two children with his second wife, Debbie Rowe, but the couple divorced within three years. Michael's third child, Prince Michael Jackson II (nicknamed "Blanket"), was born in 2002. While in Berlin that year, Michael made headlines when he presented Blanket to the throngs of press and fans outside his hotel room. However, he didn't just wave with the baby in his arms; he dangled the child over the balcony, causing yet another media frenzy: Was Michael fit to be a parent?

What Happened?
Looking at the events of Michael Jackson's life, it is understandable how a person could become a bit odd over the years. Superstardom before age ten, a demanding father who pushed his kids too hard, a record-setting career unparalleled in world history, and wealth beyond imagination—all of this contributed to the person Michael Jackson is today. Though he was acquitted of all charges brought against him, the world is still wary of the star and largely treats him like a leper. Only time will tell if the prodigal son of pop music will make a triumphant return.

Frozen Stiff

People can learn a lot from a cadaver, especially if said corpse has a body temperature hovering around –100°F and has single-handedly inspired an annual festival in its honor. Don't believe us? Check out Nederland, Colorado's Frozen Dead Guy Days, a festival guaranteed to ruin your taste for Popsicles.

Dead Man Thawing

Just after Bredo Morstoel passed away in 1989, his doting grandson Trygve Bauge transported his body from Norway to Colorado with plans of putting him on deep ice for eternity. But Trygve's luck (and visa) ran out, and he was deported in a fairly cold manner. So his mother, Aud, stepped in to keep her deceased dad on the cryogenic rocks.

Unfortunately for Aud, her dead dad wasn't the only one with ice in his veins. In 1993, when local authorities learned she was living in a home with no electricity or plumbing, they kicked her to the curb, citing violations of local ordinances. Aud decided to go public, and soon, her neighbors heard of the plight of the cryogenically frozen man slowly thawing in a backyard shed.

The case brought about an ordinance forbidding residents from keeping human body parts in their homes. But Bredo was exempted through a "grandfather" clause, and someone in town even built him a climate-controlled shed for good measure.

Lucky Stiff

In 2002, a festival was held in Bredo's honor, and since then the event has been held annually each March. One highlight of the event is the Grandpa Look-Alike Contest, wherein homely humans try to emulate Bredo, now rigid for nearly two decades.

Another popular event is the Polar Plunge. Participants jump into a frigid Colorado pond to simulate the cryogenic experience. There's also a coffin race, and at night the Blues Masquerade Ball offers up a chance to dance 'til you drop as proof that no matter how old—or dead—you are, you can still have fun.

FREAKY FACTS: BEDBUGS

Good night, sleep tight. Don't let the bedbugs bite! For decades, bedbugs were all but extinct in many places. But recently, increased travel and less-toxic modern pesticides have allowed a resurgence of these creepy crawlies.

- *When full of blood, bedbugs can swell as large as three times their normal size.*

- *It takes a bedbug five minutes to drink its fill of blood.*

- *A female bedbug can lay up to five eggs per day and 200–500 eggs in her lifetime.*

- *When bedbugs bite, proteins in their saliva prevent the wound from closing.*

- *Bedbugs can consume as much as six times their weight in blood at one feeding.*

- *Normally, a bedbug is brown. After eating, however, its body appears dark red.*

- *Bedbugs are nocturnal—they become active when humans are sleeping.*

- *Bedbugs only eat once every seven to ten days.*

- *In the last five years, calls to pest-control companies about bedbugs have increased by more than 70 percent.*

- *Other names for bedbugs include "mahogany flats," "redcoats," and "chinches."*

- *Bedbugs molt five times before reaching adulthood.*

- *Bedbugs migrated from Europe to the United States during the 1600s.*

- *Contrary to popular belief, the presence of bedbugs does not indicate a dirty house.*

Famous UFO Sightings

*Unidentified flying objects, foo fighters, ghost rockets—
whatever you call them, strange and unclassified objects in the
sky remain one of the world's truly mysterious phenomena.
Here are some of the most famous UFO sightings.*

The Battle of Los Angeles

On February 25, 1942, just weeks after Japan's attack on Pearl
Harbor and America's entry into World War II, late-night air-
raid sirens sounded a blackout order throughout Los Angeles
County in California. A silvery object (or objects) was spotted
in the sky, prompting an all-out assault from ground troops.
For a solid hour, antiaircraft fire bombarded the unidentified
craft with some 1,400 shells, as numerous high-powered search-
lights followed its slow movement across the sky. Several witnesses reported direct hits on the invader, though it was never
downed. After the "all clear" was sounded, the object vanished, and it has never been identified.

The Marfa Lights

The town of Marfa, located far out in western Texas, is home
to what many believe is the best concentration of "ghost lights"
in the nation. Almost nightly, witnesses along Highway 67
can peer across the flatland north of the Chinati Mountains
and spot glowing orbs of varying color and size, bobbing and
floating among the brush. It's an event that's reportedly been
witnessed since the 1880s. Though several scientists have conducted studies, no one has been able to determine their origin.
Nevertheless, local officials have capitalized on the phenomenon and constructed an official roadside viewing area.

The Washington Flap

In two separate incidents just days apart in 1952, numerous objects were detected high above Washington, D.C., moving erratically at speeds as fast as 7,000 miles per hour. At one point, separate military radar stations detected the same objects simultaneously. Several eyewitnesses viewed the objects from the ground and from air control towers, and three pilots spotted them at close range, saying they looked like the lit end of a cigarette or like falling stars without tails. The official Air Force explanation was "temperature inversion," and the sightings were labeled "unexplained."

The Hill Abduction, aka the Zeta Reticuli Incident

By the 1960s, a number of people had reportedly seen UFOs but hadn't actually encountered aliens personally. But on September 19, 1961, Barney and Betty Hill found themselves being chased by a spacecraft along Route 3 in New Hampshire. The object eventually descended upon their vehicle, whereupon Barney witnessed several humanoid creatures through the craft's windows. The couple tried to escape, but their car began shaking violently, and they were forced off the road. Suffering lapses in memory from that moment on, the Hills later recalled being taken aboard the ship, examined, and questioned by figures with very large eyes. The incident was known only to locals and the UFO community until the 1966 publication of *The Interrupted Journey* by John Fuller.

The Apollo 11 Transmission

When American astronauts made that great leap onto the surface of the moon on July 20, 1969, they apparently weren't alone. Although the incident has been repeatedly denied, believers point to a transmission from the lunar surface that had been censored by NASA but was reportedly picked up by private ham-radio operators: "These babies are huge, sir! Enormous!... You wouldn't believe it. I'm telling you there are other spacecraft out there, lined up on the far side of the crater edge. They're on the moon watching us!"

Fire in the Sky

After completing a job along Arizona's Mogollon Rim on
November 5, 1979, Travis Walton and six fellow loggers spotted a large spacecraft hovering near the dark forest road lead-

ing home. Walton
approached the
craft on foot and
was knocked to the
ground by a beam
of light. Then he
and the craft disap-
peared. Five days
later, Walton mysteri-
ously reappeared just
outside of town. He
said that during
his time aboard the
spacecraft, he had
struggled to escape
from the short, large-headed creatures that performed experiments on his body. Neither Walton nor any of his coworkers
has strayed from the facts of their stories in nearly 30 years.

The Rendlesham Forest Incident

In late December 1980, several soldiers at the Royal Air
Force base in Woodbridge, Suffolk, England, saw a number
of strange lights among the trees just outside their east gate.
Upon investigation, they spotted a conical or disk-shape object
hovering above a clearing. The object seemed aware of their
presence and moved away from them, but the men eventually
gave chase. No hard evidence has been provided by the military, but the event is often considered the most significant UFO
event in Britain. The Forestry Commission has since created a
"UFO Trail" for hikers near the RAF base.

JAL 1628

On November 17, 1986, as Japan Airlines flight 1628 passed
over Alaska, military radar detected an object on its tail. When

the blip caught up with the cargo jet, the pilot reported seeing three large craft shaped like shelled walnuts, one of which was twice the size of an aircraft carrier. The objects matched the airplane's speed and tracked it for nearly an hour. At one point, the two smaller craft came so close that the pilot said he could feel their heat. The incident prompted an official FAA investigation and made worldwide headlines.

The Phoenix Lights

In March 1997, hundreds, if not thousands, of witnesses throughout Phoenix, Arizona, and the surrounding area caught sight of what was to become the most controversial UFO sighting in decades. For at least two hours, Arizona residents watched an array of lights move across the sky, and many reportedly saw a dark, triangular object between them. The lights, which varied in color, were even caught on videotape. Nearby military personnel tried to reproduce the event by dropping flares from the sky, but most witnesses weren't satisfied with what was deemed a diversion from the truth.

Roswell

Undoubtedly the most famous UFO-related location, Roswell immediately brings to mind flying-saucer debris, men in black, secret military programs, alien autopsies, weather balloons, and government cover-ups. The incident that started it all occurred during the first week of July 1947, just before Roswell Army Air Field spokespersons claimed they had recovered parts of a wrecked "flying disc" from a nearby ranch. The report was quickly corrected to involve a weather balloon instead, which many insist was part of a cover-up. In later years, people claiming to have been involved in the recovery effort began to reveal insider information, insisting that not only was the wreckage of extraterrestrial origin, but that autopsies had been performed on alien bodies recovered from the site. Ever since, the name of this small New Mexico town has been synonymous with ufology, making Roswell a popular stop for anyone interested in all things alien.

The Death of John Dillinger...or Someone Who Looked Like Him

💀 💀 💀 💀 💀

On July 22, 1934, outside the Biograph Theater on Chicago's north side, John Dillinger, America's first Public Enemy Number One, passed from this world into the next in a hail of bullets. Or did he? Conspiracy theorists believe that FBI agents shot and killed the wrong man and covered it all up when they realized their mistake. So what really happened that night? Let's first take a look at the main players in this gangland soap opera.

Hoover Wants His Man

Born June 22, 1903, John Dillinger was in his early thirties when he first caught the FBI's eye. They thought they were through with him in January 1934, when he was arrested after shooting a police officer during a bank robbery in East Chicago, Indiana. However, Dillinger managed to stage a daring escape from his Indiana jail cell using a wooden gun painted with black shoe polish.

Once Dillinger left Indiana in a stolen vehicle and crossed into Illinois, he was officially a federal fugitive. J. Edgar Hoover, then director of the FBI, promised a quick apprehension, but Dillinger had other plans. He seemed to enjoy the fact that the FBI was tracking him—rather than go into hiding, he continued robbing banks. Annoyed, Hoover assigned FBI Agent Melvin Purvis to ambush Dillinger. Purvis's plan backfired, though, and Dillinger escaped, shooting and killing two innocent men in the process. After the botched trap, the public was in an uproar and the FBI was under close scrutiny. To everyone at the FBI, the message was clear: Hoover wanted Dillinger, and he wanted him ASAP.

The Woman in Red

The FBI's big break came in July 1934 with a phone call from a woman named Anna Sage. Sage was a Romanian immigrant who ran a Chicago-area brothel. Fearing that she might be deported, Sage wanted to strike a bargain with the feds. Her proposal was simple: In exchange for not being deported, Sage was willing to give the FBI John Dillinger. According to Sage, Dillinger was dating Polly Hamilton, one of her former employees. Melvin Purvis personally met with Sage and told her he couldn't make any promises but he would do what he could about her pending deportation.

Several days later, on July 22, Sage called the FBI office in Chicago and said that she was going to the movies that night with Dillinger and Hamilton. Sage quickly hung up but not before saying she would wear something bright so that agents could pick out the threesome in a crowd. Not knowing which movie theater they were planning to go to, Purvis dispatched several agents to the Marbro Theater, while he and another group of agents went to the Biograph. At approximately 8:30 P.M., Purvis believed he saw Dillinger, Sage, and Hamilton enter the Biograph. As she had promised, Sage indeed wore something bright—an orange blouse. However, under the marquee lights, the blouse's color appeared to be red, which is why Sage was forever dubbed "The Woman in Red."

Purvis tried to apprehend Dillinger right after he purchased tickets, but he slipped past Purvis and into the darkened theater. Purvis went into the theater but was unable to locate Dillinger in the dark. At that point, Purvis left the theater, gathered his men, and made the decision to apprehend Dillinger as he was exiting the theater. Purvis positioned himself in the theater's vestibule, instructed his men to hide outside, and told them that he would signal them by lighting a cigar when he spotted Dillinger. That was their cue to move in and arrest Dillinger.

"Stick 'em up, Johnny!"

At approximately 10:30 P.M., the doors to the Biograph opened and people started to exit. All of the agents' eyes were on Purvis. When a man wearing a straw hat, accompanied by two women, walked past Purvis, the agent quickly placed a cigar in his mouth and lit a match. Perhaps sensing something was wrong, the man turned and looked at Purvis, at which point

Purvis drew his pistol and said, "Stick 'em up, Johnny!" In response, the man turned as if he was going to run away, while at the same time reaching for what appeared to be a gun. Seeing the movement, the other agents opened fire. As the man ran away, attempting to flee down the alleyway alongside the theater, he was shot four times on his left side and once in the back of the neck before crumpling on the pavement. When Purvis reached him and checked for vitals, there were none. Minutes later, after being driven to a local hospital, John Dillinger was pronounced DOA. But as soon as it was announced that Dillinger was dead, the controversy began.

Dillinger Disputed

Much of the basis for the conspiracy stems from the fact that Hoover, both publicly and privately, made it clear that no matter what, he wanted Dillinger caught. On top of that, Agent Purvis was under a lot of pressure to capture Dillinger, especially since he'd failed with a previous attempt. Keeping that in mind, it would be easy to conclude that Purvis, in his haste to capture Dillinger, might have overlooked a few things. First, it was Purvis alone who pointed out the man he thought to be Dillinger to the waiting agents. Conspiracy theorists contend that Purvis fingered the wrong man that night, and an innocent man ended up getting killed as a result. As evidence, they point to Purvis's own statement: While they were standing at close range, the man tried to pull a gun, which is why the agents had to open fire. But even though agents stated they recovered a .38-caliber Colt automatic from the victim's body (and even had it on display for many years), author Jay Robert Nash discovered that that particular model was not even available until a good five months after Dillinger's alleged death! Theorists believe that when agents realized they had not only shot the wrong man, but an unarmed one at that, they planted the gun as part of a cover-up.

Another interesting fact that could have resulted in Purvis's misidentification was that Dillinger had recently undergone plastic surgery in an attempt to disguise himself. In addition to work on his face, Dillinger had attempted to obliterate his fingerprints by dipping his fingers into an acid solution. On top of that, the man who Purvis said was Dillinger was wearing a straw hat the entire time Purvis saw him. It is certainly possible that Purvis did not actually recognize Dillinger but instead picked out someone who merely looked like him. If you remember, the only tip Purvis had was Sage telling him that she was going to the movies with Dillinger and his girlfriend. Did Purvis see Sage leaving the theater in her orange blouse and finger the wrong man simply because he was standing next to Sage and resembled Dillinger? Or was the whole thing a setup orchestrated by Sage and Dillinger to trick the FBI into executing an innocent man?

So Who Was It?

If the man shot and killed outside the theater wasn't John Dillinger, who was it? There are conflicting accounts, but one speculation is that it was a man named Jimmy Lawrence, who was dating Polly Hamilton. If you believe in the conspiracy, Lawrence was simply in the wrong place at the wrong time. Or possibly, Dillinger purposely sent Lawrence to the theater hoping FBI agents would shoot him, allowing Dillinger to fade into obscurity. Of course, those who don't believe in the conspiracy say the reason Lawrence looked so much like Dillinger is because he *was* Dillinger using an alias. Further, Dillinger's sister, Audrey Hancock, identified his body. Finally, they say it all boils down to the FBI losing or misplacing the gun Dillinger had the night he was killed and inadvertently replacing it with the wrong one. Case closed.

Not really, though. It seems that whenever someone comes up with a piece of evidence to fuel the conspiracy theory, someone else has something to refute it. Some have asked that Dillinger's body be exhumed and DNA tests be performed, but nothing has come of it yet. Until that happens, we'll probably never know for sure what really happened on that hot July night back in 1934. But that's okay, because real or imagined, everyone loves a good mystery.

Underground Cities: What's Going on Down There?

Most of us give little thought to what is going on beneath our feet. Under many cities, however, there exists another city that contains other people—or did at one time.

Edinburgh, Scotland

In the 1700s, space was at a premium in Edinburgh. Hemmed in by hills and surrounded by protective walls, Edinburgh had no more clear land to build upon within the city limits. Arched bridges, such as South Bridge, were built to connect hilltop to hilltop, and, in a marvel of architectural design, small honeycombed chambers and tunnels were built into the vaults. At first, fashionable shops used these rooms for storage and workspace areas. But their underground nature attracted the seedier members of society, and the area quickly became a breeding ground for disease and crime. Although the vaults were closed in the mid-1800s, they were rediscovered and excavated in 1995. Today, a few restaurants, nightclubs, and ghost tours operate in the vaults.

Seattle, Washington

In 1889, the Great Seattle Fire destroyed more than 25 city blocks near the waterfront. In rebuilding the Pioneer Square area, city leaders decided to raise the street level to avoid flooding. With street level now a full story higher, merchants moved most of their businesses to their second (now ground) floors. Sidewalks built at the new street level created underground tunnels connecting the taverns and businesses that remained open. In 1907, fear of crime and disease caused the underground to be condemned, but a few of these abandoned tunnels and rooms have been restored and are currently open to the public.

Cappadocia, Turkey
It is believed that hundreds of underground cities exist underneath the Cappadocia rock, although only 40 have been found and a mere six are open to visitors. These cities first appeared in literature around 400 B.C., and were used for storage and protection. Carved out of soft volcanic rock, the largest of these cities has 600 doors leading to the surface, as well as connecting rooms that tunneled underground eight excavated stories—and possibly as many as 12 unexcavated levels below those—and could hold as many as 30,000 people.

Paris, France
Built upon a network of 12th-century quarries, Paris sits atop 170 miles of tunnels. From 1785 until the 1880s, these tunnels received the bones of nearly six million people from condemned or overcrowded cemeteries around the city. During World War II, the tunnels were used to hide Resistance fighters. Today, a portion of the catacombs is open as a museum to visitors, but the rest is left to foolhardy explorers, illegal partiers, and the dead.

Montreal, Quebec, Canada
Montreal is sometimes called two cities in one due to its subterranean counterpart. The underground city was started in 1962 as a shopping center, and it eventually grew to connect important buildings and house more shopping space. Now, 60 percent of offices in Montreal are linked to the underground city and there are more than 200 entrances. The underground city's 22 miles of corridors are used by more than 500,000 people every day to go to work, school, or any of the bus terminals, metro stations, 1,700 shops, 1,615 apartments, 200 restaurants, 40 banks, 40 cinemas and entertainment venues, 8 hotels, or other places that are part of the network.

Rebel with a Curse: James Dean and "Little Bastard"

💀   💀   💀   💀   💀

From the moment James Dean first walked onto a Hollywood set, countless people have emulated his cool style and attitude. When Dean died in a car crash in 1955 at age 24, his iconic status was immortalized. Perhaps this is partly due to the strange details that surrounded his death. Did a cursed car take the rising star away before his time?

How Much Is that Porsche in the Window?

In 1955, heartthrob James Dean purchased a silver Porsche 550 Spyder, which he nicknamed "Little Bastard." Dean painted the number "130" on the hood and the car's saucy name on the back.

On the morning of September 30, Dean drove the Porsche to his mechanic for a quick tune-up before heading to a race he was planning to enter. The car checked out, and Dean left, making plans to meet up with a few friends and a *Life* magazine photographer later that day.

Everyone who knew Dean knew he liked to drive fast. The movie star set out on the highway, driving at top speeds in his beloved Porsche. He actually got stopped for speeding at one point but got back on the road after getting a ticket.

But when the sun got in his eyes and another car made a quick left turn, Dean couldn't stop in time. Screeching brakes, twisted metal, and an ambulance that couldn't make it to the hospital in time signaled the end of James Dean's short life.

You Need Brake Pads, a New Alternator, and a Priest

Within a year or so of Dean's fatal car crash, his Porsche was involved in a number of unusual—and sometimes deadly—incidents. Were they all coincidental, or was the car actually cursed? Consider the following:

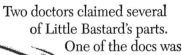

Two doctors claimed several of Little Bastard's parts. One of the docs was killed and the other seriously injured in separate accidents. Someone else purchased the tires, which blew simultaneously, sending their new owner to the hospital.

The Fresno garage where the car was kept for a while after Dean's death was the site of a major fire. The California State Highway Patrol removed the car from Fresno, figuring they could show the charred remains of Dean's car to warn teenagers about the dangers of careless driving. When the vehicle transporting the remains of the car crashed en route to the site, the driver was thrown from his vehicle and died.

The display the Highway Patrol produced was incredibly popular, of course, but it also turned out to be dangerous. The legs of a young boy looking at the car were crushed when three of the cables holding the vehicle upright suddenly broke, bringing the heavy metal down onto the boy's body. When the car left the exhibit, it broke in half on the truck used to haul it away and killed a worker involved in the loading process.

In 1959, there was another attempt to display the car. Though it was welded together, legend has it that the car suddenly broke into 11 pieces. The following year, the owner had finally had enough and decided to have the Porsche shipped from Miami back to California. Little Bastard was loaded onto a sealed boxcar, but when the train arrived in L.A., the car was gone. Thieves may have taken the car, sure, but there were reports that the boxcar hadn't been disturbed. Whether or not the car was cursed, with all the trouble it caused, perhaps it was for the best that it finally disappeared.

New Uses for Dead Malls

In the 1970s, the heyday of shopping malls, a new one opened every three or four days. Today, many existing enclosed malls are slated to close or be demolished, and few are being built. But whether we see shopping malls as self-contained fantasy worlds or climate-controlled prisons, they are a constant presence in our urban landscape and part of our cultural identity.

Dixie Square Mall, Harvey, Illinois

The Dixie Square Mall is the mall emeritus of dead malls—it's been abandoned longer than many other malls have been in existence. The 800,000-square-foot mall opened in 1966, in a great location 20 miles from downtown Chicago and minutes from three interstates. During its heyday, it was anchored by Montgomery Ward and JCPenney and was full of shoppers. But by 1978, neighborhood crime and competition from other malls forced it to close.

The lights came on once more in 1979, when Universal Pictures partially renovated the structure to film Jake and Elwood Blues leading police on a merry car chase through the mall in *The Blues Brothers.* The mall has sat empty ever since and has been the site of frequent vandalism and even a rape and murder. Although there have been several attempts to demolish the mall, they've all fallen through due to shady contractors, the expense of asbestos removal, and questions of ownership. Too expensive to tear down, the mall currently sits in limbo.

Bell Tower Mall, Greenville, South Carolina

This 300,000-square-foot mall was built in downtown Greenville in the late 1960s, complete with the brick walls and carpeted floors that were hallmarks of the era. Although it enjoyed a few years of prosperity, it suffered as the suburbs pulled shops and shoppers away from the center of town. By 1982, Woolco, one of the anchor stores, had closed, and by decade's end, the four-screen movie theater had closed as well. The space has since reopened as County Square, housing a collection of county government offices. The former movie theater now serves as a family courthouse.

The Galleria, Sherman Oaks, California

Located in the San Fernando Valley, the Galleria was the epicenter of mall culture during the Valley Girl craze of the early 1980s. In 1982, it made two pop-culture appearances: in the teen movie *Fast Times at Ridgemont High* and in the lyrics of Frank Zappa's song "Valley Girl." It was later used in the films *Commando* (1985) and *Chopping Mall* (1986).

In 1999, the mall closed because of declining business and damage from a 1994 earthquake. After a major renovation, it reopened in 2002, *sans* roof, as an open-air town center, which features a few stores, a 16-screen theater, restaurants, and offices, including the headquarters for Warner Bros. Animation.

Indian Springs, Kansas City, Kansas

This 700,000-square-foot, two-level mall has been resurrected several times, each time with a new purpose that locals hope will keep the wrecking ball from its walls. It opened in 1971 with three solid anchor stores, but a depressed economy, suburban growth, and competition forced it to close in 2001. The mall then repackaged itself as a mixed-use space with vendors, restaurants, and offices. The Kansas City School District leased the former JCPenney site for administration and classroom space, and the U.S. Postal Service used the former Dillard's store as a customer service center. The mall's tenaciousness touched some local filmmakers, who made a documentary entitled *I Saw You at the Mall* about the struggle to resurrect the dead mall. Nevertheless, Kansas City declared the mall a "blighted" property in 2006, and the city is currently planning to demolish it and redevelop the land for office buildings, a hotel, shops, housing, and athletic fields.

The Haunting of Hull House

In the late 1880s, Hull House represented a bastion in social equality and was intended to help raise the poorest residents of Chicago above their poverty and poor education. Unfortunately, it became known for its ghost stories and one infamous supernatural creature forever known as the "Devil Baby."

In 1856, wealthy businessman Charles J. Hull constructed a mansion at Halsted and Polk streets on Chicago's near west side, at the time one of the most fashionable sections of the city. But the Great Fire of 1871 sent wealthy Chicagoans to other parts of the city, and the near west side began to attract a large population of Italian, Greek, and Jewish immigrants. It became one of the most dangerous slums in the city, and by the 1880s, Hull House was surrounded by factories, bordellos, taverns, and rundown tenement houses. In 1889, it was exactly the sort of neighborhood that Jane Addams was seeking.

Jane Addams's Hull House

Born into an affluent family in 1860, Jane Addams knew nothing of poverty as a child. But when her father died, she sank into a deep depression, so she traveled to Europe to escape from her grief. It was there, in the slums of London, that she realized her life's calling.

Jane and Ellen Gates Starr, her friend and traveling companion, volunteered with the poor at Toynbee Hall, a settlement house in the poverty-stricken Whitechapel neighborhood. There, affluent students like Jane and Ellen worked alongside the most undesirable members of British society, offering food, education, and medical care while lobbying for social reform and improved standards of living for the poor. Jane was invigorated by her work at Toynbee Hall and soon made plans to start a similar project in Chicago.

By the time Addams came to the west side with the intention of starting a settlement house, the crowded neighborhood was teeming with poverty, crime, and prostitution. Numerous brothels, saloons, and dope dealers victimized the refugees and immigrants who came to America with little money and were often unable to speak English. It was to these people that Jane Addams became the "voice of humanity."

Impressed by Jane's plans for a settlement house, Helen Culver, Charles Hull's niece, offered the mansion to Addams with a rent-free lease. Addams and Starr converted the mansion into a safe and comfortable place that offered food, shelter, and education for the impoverished. As the operation increased in popularity, 12 more buildings were added, until eventually Hull House spread out over an entire city block.

When Jane Addams died in 1935, the Hull House Association took over the property and continued her efforts until the 1960s, when the University of Illinois at Chicago bought the property. Hull House was named a historic site, but the additional buildings around the mansion were torn down. And though much has changed, some things remain the same—such as the resident ghosts of Hull House, including a spirit that Jane Addams herself witnessed on numerous occasions!

The Ghost of Mrs. Hull

Charles Hull's wife had died of natural causes in a second-floor bedroom of the mansion several years before Jane Addams took up residence in the home. Addams occupied Mrs. Hull's former bedroom and was awakened by the sound of footsteps pacing back and forth. When Ellen confessed that she'd heard the same noises, too, Addams moved to another bedroom.

Jane, Ellen, and other staff members were not the only ones to witness the strange occurrences in the house. Visitors and overnight guests experienced Mrs. Hull's presence, too. Author Helen Campbell claimed to see a ghostly woman standing next to her bed when she spent the night in the haunted room. When she turned on a light, the apparition disappeared.

In Jane Addams's autobiography, *Twenty Years at Hull House,* she stated that earlier tenants of the mansion believed that the attic was haunted, so they always left a bucket of water on the steps because they thought a ghost would not be able to pass it and descend to the lower floors.

The ghostly tale of Mrs. Hull is still recounted today, but unfortunately for Jane Addams, this would not be the only supernatural tale surrounding Hull House.

The "Devil Baby"

By 1913, rumors were circulating that Hull House was the refuge of a "Devil Baby," and the organization's reputation as a great example of social reform was tarnished. According to the widely spread story, this horribly deformed child was the son of a Catholic woman whose husband was an atheist. When the young woman hung a picture of the Virgin Mary in her home, her husband angrily tore it down, screaming that he would rather have the devil himself in his home than a picture of the Virgin Mary. He soon got his wish!

When his wife became pregnant a short time later, she was carrying the "Devil Baby" in her womb. Allegedly, the baby was born with pointed ears, horns, and a tail. Unable to endure the insults and tormenting by his neighbors, the husband abandoned the child at Hull House.

The baby, who was born with the ability to speak both English and Latin, continued to be a nuisance while at Hull House. While being baptized, he purportedly leapt from the priest's arms and began dancing, laughing, and singing. Unable to make the child behave, Jane had him locked away in the attic of Hull House, safe from prying eyes.

Stories about the "Devil Baby" quickly spread around town and, believing them to be true, people flocked to Hull House in droves, hoping to get a peek at the freakish child. Jane turned away dozens of curiosity seekers every day and tried to assure them that there was no truth to the rumors. The pandemonium eventually died down, but decades later, many people still believe that the story of the "Devil Baby" had some elements of truth to it. People have speculated that the child was actually a badly deformed infant brought to Hull House by a poor, young mother who could not care for it. But once the rumors got started, they took on a life of their own.

Those who believe that the "Devil Baby" tale is true insist that the disfigured boy was hidden away in the attic of Hull

House for many years. They claim this explains why a deformed face was often seen looking out of the upstairs windows. Believers state that the boy grew up at Hull House, tucked safely out of sight, and when Jane Addams died, he was moved to another settlement house on the north side of the city, where he later died.

Hauntings Today

What remains of Hull House today is located on Halsted Street and is open as a historical site. The University of Illinois at Chicago built its campus around the mansion in the 1960s, leaving no trace of the old neighborhood that once existed. The crumbling tenements, brothels, and saloons have been replaced by loft apartments, parking lots, and ethnic restaurants.

Today, Hull House remains an attraction for tourists, history buffs, and ghost enthusiasts. It is not uncommon for motion sensors to be triggered, even when no one is at the house. Officers report that no other building on campus gets as many false alarm calls as Hull House. They have also answered calls about people looking out of the windows after the museum is closed, but they have never found anyone in the place after hours.

One incident that remains unexplained occurred when a front window of the house was shattered a few years ago. Officers rushed to the scene but found no one there. The strange thing was that the window appeared to be broken from inside the house, yet police found no evidence of a break-in and no sign that anyone had been in the house at all.

Visitors who have come to Hull House during the evening hours often report strange occurrences. There are many claims of lights turning on and off, shadowy figures seen moving inside, and shutters that open and close by themselves.

There are many possible suspects in the haunting of this house, including the ghost of Mrs. Hull, the lingering spirit of one of the poor people that Jane Addams tried to save, and, of course, the "Devil Baby," whose spirit may still be trapped in the mansion's attic. It might be any one of these restless spirits, or perhaps all of them. It's no surprise that many call Hull House the most haunted house in Chicago!

Don't Try This at Home: Body Modification Artists

Ever wish you looked different? Maybe you'd like to be a little taller or have a smaller nose. The following people wanted more than that. Read on to learn about a few of the more devoted individuals in the world of body modification.

Dennis Avner, aka Stalking Cat

One of the more publicly known body modification artists these days, Stalking Cat has undergone numerous surgeries to transform himself into a tiger. Believing that resembling his totem animal is the destiny set forth by his Native American heritage, Avner began his lifelong project at age 23 with full-body cat-stripe tattoos. Since then, he's had his hairline altered and silicone injections added to his lips; he's gotten facial implants in order to thread whiskers through his cheeks, as well as implants to alter the shape of his brow and forehead; he's had his upper lip split and his ears surgically pointed; and his teeth are filed and capped to be pointy and fanglike. Stalking Cat is a computer programmer; however, he also makes appearances on television shows to show off his odd obsession.

Paul Lawrence, aka The Enigma

As a youth, Paul Lawrence studied piano, flute, and dance. But as a teenager, he decided swallowing swords was more fun, and thus began his career in the sideshow industry as The Enigma. Lawrence's entire body is covered with tattoos of interlocking puzzle pieces of a greenish-blue hue. He's had nubby horns implanted in his forehead and sports a long goatee. Some of his sideshow work includes music, some of it involves sword swallowing, but all of it is quite puzzling.

Isobel Varley, aka The Painted Lady

Proving you don't have to be young to be wild, in 2000, Isobel Varley was noted by *The Guinness Book of Records* as being "The World's Most Tattooed Senior Woman." Varley didn't start getting inked until she was 49 years old, making her a media darling in the world of tattoo artists and aficionados. Varley makes special appearances at conventions, often appears in newspapers and magazines, and has been featured on television shows all over the world.

Eric Sprague, aka Lizardman

It's hard to say which aspect of Lizardman is most alarming: his split tongue; his green, scaly, tattooed face; or his bumpy brow and tattooed eyelids. Or maybe it's how well he articulates the reasons why he's done all this in the first place. Sprague began his transformation into Lizardman during college, after becoming interested in body-based performance art. He chose the lizard because he thought it would look good and age well. Lizardman (who has undergone more than 700 hours of tattooing) performs sideshow acts that involve suspension, drilling, sword-swallowing, and fire manipulation.

Your Name Here

If you have a really strong stomach, a lot of money, and a rather dark sense of humor, you too could join the body-modification subculture. People who aren't yet household names like the artists listed above are busy doing incredibly strange things to their bodies every day, such as ear-pointing and stretching, castration, tooth extraction, even amputations. Some claim it's a spiritual thing, some do it for sexual reasons, and some of them do it for reasons they'll never share. Whatever the case, extreme body modification is incredibly dangerous unless you have a qualified, trained professional helping out with sterile equipment and the proper tools. Don't try it at home—or anywhere—unless you're ready to make serious body alterations you can't take back.

FREAKY FACTS: PLATYPUS

With aspects of a bird, a reptile, and a mammal, the Australian platypus is one of nature's oddest animals.

- *When British naturalists examined the first platypus specimen in 1799, they thought it was a hoax. They cut it open, looking for stitches holding the bill in place.*

- *Male platypuses secrete poison from the spurs on their hind feet. The venom won't kill a human adult, but it can cause severe pain and swelling.*

- *The platypus' hair makes it effectively waterproof, with a dense, insulating undercoat similar to that of a Labrador retriever.*

- *While under water, the platypus shuts its eyes, ears, and nostrils and uses an electroreceptor system in its sensitive, ducklike bill to navigate and hunt.*

- *The platypus' fatty, beaverlike tail is used for energy storage, much like a camel's hump. When food runs short, the animal survives on the stored fat.*

- *The platypus isn't noisy, but when disturbed, it may give a call that sounds like a frog-throated puppy growl.*

- *Platypus eggs are rubbery or leathery, like turtle eggs, and are about the size of gumballs. Females generally lay only two or three eggs during the annual mating season, which occurs between June and October.*

Getting a Charge Out of Life

💀　💀　💀　💀　💀

It may seem odd to compare the human body to an electric power generator, but rare cases around the world have shown that some people are born with shocking abilities...literally. Jacqueline Priestman, a British woman, consistently produces ten times the static electricity of a normal human being.

How to "Conduct" Oneself

Priestman, who ironically married an electrician before she knew about her strange ability, grew up with no more than the usual mild electromagnetic field that surrounds every human. But when she turned 22, sparks began to fly. Priestman noticed that her mere touch would cause ordinary household appliances to short out and fizzle, while others could use the same appliances with no problem. She could also change the channels on her TV by going near it.

Priestman has had to buy at least 30 new vacuum cleaners in her married life, plus five irons and several washing machines. Michael Shallis, a lecturer at Oxford University and a former astrophysicist, studied Priestman and told a British newspaper in 1985 that she was actually able to transmit tiny bolts of "lightning" that could affect any electrical system nearby. He had no explanation for the phenomenon but did say that most similar cases he had investigated involved women. For example, Pauline Shaw flooded her house every time she tried to do laundry because the washing machine fuses would blow when she touched the dials. The washer's door would then pop open and turn the machine into a fountain.

For more than four years, Shallis studied 600 people with Priestman's condition and, eventually, wrote a book about them called *The Electric Connection*.

SLI-ding Through Life

There is a name for those like Priestman and Shaw. Because people with abnormal amounts of static electricity often cause streetlights to flicker when they pass by, scientists call the strange disorder Street Light Interference, or SLI. People with the condition are called SLI-ders, or Sliders.

An older name for the phenomenon is High Voltage Syndrome, or HVS. Around 1930, one HVS patient, Count John Berenyi of Hungary, was reportedly able to make neon light tubes glow merely by holding them. And according to author Vincent Gaddis, the National Safety Council investigates what he calls "human spark plugs"—people who can start fires with the electrical abundance of their mere presence. One woman made a rather poor vocational choice in the early 1940s when she got a job gluing shoes together with rubber cement, a highly flammable substance. She allegedly started at least five fires in the factory and could ignite a pail of rubber cement merely by standing near it. She had to quit after suffering severe burns in one of the fires.

Even babies can act as superconductors. In 1869, a child born in France was so highly charged that anyone who approached him received a sharp electric shock. He even exhibited a faint glow around his hands. The infant died from undetermined causes when he was only nine months old, and, according to witnesses, his entire body radiated light at the time of his passing.

Radiant Blood

The strange baby was not the only human known to glow. Luminous people have been reported in many circumstances, and their abilities are often tied to medical conditions. Anna Monaro, an Italian woman, gained attention in 1934, when her breasts began to spontaneously emit blue phosphorescent light while she was sleeping. The weird condition lasted for weeks and drew many eminent doctors and scientists to study her firsthand. They were even able to capture the glow on film. Many theories were offered, from "electrical and magnetic organisms in the woman's body" to "radiant blood." Eventually, the bizarre condition went away and did not return.

Through No Fault of Her Own

A Welsh woman named Mary Jones set off a religious fervor in 1905, when amazing forms of light appeared to emit from her body. Jones had already gained some notoriety as a local preacher when people began to observe glowing, exploding balls of lightning and electric-blue rectangles hovering near her as she spoke. The light show lasted for several months and attracted hundreds of believers, along with a cadre of scientific observers. Various explanations were offered for the lights, from a misidentification of the planet Venus to fault lines under the chapel where Jones preached. Scientists speculated that movements of the earth had stressed the bedrock, issuing gases that resulted in geomagnetic anomalies in the air above.

Lightning Reactions

Not everyone with an electric attraction finds the sensation enjoyable. Grace Charlesworth, a woman from the UK, had lived in a house for almost 40 years when, in 1968, she began receiving unexplainable shocks both indoors and out. The weird voltage was strong enough to spin Charlesworth's body in a complete circle, and at times, it would even make her head shake uncontrollably. The voltage was sometimes visible as sparks, and she could escape only by leaving her house or yard, as she was never bothered elsewhere.

Charlesworth blamed her problem on the noise from a compressor in a nearby factory, but fixing the compressor did not stop the mysterious electricity. One possible contributing factor was that the house had been hit by lightning five times.

Some people become so sensitive to electrical currents that they cannot even live in homes with any sort of wiring or appliances. An Irish woman named Margaret Cousins had to move to a cabin with no utilities in 1996 because her condition had become so painful. But two years later she had to move again after two cell phone towers were installed nearby and caused her pain to return.

A cow produces nearly 200,000 glasses of milk in her lifetime.

My Bloody Valentine

During the Roaring '20s, Al "Scarface" Capone ruled Chicago. Be it gambling, prostitution, bootleg whiskey, or anything else illegal or immoral, Capone and his gangsters controlled it. Almost no one dared to stand up to Capone and his men, including the police, because that meant possibly winding up on the wrong end of a gun. Still, one man was determined to dethrone Capone—George "Bugs" Moran. For a few years, Moran and his North Side Gang had been slowly muscling their way into Chicago in an attempt to force Capone and his men out. As 1929 began, rumors started to fly that Capone was fed up and was planning his revenge. As the days turned into weeks and nothing happened, Moran and his men began to relax and let their guard down. That would prove to be a fatal mistake.

Gathering for the Slaughter

On the morning of February 14, 1929, six members of the North Side Gang—James Clark, Frank Gusenberg, Peter Gusenberg, Adam Heyer, Reinhart Schwimmer, and Al Weinshank—were gathered inside the SMC Cartage Company at 2122 North Clark Street in the Lincoln Park neighborhood on Chicago's north side. With them was mechanic John May, who was not a member of the gang but had been hired to work on one of their cars. May had brought along his dog, Highball, and had tied him to the bumper of the car while he worked. Supposedly, the men were gathered at the warehouse to accept a load of bootleg whiskey. Whether that is true or not remains unclear. What is known for certain is that at approximately 10:30 A.M., two cars parked in front of the Clark Street entrance of the building. Four men—two dressed as police officers and two in street clothes—got out and walked into the warehouse.

Murderers in Disguise

Once the men were inside, it is believed they announced that the warehouse was being raided and ordered everyone to line up facing the back wall. Believing the armed men were indeed police officers, all of Moran's men, along with John May, did as they were told. Suddenly, the four men began shooting, and, in a hail of shotgun fire and more than 70 submachine-gun rounds, the seven men were brutally gunned down.

When it was over, the two men in street clothes calmly walked out of the building with their hands up, followed by the two men dressed as police officers. To everyone nearby, it appeared as though there had been a shootout and that the police had arrived and were now arresting two men.

"Nobody Shot Me"

Minutes later, neighbors called police after reportedly hearing strange howls coming from inside the building. When the real police arrived, they found all seven men mortally wounded. One of the men, Frank Gusenberg, lingered long enough to respond to one question. When authorities asked who shot him, Gusenberg responded, "Nobody shot me." The only survivor of the massacre was Highball the dog, whose howls first alerted people that something was wrong.

When word of the massacre hit the newswire, everyone suspected Al Capone had something to do with it. Capone stood strong, though, and swore he wasn't involved. Most people, however, felt that Capone had orchestrated the whole thing as a way to get rid of Moran and several of his key men. There was only one problem—Bugs Moran wasn't in the warehouse at the time of the shooting. Some believe that Moran may have driven up, seen the cars out front, and, thinking it was a raid, driven away. One thing is for certain: February 14, 1929, was Moran's lucky day.

Police launched a massive investigation but were unable to pin anything on Capone, although they did arrest two of his gunmen, John Scalise and Jack "Machine Gun" McGurn, and charged them with the murders. Scalise never saw the inside of the courthouse—he was murdered before the trial began. Charges against McGurn were eventually dropped, although he was murdered seven years later, on Valentine's Day, in what appeared to be retaliation for the 1929 massacre.

Al Capone Haunted by the Truth

Publicly, Al Capone may have denied any wrongdoing, but it appears that the truth literally haunted him until his dying day. Beginning in 1929, Al Capone began telling several of his closest friends that the ghost of James Clark, one of the men killed in the massacre, was haunting him. Several times, Capone's bodyguards heard him scream, "Get out! Leave me alone!" in the middle of the night. When they burst into the room believing Capone was being attacked, they would always find the room empty except for Capone, who would say that Clark's ghost was after him. For the rest of his life, Capone claimed Clark's ghost tormented him. Some say Clark didn't rest until Capone passed away on January 25, 1947.

Ghosts Still Linger

The warehouse at 2122 North Clark Street, where the bloody massacre took place, was demolished in 1967 and is now a parking lot. The wall against which the seven doomed men stood, complete with bullet holes, was dismantled brick by brick and sold at auction. A businessman bought the wall and reassembled it in the men's room of his restaurant. However, the business failed and the owner, believing the wall was cursed, tried getting rid of it to recoup his losses. He sold the individual bricks and was successful in getting rid of many of them, but they always seemed to find their way back to him. Sometimes they would show up on his doorstep along with a note describing all the misfortune the new owner had encountered after buying the brick.

At the former site of the warehouse, some people report hearing the sounds of gunfire and screams coming from the lot. People walking their dogs near the lot claim that their furry friends suddenly pull on their leashes and try to get away from the area as quickly as possible. Perhaps they sense the ghostly remnants of the bloody massacre that happened more than 75 years ago.

A single coffee tree produces only about one to three pounds of beans per year.

Castles, American Style

Castles aren't just for Europe anymore. Here are some
of the best castles in the good ol' U. S. of A.

Boldt Castle, Heart Island, New York

In 1900, George Boldt, owner of the luxurious Waldorf–
Astoria Hotel, purchased one of the Thousand Islands in the
St. Lawrence River and began construction on a six-story
castle in honor of his wife, Louise. Hundreds of workers were
employed in building the 120-room castle, as well as the Power
House, the Alster Tower, the Hennery, the Arch, and a stone
gazebo. But when Louise died suddenly in 1904, a broken-
hearted Boldt lost interest in his dream. He never returned
to the island, and the castle was abandoned for 73 years until
the Thousand Islands Bridge Authority purchased it in 1977,
restored it, and opened it to the public.

Herreshoff Castle, Marblehead, Massachusetts

Built in the 1920s by artist Waldo Ballard, the castle was pat-
terned after Erik the Red's castle in Qagssiarssuk, Greenland.
Local legends say that Ballard found buried treasure in his
basement, which enabled him to build his dream castle,
complete with parapets and rumors of a secret stairway and
dungeon. The small castle has only a few rooms but includes
a grand ballroom and a rooftop deck overlooking the Marble-
head harbor. Ever the artist, Ballard painted details all over
the castle, including medieval patterns, family crests, and even
an oriental rug on the floor. The castle changed hands a few
times, picking up the Herreshoff name from a previous owner
before being purchased by the current owners, who converted
the adjacent carriage house into a bed-and-breakfast.

Bishop Castle, Beulah, Colorado

Jim Bishop was not planning to be in the castle business when, in 1969, he began building a cabin out of local stone. A visitor commented that it looked like a castle, so a castle it became. Since then, Bishop has designed and built nearly every inch of the 160-foot-tall castle by himself, complete with precarious wrought-iron balconies and a basket-lift. Perhaps the most memorable feature is perched on the roof—a metallic dragon that shoots real smoke and fire through its nose.

Loveland Castle, Loveland, Ohio

Château Laroche ("stone castle") was the vision of Harry Andrews, an eccentric with a mission to propagate modern-day knighthood. Designed as a full-scale replica of a 10th-century French castle, Andrews worked on the project single-handedly from 1929 until his death in 1981. Even unfinished, the castle is a true fortification with 17 rooms, including an armory, banquet hall, chapel, master suite, great hall, and dungeon, as well as seven holes above the front door for pouring boiling oil upon invaders. Today, the castle is owned by a group of "knights"— medieval reenactors who uphold Andrews's vision. It is also reportedly home to a few resident ghosts.

Kracht's Castle Island, Junction City, Kansas

Don Kracht's castle began with a pond. After an excavation, the small island in the middle made the pond look more like a moat, so in 1988, Kracht designed a fantasy castle and began building. A retired schoolteacher, Kracht works on his unusual project every day and expects to be done by 2010. Although the castle, which is partially based on Neuschwanstein Castle in Germany, has only three actual bedrooms, it features a drawbridge, bell tower, hot tub, amphitheater, waterfall, Italianate gardens, turrets, cannons, and a dungeon.

Biltmore Castle, Asheville, North Carolina

Tucked into the rolling hills of the Blue Ridge Mountains near Asheville, North Carolina, lies Biltmore Castle, America's largest privately owned home. Construction of the country home of George Washington Vanderbilt and his wife, Edith, began in 1889, and it officially opened on Christmas Eve 1895. The 175,000-square-foot castle, which was modeled after three 16th-century French châteaux, has 250 rooms, including 34 bedrooms, 43 bathrooms, 65 fireplaces, and a basement that houses a swimming pool, gymnasium, and bowling alley. The Gilded Age estate boasted the latest amenities of the day, such as an elevator, fire alarms, mechanical refrigeration, and central heating, plumbing, and electricity. In 1930, at the request of town officials, the Biltmore estate was opened to the public in an effort to boost local tourism during the Great Depression, and today, more than a million guests tour the palatial estate and its magnificent gardens each year.

Iolani Palace, Honolulu, Hawaii

Located in downtown Honolulu, Iolani Palace is America's only official state residence lived in by royalty, serving as the home to Hawaii's last two monarchs—King Kalakaua and his sister, Queen Lili'uokalani, who succeeded him. As the first monarch to travel around the world, Kalakaua envisioned building a majestic palace like those he'd seen on his journeys. Built between 1879 and 1882, Iolani Palace featured the most modern technology of the time, such as indoor plumbing, telephones, and gas lighting.

When the U.S. government overthrew the Hawaiian monarchy in 1893, Queen Lili'uokalani was forced to abdicate her throne and was imprisoned in the palace for months. Although it was neglected for several decades, renovation of Iolani Palace took place in the 1970s, and it opened to the public in 1978, restored to its historic grandeur.

As an interesting side note, on April 30, 2008, a group of native Hawaiians, who do not recognize Hawaii as a U.S. state, occupied Iolani Palace to protest what they view as the illegal rule of the U.S. government.

Butter Battles in the Dairy State

💀　💀　💀　💀　💀

Wisconsin has long been regarded by many as a friendly place to visit. The stories of hospitality that come flooding back from a visit to "America's Dairyland" are about as sweet as whipped cream. But a portion of Wisconsin's history is not so sugary. In fact, it's downright sour.

The "Oleo Wars" between butter and the butterlike substitute oleomargarine are a little-known footnote to our nation's intrepid history. This is puzzling because skirmishes in this war are *still* being fought to this very day, some 40 years after the combatants officially laid down their "sticks."

A Likely Battleground

In a way, the Wisconsin Oleo Wars were predestined. Really, what can you expect from a dairy region that is currently ranked second in the nation in butter production?

In the early 1870s, wives on dairy farms made butter, and variations in equipment, churning skills, and cleanliness resulted in a finished product of widely varying quality. During this time, oleomargarine arrived on the scene with little fanfare. The French product was cheaper than butter, far more consistent in quality, and it kept for longer periods. Slowly but surely, oleomargarine tempted the taste buds of quality-conscious consumers, even if many hid their fondness from fellow citizens. An oleo–butter battle loomed large.

The Battle's Beginnings

In 1872, Wisconsin dairy producers banded together to form the Wisconsin Dairymen's Association (WDA). This protectionist organization eventually zeroed in on oleomargarine and the alarming headway it had made into the butter market. In 1880, former WDA president Hiram Smith warned farmers that "oleomargarine is giving better satisfaction than most dairy butter as now made." To protect their industry, Wisconsin dairy leaders decided to improve their own product and to launch a preemptive strike against oleomargarine for added insurance. The battle lines had been drawn.

In 1881, Wisconsin passed its first anti-margarine law, which required that butter and oleomargarine be marked as such to avoid confusion between the two. In 1886, the state passed even more stringent legislation, which added a stiff tax and imposed labeling and packaging restrictions upon oleomargarine. In 1895, Wisconsin brought forth yet another law. It required restaurants and hotels to display signs announcing that margarine was sold on the premises. It also prohibited the manufacture and sale of oleomargarine—whitish in its normal state—that had been colored yellow to mimic butter.

Fighting Words

To turn consumers against oleomargarine, butter proponents drew wretched pictures of farmers being economically driven off their farms by the evil spread. The "Three-Headed Hydra," drawn by A. Berghaus in 1890 for *The Rural New Yorker*, depicted a hideous serpent poised to attack an alarmed but at-the-ready farmer holding a rifle. The words *oleomargarine* and *fraud* were drawn prominently on its body.

By this time, margarine backers weary of taking it on the chin went on the offensive. They noted that their product was as "wholesome as butter" and reminded the state assembly of documented cases where spoiled butter had been reprocessed and sold as fresh. They also reminded consumers that creameries routinely colored their butter to make it more yellow. In answer to unsavory drawings depicting oleomargarine as a three-headed monster, "oleophiles" reportedly fired back with artwork that portrayed diseased and dirty dairy cows being milked in mucky barnyards.

In 1915, a new wave of anti-margarine propaganda featured illustrations of sickened rats that had ingested vegetable oils—a prime ingredient in oleomargarine. This opportunity to further demean oleomargarine presented itself after a University of Wisconsin research study of vitamins went public. It suggested that laboratory rats fed milk fat were healthier than those that had ingested vegetable oils. A margarine supporter said of the incident: "Some [anti-margarine propaganda] is put out by persons who actually think that any industry, domestic or foreign, that is at all in competition with dairy farming, has no rights in our economic system and ought to be outlawed."

Oleo Makes Headway

World War II saw a changing tide in the Oleo Wars. Due to stronger food rationing penalties against fats than those against vegetable oil, oleomargarine made substantial inroads into the butter market. By war's end, oleomargarine was commonly found on tables throughout Wisconsin, and the stigma of being a poor man's spread had all but vanished.

A growing resentment against unfair taxation on oleomargarine was also gathering steam. More than a few consumers were irked that an economical food source was being effectively denied to them due to petty, protectionist policies. Plainly, the war had battles left to fight.

In the mid-1950s, oleomargarine was still being heavily taxed in Wisconsin. The uncolored oleomargarine tax rate of 15 cents per pound was significant in a day and age when the minimum wage was just 75 cents per hour. This caused oleomargarine-loving Wisconsinites to smuggle the product in from out-of-state sources. Newspaper photos from the period show value-minded people cramming their cars with Illinois-bought oleomargarine to take back into Wisconsin. A state official estimated that a ton of colored margarine came across the Illinois–Wisconsin border each week. Butter may have looked like it was winning the present battle, but if such underground trends continued, many felt it would eventually lose the war.

Concessions

By 1967, opinions among Wisconsin state legislators were starting to change. Aware of oleomargarine's popularity, lawmakers brought forth a bill that would eliminate the ban on the sale of colored margarine but still retain a tax of 5 ¾ cents per pound through 1972 (the tax was ultimately extended to December 31, 1973). After that, oleomargarine would be tax-free. The bill passed in the state assembly on April 6, 1967, and went into law on July 1, 1967. For the first time in 72 tumultuous years, colored oleomargarine was legal in Wisconsin. But was it?

Despite the repealed ban, dairy protectionism continued well beyond the 1960s. In fact, butter's parting shot has survived right up to this day. As proof, an obscure law officially designated Wisconsin Statute 97.18(4) states: "The serving of colored oleomargarine or margarine at a public eating place as a substitute for table butter is prohibited unless it is ordered by the customer." The law is used as a sort of trump card by dairy-backers and is applied sporadically, usually coming into play only after a butter-loving patron turns in an offending restaurant.

Such a violation occurred in 2004. Wisconsin citizen Nels Harvey ordered a baked potato at a Ponderosa Steakhouse in Menomonee Falls and was horrified to see that it was dripping with margarine. When he asked for butter in its place, the server replied, "We don't have any butter." Treating this admission like a shot fired across the bow, Harvey sprang into action.

The 71-year-old, who had lived half his life under the rules set by the Oleo Wars, filed a complaint with the Waukesha County Department of Health and Human Services. Within hours an inspector was dispatched to the offending restaurant. When she arrived, she demanded that butter be made available to customers. Despite the steeper price of the dairy product and the fact that no one other than Harvey seemed to care, the owner complied with the request.

Perhaps supporters on either side of the stick shouldn't behave so indignantly, particularly this late into the Oleo Wars. Wisconsin is dairy country, after all.

A Different Kind of Diagnostic

A courthouse security officer in New Hampshire was convicted of persuading a couple that he was a tester for an insurance company. In 2007, he offered to pay them $20 to have sex in front of him so he could evaluate a certain bed sheet and condom.

The Weird World of Sports

Wrong-Way Nicholl
On March 20, 1976, while playing for Britain's Aston Villa soccer team, Chris Nicholl began scoring like crazy. Amazingly, the footballer scored every goal in a 2–2 draw against Leicester City, including two "own goals," or goals for the opposing team.

Dubious Distinction
During the 1998 home run battle between Sammy Sosa and Mark McGwire, pitcher Rafael Roque had the dubious distinction of giving up home run number 64 to both hitters. McGwire hit his 64th dinger off the Milwaukee Brewers slinger on September 18, and Sosa did the same on September 23.

Davey Decks Goliath
During a 1970s-era basketball game between the Boston Celtics and the Houston Rockets, 6'9" Sidney Wicks threw an elbow at 5'9" Calvin Murphy. It was a costly mistake. With a ferocity that belied his smaller stature, Murphy "chopped down" the giant with dozens of unanswered blows thrown in flurries and combinations. It took four players to dislodge Murphy from his victim. Wicks, who appeared dumbfounded, needed several stitches to close a gaping wound on his nose. He honestly didn't know what hit him.

Cantankerous Coaches
In 1978, two college football coaches from different teams stepped way out of bounds. Ohio State's legendary coach Woody Hayes tackled Clemson's middle linebacker Charlie Bauman as he ran out of bounds during the Gator Bowl. To top it off, the crazed coach then slugged the player.

At another game, Fairfield University's football coach, Ed Hall, 48, did Hayes one better. When he saw that Western New England's Jim Brown had eluded every Fairfield defender while on his way to a touchdown, Hall took action. The angered coach bolted from the sideline and tackled Brown at midfield. A stunned Brown asked, "Are you out of your mind, coach?"

Later, Hall explained the incident. "Something just happened to me and the next thing I knew, the referee was standing over me and screaming at me to get out of the game. As I started walking to the rear of the bleachers, with the crowd booing me, I broke down and cried."

The Sultan of Swat

On June 23, 1917, while pitching against the Washington Senators at Fenway Park, Red Sox pitcher Babe Ruth got into an argument with umpire Brick Owens after walking the first batter. Owens ejected Ruth, and the livid Sultan of Swat lived up to his nickname by slugging the umpire. As luck would have it, Ruth's replacement, Ernest Shore, was able to retire the next 26 Senators, and the Red Sox won the game, 4–0.

That's the Way the Ball Bounces

During a May 26, 1993, night game between the Cleveland Indians and the Texas Rangers, the Indians' Carlos Martinez hit a long fly ball. Rangers' right-fielder Jose Canseco tried to make the catch, but he lost the ball in the lights, and, instead, it struck him on top of the head, took an improbable bounce, and landed over the outfield wall for a home run.

Rattlesnakes can mate for 23 hours, and soapberry bugs can go for 11 days. But that's nothing compared to stick insects—they can go on for 2½ months!

Thomas Tresham
Ties Triangles Together

💀　💀　💀　💀　💀

Nothing prompts a person to build a bizarre, triangular stone lodge in the middle of nowhere quite like religious persecution. At least, that's how Sir Thomas Tresham felt back in 1593 when he began work on what would become the mysterious Rushton Triangular Lodge, a structure that he hoped would be much more than a place to hang his hat.

But Why?

At the end of the 16th century, life wasn't much fun for Catholics living in England, as Tresham could attest. As a devout Catholic, he'd spent 15 years in prison—his faith had made him a criminal in the eyes of the law. Once he was a free man, Tresham figured he'd better keep his mouth shut about his religion, but that didn't keep him from professing his faith in other ways.

Tresham decided to build a secretly Catholic monument near Rushton that would encode messages to keep it safe from Protestant adversaries. The bricks and mortar of his lodge would showcase aspects of his faith without betraying his freedom. The man stuck to his plan so diligently that the details of Rushton Triangular Lodge are downright weird.

The Rule of Three

To represent the Holy Trinity, Tresham designed the building with only three walls. The structure is itself a perfect equilateral triangle, its walls meeting at 60-degree angles. Glorifying the Holy Trinity via the rule of three is repeated (and repeated and repeated) throughout the whole building. Check this out:

- Each of the three walls is 33.3 feet.

- Each floor of the three-story building has three windows.

- Each wall has three gables. Each gable is 3 feet × 3 feet with three-sided pinnacles.

- There are nine gargoyles (three sets of three).

- Friezes run along the walls on each side of the building, containing a phrase in Latin—each phrase contains exactly 33 letters.

- And though the main room on each floor is hexagonal in shape, if you draw three bisecting lines through a hexagon, you get six more equilateral triangles.

And if all those threes are making you a little dizzy, just wait—Tresham was far from content with a few triangular tricks. The building's ornaments were where Tresham spared no expense to work in secret codes for the glory of the Lord.

Gables, and Windows, and Math, Oh My!

Two of the gables of Tresham's lodge are inscribed with dates. One of the dates is 1641, one is 1626. Indeed, Tresham carved future dates into the side of the building for a reason. If you subtract 1593 (the year he started building) from 1626, you get 33. Subtract 1593 from 1641, and you get 48. Both numbers are divisible by three—no big surprise there—but there's something more. If you add the *anno domani* (commonly known as "A.D.") you get the years of Jesus' death and the Virgin Mary's death, respectively. The second gable shows the dates 3898 B.C. and 3509 B.C., dates that are said to be the years of the Great Flood and the call of Abraham.

The windows provided another place for Tresham to work in his code magic. The three windows on the first floor are in the shape of a Gothic trefoil, a vaguely triangular-shape Christian symbol that also happened to be the Tresham family crest.

The trefoil-shape is carried through to the basement windows as well, all of which are, of course, repeated in threes.

Double Entendres

As mentioned before, there were three 33-character-long inscriptions on the Rushton Lodge, one on each side. The inscriptions and their respective translations read as follows:

- *"Aperiatur terra & germinet salvatorem"* means "Let the earth open and let them bring forth a Savior."

- *"Quis seperabit nos a charitate Christi"* means "Who shall separate us from the love of Christ."

- *"Consideravi opera tua domine at expavi"* means "I have considered your works and am sorely afraid."

In addition, if you inspect all the waterspouts at Tresham's place, you'll find a letter above each one. Together, they create an acronym for the first three letters of a Latin mass. An inscription above the main door to the lodge reads *Tres Testiminium Dant,* which means "these three bear witness." But Tresham's wife is said to have called him "Tres" for short; knowing that, one might interpret this as: "Tresham bears witness," which was certainly the point of all this obsessive building.

Even More Hidden Meaning?

Tresham got away with his secretly Catholic building—though it certainly raised a few eyebrows. In fact, the building (which is now maintained as a historical site by the English Heritage organization) is still a source of much discussion. Some people don't think Tresham was über-Catholic at all, that all those numbers and all that funky math were rooted in black magic.

Either way, the building is a great example of the era's love of allegory—using something to represent something else entirely. After the Triangular Lodge was done, Tresham started *another* building full of secret codes and mysterious math called Lyveden New Bield but died before it was finished. It still sits in England exactly as it was left, half-built and full of its own mystery.

A Bump in the Light:
America's Haunted Lighthouses

More than 60 lighthouses in the United States are believed to be haunted. Some are home to eerie ghosts, while others host more playful spirits. Whether they stick around because of tragedy, love, or some other reason, these spectral visitors add an otherworldly element to already-fascinating places.

St. Simons Island Lighthouse, Georgia

This lighthouse may have been cursed from the start. Originally constructed in 1811, the first building was destroyed by Confederate soldiers. While the lighthouse was being rebuilt, the architect fell ill and died of yellow fever. Then, on a stormy night in 1880, a dispute between the lighthouse keeper and his assistant resulted in gunshots. The keeper died after days of suffering from his wounds, but the assistant was never charged with the crime. The new keeper maintained he could hear strange footsteps on the spiral staircase to the tower. To this day, subsequent lighthouse keepers, their families, and visitors have also heard the same slow tread on the tower's 129 steps.

Minots Ledge Lighthouse, Massachusetts

Despite the sweet nickname, the ghosts of the "I Love You" lighthouse tell a tragic story. The first Minots Ledge Lighthouse began operating in 1850, and being its keeper was arguably the most frightening assignment around. Built directly in the rough waters around the Cohasset Reefs, the spidery metal skeleton swayed and buckled in the wind and waves. On April 17, 1851, a sudden nor'easter stranded the keeper on the mainland—he could only watch as the storm slowly destroyed the lighthouse, with his two assistants inside. Their bodies were found after the storm cleared.

A new storm-proof stone tower was built, and the spirits of those who perished in the first lighthouse seem to reside in the new building. Subsequent keepers have heard them working, and sailors see them waving from the external ladder. On stormy nights the light blinks "1–4–3," which locals say is code for "I love you." They believe this is the assistants' message to their loved ones, passing ships, and anyone caught in a storm.

Yaquina Bay Lighthouse, Oregon

In 1899, Lischen M. Miller wrote a story for *Pacific Monthly* about a girl who disappeared at the Yaquina Bay Lighthouse. The girl, a captain's daughter, was left with a caretaker while her father was at sea. One day she and her friends went to explore the abandoned lighthouse. When she got separated from her friends, they heard her shriek. They searched for her but only found some blood and her handkerchief. A door that had been open only moments before was locked. Although many maintain that this story is pure fiction, the spectral figure of a girl has been seen around the tower.

St. Augustine Lighthouse, Florida

St. Augustine is often called America's most haunted city, and the lighthouse there might claim its own "most haunted" title. So many different spirits are rumored to haunt this light that it's probably a bit crowded. Visitors report seeing a young girl with a bow in her hair. She is thought to be the ghost of a girl who died during the tower's construction. A tall man is often seen in the basement of the keeper's house, and doors unlock mysteriously, footsteps follow visitors, and cold spots move around the buildings. The spirits seem harmless, but construction workers have complained of foreboding feelings and freak accidents.

Owls Head Lighthouse, Maine

An older woman dubbed "Little Lady" is frequently seen in the kitchen of this lighthouse. Although most spirits tend to bring cold spots or unease, this one reportedly causes a feeling of calm and warmth. No one is sure who she is, but it is possible that she's keeping the other Owls Head ghost company. Believed to be a previous keeper known for his frugal nature and attention to his post, this ghost makes himself known by turning thermostats down, polishing the brass, leaving footprints in the snow, and occasionally appearing in the tower. He seems to be training his replacement: A resident's young daughter announced one day that fog was coming in and that they should turn on the beacon, something she claimed to have learned from her "imaginary friend."

Fairport Harbor Light, Ohio

This lighthouse is rumored to have two rather playful ghosts. The first is of a keeper's young son who died. The second appears to be a charming gray kitten that routinely seeks out museum staff and visitors to play. Its spectral nature becomes apparent when visitors realize the kitten has no feet—it simply hovers above the ground. Although a former keeper's wife had a beloved kitten while she lived in the lighthouse, the "ghost cat" story was dismissed as silly until workers found the body of a cat in a crawl space there.

Old Presque Isle Lighthouse, Michigan

This lighthouse was decommissioned in 1870 and became a museum. In 1977, when George and Lorraine Parris were hired as caretakers, they ran the light regularly until the Coast Guard warned that running a decommissioned light was hazardous and illegal. To ensure it wouldn't happen again, the machinery that rotated the light was removed. But since George's death in 1992, the lighthouse has frequently glowed at night—not so brightly as to cause harm but bright enough to be seen by passing ships and across the bay. Although the Coast Guard has classified it as an "unidentified" light, Lorraine believes that it is George, still happily working in his lighthouse.

An Underground Mystery: The Hollow Earth Theory

For centuries, people have believed that Earth is hollow. They claim that civilizations may live inside Earth's core or that it might be a landing base for alien spaceships. This sounds like fantasy, but believers point to startling evidence, including explorers' reports and modern photos taken from space.

A Prize Inside?

Hollow Earth believers agree that our planet is a shell between 500 and 800 miles thick, and inside that shell is another world. It may be a gaseous realm, an alien outpost, or home to a utopian society.

Some believers add a spiritual spin. Calling the interior world Agartha or Shambhala, they use concepts from Eastern religions and point to ancient legends supporting these ideas.

Many Hollow Earth enthusiasts are certain that people from the outer and inner worlds can visit each other by traveling through openings in the outer shell. One such entrance is a hole in the ocean near the North Pole. A November 1968 photo by the ESSA-7 satellite showed a dark, circular area at the North Pole that was surrounded by ice fields.

Another hole supposedly exists in Antarctica. Some Hollow Earth enthusiasts say Hitler believed that Antarctica held the true opening to Earth's core. Leading Hollow Earth researchers such as Dennis Crenshaw suggest that President Roosevelt ordered the 1939 South Pole expedition to find the entrance before the Germans did.

The poles may not hold the only entrances to a world hidden deep beneath our feet. Jules Verne's famous novel *Journey to the Center of the Earth* supported yet another theory about passage between the worlds. In his story, there were many access points, including waterfalls and inactive volcanoes. Edgar Allan Poe and Edgar Rice Burroughs also wrote about worlds inside Earth. Their ideas were based on science as well as fantasy.

Scientists Take Note

Many scientists have taken the Hollow Earth theory seriously. One of the most noted was English astronomer Edmund Halley, of Halley's Comet fame. In 1692, he declared that our planet is hollow, and as evidence, he pointed to global shifts in Earth's magnetic fields, which frequently cause compass anomalies. According to Halley, those shifts could be explained by the movement of rotating worlds inside Earth. In addition, he claimed that the source of gravity—still debated in the 21st century—could be an interior world.

In Halley's opinion, Earth is made of three separate layers or shells, each rotating independently around a solid core. We live on the outer shell, but the inner worlds might be inhabited, too.

Halley also suggested that Earth's interior atmospheres are luminous. We supposedly see them as gas leaking out of Earth's fissures. At the poles, that gas creates the *aurora borealis*.

Scientists Look Deeper

Hollow Earth researchers claim that the groundwork for their theories was laid by some of the most notable scientific minds of the 17th and 18th centuries. Although their beliefs remain controversial and largely unsubstantiated, they are still widely discussed and have a network of enthusiasts.

Some researchers claim that Leonhard Euler (1707–1783), one of the greatest mathematicians of all time, believed that Earth's interior includes a glowing core that illuminates life for a well-developed civilization, much like the sun lights our world. Another mathematician, Sir John Leslie (1766–1832), suggested that Earth has a thin crust and also believed the interior cavity was filled with light.

In 1818, a popular lecturer named John Cleves Symmes, Jr., proposed an expedition to prove the Hollow Earth theory. He believed that he could sail to the North Pole, and upon reaching the opening to Earth's core, he could steer his ship over the lip of the entrance, which he believed resembled a waterfall.

Then he would continue sailing on waters inside the planet. In 1822 and 1823, Symmes petitioned Congress to fund the expedition, but he was turned down. He died in 1829, and his gravestone in Hamilton, Ohio, is decorated with his model of the Hollow Earth.

Proof Gets Woolly and Weird

In 1846, a remarkably well-preserved—and long extinct—woolly mammoth was found frozen in Siberia. Most woolly mammoths died out about 12,000 years ago, so researchers were baffled by its pristine condition.

Hollow Earth enthusiasts say there is only one explanation: The mammoth lived inside Earth, where those beasts are not extinct. The beast had probably become lost, emerged into our world, and froze to death shortly before the 1846 discovery.

Eyewitnesses at the North Pole

Several respected scientists and explorers have visited the poles and returned with stories that suggest a hollow Earth.

At the start of the 20th century, Arctic explorers Dr. Frederick A. Cook and Rear Admiral Robert E. Peary sighted land—not just an icy wasteland—at the North Pole. Peary first described it as "the white summits of a distant land." A 1913 Arctic expedition also reported seeing "hills, valleys, and snow-capped peaks." All of these claims were dismissed as mirages but would later be echoed by the research of Admiral Richard E. Byrd, the first man to fly over the North Pole. Hollow Earth believers suggest that Byrd actually flew into the interior world and then out again, without realizing it. They cite Byrd's notes as evidence, as he describes his navigational instruments and compasses spinning out of control.

Unidentified Submerged Objects

Support for the Hollow Earth theory has also come from UFO enthusiasts. People who study UFOs have also been documenting USOs, or unidentified submerged objects. These mysterious vehicles have been spotted—mostly at sea—since the 19th century.

USOs look like "flying saucers," but instead of vanishing into the skies, they plunge beneath the surface of the ocean. Some are luminous and fly upward from the sea at a fantastic speed...and without making a sound.

UFO enthusiasts believe that these spaceships are visiting worlds beneath the sea. Some are certain that these are actually underwater alien bases. Other UFO researchers think that the ocean conceals entries to a hollow Earth, where the aliens maintain outposts.

The Search Continues

Scientists have determined that the most likely location for a northern opening to Earth's interior is at 84.4 N Latitude, 141 E Longitude. It's a spot near Siberia, about 600 miles from the North Pole. Photos taken by *Apollo 8* in 1968 and *Apollo 16* in 1972 show dark, circular areas confirming the location.

Some scientists are studying seismic tomography, which uses natural and human-made explosions as well as earthquakes and other seismic waves to chart Earth's interior masses. So far, scientists confirm that Earth is comprised of three separate layers. And late 20th-century images may suggest a mountain range at Earth's core.

What may seem like fantasy from a Jules Verne novel could turn out to be an astonishing reality. Hollow Earth societies around the world continue to look for proof of this centuries-old legend...and who knows what they might find?

Dazed and Confused

In McAllen, Texas, in 2007, police discovered a home with its door bashed in and entered to investigate. They learned that the residence had been burglarized, and they found nearly 15 pounds of marijuana lying on the floor. In a bizarre twist, the home's occupant (who had escaped while the intruders went about their robbery) later returned to talk to deputies. He casually explained that he had been wrapping the marijuana for shipment when the bad guys showed up. He was subsequently charged with felony possession of marijuana.

Eerie Haunted Objects

☠ ☠ ☠ ☠ ☠

Many ghost hunters believe that solid objects, such as build-ings, furnishings, and decorative items, retain psychic energy. People who come into contact with these objects may sense stored emotions, as though they're revisiting the original events surrounding the items. Usually these "flashbacks" are associ-ated with past tragedies and death. Others objects appear to channel actual spirits. Either way, they're just plain creepy.

Robert, the Haunted Doll

Few dolls are as haunted as "Robert," a straw doll once owned by Florida artist Robert "Gene" Otto. During Otto's lifetime (he died in 1974), the doll was often heard walking, humming, and singing in the attic. Some witnesses even claim they saw the doll staring out the window at them. Today, the doll resides in the Fort East Martello Museum in Key West, where he continues to frighten visitors. As ghost hunter David Sloan quipped after investigating Robert, "Be careful of the objects you possess, or one day they may end up possessing you."

A Haunted Painting

A disturbing—and apparently haunted—painting entitled *Hands Resist Him* became famous on eBay in February 2000. The painting portrayed a little boy standing in front of a win-dow and next to a girl with jointed, doll-like arms.

Artist Bill Stoneham painted the picture in 1972. Within a year of the art's first showing, both the gallery owner and the Los Angeles critic who reviewed it were dead. No one is certain what happened after the painting's original owner, actor John Marley, died on May 22, 1984, but years later, the art was found behind a brewery.

People continue to report strange events after merely viewing photos of the painting online. (An Internet search for "haunted painting" will lead you to such photos.) One person heard an eerie, disembodied voice when viewing the artwork. Others talk about fainting as soon as they look at it. Some say that they have been visited by spirits from the painting.

Comte LeFleur's Ghostly Portrait

If you dine at Brennan's Restaurant in New Orleans, be sure to visit the Red Room upstairs and watch the portrait of Comte LeFleur for several minutes. Many guests watch his smile change to an expression far more sinister.

Wealthy Comte LeFleur was well liked in colonial New Orleans. One day, he cheerfully went around town making funeral and burial arrangements for three people. Then he returned home and killed his wife and his college-age son. The count then hanged himself from the sturdy gas chandelier overlooking the corpses of his family.

Today, the LeFleur residence is home to Brennan's Restaurant. Like the ghosts of the count and his family, the chandelier is still there. But it is the painting of Comte LeFleur that catches the eye of most visitors. Those who spend a few minutes watching the killer's image understand why it is one of America's most frightening portraits. LeFleur's head tilts slightly, and his expression changes from a mild smile to an evil grin until you blink or glance away.

An Especially Spooky Ouija Board

Many people avoid Ouija boards because they may connect us with "the other side" or with evil entities. This certainly seemed to be the case with the board Abner Williams loaned to a group of El Paso "Goths." In mid-2000, after the board was returned to him, Williams complained of scratching noises coming from the board, along with a man's voice addressing him, followed by the sound of children chanting nursery rhymes at his window. When Williams tried to throw the board in the trash, it reappeared in his house. A paranormal investigator borrowed the board, and a hooded figure appeared from nowhere and growled at his son.

When a paranormal research team investigated the Ouija board, they found spots of blood on the front of it and a coating of blood on the back. They measured several cold spots over areas of the board, and photos revealed a strange ectoplasm rising from it. The board was eventually sent to a new owner, who did not want it cleared of negative energy. That person has remained silent about more recent activity surrounding the board.

Although this is an unusually well-documented haunted Ouija board, this is not an uncommon tale. Many psychics warn that, if you ask a spirit to communicate with you through a Ouija board, it's like opening a door between the worlds. You never know what kind of spirits—good or evil—will use that Ouija board to visit you. In general, it's wise to be cautious with "spirit boards" of any kind.

Nathaniel Hawthorne and the Haunted Chair

You may have seen a creepy old chair or two, but when author Nathaniel Hawthorne encountered one that was actually haunted, he wrote a short story about it. Hawthorne's "true family legend," which he titled "The Ghost of Dr. Harris," wasn't published until 30 years after the author's death.

According to Hawthorne, Dr. Harris used to sit and read the newspaper in the same chair at the Boston Athenaeum each morning. When the old man died, his ghost continued to visit, and Hawthorne, who was researching at the library, saw it daily until he had the courage to look him in the eye. There, the author reported a "melancholy look of helplessness" that lingered for several seconds. Then the ghost vanished.

So if you visit the Boston Athenaeum, be careful where you sit. Dr. Harris may be in that "empty" chair.

FREAKY FACTS: CRAZY CRITTERS

- *Through balloonlike air sacs in its mouth, the African bullfrog can make a bellowing sound that can be heard as far as a half mile away.*

- *The 6.5-inch-long, deep-sea creature known as the dragonfish has long, fanglike upper and lower teeth. It also swims with its own attached fishing line, known as a "barbel," hanging from its chin to catch small fish and haul them straight up to its gaping mouth.*

- *The male Australian lyrebird is such a skilled mimic that he can reproduce mechanical sounds, such as automobile horns, and is famous for his 24-inch tail feathers that assume the shape of a lyre when fanned.*

- *Oysters must hitchhike on fish if they want to grow up. Oyster larvae catch a ride on a passing fin and hang on for several months, feeding on their benefactor's body until they grow large enough to let go and settle into a spot of their own on the river bottom.*

- *The monkeylike common potto is the only mammal that keeps part of its backbone on the outside, with a row of bare bones protruding slightly from its back. The potto has a defensive pose where it clamps down its feet and hands and lowers its head to bring forth the exposed vertebrae.*

- *Africa's multi-mammate mouse might appropriately be called the "mother of all mice," although it's more closely related to the rat. Females boast eight to twelve pairs of teats, many more than the average five pairs found on most rodents. This allows the multi-mammate mouse to breed at a furious rate, bearing litters of as many as 20 at a time.*

Precious Cargo:
Airplane Stowaways

*Some people are so desperate to flee their home country that
they're willing to risk their lives. One method of escape is to
stow away in the wheel well of a jet plane. The odds of pulling
off such a stunt are staggering, but there appears to be little that
U.S. regulators can do to prevent the practice on international
flights. Despite the risks, people such as Pardeep Saini of India
and Fidel Maruhi of Tahiti were willing to take the chance.*

A New Beginning
In 1996, Pardeep Saini, 22, and his brother Vijay, 19, were desperate to escape their native India. Details surrounding their
motives are cloudy (Pardeep claims he was persecuted for
alleged links with Sikh separatists), but their method of "flight"
is clear. According to the elder Saini, a smuggling agent in Delhi
told the brothers they could stow away in the undercarriage of
a jumbo jet and wing it to England, where they could request
political asylum. On paper, the idea seemed entirely workable,
but such things rarely go according to plan.

In October 1996, the brothers climbed high up into the
wheel well of a British Airways Boeing 747 and crossed their
fingers. They were in for the ride of their lives.

In 2000, Fidel Maruhi of Tahiti set his sights on a new life
in the United States. At Tahiti's Faa'a International Airport,
Maruhi crawled into the wheel well of a Los Angeles-bound Air
France jet and hunkered down for the forthcoming onslaught.

The Death Zone
At 29,035 feet, Mt. Everest is considered a killer mountain,
not for its steepness or avalanche dangers, but because of the
peak's extreme height. Simply put, humans can't survive long
at an altitude where oxygen density is about one-third that
found at sea level. During their odyssey, the Saini brothers

spent ten hours at heights approaching 39,000 feet—nearly 10,000 feet *higher* than the celebrated death summit.

Shortly after takeoff, Pardeep lost consciousness, sparing him the panic of gasping for air and consciously freezing in temperatures that would eventually reach –40°Fahrenheit.

On his way to Los Angeles, Maruhi's airliner reached its cruising altitude in approximately 20 minutes. During the plane's ascent, the outside air temperature quickly plunged, and oxygen in the air decreased as Maruhi's airplane cruised at 38,000 feet for nearly eight hours.

Tragedy Strikes

After ten agonizing hours, the Saini brothers' plane prepared to land at Heathrow Airport. At 2,000 feet, the pilot lowered the landing gear, and, in an instant, Vijay was sucked out of the airplane. His limp body was later recovered in Richmond, a neighborhood in southwestern London. He had frozen to death before he fell from the plane.

This left only Pardeep. Surely no one could survive this double whammy of oxygen deprivation and extreme cold. But survive he did. Baggage handlers found him dazed and suffering from extreme hypothermia. By a fateful stroke, the 22-year-old stowaway had defied monumental odds and made it to Britain. Saini was initially denied asylum, but, upon appeal, he was later granted "compassionate leave" to remain in England.

A Shocking Discovery

When Maruhi's plane landed at LAX Airport, shocked workers spotted his body tucked deep into the wheel well. He was alive, but just barely. The ordeal had lowered the Tahitian's body temperature to an astounding 79 degrees—six degrees *below* that which is generally considered fatal. Maruhi was transported to a hospital where he was treated for hypothermia and frostbite. Miraculously, he survived.

Maruhi remembers nothing about the trip, which is understandable because he'd blacked out just after takeoff. Despite his ordeal, U.S. authorities shipped him back to Tahiti. His dream of a life in the United States remains unfulfilled.

A Doll of a Woman: Cindy Jackson

Cindy Jackson is living proof that any woman can achieve a little girl's fantasy of resembling a Barbie doll—provided she is willing to put forth the time, money, and determination to undergo dozens of procedures on her face and body.

Coming Up Barbie

Jackson's platinum-haired perfection may invite comparison to stereotypes, but she is no dumb-blonde-joke punch line. On the contrary, the Ohio farm girl turned world celebrity is a member of MENSA. However, Jackson has refused to accept the idea that a brainiac can't also be a beauty, so she has spent around "the cost of a mid-size family car" on dozens of cosmetic procedures since 1988. She says it all goes back to the Barbie doll she received from her parents at age six. "Through Barbie I could glimpse an alternative destiny," Jackson says on her Web site.

Although photos of Jackson at age eight reveal a relatively attractive little girl, Jackson felt homely compared to her beautiful mother and sister. She also felt unloved by an undemonstrative father and misunderstood by schoolmates, who took her habit of daydreaming for standoffishness. At home, she would pore over her mother's issues of *Vogue* magazine and imagine a life filled with glamour and excitement…a life like Barbie's.

Jackson studied art and photography after graduating from high school and then worked several jobs until she could buy a one-way ticket from Ohio to London. She left in 1977 and spent ten years rocking with British punk bands. When her father died in 1988 and left her an inheritance, a lightbulb went on…she could now afford to lift her heavy eyelids, reduce her chin and nose, and add breast implants. At last she could become Barbie—or at least a reasonable facsimile.

Globetrotter Barbie

That year, Jackson methodically set about going under the knife and soon had more plastic than the original Barbie. Her official "wish list" included a smaller, more feminine nose, fuller lips, whiter teeth, a smaller jaw, less "tired-looking" eyes, a more defined waistline and flatter stomach, higher cheekbones, slimmer thighs, and larger breasts. She's undergone nine major surgeries, often with multiple procedures during each operation. She's also had numerous minor procedures, such as dermabrasion. But not every operation went well—her first breast implants solidified into cementlike bags and had to be removed.

After only a few years, she achieved Barbie doppelganger status to the extent that TV talk shows began to invite her on as a guest. The BBC even paid for a live breast implant procedure, which was viewed by millions.

She has written an autobiography, *Living Doll*, and another book on cosmetic surgery tips, which she offers along with her own beauty products on her Web site. She models designer fashions, makes appearances around the world, champions a number of animal protection charities, and writes articles for *Cosmopolitan, The Daily Telegraph*, and other publications. Yet Jackson somehow finds several days a week to devote to researching cosmetic surgery. Now in her fifties, she looks decades younger and says she is still toying with final improvements. And though it may look as though her ideas of beauty are only skin-deep, she contributes a portion of her book earnings toward the prevention of cruelty to animals.

This Little Piggy Went Kaboom!

Japanese parents, like most, encourage their children to save money. But they're not onboard with a quirky piggy bank introduced by TOMY toys in 2007. If the money-hungry porker isn't fed with coins on a regular basis, it explodes, showering those around it with loose change.

Gettysburg's Ghosts

The Battle of Gettysburg holds a unique and tragic place in the annals of American history. It was the turning point of the Civil War and its bloodiest battle. From July 1 through July 3, 1863, both the Union and Confederate armies amassed a total of more than 50,000 casualties (including dead, wounded, and missing) at the Battle of Gettysburg. All that bloodshed and suffering is said to have permanently stained Gettysburg and left the entire area brimming with ghosts. It is often cited as one of the most haunted places in America.

First Ghostly Sighting

Few people realize that the first sighting of a ghost at Gettysburg allegedly took place before the battle was over. As the story goes, Union reinforcements from the 20th Maine Infantry were nearing Gettysburg but became lost as they traveled in the dark. As the regiment reached a fork in the road, they were greeted by a man wearing a three-cornered hat, who was sitting atop a horse. Both the man and his horse appeared to be glowing. The man, who bore a striking resemblance to George Washington, motioned for the regiment to follow. Believing the man to be a Union general, Colonel Joshua Chamberlain ordered his regiment to follow the man. Just about the time Chamberlain starting thinking there was something odd about the helpful stranger, the man simply vanished.

As the regiment searched for him, they suddenly realized they had been led to Little Round Top—the very spot where, the following day, the 20th Maine Infantry would repel a Confederate advance in one of the turning points of the Battle of Gettysburg. To his dying day, Chamberlain, as well as the roughly 100 men who saw the spectral figure that night, believed that they had been led to Little Round Top by the ghost of George Washington himself.

Devil's Den

At the base of Little Round Top and across a barren field lies an outcropping of rocks known as Devil's Den. It was from this location that Confederate sharpshooters took up positions and fired at the Union soldiers stationed along Little Round Top. Eventually, Union soldiers followed the telltale sign of gun smoke and picked off the sharpshooters one by one.

After Devil's Den was secured by Union forces, famous Civil War photographer Alexander Gardner was allowed to come in and take photos of the area. One of his most famous pictures, "A Sharpshooter's Last Sleep," was taken at Devil's Den and shows a Confederate sharpshooter lying dead near the rocks. There was only one problem: The photograph was staged. Gardner apparently dragged a dead Confederate soldier over from another location and positioned the body himself. Legend has it that the ghost of the Confederate soldier was unhappy with how his body was treated, so his ghost often causes cameras in Devil's Den to malfunction.

Pickett's Charge

On July 3, the final day of the battle, Confederate General Robert E. Lee felt the battle slipping away from him, and in what many saw as an act of desperation, ordered 12,000 Confederate soldiers to attack the Union forces who were firmly entrenched on Cemetery Ridge. During the attack, known as Pickett's Charge, the Confederates slowly and methodically marched across open fields toward the heavily fortified Union lines. The attack failed miserably, with more than 6,000 Confederate soldiers killed or wounded before they retreated. The defeat essentially signaled the beginning of the end of the Civil War.

Today, it is said that if you stand on top of Cemetery Ridge and look out across the field, you might catch a glimpse of row after ghostly row of Confederate soldiers slowly marching toward their doom at the hands of Union soldiers.

Jennie Wade

While the battle was raging near Cemetery Ridge, 20-year-old Mary Virginia "Ginnie" Wade (also known as Jennie Wade) was at her sister's house baking bread for the Union troops stationed nearby. Without warning, a stray bullet flew through the house, struck the young woman, and killed her instantly, making her the only civilian known to die during the Battle of Gettysburg. Visitors to the historical landmark known as the Jennie Wade house often report catching a whiff of freshly baked bread. Jennie's spirit is also felt throughout the house, especially in the basement, where her body was placed until relatives could bury her when there was a break in the fighting.

Farnsworth House

Though it was next to impossible to determine who fired the shot that killed Jennie Wade, it is believed that it came from the attic of the Farnsworth house. Now operating as a bed-and-breakfast, during the Battle of Gettysburg the building was taken over by Confederate sharpshooters. One in particular, the one who may have fired the shot that killed Jennie Wade, is said to have holed himself up in the attic. No one knows for sure because the sharpshooter didn't survive the battle, but judging by the dozens of bullet holes and scars along the sides of the Farnsworth house, he didn't go down without a fight. Perhaps that's why his ghost is still lingering— to let us know what really happened in the Farnsworth attic. Passersby often report looking up at the attic window facing the Jennie Wade house and seeing a ghostly figure looking down at them.

Spangler's Spring

As soon as the Battle of Gettysburg was over, soldiers began relating their personal experiences to local newspapers. One story that spread quickly centered on the cooling waters of Spangler's Spring. It was said that at various times during the fierce fighting, both sides agreed to periodic ceasefires so that Union and Confederate soldiers could stand side-by-side and drink from the spring. It's a touching story, but in all likelihood, it never actually happened. Even if it did, it doesn't explain the ghostly woman in a white dress who is seen at the spring. Some claim that the "Woman in White" is the spirit of a woman who lost her lover during the Battle of Gettysburg. Another theory is that she was a young woman who took her own life after breaking up with her lover years after the war ended.

Pennsylvania Hall at Gettysburg College

One of the most frightening ghost stories associated with the Battle of Gettysburg was originally told to author Mark Nesbitt. The story centers around Gettysburg College's Pennsylvania Hall, which was taken over during the battle by Confederate forces, who turned the basement into a makeshift hospital. Late one night in the early 1980s, two men who were working on an upper floor got on the elevator and pushed the button for the first floor. But as the elevator descended, it passed the first floor and continued to the basement. Upon reaching the basement, the elevator doors opened. One look was all the workers needed to realize that they had somehow managed to travel back in time. The familiar surroundings of the basement had been replaced by bloody, screaming Confederate soldiers on stretchers. Doctors stood over the soldiers, feverishly trying to save their lives. Blood and gore were everywhere.

As the two men started frantically pushing the elevator buttons, some of the doctors began walking toward them. Without a second to spare, the elevator doors closed just as the ghostly figures reached them. This time the elevator rose to the first floor and opened, revealing modern-day furnishings. Despite repeated return visits to the basement, nothing out of the ordinary has ever been reported again.

Have You Had Your McAloo Tikki Break Today?

💀　💀　💀　💀　💀

The sun never sets on the McDonald's empire. Because the behemoth has restaurants on every continent (except Antarctica) and in more than 100 countries, it needs to adapt to local tastes and customs. Whether it's called "McDo," "Mackedonkan," or "de Mac," you'll find some menu items that are reassuringly familiar—and some, not so much.

- **McAloo Tikki (India):** This vegetarian sandwich consists of a breaded, fried patty of spiced potatoes and peas topped with fresh tomato, onion, and vegan tomato mayonnaise on a toasted bun.

- **Twisty Pasta (Hong Kong):** Tired of pancakes for breakfast? Try this meal-in-a-bowl that contains chicken broth, pasta, tomatoes, cabbage, corn, greens, ham (or breakfast sausage), and a fried egg.

- **Rice Fantastic (Hong Kong):** Sometimes you feel like a bun; sometimes you don't. This sandwich is made from two flattened patties of sticky rice.

- **McOz (Australia):** This burger is made from Australian beef and "mouthwatering beetroot."

- **McShawarma (Israel):** In Israel, McDonald's offers kosher and nonkosher restaurants, but they all serve the McShawarma—a sandwich of shaved lamb wrapped in fluffy flatbread.

- **Tamago Double Mac (Japan):** This burger starts with the classic two all-beef patties, throws on some fairly typical bacon, but then finishes it with hot pepper sauce and a poached egg. Cheese is optional.

- **Seasoned Fries (Japan):** McDonald's famous french fries are shaken with powdered seasoning in a paper bag and are available in nori (seaweed), curry, BBQ, and Mexican flavors.

- **McKroket (The Netherlands):** This breaded, deep-fried patty of beef and potato topped with Dijon mustard sauce is the McDonald's version of the traditional Dutch croquette.

- **Creamy Corn Ice Mix Sundae (Philippines):** When chocolate or caramel become too boring, consider corn. This sundae layers vanilla ice cream and sweet corn.

- **Spam Musubi (Hawaii):** Fancy some Spam in the morning? This breakfast dish consists of a slice of fried Spam on top of sticky rice, tied with a strip of seaweed.

- **McPoutine (Canada):** Poutine—the combination of french fries, gravy, and cheese curds—is practically the official dish of Quebec.

- **McCalabresa (Brazil):** This sandwich is the McDonald's take on a traditional Brazilian sandwich, consisting of a slab of pepperonilike sausage covered in vinaigrette.

- **Chicken McCurry Pan (India):** This dish is made of spicy bread filled with tomato curry, chicken, and peppers and topped with cheese.

- **McPalta (Chile):** This local favorite includes avocado paste smeared on pork or beef.

- **McChutney (Pakistan):** Ground meat and chutney are combined to make the patty for this sandwich.

- **McSpaghetti (Philippines):** This dish sounds like a small child's fantasy—a plate of spaghetti tossed with a sweet tomato sauce, chunks of hot dog, and powdered cheese.

Phantom Ships and Ghostly Crews

Ghost ships come in a variety of shapes and sizes, but they all seem to have the ability to slip back and forth between the watery veil of this world and the next, often making appearances that foretell of impending doom. Come with us now as we set sail in search of some of the most famous ghost ships in maritime history.

The *Palatine*

According to legend, shortly after Christmas 1738, the *Princess Augusta* ran aground and broke into pieces off the coast of Block Island, Rhode Island. Roughly 130 years later, poet John Greenleaf Whittier renamed the European vessel and told his version of the shipwreck in his poem *The Palatine*, which was published in *Atlantic Monthly*. Today, strange lights, said to be the fiery ghost ship, are still reported in the waters surrounding Block Island, especially on the Saturday between Christmas and New Year's Day.

Mary Celeste

The *Amazon* was cursed from the beginning. During her maiden voyage, the *Amazon*'s captain died. After being salvaged by an American company that renamed her the *Mary Celeste,* the ship left New York on November 7, 1872, bound for Genoa, Italy. Onboard were Captain Benjamin Briggs, his family, and a crew of seven.

Nearly a month later, on December 4, the crew of the *Dei Gratia* found the abandoned ship. There was plenty of food and water onboard the *Mary Celeste,* but the only living soul on the ship was a cat. The crew and the captain's family were missing, and no clues remained as to where they went. The last entry in the captain's logbook was dated almost two weeks prior to the ship's discovery, meaning it had somehow piloted itself all that time.

To this day, the fate of the members of the *Mary Celeste* remains unknown, as does how the ship piloted its way across the ocean non-crewed for weeks. Many believe she was piloted by a ghostly crew that kept her safe until she was found.

Iron Mountain

A ship disappearing on the high seas is one thing, but on a river? That's exactly what happened to the *Iron Mountain*. In June 1872, the 180-foot-long ship left New Orleans heading for Pittsburgh via the Mississippi River with a crew of more than 50 men. A day after picking up additional cargo, which was towed behind the ship in barges, the *Iron Mountain* steamed its way north and promptly vanished. Later that day, the barges were recovered floating in the river, but the *Iron Mountain* and its entire crew were never seen nor heard from again. For years after it disappeared, ship captains would whisper to each other about how the *Iron Mountain* was simply sucked up into another dimension through a ghostly portal.

Edmund Fitzgerald

When it comes to ghost ships, the *Edmund Fitzgerald* is the biggest—literally. At more than 720 feet long, the freighter

shuttled iron ore across the Great Lakes beginning in the late 1950s. On November 9, 1975, Captain Ernest M. McSorley and his crew pulled the *Edmund Fitzgerald* out of dock at Superior, Wisconsin, with a load of iron ore to be delivered to a steel mill near Detroit. The following day, *"The Fitz"* sank during a violent storm without ever issuing a distress signal. All 29 members of the crew were presumed dead, but their bodies were never found.

Almost ten years to the day after it sank, a strange, dark ship was seen riding along the waves of Lake Superior. One look at the monstrous ship was all witnesses needed to recognize it as the *Edmund Fitzgerald.*

Flying Dutchman

Easily the world's most famous ghost ship, the story of the *Flying Dutchman* is legendary. Stories say that during the 1800s, a Dutch ship captained by Hendrick Vanderdecken was attempting to sail around the Cape of Good Hope when a violent storm came up. Rather than pull into port, the *Dutchman*'s stubborn captain claimed he would navigate around the Cape even if it took him all of eternity to do so. The ship and all of the crew were lost in the storm, and as foreshadowed by Vanderdecken, they were, indeed, condemned to sail the high seas for all eternity.

Almost immediately, people from all over the world began spotting the Dutch ship silently moving through the ocean, often cast in an eerie glow. Because of the legend associated with Captain Vanderdecken, sightings of the *Flying Dutchman* are now thought to be signs of bad things to come. Case in point: The most recent sighting of the vessel occurred off the coast of North Carolina's Outer Banks prior to Hurricane Isabel in 2003.

Not Too Ruff

When wealthy Maryland man Ken Kemper died in 2006, he left his three dogs $400,000. The dogs remain at the house with a caretaker and are treated to spaghetti with meatballs and garlic bread for dinner every Friday night. This story may remind some of Leona Helmsley's pooch, Trouble, who inherited $12 million from the infamous hotel maven when she died in 2007, although a judge subsequently reduced the trust fund to $2 million.

The Collyer Brothers:
Pack Rats Extraordinaire

💀   💀   💀   💀   💀

It all started out so well. The Collyer boys were born into a fairly prominent New York family: Homer in 1881 and Langley in 1885. Their father, Herman, was a doctor; their mother was an educated woman who worked occasionally as an opera singer. Both boys attended Columbia University and earned degrees in law and engineering, respectively.

In 1909, the family broke apart when Dr. Collyer left for unknown reasons. Homer, Langley, and their mother stayed in the family house at 2078 Fifth Avenue, smack in the middle of Harlem, which at the time was an affluent white neighborhood. But as the neighborhood changed, so did the boys. When their mother died in 1929, the boys were left to fend for themselves, and that's when things got really bizarre.

What's Up with the Quirky Neighbors?

The Collyer boys weren't very good with details like paying bills, so they had no telephone, electricity, or running water in the house. Paranoid about burglars, the eccentric brothers boarded up all the windows in the house and put iron gates over the doors. Kerosene lamps lit the house, and a kerosene stove provided nominal heat during the frigid New York winters. Water was retrieved from a pump at a nearby park—but only under the cover of darkness. This is also when they did their junk collecting.

In 1933, Homer went blind, and he would later be crippled by a battle with rheumatism. Langley prescribed his ailing brother a treatment: He was to eat 100 oranges per week, supplemented with a few peanut butter sandwiches for good measure. It's no surprise that Homer never regained his eyesight.

On top of all the reclusiveness, home remedies, and water fetching, the Collyer brothers were constantly hoarding. Individuals who suffer from this "pack rat syndrome" (also known as syllogomania) save *everything*. This is never done in a neat, organized way—one of the hallmarks of a compulsive hoarder is a totally chaotic, stuffed-to-the-rafters home. Hoarders have so many possessions that they are usually rendered incapable of carrying out basic living functions like washing dishes or cleaning the house.

Such was the case with Homer and Langley. Hoping that one day his brother would regain his eyesight, for several decades, Langley saved every New York newspaper he could find—by the end he had several tons of newspapers. The brothers also amassed a collection that included sewing machines, baby carriages, rusted car parts, chandeliers, mannequins, old bicycles, thousands of books, and five pianos. If one of the two happened upon something, it went into the house, piled on top of everything else. Over the years, they created a palace of junk.

Knock, Knock

In 1942, after the Collyers had neglected to pay their mortgage for some time, the bank set eviction proceedings in motion, and a cleanup crew was sent to 2078 Fifth Avenue. They were met by an irate Langley, and the police were summoned.

The police eventually entered the fortress but not without a struggle. All entrances to the house were blocked with what the officers identified as "refuse" and "garbage" that was "neck-deep." When they finally found Langley, he wrote a check for the remainder of the mortgage and sent the authorities on their merry way. For the next five years, the Collyer brothers lived in an increasingly hermitlike manner, and sightings of the eccentric men became less frequent.

Then in 1947, the police received a phone call from a man identifying himself as Charles Smith, who claimed there was a dead body in the Collyer house. When police arrived, they found it more impenetrable than before. The only way into the house was through an upper-story window, and even then, gaining access involved removing huge chunks of junk and throwing them to the street below.

When one of the officers finally got inside the cavernous house, he went through the labyrinthine rooms searching for the source of a nasty odor. Between several piles of trash, the officer found Homer. Police reports stated that he'd died from a combination of malnutrition and cardiac arrest and had only been dead for a few hours. Langley, however, was nowhere to be found.

A manhunt was deployed in New York, but most people figured Langley was still inside the house, waiting to catch one of the officials with his homemade booby traps. As it turned out, they were right—sort of. Langley was indeed in the house, but he wasn't about to catch anyone. His body was found about ten feet from his brother's and had been providing lunch for the neighborhood rats for a couple of weeks by the time he was found. It appeared that Langley was trying to bring food to Homer when he was caught in one of his own traps.

The Numbers
In the end, more than 100 tons of junk were removed from the Collyer house. That's more than 200,000 pounds of shoes, medical equipment, suitcases, phonebooks, tapestries, newspapers, animal parts, etc.

The house was razed, and Collyer Brothers Park now stands in its place. Over the years, the obsessive brothers have been the subject of several books and plays, and even a comic book, though no one's made a movie of their lives just yet.

Shop at Slip 'n' Save!

If you're a scam artist in the 21st century, you're going to have to try a little harder than the Florida woman who tried the old "slip 'n' sue" scam in a convenience store. In 2007, surveillance cameras recorded her pouring a bottle of olive oil on the floor before returning to the spot a few minutes later to "fall." She even tried falling a second time, but when authorities watched the video, they saw she was actually falling incorrectly—slips usually take you down bottom first, not face first. Needless to say, the camera didn't lie, and the woman didn't get away with her scam.

Animals Behaving Badly

They're brave, beautiful, and often loving…that is, until you cross them. Sometimes it's unprovoked, but other times it's hard to tell who is the bigger animal—man or beast.

Now Who's King of the Jungle?
Moses Lekalau, a 35-year-old Kenyan herdsman, was walking home from a neighboring village in 2007 when he was attacked by a lion. He fought the beast for a half hour with just a spear and a club, eventually killing it. Turning from his ordeal, however, Lekalau was set upon by a pack of hyenas. The animals bit off his hands and toes, and he died from his injuries.

Leave Me Alone!
In South Africa in 2005, 49-year-old animal-lover Elsie Van Tonder was only trying to help a cute young seal return to the ocean when the animal informed her in no uncertain terms to leave it alone—by biting off her nose! Volunteers located the nose, but doctors were unable to reattach it. After Van Tonder underwent reconstructive surgery, a coastal management official said the seal was using its own way of telling the woman it didn't want to go back into the water.

A Rough First Day on the Job
On his first day as a cage cleaner at the Shanghai Wild Animal Park, Zhang Huabang decided to take a shortcut. However, his new path led him straight into a cage containing several lions. The animals immediately turned on Huabang, mauling his legs, chest, and head. The zoo used water hoses to get the lions off their prey, who survived the 2005 incident, but it will likely take years for Huabang to recover from his injuries.

Don't Play with Your Food

In 2005, after robbing a couple at knifepoint, a thief in Bloem-
fontein, South Africa, found himself cornered after being
chased by security guards. With nowhere to go, he took the
only route open to him: over a fence and into a Bengal tiger
cage at the city zoo, where the animals made short work of
him. When the crook's body was removed, officials noted that
because the tigers had already been fed, they merely killed the
intruder instead of making a meal out of him.

What Goes Around, Comes Around

Carl Hulsey, a retired poultry worker from Canton, Georgia,
wanted to turn his goat Snowball into a watchdog, so he beat
the animal with a stick to make it more aggressive. His wife
warned him: "This goat's going to kill you if you keep that
up." In 1991, Hulsey approached the goat with his stick, but
this time Snowball was ready. The 110-pound animal repeatedly butted Hulsey in the stomach until it knocked him off
the porch and five feet to the ground. The goat had ruptured
the man's stomach, and Hulsey died where he fell. As officials
were debating whether or not to put Snowball down, they
were besieged by hundreds of calls to spare the goat, insisting
it was only defending itself against a cruel owner. Snowball was
turned over to a private shelter for abused animals, neutered,
and renamed "Snow."

Well...Duh

In 1995, someone brought a gopher to three custodians at the
Carroll Fowler Elementary School in Ceres, California, and
asked them to deal with the rodent. The men decided to kill
the animal and took it into a small supply room where they
sprayed it with solvent. The gopher hung on, even after being
subjected to three cans of the chemical. As the custodians took
a break to discuss their next move, one of the men lit a cigarette and the shed exploded, injuring all three men as well as
16 nearby students. After the explosion, the frightened gopher
was found clinging to a wall. It was released into the wild,
while all three custodians were sent to the hospital.

Attack of the Killer Monkeys

While reading the newspaper on his terrace in 2007, Delhi Deputy Mayor Surinder Singh Bajwa was attacked by monkeys. He tried to scare away the Rhesus macaques with a stick but fell from the balcony and suffered fatal injuries. This sort of attack is becoming more common as Indian officials struggle to deal with the brash simians, which are seen as manifestations of the Hindu monkey god, Hanuman. Locals give the animals food and allow them to roam as they please due to their holy status.

Caught in a Web of Deceit

Thirty-year-old Mark Voegel wanted nothing more than to have his own botanical garden in his apartment in Dortmund, Germany. He filled it with more than 200 spiders, including a black widow named Bettina, as well as poisonous frogs, a boa constrictor, and other snakes and lizards. In 2004, neighbors finally complained about the smell and alerted police. When authorities entered the apartment, they found the odor was not from the animals but from Voegel himself. He had died from a black widow bite, and his animal friends had turned on him, using his corpse as their food source. Police said the scene resembled a horror movie: Voegel's body was covered in webs, spiders, and insects—inside and out.

Minks Gone Wild

In 1998, the Animal Liberation Front invaded the Crow Hill Farm in England and released 6,500 minks with the belief they would disappear into the countryside, mate with the wild mink population, and live happily ever after. Instead, the minks used the surrounding area as a buffet. They attacked a local wild bird sanctuary and went after a local dog. Some minks were found holed up at a pub, while others were shot by locals worried about the safety of their livestock. Ironically, the animal rights activists stood by their actions: "Had they stayed where they were, they would have been killed in a barbarous manner," activist Robin Webb said.

It Was Self-Defense

In 2004, Jerry Bradford of Florida decided to shoot a litter of three-month-old puppies because he couldn't find them a home. However, one of the dogs had other ideas. After killing three of them, Bradford prepared to shoot another when the puppy he was holding slipped its paw into the trigger of the man's .38-caliber revolver and shot him in the wrist. Bradford was hospitalized before being charged with felony animal cruelty, and the surviving puppies were placed in loving homes.

Playing with Fire

In 2006, 81-year-old Luciano Mares had a mouse problem in his house. After finally catching one of the little rascals in a glue trap, he threw it into a leaf fire outside his New Mexico home. The fire melted the glue and the mouse was able to escape, but its fur had caught fire. It ran into Mares's house, and within minutes the home was ablaze, leaving Mares homeless.

Turkey Takes a Stand

When Nancy Arena arrived at her video store near Buffalo, New York, in 2002, she was astonished to find the front window smashed and feathers littering the floor. She called police thinking the store had been vandalized. When authorities arrived they found the mischievous individual still lurking about—a 12-pound turkey. As they grabbed the bird, officers noticed something odd about the section where it had decided to do its damage: The turkey had destroyed several hunting videos and defecated on them.

A Match Made in Heaven?

In 2006, a 31-year-old woman in India married a cobra, which stays under a tree. "Whenever we arranged marriage for her elsewhere, she refused and said she would only marry the snake. So we got her married to the snake," said the woman's mother. This was not the first odd marriage in the area; there have also been instances of girls marrying trees and dogs for superstitious beliefs.

Gearing Up for Ghosts

So you've decided you want to go ghost-hunting. Here's a handy list of essential tools every good ghost hunter should have during an investigation.

- **Electromagnetic Field (EMF) Detector**—Generally speaking, a ghost is nothing more than a form of energy. Therefore, it is believed that such energy can be measured as it interacts with other forms of energy, such as those with an electric or a magnetic charge. An EMF detector allows ghost hunters to measure and track anything with these types of charges in a specific area. Look for strange spikes that could be paranormal in nature. EMF detectors, which range in cost from $20 to $75, come in a variety of shapes and sizes, and some even come with LED screens.

- **Digital Voice Recorder**—If you're interested in capturing the voices of the dead, known as electronic voice phenomena (EVP), you'll want to bring along a digital voice recorder. These devices allow you to record voices and otherworldly sounds that the unaided human ear can't detect.

- **Still Camera**—They say a picture is worth a thousand words, so make sure you have a camera at the ready if and when a ghost decides to make an appearance. Any camera will do, but digital cameras are more appealing because the results can be viewed immediately.

- **Video Camera**—If your budget allows (or if you can borrow one), a video camera can serve multiple purposes during an investigation. Not only can you possibly capture paranormal activity, but the built-in microphone can also help pick up ghostly voices and sounds.

- **Thermometer**—Some people believe that a ghost can draw heat energy out of the air, which results in the infamous "cold spot." Therefore, many ghost hunters bring along thermometers to track sudden drops in temperature that might be otherworldly in nature. There are two main types of thermometers: noncontact "spot" thermometers, which measure the temperature of a specific solid object, and ambient thermometers, which measure the temperature of a general area.

- **Household Items**—There are a few household items you might want to bring along on an investigation:
  - **Watch**—to note the time of any ghostly activity
  - **Notebook**—to record the time and location of above-mentioned activity
  - **Flashlight**—to avoid having to walk into dark, haunted rooms

STRANGE STATS

- *Each day, a healthy individual releases a minimum of 17 ounces of gas due to flatulence.*

- *A human can survive weeks without food but only about ten days without sleep.*

- *The left lung is smaller than the right lung in order to provide room for the heart.*

- *The average human body contains enough fat to create seven bars of soap and enough iron to form a three-inch-long nail.*

- *A tiny flea only a few millimeters in size can jump nearly eight inches high. If a five-foot human jumped a proportionate distance, the intrepid leaper would have to reach a zenith of 1,000 feet to equal the flea's feat.*

- *Synesthesia is a rare occurrence where an individual's senses are linked. It is estimated that the phenomena affects about one person out of 20,000—this person can taste colors and hear shapes.*

Watt an Accomplishment: Obsessive Art in Los Angeles

What is nearly 100 feet tall, is comprised of 17 pieces, was decorated mostly from recycled materials, can withstand a force equivalent to nearly 80 mile-per-hour winds, and lives in Los Angeles? No, it's not some computer-generated monster starring in the latest summer blockbuster: It's Watts Towers, the strange but oddly attractive creation of an Italian immigrant who became a bit obsessed with an extracurricular art project.

Buon Giorno, Signor Rodia

Born in southern Italy in 1879, Simon Rodia immigrated to the United States with his older brother in the mid-1890s. The boys settled on the East Coast, where they worked various jobs in coalfields, rock quarries, and railroad camps. When his brother was killed in a jobsite accident, Rodia relocated to Seattle, where he met his wife and started a family before moving to Watts, a section of Los Angeles. Soon after, Rodia began an art project in his backyard to pay tribute to his adopted country. It would take him 33 years to complete.

The Towers

Rodia had been trained as a tile-layer, not as a carpenter or an engineer, so when he decided to build super tall towers on his modest one-tenth of an acre plot, he had to get creative. By tying beams together with chicken wire and scaling the sides of the towers (which were glued together with cement) as he built them, he got the job done. The steel pipes and rods, wire mesh, and crude mortar used for support might have been primitive and rather unorthodox, but they worked for Rodia.

As he built the structure, he decorated it. Way before "going green" was cool, Rodia chose to recycle old materials to adorn his edifice. By pressing broken dishes, glass, ceramic bits, and other shiny stuff into the concrete, he created a mosaic over every inch of Watts Towers—he even inlaid the floor. The multicolored chips form hearts, Rodia's initials, the dates 1921 and 1923 (the years his children were born), and flowers, but most of the tiles create swirls of random, free-form designs.

When he stepped off the final tower and declared he was finished, Rodia was 75 years old. Unfortunately, a general lack of understanding had plagued the structures for some time. During the 1930s and 1940s, rumors had spread that the towers were transmitting signals to the Communists and the Japanese. Annoyed by government officials and disheartened by a steady stream of vandals, Rodia signed the property over to his neighbor and friend, Louis H. Saucedo, and left town in the mid-1950s.

Trouble in Cement Paradise

Though the Watts Towers had survived numerous earthquakes throughout the years, in 1959, the city of Los Angeles threatened to raze the structures on account of them being an "unauthorized public hazard." Public outcry demanded that the towers be tested before being demolished, and the city agreed. More than a thousand people watched as 10,000 pounds of force were applied to the tallest tower. Ironically, the testing apparatus itself bent from the force, but the tower withstood the pressure just fine. The towers were reopened a year later and soon the Los Angeles community felt a sense of pride toward their unique landmark.

In 1978, the land on which the Watts Towers stood was deeded to the state of California, and the structures underwent extensive repair for seven years. After that, the towers were named a national historic landmark and were later named an official California State Park. Today, the towers are visited by thousands of people every year who enjoy the bizarre but fascinating work of the Italian-American folk artist.

Centralia, Pennsylvania: It's Hot, Hot, Hot

😀 😀 😀 😀 😀

There's a lot going on underfoot in any given place: sewage systems, tree roots, animal dens, subway tunnels, maybe even some caves, depending on where you live. But if you're one of the few people who still happen to live in Centralia, Pennsylvania, you've got a lot more going on beneath the ground. Read on to discover the stranger-than-fiction truth about this now-defunct mining community.

Whoops!

For most of the first half of the 20th century, the northeastern Pennsylvania mining town of Centralia was a perfectly functional Smalltown, U.S.A. The population hovered around 3,000, and there were shops and cafés, businesses and schools. Miners worked hard in the coal-rich region, and all was well.

Then in 1962, the fate of Centralia changed forever. Though the logic seems dubious now, it was common practice in those days to turn open mine pits into garbage dumps. After all, the mining holes were wide dips in the earth, which made for perfect fire pits—there was little risk of starting forest fires because the garbage would burn below ground level. No one thought about the possibility of the fire going underground. But that's exactly what happened.

The garbage dumpers picked a very, very bad place to set their trash alight. As it turns out, the pit, an abandoned mine in the southeastern part of town, was smack in the middle of a robust coal vein. And what does coal do best? Burn. The trash ignited the trail of coal, and the coal began to slowly burn underground, spidering out to other coal veins beneath the surface of Centralia. This was not good.

Everybody Out

The underground fire sizzled its way into coal veins under the businesses, schools, and homes of Centralia. Over time, the fire started causing health problems for residents. Carbon monoxide gases caused lightheadedness and hacking coughs as the smoke continued to curl up from the ground. Wildlife was making a mass exodus, and the air smelled bad. Pavement started to crack, building foundations were at risk, and it began to dawn on the people of Centralia that this underground fire wasn't going to fizzle out on its own.

The next two decades were spent trying to extinguish the fire but to no avail. Firefighters, engineers, and concerned individuals came up with plan after failed plan. Some thought the best solution was to flush the mines with water; others tried to excavate the burning material. Some figured that drilling holes into the ground might help locate the boundaries of the fire, but that only fed the fire with more oxygen.

By the early 1980s, the fire was burning under a few hundred acres. After a young boy fell into a burning sinkhole in the sidewalk, the government stepped in to help Centralians relocate. Eventually, the few remaining buildings in town were condemned, and the government took ownership of the land.

Pennsylvania's government seriously looked into putting the fires out for good, but ultimately, it seemed more reasonable to just move people out rather than shell out the $660 million price tag for trenching the entire area, which was not guaranteed to work. Several million dollars had already been spent on the fire, and apparently, that was enough.

Visit Scenic Centralia...or Not

An engineering study in 1983 concluded that the mine fires could burn for another couple of centuries or more, perhaps spreading over more than 3,500 acres before burning out.

That means that if you want to visit a slow-roasted town, you've got plenty of time. You'll have to look hard for Centralia, though—the town doesn't even exist on a lot of maps these days. Visitors will occasionally see smoke rising from cracks in the road or catch a whiff of sulfur here and there. Though tourism is obviously not encouraged—and we certainly don't advise it—it's not against the law to explore the town. Just keep an eye out for burning sinkholes, of course.

The Greenbrier Ghost:
Testimony from the Other Side

💀　　💀　　💀　　💀　　💀

The strange tale of the Greenbrier Ghost stands out in the annals of ghost lore. Not only is it part of supernatural history, it is also part of the history of the U.S. judicial system. To this day, it is the only case in which a crime was solved and a murderer convicted based on the testimony of a ghost.

A Doomed Marriage

Little is known about her life, but it is believed that Zona Heaster was born in Greenbrier County, West Virginia, around 1873. In October 1896, she met Erasmus "Edward" Stribbling Trout Shue, a drifter who had recently moved to the area to work as a blacksmith. A short time later, the two were married, despite the animosity felt toward Shue by Zona's mother, Mary Jane Heaster, who had instantly disliked him.

Unfortunately, the marriage was short-lived. In January 1897, Zona's body was discovered at home by a young neighbor boy who had come to the house on an errand. After he found Zona lying on the floor at the bottom of the stairs, he ran to get the local doctor and coroner, Dr. George W. Knapp. By the time Dr. Knapp arrived, Shue had come home, found his wife, and carried her body upstairs where he laid her on the bed and dressed her in her best clothing—a high-necked, stiff-collared dress with a big scarf tied around her neck and a veil placed over her face.

While Dr. Knapp was examining Zona's body in an attempt to determine the cause of death, Shue allegedly stayed by his wife's side, cradling her head, sobbing, and clearly distressed over anyone touching her body. As a result, Knapp did not do a thorough examination. Although he did notice some bruising on Zona's neck, he initially listed her cause of death as "everlasting faint" and then as "childbirth." Whether or not Zona was pregnant is unknown, but Dr. Knapp had been treating her for some time prior to her death.

When Mary Jane Heaster was informed of her daughter's death, her face grew dark as she uttered: "The devil has killed her!" Zona's body was taken to her parents' home where it was displayed for the wake.

Those who came to pay their respects whispered about Shue's erratic behavior—one minute he'd be expressing intense grief and sadness, then displaying frenetic outbursts the next. He would not allow anyone to get close to the coffin, especially when he placed a pillow and a rolled-up cloth around his wife's head to help her "rest easier." Still, when Zona's body was moved to the cemetery, several people noted a strange looseness to her head. Not surprisingly, people started to talk.

Ghostly Messages from the Other Side
Mary Jane Heaster did not have to be convinced that Shue was acting suspiciously about Zona's death. She had always hated him and wished her daughter had never married him. She had a sneaking suspicion that something wasn't right, but she didn't know how to prove it.

After the funeral, as Heaster was folding the sheet from inside the coffin, she noticed that it had an unusual odor. When she placed it into the basin to wash it, the water turned red. Stranger still, the sheet turned pink and then the color in the water disappeared. Even after Heaster boiled the sheet, the stain remained. To her, the bizarre "bloodstains" were a sign that Zona had been murdered.

For the next four weeks, Heaster prayed fervently every night that Zona would come to her and explain the details of her death. Soon after, her prayers were answered. For four nights, Zona's spirit appeared at her mother's bedside, first as a bright light, but then the air in the room got cold and her apparition took form. She told her mother that Shue had been an abusive and cruel husband, and in a fit of rage, he'd attacked her because he thought she had not cooked any meat for supper. He'd broken her neck, and as evidence, Zona's ghost spun her head around until it was facing backward.

Heaster's suspicions were correct: Shue had killed Zona and she'd come back from beyond the grave to prove it.

Opening the Grave

After Zona's ghostly visit, Heaster tried to convince the local prosecutor, John Alfred Preston, to reopen the investigation into her daughter's death. She pleaded that an injustice was taking place and, as evidence, she told him about her encounters with Zona's spirit. Although it seems unlikely that he would reexamine the case because of the statement of a ghost, the investigation was, in fact, reopened. Preston agreed to question Dr. Knapp and a few others involved in the case. The local newspaper reported that a number of citizens were suspicious of Zona's death, and rumors were circulating throughout the community.

Dr. Knapp admitted to Preston that his examination of Zona's body was cursory at best, so it was agreed that an autopsy would be done to settle any lingering questions. They could find out how Zona really died, and, if he was innocent, ease the suspicions surrounding Shue.

The local newspaper reported that Shue "vigorously complained" about the exhumation and autopsy of his wife's body, but he was required to attend. A jury of five men gathered together in the chilly building to watch the autopsy along with officers of the court, Shue, and other witnesses.

The autopsy findings were rather damning to Shue. When the doctors concluded that Zona's neck had been broken, Shue's head dropped, and a dark expression crossed his face. "They cannot prove that I did it," he said quietly.

A March 9 report stated: "The discovery was made that the neck was broken and the windpipe mashed. On the throat were the marks of fingers indicating that she had been choken [sic]... The neck was dislocated between the first and second vertebrae. The ligaments were torn and ruptured. The windpipe had been crushed at a point in front of the neck."

Despite the fact that—aside from Zona's ghost—the evidence against Shue was circumstantial at best, he was arrested, indicted, and formally arraigned for murder. All the while, he maintained his innocence and entered a plea of "not guilty." He repeatedly told reporters that his guilt in the matter could not be proven.

While awaiting trial, details about Shue's unsavory past came to light. Zona was actually his third wife. In 1889, while he was in prison for horse theft, he was divorced from his first wife, Allie Estelline Cutlip, who claimed that Shue had frequently beaten her during their marriage. In fact, at one point, Shue allegedly beat Cutlip so severely that a group of men had to pull him off of her and throw him into an icy river.

In 1894, Shue married his second wife, Lucy Ann Tritt, who died just eight months later under mysterious circumstances. Shue left the area in the autumn of 1896 and moved to Greenbrier. When word got out that Shue was suspected of murdering Zona, stories started circulating about the circumstances behind Tritt's death, but no wrongdoing was ever proven.

Despite the fact that he was in jail, Shue seemed in good spirits. Remarking that he was done grieving for Zona, he revealed that it was his life's dream to have seven wives. Because Zona was only wife number three and he was still fairly young, he felt confident that he could achieve his goal.

Testimony from a Ghost

When Shue's trial began in June 1897, numerous members of the community testified against him. Of course, Heaster's testimony was the highlight of the trial. She testified as both the mother of the victim and as the first person to notice the unusual circumstances of Zona's death. Preston wanted her to come across as sane and reliable, so he did not mention the spirit encounter, which would make Heaster look irrational and was also inadmissible as evidence. Zona's testimony obviously could not be cross-examined by the defense and, therefore, was hearsay under the law.

But unfortunately for Shue, his attorney *did* ask Heaster about her ghostly visit. Certainly, he was trying to destroy her credibility with the jury, characterizing her "visions" as the overactive imagination of a grieving mother. He was tenacious in trying to get her to admit that she was mistaken about what she'd seen, but Heaster zealously stuck to her story. When Shue's attorney realized that she was not going to budge from her story, he dismissed her.

But by then, the damage was done. Because the defense—not the prosecution—had brought up Zona's otherworldly testimony, the judge had a difficult time ordering the jury to ignore it. Clearly, most of the townspeople believed that Heaster really had been visited by her daughter's ghost. Shue testified in his own defense, but the jury quickly found him guilty. Ten of the jury members voted for Shue to be hanged, but because they could not reach a unanimous decision, he was sentenced to life in prison.

Shue didn't carry out his sentence for long—he died in March 1900 at the West Virginia State Penitentiary in Moundsville. Until her death in 1916, Heaster told her tale to anyone who would listen, never recanting her story of her daughter's ghostly visit.

It seems that after visiting her mother to offer details of her murder, Zona was finally able to rest in peace. Although her ghost was never seen again, she did leave a historical mark on Greenbrier County, where a roadside marker still commemorates the case today. It reads:

> "Interred in nearby cemetery is Zona Heaster Shue. Her death in 1897 was presumed natural until her spirit appeared to her mother to describe how she was killed by her husband Edward. Autopsy on the exhumed body verified the apparition's account. Edward, found guilty of murder, was sentenced to the state prison. Only known case in which testimony from ghost helped convict a murderer."

Anger Mismanagement at the Golden Arches

Had he asked nicely, McDonald's employees would have gladly just given David Spillers his fries. But when he opened his bag and found them missing, drive-thru rage took over.

In January 2008, Spillers plowed his car through the play area and into the Jacksonville, Florida, store before fleeing the scene. No one was injured, but Spillers left a trail of shattered glass, which enabled police to track him down and arrest him.

FREAKY FACTS: OPOSSUMS

- *The rat-tailed opossum is the only marsupial native to North America.*

- *A female opossum can bear as many as 20 babies in one litter, but because she only has about a dozen teats, every birthing is followed by an epic race through her fur to reach the safety of her pouch and find a nipple. Because each baby clamps onto the same nipple every time they feed, those that arrive too late will perish.*

- *Baby opossums, about the size of a honeybee at birth, are so undeveloped that they can't even suck milk. The mother has to use her own muscles to "pump" the milk into their tiny gullets.*

- *A mother opossum gestates her young for only 13 days before they are born.*

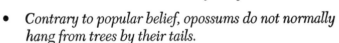

- *After baby opossums leave the pouch (at between two and three months), the mother carries all of them on her back for the next month or so whenever the family leaves their den.*

- *Contrary to popular belief, opossums do not normally hang from trees by their tails.*

- *Opossums possess a whopping 50 teeth—more than any other land-dwelling North American mammal.*

- *Although humans often believe they are the only species with opposable thumbs, the lowly possum has opposable, thumblike digits on all four paws and a tail that can grasp food and tree branches.*

The Mysterious 27 Club

If you're a rock star approaching your 27th birthday, perhaps you should take a year-long hiatus. The curse known as the 27 Club is a relatively new one, but that doesn't make it any less freaky. For those about to blow out 27 candles, good luck.

Founding Members

Keith Richards and Eric Clapton both cite guitarist Robert Johnson as a major musical influence. Born on May 8, 1911, Johnson played guitar so well at such a young age that some said he must have made a deal with the devil. Those spooky speculations have survived in part due to Johnson's untimely death. The blues guitar legend died on August 16, 1938, at age 27, after the husband of a woman Johnson was involved with allegedly poisoned him.

After Johnson, the next rocker to join the 27 Club was Brian Jones, one of the founding members of the Rolling Stones. Jones was a lifelong asthma sufferer, so his descent into drug and alcohol addiction was probably not the wisest choice. Still, the sex and drugs inherent in the music biz proved to be too much for Jones to pass up. Some believe he committed suicide because his time with the Stones had recently come to an end. Due to his enlarged liver, autopsy reports led others to believe he overdosed. Either way, when Jones's body was found lifeless in a swimming pool in 1969, the British Invasion rocker was dead at age 27. Jones, another person who cited Johnson as a musical influence, was unfortunately following in his idol's footsteps—and he would soon have company.

A Trio of Inductees

About a year later, the 27 Club would claim its biggest star yet. The counterculture of the late 1960s had embraced the incredibly talented Jimi Hendrix. Legions of fans worshipped the man and his music and sang along to "Purple Haze" at Woodstock. On September 18, 1970, the rock star—who, like so many before him and since, had an affinity for drugs and alcohol—died in London at age 27. Hendrix aspirated on his own vomit after taking too many sleeping pills.

Texas-born singer-songwriter Janis Joplin was another megastar at the time and a friend of Jimi. Largely regarded as one of the most influential artists in American history, Joplin's gravelly voice and vocal stylings were unique and incredibly popular. She screeched, growled, and strutted through numbers like "Me and Bobby McGee" and "Piece of My Heart." She also tended to play as hard as she worked, typically with the aid of drugs (including psychedelics and methamphetamines) and her signature drink, Southern Comfort whiskey.

On October 4, 1970, when Joplin failed to show up for a recording session for her upcoming album *Pearl,* one of her managers got worried and went to her motel room to check on her. He found the singer dead—at age 27—from a heroin overdose. After Joplin's death, rumors about this strange and tragic "club" began to take hold in the superstitious minds of the general public. Another tragic death less than a year later didn't help.

Florida-born Jim Morrison was yet another hard-living, super famous, devil-may-care rock star. He skyrocketed to fame as the front man for the 1960s band The Doors. The young musician was known for his roguish good looks, his dark, curly hair, and his charismatic and mysterious attitude. But his fans didn't have much time to love him. The Doors hit their peak in the late 1960s, and Morrison died (at age 27) from an overdose on July 3, 1971.

The Latest Inductee

If you were a fan of rock 'n' roll music in 1994 (especially if you were younger than 30), you probably remember where you were when you heard that Kurt Cobain had died. The tormented lead singer of the incredibly popular alternative rock band Nirvana had committed suicide after a lifelong battle with drug addiction, chronic pain, and debilitating depression.

At the tender age of (you guessed it) 27, Cobain had ended his life and had become the most recent member of the 27 Club. Cobain seemed to have known about the "elite" group of young, dead rock musicians: His mother told reporters, "Now he's gone and joined that stupid club. I told him not to join that stupid club."

Rock Steady? Probably Not

It is odd that these incredibly influential, iconic figures in music would all die before their time and all at age 27. However, when you think about all of the other rock stars who *didn't* die—Keith Richards, Paul McCartney, and Ozzy Osbourne, to name a few—the odds don't seem so bad. Plus, when you consider how hard these individuals lived while they were alive, it seems extraordinary that they lived as long as they did.

Rock musicians are shrouded in speculation and the all-powerful effects of idol worship, so it's no wonder that fans have elevated what's probably just a strange coincidence into the stuff of legend or curse. Whether you believe in the 27 Club or not, you can still rock out to the music these tragic stars left behind.

Take That, Christmas!

Sometimes one more Christmas decoration is just one too many. In January 2008, a home security camera in Calgary, Alberta, captured footage of a man slashing through a couple's outdoor Christmas decorations with a machete. The huge inflatable Santa, polar bear, and train belonged to a mild-mannered couple. The camera didn't get a very good look at the grinch who also destroyed the sound system playing holiday classics, and the masked bandit responsible has yet to be brought to justice.

The House of David—
God's Hairy Messengers

💀 💀 💀 💀 💀

The only thing more startling than seeing men with waist-length hair and long beards playing baseball in the early 1900s might have been knowing every player on this early barnstorming team was a member of a highly controversial religious sect known as the House of David.

From Kentucky to the Second Coming

Based in Benton Harbor, Michigan, this religious sect centered around its charismatic leader, Benjamin Franklin Purnell, and his wife, Mary. The couple believed that they were God's appointed messengers for the Second Coming of Christ, and that the human body could have eternal life on Earth. They also believed that both men and women should imitate Jesus by never cutting their hair. Purnell based his teachings on those of an 18th-century English group called the Philadelphians, which were developed from the prophecies of a woman named Joanna Southcott who claimed she was the first of seven messengers to proclaim the Second Coming. Purnell somehow deduced that he was also one of those seven.

Growing Hair, Religion, and Crowds

Born in Kentucky in March 1861, Purnell and Mary traveled around the country for several years while polishing their doctrine. After being booted out of a small town in Ohio, possibly because Benjamin was accused of adultery with a local farmer's wife, they landed in Benton Harbor in March 1903. Members of a sect related to the Philadelphians called the Jezreelites lived in nearby Grand Rapids, and Purnell had been in touch with the Bauschke brothers of Benton Harbor, who were sympathetic to his cause.

With the backing of the Bauschkes and other prominent local citizens, Purnell soon attracted a crowd of believers and called his group the Israelite House of David. The 700 or so members lived chaste, commune-style lives on a cluster of farms and land, served vegetarian meals, and started successful cottage industries, such as a toy factory, greenhouse, and canning facility called House of David Jellies and Jams.

As word spread of the long-haired, oddly dressed members and their colony, the curious began making Sunday trips to observe them. Purnell turned this into a cash opportunity by opening an aviary, a small zoo, a vegetarian restaurant, an ice cream parlor, and, ironically, a barber shop. The crowds grew, and, in 1908, he started work on his own amusement park, which included an expanded zoo and a miniature, steam-powered railway whose trains ran throughout the grounds.

Entertainment Evangelism

In the meantime, some members of the group had formed a baseball team that also drew crowds, so Purnell added a large stadium next to the amusement park. The team traveled, as well, and added to their popularity with comical routines, such as hiding the ball under their beards. Building on the sports theme, the colony also featured exhibition basketball, and later, miniature car racing.

The colony also boasted a popular brass band, whose members capitalized on their showy long tresses by starting each concert facing away from the audience, hair covering half of their snazzy uniforms. They often played jazzy, crowd-pleasing numbers rather than the expected somber religious tunes.

Religious activities continued, too. Adopting the title "The Prince of Peace," Purnell often held teaching sessions, including one in which he was photographed allegedly changing water into wine.

Problems in Paradise

As happens with any large social enterprise, some members became disgruntled and left. Purnell referred to them as "scorpions." Rumors flew concerning improper relations between Purnell and young females in the group, especially when the colony purchased an island in northern Michigan where they ran a prosperous lumber business. Newspaper reports alleged that rebellious group members were killed and buried there and that Purnell kept a group of young girls as sex slaves. The public was also suspicious of mass weddings he conducted. Lawsuits had begun against Purnell in Ohio, and continued to mount even as the Michigan colony progressed.

In 1926, Purnell was finally arrested on charges that included religious fraud and statutory rape. He endured a lengthy trial, but he was ill for most of it, and much of his testimony was deemed incoherent. Most charges were eventually dismissed.

Purnell died in Benton Harbor on December 16, 1927, at age 66. But shortly before passing, he told his followers that, like Jesus, he would be back in three days. As far as anyone knows, he wasn't. His preserved remains were kept in a glass-covered coffin on the colony grounds for decades, although at one time Mary's brother reportedly insisted that the body was not Purnell's but that of another colony member.

Remains of the Day

After his death, some of the believers switched their allegiance to Purnell's widow, Mary, who lived until 1953 and started a new colony called Mary's City of David, which still plays baseball and runs a museum in Benton Harbor. The grounds and businesses were split between the two groups, and only a handful of members remain in either. The zoo closed in 1945, with the animals given to Chicago's Lincoln Park Zoo, and the amusement park, remembered fondly by many local residents, closed in the early 1970s. The original area east of Benton Harbor's city limits still serves as the headquarters for the two groups. And many credit Benjamin Purnell as the forerunner of later, high-style evangelical leaders such as Jim Bakker and Oral Roberts.

The female platypus has no teats. Instead, milk seeps out of pores onto her body, where her babies slurp it up.

Europe's Most Haunted Hotels

Many of Europe's haunted hotels are located in Britain and Ireland, where ghosts are often considered as friends or even members of the family, and are given the same respect as any living person—or even more. Other European cultures aren't as comfortable with ghosts—opting to tear down haunted hotels instead of coexisting with spirits—but there are still a few places in Europe where ghost hunters can explore.

Comlongon Castle, Dumfries, Scotland

Lady Marion Carruthers haunts Scotland's beautiful Comlongon Castle. On September 25, 1570, Lady Marion leaped to her death from the castle's lookout tower rather than submit to an arranged marriage. Visitors can easily find the exact spot where she landed; for more than 400 years, it's been difficult to grow grass there. Because Lady Marion's death was a suicide, she was denied a Christian burial, and it seems her spirit is unable to rest in peace. Dressed in green, her ghost wanders around the castle and its grounds. In 2007, Comlongon Castle was voted the "Best Haunted Hotel or B&B" in the UK and Ireland.

Ettington Park Hotel, Alderminister, England

You may feel chills when you see the Ettington Park Hotel, where the classic 1963 horror movie *The Haunting* was filmed. It was an apt choice for the movie locale because the hotel features several ghosts.

The Shirley family rebuilt this Victorian Gothic structure in the mid-1800s, and the ghost of the "Lady in Gray" has appeared on the staircase regularly since that time. Her identity is unknown, unlike the phantom "Lady in White," who was supposedly a former governess named Lady Emma. The voices of crying children are probably the two Shirley children who drowned nearby in the River Stour; they're buried by the church tower.

Watch out for poltergeists in the Library Bar, where books fly across the room. And don't be alarmed if you hear a late-night snooker game when no one is in the room—it's just the ghosts having fun.

Ye Olde Black Bear, Tewkesbury, England
If you're looking for headless ghosts dragging clanking chains, Ye Olde Black Bear is just the place. Built in the early 1300s, the structure is the oldest inn in Gloucestershire. The hotel's headless ghost may be one individual or several—without a head, it's difficult to tell. However, the ghost's uniform suggests that he was a soldier killed in a battle around the 1470s. Those who've seen the figure at the hotel suspect he doesn't realize he's dead—Ye Olde Black Bear was supposedly a favorite hangout for soldiers during his era.

Renvyle House Hotel, Galway, Ireland
Renvyle House Hotel is not old by haunted hotel standards. The site has been built on, destroyed, built again, destroyed again—once by a fire set by the IRA—and so on, until the current hotel was erected in the 1930s. But its ghosts have an impressive pedigree, dating back to a 16th-century Irish pirate queen, Gráinne O'Malley. A redheaded boy is a more recent spirit, possibly a son of the Blake family who owned the site in the 19th century. The hotel is haunted by so many spirits that it was regularly visited by celebrities, such as poet W. B. Yeats, who conducted séances there. Today, Renvyle House Hotel is still a favorite destination for ghost hunters, and it is included in many "haunted hotel" tours.

Royal Lion Hotel, Lyme Regis, England
The Royal Lion Hotel was built in 1601 as a coaching inn, but some of its ghosts may visit from across the street, where executions allegedly took place. Other misty, ghostly figures

around the hotel may be the spirits of pirates who sailed into the port, or they could be some of the rebels who were hung and quartered on the nearby beach after trying to overthrow King James II in 1685. Waterfront hotels are often haunted due to their association with pirates and wrecked ships. However, with several dozen different spirits, this site reports more ghosts than most.

Dragsholm Slot Hotel, Nekselø Bay, Denmark

In Danish, the word *slot* means "castle," and the Dragsholm is one of the world's great haunted castle hotels. According to legend, Dragsholm's "Gray Lady"—a 12th-century maid who loved working at the hotel—visits on most nights. She silently checks on guests to be sure they are comfortable. The "White Lady" haunts the corridors nightly. She may be the young woman who was allegedly walled up inside the castle; her ancient corpse was found during 19th-century renovations.

James Hepburn, the Fourth Earl of Bothwell, is the castle's most famous ghost. Hepburn became the third husband of Mary, Queen of Scots, after he helped murder her previous spouse. For his role in that crime, Bothwell spent the last ten years of his life chained to a pillar in Dragsholm. If you think you've seen his ghostly apparition, you can compare it to his mummified body in a nearby church in Faarevejle.

Hotel Scandinavia, Venice, Italy

The Hotel Scandinavia is in a building dating back to the year 1000, and it's surrounded by stories of ghosts and apparitions. In the 15th century, the apparition of a wealthy (and rather buxom) Madonna first appeared close to the hotel's palazzo. Witnesses report hearing sounds from the sorrowful ghosts of condemned prisoners who long ago crossed the nearby Bridge of Sighs. This famous bridge was where convicts caught a final glimpse of Venice before being imprisoned. These spirits apparently visit the hotel, and their voices are most often heard in the lobby. Because of the location's unique ghosts and how often they're heard, the Hotel Scandinavia is consistently ranked as one of the world's top five haunted hotels.

Bigfoot: The King of All Monsters

💀 💀 💀 💀 💀

Let's face it—if you had to pick one monster that stands head (and feet) above all others, it would be Bigfoot. Not only is it the stuff of legends, but its likeness has also been used to promote everything from pizza to beef jerky. Bigfoot has had amusement park rides and monster trucks named after it and is even slated to be one of the mascots for the 2010 Winter Olympics in Vancouver, British Columbia.

Early Sightings

Folktales from Native American tribes throughout the Northwest, the area that Bigfoot traditionally calls home, are filled with references to giant, apelike creatures roaming the woods. They described the beast as between seven and ten feet tall and covered in brown or dark hair. (Sasquatch, a common term used for the big-footed beast, is actually an anglicization of a Native American term for a giant supernatural creature.)

Walking on two legs, there was something humanlike about Sasquatch's appearance, although its facial features more closely resembled that of an ape, and it had almost no neck. With looks like that, it's not surprising that Native American folklore often described the creature as cannibalistic, supernatural, and dangerous. Other tales, however, said Sasquatch appeared to be frightened of humans and mostly kept to itself.

It wasn't until the 1900s, when more and more woodlands were being devoured in the name of progress, that Sasquatch sightings started to increase. It was believed that, though generally docile, the beast did have a mean streak when feeling threatened. In July 1924, Fred Beck and several others were mining in a mountainous area of Washington State. One evening, the group spotted and shot at what appeared to be an apelike creature. After fleeing to their cabin, the group was startled when several more hairy giants began banging on the walls, windows, and doors. For several hours, the creatures pummeled the cabin and threw large rocks at it before disappearing shortly before dawn. After several such encounters in the same general vicinity, the area was renamed Ape Canyon.

My, What Big Feet You Have!

In August 1958, Jerry Crew, a bulldozer operator, showed up for work at a wooded site in Bluff Creek, California. Walking up to his bulldozer, which had been left there overnight, Crew found giant footprints in the dirt. At first, they appeared to be the naked footprints of a man, but with one major difference —these feet were huge! After the tracks appeared on several

occasions, Crew took a cast of one of them and brought it to *The Humboldt Times* in Eureka, California. The following day, the newspaper ran a front-page story, complete with photos of the footprint and a name for the creature: Bigfoot. The story and photographs hit the Associated Press, and the name stuck.

Even so, the event is still rife with controversy. Skeptics claim that it was Ray Wallace, not

Bigfoot, who made the tracks as a practical joke on his brother Wilbur, who was Crew's supervisor. Apparently the joke backfired when Crew arrived at the site first and saw the prints before Wilbur. However, Ray Wallace never admitted to faking the tracks or having anything to do with perpetrating a hoax.

Video Evidence?

In 1967, in response to numerous Bigfoot sightings in northern California, Roger Patterson rented a 16mm video camera in hopes of filming the elusive creature. Patterson and his friend, Robert Gimlin, spent several days on horseback traveling though the Six Rivers National Forest without coming across as much as a footprint.

Then, on October 20, the pair rounded a bend and noticed something dark and hairy crouched near the water. When the creature stood up on two legs and presented itself in all its hairy, seven-foot glory, that's when Patterson said he knew for sure he was looking at Bigfoot. Unfortunately, Patterson's horse saw the creature, too, and suddenly reared up. Because of this, it took Patterson several precious seconds to get off the horse and remove the video camera from his saddlebag. Once he did that, he ran toward the creature, filming as he went.

As the creature walked away, Patterson continued filming until his tape ran out. He quickly changed his film, and then both men retrieved their frightened horses and attempted to follow Bigfoot further before eventually losing sight of it.

When they arrived back in town, Patterson reviewed the film. Even though it was less than a minute long and extremely shaky in spots, the film appeared to show Bigfoot running away while occasionally looking toward the camera. For most Bigfoot enthusiasts, the Patterson–Gimlin film stands as the Holy Grail of Bigfoot sightings—physical proof captured on video. Skeptics, however, alleged that Patterson and Gimlin faked the entire incident and filmed a man in an expensive monkey suit. Nevertheless, more than 40 years after the event occurred, the Patterson–Gimlin film is still one of the most talked about pieces of Bigfoot evidence, mainly because neither man ever admitted to a hoax and the fact that no one has been able to figure out how they faked it.

Gone Sasquatching

The fact that some people doubt the existence of Bigfoot hasn't stopped thousands of people from heading into the woods to try to find one. Even today, the hairy creature makes brief appearances here and there. Of course, sites like YouTube have given rise to dozens of "authentic" videos of Bigfoot, some of which are quite comical.

Still, every once in a while, a video that deserves a second look pops up. For example, in 2005, ferry operator Bobby Clarke filmed almost three minutes of video of a Bigfoot-like creature on the banks of the Nelson River in Manitoba. And in late 2007, photos taken by a hunter in Pennsylvania's Allegheny National Forest were being analyzed.

Weird Weather

💀   💀   💀   💀   💀

We've all heard that neither rain, snow, sleet nor hail, will stop our determined mail carriers, but how about a few rounds of ball lightning or tiny frogs dropping from the sky? Apparently, Mother Nature has a sense of humor. Here are some of the weirdest weather phenomena encountered on Planet Earth.

Goodness, Gracious, Great Balls of Lightning!

Perhaps it was ball lightning, an unexplained spherical mass of electrical energy, that Jerry Lee Lewis was singing about in the popular tune "Great Balls of Fire." In 1976, the strange phenomenon supposedly attacked a woman in the UK as she ironed during an electrical storm. A ball of lightning emerged from her iron, spun around the room, then threw her across the room, ripping off half her clothes in the process. In 1962, a Long Island couple was astounded to see a fiery, basketball-size orb roll into their living room through an open window. The fireball passed between the pair, continued through the room, and disappeared down an adjacent hallway. Exactly how lightning or any other electrical anomaly can form itself into a ball and zigzag at different speeds is not well understood.

Otherworldly Lights: St. Elmo's Fire

A weird haze of light glimmering around a church steeple during a storm, a rosy halo over someone's head, or a ghostly light swirling around the mast of a wave-tossed ship—these are all possible manifestations of the strange, bluish-white light known as St. Elmo's Fire, which may be a signal that a lightning strike to the glowing area is imminent. The light is a visible, electric discharge produced by heavy storms. It was named after St. Erasmus, aka St. Elmo, the patron saint of sailors.

When the Moon Gets the Blues

Everyone understands that the phrase "once in a blue moon" refers to a very unusual occurrence, since blue moons are rare. But a blue moon is not actually blue. In fact, a blue moon is determined by the calendar, not by its color. Typically, there is one full moon per month, but occasionally, a second full moon will sneak into a monthly cycle. When this happens, the second full moon is referred to as a "blue moon," which happens every two to three years. But at times, the moon has been known to appear blue, or even green, often after a volcanic eruption leaves tiny ash and dust particles in the earth's atmosphere.

Green Flash: When the Sun Goes Green

The term *green flash* may sound like a comic book superhero, but it is actually a strange flash of green light that appears just before the setting sun sinks into the horizon. Some have suggested that rare fluctuations in solar winds may be responsible for green glows and flashes that sometimes appear in the atmosphere just before sunset. Some believe it's just a mirage. But others contend that a green flash occurs when layers of the earth's atmosphere act like a prism. Whatever causes the emerald hue, seeing a flash of green light along the horizon can be an eerie and unsettling experience.

Double the Rainbows, Double the Gold?

Rainbow stories abound; ancient Irish lore promises a pot of leprechaun's gold at the end of a rainbow, and Biblical tradition says God set a rainbow in the sky as a promise to Noah that Earth would never again be destroyed by water. Rainbows are formed when sunlight passes through water droplets, usually at the end of a rainstorm, and the droplets separate the light like tiny prisms into a spectrum from red to violet. A secondary rainbow, set outside the first one and in the reverse order of colors, is formed by a second set of light refractions to create the spectacular double rainbow. Conditions have to be just right to see the double rainbow because the secondary arch of colors is much paler than the primary rainbow and is not always visible.

Lava Lamps in the Sky: *Aurora Borealis*

Like a neon sign loosened from its tubing, the *aurora borealis* sends multicolored arches, bands, and streams of luminous beauty throughout the northern skies whenever solar flares are at their height. This occurs when electrons ejected from the sun's surface hit Earth's atmospheric particles and charge them until they glow. The electrons are attracted to Earth's magnetic poles, which is why they are seen mainly in the far northern or southern latitudes. In the southern hemisphere, they are called *aurora australis*. *Aurora polaris* refers to the lights of either pole.

It's Raining Frogs!

Startling as the thought of being pelted from above by buckets of hapless amphibians may be, reports of the sky raining frogs have occurred for so long that the problem was even addressed in the first century A.D., when a Roman scholar, Pliny the Elder, theorized that frog "seeds" were already present in the soil. But in 2005, residents of Serbia were shocked when masses of teensy toads tumbled out of a dark cloud that suddenly appeared in the clear blue sky. *Scientific American* reported a frog fall over Kansas City, Missouri, in July 1873, in numbers so thick they "darkened the air." And in Birmingham, England, the froglets that reportedly dropped from the heavens on June 30, 1892, were not green but a milky white. In 1987, pink frogs fell in Gloucestershire, England. No one knows for certain why this happens, but one theory is that the small animals—fish, birds, and lizards are also common—are carried from other locations by tornadoes or waterspouts.

Spouting Off

Ancient people feared waterspouts and understandably so. Waterspouts are actually tornadoes that form over a body of water, whirling at speeds as fast as 190 miles per hour. Water-spouts start with parent clouds that pull air near the surface into a vortex at an increasing rate, until water is pulled up toward the cloud. One of the world's top waterspout hot spots is the Florida Keys, which may see as many as 500 per year. They can also occur in relatively calm areas such as Lake Tahoe, on the California–Nevada border. There, a Native American legend said that waterspouts, which they called "waterbabies," appeared at the passing of great chiefs to take them to heaven.

Mirages: Optical Confusion

Mirages have been blamed for everything from imaginary waterholes in deserts to sightings of the Loch Ness Monster. They come in two forms: hallucinations or environmental illusions based on tricks of light, shadow, and atmosphere. In April 1977, residents of Grand Haven, Michigan, were able to plainly see the shimmering lights of Milwaukee, Wisconsin, some 75 miles across Lake Michigan. The sighting was confirmed by the flashing pattern of Milwaukee's red harbor beacon. Another rare type of water mirage is the *fata morgana,* which produces a double image that makes mundane objects look gigantic and may account for some reports of sea monsters.

Cobwebs from Heaven?

On their 40-year desert tour with Moses, the Israelites were blessed with a strange substance called *manna* that fell from the sky. People in other places have also witnessed falls of unknown material, often resembling cobwebs. In October 1881, great quantities of weblike material fell around the cities of Milwaukee, Green Bay, and Sheboygan, Wisconsin. Newspapers speculated that the strong, white strands had come from "gossamer spiders" due to their lightness. The same thing allegedly happened in 1898 in Montgomery, Alabama. Not all falls of unknown material have been so pleasant—a yellowish, smelly substance fell on Kourianof, Russia, in 1832, and something similar was reported in Ireland around 1695.

Canada's Most Haunted Resort

💀   💀   💀   💀   💀

The Fairmont Banff Springs Hotel looks like an elegant castle fit for a fairy tale. Truly one of the most luxurious resorts in the world, it is also one of the most haunted.

Wandering Spirits

The story begins in 1883, when three off-duty Canadian Pacific Railway workers were hiking around Banff and discovered the now-famous hot springs. Construction of a hotel was started about four years later, and in 1888, the Banff Springs Hotel opened. It was a large, partly wooden structure nestled in spectacular mountains about two hours from Calgary. For years, the only way to visit the hotel was by rail, making it an ideal, scenic getaway for tourists...and for ghosts.

From the hotel's earliest days, security staff noticed dark, shadowy figures floating in the hallways. The apparitions seemed to linger in one area before vanishing into a nearby wall where no hotel room existed. Banff's staff and owners were baffled, and guests were a little frightened.

Then in 1926, a fire destroyed part of the hotel. During the cleanup, workers uncovered a builder's mistake. At the exact location where ghosts had been sighted, the cleanup crew found an interior room with no windows or doors. People speculated that the secluded room had been the ghosts' home, or a portal to "the other side." The hotel was rebuilt without the odd, hidden room, so when it reopened in 1928, most people thought the phantom figures were gone for good, but they were wrong....

The Ghostly Bride

According to legend, during the 1920s, a woman left the hotel's bridal suite wearing her wedding gown. As she walked down the candlelit staircase, a gust of wind lifted the train of her gown and caught it on fire. Struggling to put out the flames, the bride lost her balance and fell, which caused her to break her neck and killed her instantly. Scorch marks on the marble stairs still indicate where she fell.

Since then, staff and guests have seen the ghostly bride on the stairs. Witnesses say she appears as a translucent figure before bursting into flames and vanishing. People have also noticed unexplained gusts of wind around the haunted staircase. Others have seen the ghostly bride dancing alone in the ballroom or seemingly waiting for someone at the hotel's Rob Roy Lounge. She fades away slowly if you continue to watch her. She may also haunt the bridal suite, where guests have reported recurring "cold spots." But the bridal suite isn't nearly as haunted as another room at the hotel.

Ghosts on the Eighth Floor

If you're looking for a murder mystery, visit the eighth floor of the Banff Springs Hotel. Staff members won't talk about it, but Room 873 has been sealed and its number removed. Nearby doors are numbered 871 and 872, followed by 874 and 875.

According to rumors, a family was murdered in Room 873. Afterward, the hotel cleaned the room and prepared it for new guests. However, each time the staff cleaned the large mirror in Room 873, a child's fingerprints reappeared. Eventually, the hotel closed the room and sealed it. Some guests say the outline of the door is still visible. Others have taken photos outside the sealed room, and vivid, unexplained orbs have reportedly appeared in the pictures.

Those orbs are dramatic, but there's an even more intense, ghostly manifestation at Banff. The ghost of a former hotel bellman, Sam McCauley, appears so real that guests often think he's a regular hotel employee.

Some Scots Never Leave

McCauley arrived from Scotland in the 1930s and worked as a porter at the Banff Springs Hotel for nearly 40 years. Before he died, he promised to return to the hotel as a ghost. It seems he kept his word: McCauley has been seen in the hallways and sometimes helps guests with their luggage. When they turn to tip the elderly man, he vanishes. McCauley is popular with staff and guests alike and is spotted regularly in the lobby and on the ninth floor, where he used to store his tips.

Another Scotsman haunts the Banff Springs Hotel, too. Very late at night, a Scottish piper appears around the Rob Roy Lounge. Some people apparently see him in full Scottish garb, but because this ghost is headless, his real identity is unknown.

In addition, a portrait hanging in the MacKenzie Room appears to be haunted. According to legend, a ghost comes out of the portrait's eyes. First, the eyes seem to light up slightly, then something with jagged edges appears to swirl out of the eyes. The apparition is so scary that no one has remained in the room long enough to see what happens next. Some say this ghost was partly responsible for a fire in the hotel in 1946.

The Helpful Housekeeper and the Singing Men

One of the hotel's newest ghosts is a former housekeeper. She allegedly visits rooms and straightens the covers on the beds—sometimes while guests are still sleeping! She's harmless, but it can be unsettling to wake up in the morning and find the bed *more* tidy than when you went to sleep.

For your listening pleasure, it has been reported that around 3:00 A.M., a male voice sings loudly in the downstairs ladies' washroom. He's never seen, nor is the male chorus that sings in the men's washroom near the ballrooms.

Other Figures and Phantom Lights

Though most people believe the hotel's earliest shadowy ghosts left when the resort was rebuilt in the 1920s, some have reported seeing those fleeting forms again. They're dark and move silently through the halls, like something out of a movie, then they vanish, passing through walls and locked doors. Other guests describe eerie, unexplained lights hovering outside their hotel room windows. These guests say that the lights aren't frightening, merely odd.

One thing is certain: Banff Springs Hotel is popular with everyone who visits it…including ghosts.

Mysterious Disappearances in the Bermuda Triangle

The Bermuda Triangle is an infamous stretch of the Atlantic Ocean bordered by Florida, Bermuda, and Puerto Rico where strange disappearances have occurred throughout history. The Coast Guard doesn't recognize the Triangle or the supernatural explanations for the mysterious disappearances. There are some probable causes for the missing vessels—hurricanes, undersea earthquakes, and magnetic fields that interfere with compasses and other positioning devices. But it's much more interesting to think they were sucked into another dimension, abducted by aliens, or simply vanished into thin air.

Flight 19

On the afternoon of December 5, 1945, five Avenger torpedo bombers left the Naval Air Station at Fort Lauderdale, Florida, with Lt. Charles Taylor in command of a crew of 13 student pilots. About 90 minutes into the flight, Taylor radioed the base to say that his compasses weren't working, but he figured he was somewhere over the Florida Keys. The lieutenant who received the signal told Taylor to fly north toward Miami, as long as he was sure he was actually over the Keys. Although he was an experienced pilot, Taylor got horribly turned around, and the more he tried to get out of the Keys, the further out to sea he and his crew traveled. As night fell, radio signals worsened, until, finally, there was nothing at all from Flight 19. A U.S. Navy investigation reported that Taylor's confusion caused the disaster, but his mother convinced them to change the official report to read that the planes went down for "causes unknown." The planes have never been recovered.

The *Spray*

Joshua Slocum, the first man to sail solo around the world, never should have been lost at sea, but it appears that's exactly what happened. In 1909, the *Spray* left the East Coast of the United States for Venezuela via the Caribbean Sea. Slocum was never heard from or seen again and was declared dead in 1924. The ship was solid, and Slocum was a pro, so nobody knows what happened. Perhaps he was felled by a larger ship or maybe he was taken down by pirates. No one knows for sure that Slocum disappeared within the Triangle's waters, but Bermuda buffs claim Slocum's story as part of the area's mysterious and supernatural legacy.

USS *Cyclops*

As World War I heated up, America went to battle. In 1918, the *Cyclops*, commanded by Lt. G. W. Worley, was sent to Brazil to refuel Allied ships. With 309 people onboard, the ship left Rio de Janeiro in February and reached Barbados in March. After that, the *Cyclops* was never seen or heard from again. The navy says in its official statement, "The disappearance of this ship has been one of the most baffling mysteries in the annals of the navy, all attempts to locate her having proved unsuccessful. There were no enemy submarines in the western Atlantic at that time, and in December 1918, every effort was made to obtain from German sources information regarding the disappearance of the vessel."

Star Tiger

The *Star Tiger*, commanded by Capt. B. W. McMillan, was flying from England to Bermuda in early 1948. On January 30, McMillan said he expected to arrive in Bermuda at 5:00 A.M., but neither he nor any of the 31 people onboard the *Star Tiger* were ever heard from again. When the Civil Air Ministry launched an investigation, they learned that the S.S. *Troubadour* had reported seeing a low-flying aircraft halfway between Bermuda and the entrance to Delaware Bay. If that aircraft was the *Star Tiger*, it was drastically off course. According to the Civil Air Ministry, the fate of the *Star Tiger* remains unknown.

Star Ariel

On January 17, 1949, a Tudor IV aircraft like the *Star Tiger* left Bermuda with seven crew members and 13 passengers en route to Jamaica. That morning, Capt. J. C. McPhee reported that the flight was going smoothly. Shortly afterward, another more cryptic message came from the captain, when he reported that he was changing his frequency, and then nothing more was heard—ever. More than 60 aircraft and 13,000 people were deployed to look for the *Star Ariel*, but no hint of debris or wreckage was ever found. After the *Star Ariel* disappeared, production of Tudor IVs ceased.

Flight 201

This Cessna left for Fort Lauderdale on March 31, 1984, en route for Bimini Island in the Bahamas, but it never made it. Not quite midway to its destination, the plane slowed its airspeed significantly, but no distress signals came from the plane. Suddenly, the plane dropped from the air into the water, completely vanishing from the radar. A woman on Bimini Island swore she saw a plane plunge into the sea about a mile offshore, but no wreckage has ever been found.

Teignmouth Electron

Who said that the Bermuda Triangle only swallows up ships and planes? Who's to say it can't also make a man go mad? Perhaps that's what happened on the *Teignmouth Electron* in 1969. The Sunday Times Golden Globe race of 1968 left England on October 31 and required each contestant to sail his ship solo. Donald Crowhurst was one of the entrants, but he never made it to the finish line. The *Electron* was found abandoned in the middle of the Bermuda Triangle in July 1969. Logbooks recovered from the ship reveal that Crowhurst was deceiving organizers about his position in the race and going a little bit nutty out there in the big blue ocean. The last entry of his log was dated June 29—it is believed that Crowhurst jumped overboard and drowned himself in the Triangle.

The Curse of King Tut's Tomb

💀   💀   💀   💀   💀

If you discovered a mummy's tomb, would you go in? The curse of King Tut's tomb is a classic tale, even if there's a lot of evidence that says there was never anything to worry about. Still…would you wanna go in there?

Curse, Schmurse!

In the early 1920s, English explorer and archeologist Howard Carter led an expedition funded by the Fifth Earl of Carnarvon to unearth the tomb of Egyptian King Tutankhamun. Most of the tombs of Egyptian kings had been ransacked long ago, but Carter had reason to believe that King Tut's 3,000-year-old tomb was probably still full of artifacts from the ancient world. He was right.

Within the king's burial chamber were vases, precious metals, statues, even whole chariots—all buried with the king to aid him in the afterlife. Carter and his team excavated to their heart's content, and due to their hard work, we now know a great deal more about the life of ancient Egyptian people during King Tut's time.

Carter had been warned about the dangers of disrupting an ancient tomb, but he didn't buy into the rumors of curses and hexes. After opening the tomb, however, it was hard to deny that some strange, unpleasant events began to take place in the lives of those involved in the expedition.

Curse or Coincidence?

During the 1920s, several men involved in the excavation died shortly after entering King Tut's tomb. The first one to go—the Fifth Earl of Carnarvon—died only a few months after completing the excavation. Legend has it that at the exact moment the earl died, all the lights in the city of Cairo mysteriously went out. That morning, his dog allegedly dropped dead, too.

Egyptologists claim that the spores and mold released from opening an ancient grave are often enough to make a person sick or worse. The earl had been suffering from a chronic illness before he left for Egypt, which could have made him more susceptible to the mold, and, therefore, led to his death.

Other stories say that the earl was bitten by a mosquito. Considering the sanitary conditions in Egypt at the time, a mosquito bite in Cairo could have some serious consequences, including malaria and other deadly diseases. Some reports indicate that the bite became infected and he died as a result—not because an ancient pharaoh was annoyed with him.

There were other odd happenings, and the public, already interested in the discovery of the tomb itself, was hungry for details of "the curse of the pharaohs." Newspapers reported all kinds of "proof": the earl's younger brother died suddenly five months after the excavation, and on the morning of the opening of the tomb, Carter's pet bird was swallowed by a cobra—the same kind of vicious cobra depicted on the mask of King Tut. Two of the workers hired for the dig died after opening the tomb, though their passing was likely due to malaria, not any curse.

Six of the 26 explorers involved died within a decade. But many of those involved in the exploration lived long, happy lives, including Carter. He never paid much attention to the curse, and, apparently, it never paid much attention to him. In 1939, Carter died of natural causes at age 64, after working with King Tut and his treasures for more than 17 years.

Yeah, Right

King Tutankhamun's sarcophagus and treasures have toured the world on a nearly continual basis since their discovery and restoration. When the exhibit went to America in the 1970s, some people tried to revive the old curse. When a San Francisco police officer suffered a mild stroke while guarding a gold funeral mask, he unsuccessfully tried to collect compensation, claiming his stroke was due to the pharaoh's curse.

Creepy Coincidences

From a prophetic book written decades before a tragic event took place to a man struck repeatedly by lightning, life's great coincidences are often truly mind-boggling.

The Numbers Don't Lie

The terror attacks of September 11, 2001, brought with them much speculation. Was this heinous act perpetrated by a group of rogue extremists or part of a larger conspiracy? Did everything happen precisely as reported, or was the public being misled? While these questions and others were being pondered, a curious and underreported event took place.

On September 11, 2002, the one-year anniversary of the attacks, the New York State Lottery conducted one of two standard daily drawings. In the three-number contest, the balls drawn were 9–1–1. Statisticians point out that this isn't particularly astounding, given the less than astronomical odds in a three-ball draw. Even so, that's one creepy coincidence.

Womb for One More

As if one womb were no longer good enough to get the job done, Hannah Kersey of Great Britain was born with two. Then, in 2006, to confound the medical world even more, the 23-year-old woman gave birth to triplets—identical twins Ruby and Tilly were delivered from one of Kersey's wombs, while baby Gracie was extracted from the other. All three girls came into the world seven weeks premature via cesarean section and were quite healthy upon arrival. For the record, there have been about 70 known pregnancies in separate wombs in the past 100 years, but the case of triplets is the first of its kind and doctors estimate the likelihood is about one in 25 million.

He's Awl That

Most people recognize the name Louis Braille, the world-renowned inventor of the Braille system of reading and writing for the blind. But what many people don't know is how Braille himself became blind and how it led to his invention.

When he was only three years old, Braille accidentally poked himself in the eye with a stitching awl owned by his father, a saddle maker. At first his injury didn't seem serious, but when an autoimmune disease known as sympathetic ophthalmia set in, he went blind in both eyes.

Over the years, Braille adapted well to his disability. Then, in 1824, at age 15, he invented a system of raised dots that enabled the blind to read and write through use of their fingertips. To form each dot on a page, Braille employed a common hand tool found at most saddle maker's shops—a stitching awl, the same tool that had injured him as a child.

Lotsa Luck

Evelyn Adams had a couple of bucks and a dream. In 1985, she purchased a New Jersey lottery ticket and crossed her fingers. When the winning numbers were called, she realized she had hit the jackpot. The following year, Adams amazingly hit the jackpot once more. Her combined take for both wins totaled a cool $5.4 million. It was enough money to easily live out her days in comfort. But it wasn't to be.

Due to Adams's innate generosity and love of gambling, she eventually went broke. Today, she lives in a trailer and laments the past: "I wish I had the chance to do it all over again. I'd be much smarter about it now."

Think of Laura

On a whim, ten-year-old Laura Buxton of Burton, Staffordshire, England, jotted her name and address on a luggage label in 2001. She then attached it to a helium balloon and released it into the sky. Supported by air currents for 140 miles, the balloon eventually touched down in a garden in Pewsey, Wiltshire, England. Bizarrely, another ten-year-old girl named Laura Buxton read the note, got in touch with its sender, and the girls became fast friends. In addition to their identical names and ages, each child had fair hair and owned a black Labrador retriever, a guinea pig, and a rabbit.

Attractive Gent

Do some people attract lightning the way a movie star attracts fans? In the case of Major Walter Summerford, an officer in the British Army, the evidence nods toward the affirmative. In 1918, Summerford received his first jolt when he was knocked from his horse by a flash of lightning. Injuries to his lower body forced him to retire from the military, so he moved to Vancouver, British Columbia.

In 1924, Summerford spent a day fishing beside a river. Suddenly, a bolt of lightning struck the tree he was sitting beneath, and he was zapped again. But by 1926, Summerford had recovered from his injuries to the degree that he was able to take walks. He continued with this therapy until one tragic summer's day in 1930 when, unbelievably, lightning found him yet again. This time it paralyzed him for good. He died two years after the incident.

The story should end there, but it doesn't. In 1936, a lightning bolt took aim at a cemetery and unleashed its 100,000-volt charge. Luckily, no living soul was nearby at the time, and the bolt passed its energy harmlessly into the ground, as do the vast majority of lightning strikes. Still, before hitting the ground, the lightning bolt injected its fearsome energy into Major Summerford's headstone.

Four's a Crowd

In 1838, Edgar Allan Poe, famous author of the macabre, penned a novel entitled *The Narrative of Arthur Gordon Pym of Nantucket.* His fictitious account centers around four survivors of a shipwreck who find themselves adrift in an open lifeboat. After many days of hunger and torment, they decide the only way for any of them to survive is if one is sacrificed for food. They draw straws, and cabin boy Richard Parker comes up short. He is subsequently killed, and the three remaining seamen partake of his flesh.

In 1884, some 46 years after the tale was first told, the yacht *Mignonette* broke apart during a hurricane in the South Atlantic. Its four survivors drifted in a lifeboat for 19 days before turning desperate from hunger and thirst. One sailor, a cabin boy, became delirious after guzzling copious quantities of seawater. Upon seeing this, the other three determined that the man was at death's door and decided to kill him. They then devoured his remains. His name: Richard Parker.

Downed Damsels

Mary Ashford was born in 1797, and Barbara Forrest in 1954, yet circumstances surrounding their eventual murders are eerily similar. On May 27, 1817, Ashford was raped and killed in Erdington, England. On May 27, 1974, Forrest was also raped and murdered in Erdington, just 400 yards away from the site of Ashford's murder. The day preceding both of the murders was Whit Monday, a floating religious holiday on the Christian calendar celebrated mostly in Europe. The murders occurred at approximately the same time of day, and attempts had been made to conceal both bodies.

That's not all. Each woman had visited a friend on the night before Whit Monday, changed into a new dress during the evening, and attended a dance. Curiously, suspects in both cases shared the surname "Thornton." Both were subsequently tried and acquitted of murder. Paintings and photos show that the two women also shared very similar facial features.

Naughty but Nice

Whenever Brownsville, Texas, waitress Melina Salazar saw cantankerous customer Walter "Buck" Swords walking into her café, she felt an urge to walk out. Nevertheless, Salazar persevered through a fusillade of demands and curses heaped upon her by her most demanding, albeit loyal, customer.

When 89-year-old Swords passed away, no one was more shocked than Salazar to learn that he'd bequeathed her $50,000 and his car. Describing Swords as, "kind of mean," the waitress told a television news crew, "I still can't believe it."

The World's Weirdest Cocktails

💀   💀   💀   💀   💀

In the good old days, those who bellied up to the bar were fairly limited—whisky, vodka, and maraschino cherries could only yield so many combinations. But these days, with technological advancements in liquor distilling, flavor infusing, and general food and beverage manipulation, bartenders come up with funkier cocktails every day and late into the night.

The Titanic

At Citarella: The Restaurant in the Big Apple, you can enjoy this concoction made with mashed grapes, elderflower syrup, vodka, and scoops of champagne sorbet. You'll need to hail a cab after this one for sure.

The Mayoty Dog

Koji Nakamura owns the Mayonnaise Kitchen restaurant in suburban Tokyo. Here, mayo is featured in everything on the menu, including beverages like the Mayoty Dog—a version of the classic "Salty Dog" cocktail but with mayo on the rim instead of salt.

92 in the Shade

Mango puree, tequila, and red habañero pepper syrup is what patrons at the Blue Water Grill in NYC get when they order this martini. What, no guacamole garnish?

The Hunter

At Kirkland, Washington's Jager Bar & Restaurant, order this martini made with horseradish-infused vodka, Grand Marnier, and a grilled beef tenderloin tip garnish. We're guessing it comes well-done.

The Amaretto Cheesecake
Who needs regular old cheesecake when you can have a cheesecake cocktail? A consulting company called Drink Tank develops "Caketails" and "Pietinis." This particular offering contains cream cheese, amaretto, roasted almonds, and graham cracker crumbs.

Rhubarb & Vanilla
The manager of San Francisco's Aziza Restaurant wanted to increase bar traffic with some eye-catching cocktails, so he developed this one. With rhubarb-infused vodka, bourbon, vanilla bean, Stoli Vanil, lime juice, and black peppercorns, this cocktail is sweet, salty, *and* weird!

Brain Hemorrhage
This shot is good for Halloween, owing to its name and bizarre appearance. When Irish cream is poured into peach schnapps, the cream curdles instantly. With a dash of bright red grenadine, you've got a violent looking beverage with a sweet aftertaste. Mmm…hemorrhage.

The Man from Nantucket
This martini, served at the Biltmore Room in New York City, features Nantucket-made Triple 8 vodka and garlic-stuffed black olives. Pucker up!

History's Most Expensive Cocktail?
In 2007, a cocktail fetched £35,000 (nearly $70,000) at a nightclub in London. The beverage was made of Louis XII cognac, Cristal Rosé champagne, sugar, angostura bitters, and a few flakes of 24-carat edible gold leaf. There was an 11-carat white diamond ring at the bottom of the glass, too. If anyone's up for another round, we're *not* buying.

Frog hormones can be so strong that they will drive males to mate with anything, including fish and other male frogs.

Ghost Lights

The legends are similar, no matter the locale. It's whispered that mysterious lights that blink and wink in the night are the spirits of long-dead railroad workers, jealous and jilted lovers, or lost children. They go by many names: marsh lights, ghost lights, will-o'-the-wisp, *feu follet*, earth lights, and even, to the skeptical, swamp gas. They occur in remote areas, often near old railway tracks or power transmitters. Some are thought to issue from the geomagnetic fields of certain kinds of rock. But tales of lights that change color, follow people, foil electrical systems, or perform acrobatic stunts are harder to explain.

Mysterious Marfa Lights

The famed Marfa Lights of Marfa, Texas, have become almost synonymous with the term *ghost lights.* Since 1883, they have been spotted in an area southwest of the Chisos Mountains, some 200 miles south of El Paso. The lights appear almost playful in their gyrations, skimming over the fields, bobbing like a yo-yo, or chasing visitors. One woman reportedly witnessed a white ball of light three feet in diameter that bounced in slow motion alongside her car as she drove through the Chisos one night. Some of the lights have been attributed to auto headlights miles away across the desert, but the Marfa Lights were witnessed long before automobiles came to the area.

The Peculiar Paulding Light

According to legend, an old railway brakeman was killed near the Choate Branch Railroad tracks that used to run near Paulding, Michigan, along the northern Wisconsin–Michigan border. People have observed strange lights near the tracks for decades, and it is said that they're from the railman's ghostly lantern swinging as he walks his old beat. Others, armed with telescopes and binoculars, believe that the famed Paulding Light is actually caused by headlights shining from a highway a few miles away.

Still, many claim that the lights behave like anything but distant reflections. The lights are said to change from red to green, zoom up close as if peering into people's cars, chase people, flash through automobiles either cutting off all electric power or turning radios off and on, and zigzag through the nearby woods. Crowds flock to the Robins Wood Road site off Highway 45 to see the phenomenon for themselves, and a wooden sign has been erected complete with a drawing of a ghost swinging a lantern.

The Fiery Feu Follet

During the mid-18th century, when Detroit was being settled by the French, aristocrats and working folks feared the *feu follet*—spirit lights of the marshy river area. One local legend tells of a rich landowner who nearly drowned one stormy night when the brilliant lights lured him into a swamp. Luckily, two guests staying at his house heard his terrified cries and managed to rescue him. At the time, the prevailing theory of the marsh lights was that windows had to be closed when the *feu follet* were near or they would enter the house, snake their way into the windpipes of those present, and choke them to death.

Baffling Brown Mountain Lights

Although scoffed at as nothing more than reflected train lights, the multicolored light show in the foothills of North Carolina's Blue Ridge Mountains has fascinated humans since an early explorer reported it in 1771, and even earlier according to Native American legend. Several centuries ago, many people were killed during a battle between the Cherokee and the Catawba tribes. Legend has it that the Brown Mountain Lights are the spirits of those lost warriors.

Another tale states that a plantation owner got lost hunting on Brown Mountain and that one of his slaves came looking for him, swinging a lantern to light his way. The slave never found his owner but still walks the mountainside with his eternal lantern. Still another legend claims the lights come from the spirit of a woman murdered on the mountain by her husband in 1850.

Whatever the source of the colorful lights, they come in many shapes, from glowing orbs to trailing bursts to still, white areas. Crowds flock to at least three locations to view the lights, but one of the most popular is the Brown Mountain overlook on Highway 181, 20 miles north of Morganton.

Glowing in Great Britain

For a week before Cornwall, England, suffered an earthquake in November 1996, people of the region began seeing unexplained lights in the sky that ranged from circular to rectangular in shape. Some saw the lights as precursors to the quake, but that didn't explain why several witnesses observed large golden spheres dropping from the clouds two years earlier or why others saw purple pixie lights hovering around the area's old tin mines.

The Lincolnshire region was notorious in the mid-1960s as the site of unexplained balls of colored light. On August 10, 1965, a woman named Rachel Atwill woke up just before 4:00 A.M. to see a reddish light over some nearby hills. The light persisted for almost a half hour, and Atwill reported that the experience gave her a headache.

The same light was seen about an hour later by a truck driver, but he had a more harrowing experience as the light hovered only 50 yards from his truck. The situation grew worse when the light zoomed right up to his windshield and sat there, lighting up the inside of the truck and waking his sleeping wife and daughter. Luckily, it soon lifted back into the atmosphere and disappeared. Others in the area also reported seeing lights of the same description, and one was even able to capture a photo that was published in a London newspaper.

The hummingbird moth, or hawk moth, can reportedly zoom around at 45 miles per hour.

The Ghost of the Sausage Vat Murder

💀 💀 💀 💀 💀

The story of Louisa Luetgert, the murdered wife of "Sausage King" Adolph Luetgert, is a gruesome tale of betrayal, death, and a lingering specter. It is also one of the greatest stories in Chicago lore. According to legend, each year on the anniversary of her death, Louisa appears on the corner of Hermitage Avenue where it once crossed Diversey Parkway. But her ghost not only haunts her old neighborhood; allegedly, she also coaxed her treacherous husband into an early grave.

Land of Opportunity

Adolph Luetgert was born in Germany and came to America after the Civil War. He arrived in Chicago around 1865 and worked in tanneries for several years before opening his first business—a liquor store—in 1872. Luetgert married his first wife, Caroline Roepke, that same year. She gave birth to two boys, only one of whom survived childhood. Just two months after Caroline died in November 1877, Luetgert quickly remarried a much younger woman, Louisa Bicknese, and moved to the northwest side of the city. As a gift, he gave her an unusual gold ring that had her initials inscribed inside the band. Little did Luetgert know that this ring would prove to be his downfall.

Trouble for the "Sausage King"

In 1892, Luetgert built a sausage factory at the southwest corner of Hermitage and Diversey. But just a year later, sausage sales declined due to an economic depression. Luetgert had put his life's savings into the factory, along with plenty of borrowed money, so when his business suffered, creditors started coming after him.

Instead of trying to reorganize his finances, however, Luetgert answered a newspaper ad posted by an English millionaire who made a deal with him to buy out the majority of the sausage business. The Englishman proved to be a con-man, and Luetgert ended up losing even more money in the deal. Luetgert eventually laid off many of his workers, but a few remained as he attempted to keep the factory out of the hands of creditors for as long as possible.

Luetgert's business losses took a terrible toll on his marriage. Friends and neighbors frequently heard the Luetgerts arguing, and things became so bad that Luetgert eventually started sleeping in his office at the factory. He carried on with several mistresses and even became involved with a household servant who was related to his wife. When Louisa found out about his involvement with her relative, she became enraged.

Luetgert soon gave the neighbors even more to gossip about. One night, during another shouting match with Louisa, he allegedly took his wife by the throat and began choking her. After noticing alarmed neighbors watching him through the parlor window, Luetgert reportedly calmed down and released his wife before she collapsed. A few days later, Luetgert was seen chasing his wife down the street, shouting at her and waving a revolver.

Vanishing Louisa

Louisa disappeared on May 1, 1897. When questioned about it days later, Luetgert stated that Louisa had left him and was possibly staying with her sister or another man. When Louisa's brother, Dietrich Bicknese, asked Luetgert why he had not informed the police of Louisa's disappearance, the sausage maker told him that he'd hired a private investigator to find her because he didn't trust the police.

When Bicknese informed the police of his sister's disappearance, Captain Herman Schuettler and his men began to search for Louisa. They questioned neighbors and relatives, who detailed the couple's violent arguments. Schuettler summoned Luetgert to the precinct house on a couple of occasions and each time pressed him about his wife's disappearance. Luetgert stated that he did not report Louisa's disappearance because he could not afford the disgrace and scandal.

During the investigation, a young German girl named Emma Schimke told police that she had passed by the factory with her sister at about 10:30 P.M. on May 1 and remembered seeing Luetgert leading his wife down the alleyway behind the factory.

Police also questioned employees of the sausage factory. Frank Bialk, a night watchman at the plant, told police that when he arrived for work on May 1, he found a fire going in one of the boilers. He said Luetgert asked him to keep the fire going and then sent him on a couple of trivial errands while Luetgert stayed in the basement. When Bialk returned to the factory, he went back to the boiler fire and heard Luetgert finishing his work at around 3:00 A.M.

Later that morning, Bialk saw a sticky, gluelike substance on the floor near the vat. He noticed that it seemed to contain bits of bone, but he thought nothing of it. After all, Luetgert used all sorts of waste meats to make his sausage, so he assumed that's what it was.

On May 3, Luetgert asked another employee, Frank Odorofsky, to clean the basement and told him to keep quiet about it. Odorofsky put the slimy substance into a barrel, and scattered it near the railroad tracks as Luetgert had requested.

A Gruesome Discovery

On May 15, the police search was narrowed to the factory basement and a vat that was two-thirds full of a brownish, brackish liquid. Using gunnysacks as filters, officers drained the greasy paste from the vat and began poking through the residue with sticks. Officer Walter Dean found several bone fragments and two gold rings—one a heavy gold band engraved with the initials "L. L."

Luetgert, proclaiming his innocence, was questioned again shortly after the search and was subsequently arrested for the murder of his wife several days later. Despite the fact that Louisa's body was never found and there was no real evidence to link her husband to the crime, the police and prosecutors believed they had a solid case against Luetgert. He was indicted for Louisa's murder, and the details of the crime shocked the city. Even though he had been charged with boiling Louisa's body, rumors circulated that she had actually been ground up into sausage that was sold to local butcher shops and restaurants. Not surprisingly, sausage sales dropped dramatically in Chicago in 1897.

Hounded to the Grave?

Luetgert's trial ended in a hung jury on October 21. The judge threw out the case, and prosecutors had to try the whole thing over again. A second trial was held in 1898, and this time Luetgert was convicted and sentenced to a life term at Joliet Prison.

While in prison, Luetgert continued to maintain his innocence and was placed in charge of meats in the cold-storage warehouse. Officials described him as a model prisoner. But by 1899, Luetgert began to speak less and less and often quarreled with other convicts. He soon became a shadow of his former, blustering self, fighting for no reason and often babbling incoherently in his cell at night. But was he talking to himself or to someone else?

Legend has it that Luetgert claimed Louisa haunted him in his jail cell, intent on having revenge for her murder. Was she really haunting him, or was the ghost just a figment of his rapidly deteriorating mind? Based on the fact that neighbors also reported seeing Louisa's ghost, one has to wonder if she did indeed drive Luetgert insane.

Luetgert died in 1900, likely from heart trouble. The coroner who conducted the autopsy also reported that his liver was greatly enlarged and in such a condition of degeneration that "mental strain would have caused his death at any time."

Perhaps Louisa really did visit him after all.

The Ghost of Louisa Luetgert

Regardless of who killed Louisa, her spirit reportedly did not rest in peace. Soon after Luetgert was sent to prison, neighbors swore they saw Louisa's ghost inside her former home, wearing a white dress and leaning against the fireplace mantel.

The sausage factory stood empty for years, looming over the neighborhood as a grim reminder of the horrors that had taken place there. Eventually, the Library Bureau Company purchased the factory for a workshop and storehouse for library furniture and office supplies. During renovations, they discarded the infamous vats in the basement.

On June 26, 1904, the old factory caught on fire. Despite the damage done to the building's interior, the Library Bureau reopened its facilities in the former sausage factory. In 1907, a contracting mason purchased the old Luetgert house and moved it from behind the factory to another lot in the neighborhood, hoping to dispel the grim memories—and ghost—attached to it.

Hermitage Avenue no longer intersects with Diversey, and by the 1990s, the crumbling factory stood empty. But in the late '90s, around the 100th anniversary of Louisa's death, the former sausage factory was converted into condominiums and a brand-new neighborhood sprang up to replace the aging homes that remained from the days of the Luetgerts. Fashionable brick homes and apartments appeared around the old factory, and rundown taverns were replaced with coffee shops.

But one thing has not changed. Legend has it that each year on May 1, the anniversary of her death, the ghost of Louisa can still be spotted walking down Hermitage Avenue near the old sausage factory, reliving her final moments on this earth.

Nose-Picker's Deal

A video was circulating for a time amongst Las Vegas and Atlantic City gaming industry professionals. It was somewhat of a "best of" bloopers reel that featured disgusting behavior by casino patrons. Among the highlights: A woman playing blackjack removed the lower plate of her false teeth, picked out something wedged in the plate with her finger, wiped it on her pants, and put the plate back in her mouth. Other clips showed people cleaning their ears with matches, armpit "farting," and more nose-picking than anyone would care to see.

Index

Jeff Bahr is a reporter for the *The County Seat* and a contributing writer on four books, including *Weird Virginia* and *Weird U.S.* As a frequent contributor to magazines, such as *Backroads, Great Outdoors,* and *Pennsylvania Magazine,* this self-described "hired pen" finds infinite potential in the creative process.

Fiona Broome is a highly respected ghost hunter with more than 20 years of experience as a paranormal researcher. As the founder and lead investigator of HollowHill.com, she has also written several books, is a popular guest at annual conferences, such as Dragon*Con, and has appeared on numerous TV and radio shows.

Mary Fons is a freelance writer who creates snazzy content for clients such as Varitalk, Jellyvision, and Content That Works. She is a nationally ranking slam poet and a regular performer in Chicago's longest-running theater show, the Neo-Futurist's *Too Much Light Makes the Baby Go Blind.* Check out www.maryfons.com for more on Mary and to read her juicy blog, PaperGirl.

Linda Godfrey is an award-winning journalist-turned-author, radio host, and artist. She has published several books, including *The Beast of Bray Road, The Poison Widow, Strange Wisconsin,* and *Lake and Sea Monsters.* She has appeared on national TV and radio shows, such as *Inside Edition* and The History Channel's *Monsterquest.* Her radio show, *Uncanny Radio* (www.uncannyradio.com), airs weekly.

Susan McGowan lives in Columbus, Ohio, with her husband, daughter, and too many orange cats. A writer by day, in her free time, Susan travels in pursuit of all things quirky, kitschy, and haunted and hopes eventually to visit every bone chapel and ossuary in the world.

Troy Taylor is the author of more than 50 books on ghosts and crime and is the founder of the American Ghost Society. With a morbid interest in both historical murders and things that go bump in the night, he travels all over America in search of authentic tales of horror. He and his wife, Haven, reside in central Illinois.

James Willis coauthored *Weird Ohio* and *Weird Indiana,* and was a contributing writer for *Weird U.S.* and *Weird Hauntings.* He is also the founder of The Ghosts of Ohio (www.ghostsofohio.org), a nationally recognized paranormal research organization. As a sought-after public speaker, James entertains crowds with tales of his strange and spooky travels across the country. He lives in Columbus, Ohio, with his wife, a Queen-loving parrot, and three narcoleptic cats.

Hope you enjoyed this Armchair Reader™

You'll find the rest of the collection quite exciting.
Please look for these titles wherever books are sold.

ARMCHAIR
• READER™ •

The Colossal Reader

The Book of Incredible Information

The Amazing Book of History

The Extraordinary Book of Lists

Civil War • World War II

Grand Slam Baseball

Coming Attractions
The Book of Myths and Misconceptions
The Origins of Everything

Visit us at *www.armchairreader.com*
to learn all about our other great books from
West Side Publishing, or just to let us know
what your thoughts are about our books.
We love to hear from all our readers.

WEST
SIDE
PUBLISHING